Town Courts and Urban Society in Late Medieval England, 1250–1500

Town Courts and Urban Society in Late Medieval England, 1250–1500

Edited by
Richard Goddard and Teresa Phipps

THE BOYDELL PRESS

First published 2019
The Boydell Press, Woodbridge

ISBN 978 1 78327 425 3

The Boydell Press is an imprint of Boydell & Brewer Ltd
PO Box 9, Woodbridge, Suffolk IP12 3DF, UK
and of Boydell & Brewer Inc.
668 Mt Hope Avenue, Rochester, NY 14620–2731, USA
website: www.boydellandbrewer.com

A CIP catalogue record for this book is available
from the British Library

This publication is printed on acid-free paper

CONTENTS

ILLUSTRATIONS

Maps

Figures

Tables

CONTRIBUTORS

Esther Liberman Cuenca is an Assistant Professor of History at the University of Houston-Victoria. She received her PhD in History from Fordham University. She is the recipient of the Schallek Fellowship from the Medieval Academy of America and was a Visiting Scholar at the Institute of Historical Research in 2016/17. She has published in peer-reviewed journals, including *Urban History* and *The Digital Medievalist*. Her PhD dissertation, 'The Making of Borough Customary Law in Medieval Britain', examines the development of town law from the twelfth to the sixteenth centuries.

Christopher Dyer is Emeritus Professor of History at the University of Leicester, having previously worked at the universities of Edinburgh and Birmingham. He has researched the society, economy, landscape and material culture of the Middle Ages, and his books include *Standards of Living in the Later Middle Ages* (Cambridge, 1989; 1998), *Making a Living in Medieval England* (New Haven and London, 2002) and *A Country Merchant, 1495–1520* (Oxford, 2012). He has edited two historical journals and has contributed articles to periodicals and chapters to many edited volumes.

Richard Goddard is Associate Professor of Medieval History at the University of Nottingham. He has written extensively on the economic and social history of later medieval England in peer-reviewed journals. His books include *Lordship and Medieval Urbanisation: Coventry, 1043–1355* (Woodbridge, 2004); with John Langdon and Miriam Müller (eds), *Survival and Discord in Medieval Society: Essays in Honour of Christopher Dyer* (Turnhout, 2010) and *Credit and Trade in Later Medieval England* (Basingstoke, 2016).

Jeremy Goldberg has published extensively on gender, family, culture and society in later medieval England. His books include *Women, Work, and Life Cycle: Women in York and Yorkshire c. 1300–1520* (Oxford, 1992) and *Communal*

Discord, Child Abduction, and Rape in the Later Middle Ages (New York, 2008). He is currently working on the relationship between people and buildings. He teaches in the Centre for Medieval Studies and the Department of History at the University of York.

Alan Kissane earned his doctorate in medieval history from the University of Nottingham. He has written extensively on the later Middle Ages, with a specific focus on urban society and culture. His books and articles include *Civic Community in Late Medieval Lincoln: Urban Society and Economy in the Age of the Black Death, 1289–1409* (Woodbridge, 2017); '"Unnatural in Body and a Villain in Soul": Rape and Sexual Violence Towards Girls Under the Age of Canonical Consent in Late Medieval England', in *Fourteenth Century England X* (Woodbridge, 2018); and 'Aliens and the Law in Late Medieval Lincolnshire', in *Resident Aliens in Later Medieval England* (Turnhout, 2017).

Maryanne Kowaleski is Joseph Fitzpatrick SJ Distinguished Professor of History and Medieval Studies at Fordham University. Her publications include *Local Markets and Regional Trade in Medieval Exeter* (Cambridge, 1995), editions of *The Local Customs Accounts of the Port of Exeter* (1993) and *The Havener's Accounts of the Earldom and Duchy of Cornwall* (2001), a reader on *Medieval Towns* (Toronto, 2006), several co-edited essay collections, and a wide variety of articles and book chapters on economic, urban, maritime and demographic history.

Jane Laughton was a leading authority on later medieval Chester and its courts. She published extensively on the economy and society of the medieval city, as well as on urban hierarchies and patterns of trade more widely in the English Midlands. She contributed to the *Victoria County History* of Cheshire with an important chapter on the city of Chester. Her well-known book, *Life in a Late Medieval City: Chester 1275–1520* (Oxford, 2008), has become the standard single-volume work on late medieval Chester. Jane died in 2017 during the preparation of this book.

Susan Maddock is an Honorary Research Fellow in the School of History at the University of East Anglia. A former archivist in the Norfolk Record Office, she was responsible for King's Lynn's borough archives for more than thirty years and curated exhibitions on many aspects of Lynn's history, including the medieval borough's relationship with the Hanse. Her current research focuses on the social milieu of late medieval Lynn, including family and other connections of Margery Kempe of Lynn. Recently published articles include 'Brewers, Bawds and Burgess Wives: The Lives of Women in Medieval Lynn', in *Women in the Archaeology and History of West Norfolk*, edited by Clive Bond (Cromer, 2017).

Teresa Phipps studied at the University of Nottingham (Ph.D. 2015) and was part of the AHRC-funded project, 'Women Negotiating the Boundaries of Justice: Britain and Ireland c. 1100 – c. 1750', based at Swansea University from 2016 to 2018. She researches and writes on urban women and local justice, with particular reference to litigation in late medieval English towns. She is the author of *Women and Urban Justice in Late Medieval England* (forthcoming with Manchester University Press) and has also published on trespass litigation, women and credit, and coverture.

Samantha Sagui is a doctoral candidate at Fordham University. Her dissertation, written under the direction of Maryanne Kowaleski, is entitled 'Law, Order and the Development of Urban Policing in Later Medieval England'. She has also studied at the University of East Anglia as a Fulbright Scholar. Her articles focusing on urban administrative history can be found in several scholarly journals.

ACKNOWLEDGEMENTS

The editors wish to thank the Scouloudi Foundation in association with the Institute of Historical Research for making this publication possible. We would also like to thank the Institute for Medieval Research and the Centre for Economic and Business History at the University of Nottingham for funding the original workshop and conference in 2014 and 2015 from which the creation of this volume stemmed. We also wish to thank all the participants at these two events for sharing their enthusiasm and ideas, not only for medieval urban history and town courts, but also for the publication of this volume.

legal issues that these courts were concerned with. Thirdly, we consider the practicalities of court action, through the way that the various chapters in the volume exemplify how justice worked for litigants, the role of officials and the nature of court procedure. Finally, we highlight the value of town courts beyond the direct issue of law and legal practice, by drawing attention to the numerous approaches taken in the study of medieval town court records.

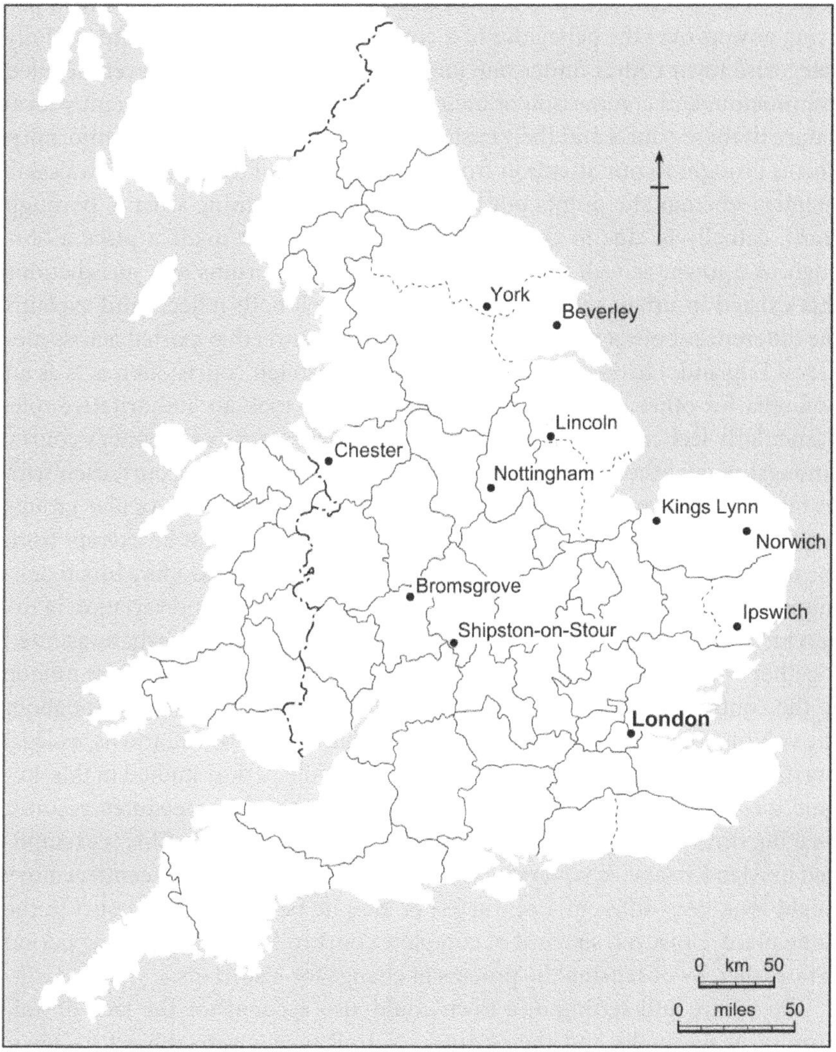

MAP 0.1: PRINCIPAL TOWN COURTS DISCUSSED IN THIS VOLUME

The Nature of Town Courts: Similarities and Differences

England's medieval town courts and their records shared many common features, including general aspects of their jurisdictions, procedures, the nature of litigation and the style of record-keeping, as the chapters of this volume demonstrate. The courts typically dealt mostly with civil pleas of debt and trespass, were governed and operated by a combination of local officials, had the power to assess damages and extract fines as punishment, and often held policing powers over the behaviour of town residents. We can, therefore, usefully categorise town courts under one jurisdictional grouping. However, detailed examination and comparison of their rolls also highlights the inherently local nature of these courts and their customs, and their distinct lack of uniformity. This is brought to our attention from the beginning of Maryanne Kowaleski's chapter, wherein she points out the difficulties in defining what a 'borough court' actually is, due to contested definitions of what made a place a borough or a town, as well as the wide range of legal forums and jurisdictions that existed in urban settings. It is this fact which both reflects and explains the differences between the innumerable urban courts that existed across medieval England. Furthermore, the category of borough courts often acts as an umbrella for other courts in which civic officials took an authoritative role, particularly leet courts, but also fair courts, staple courts or coroner's courts, amongst many others. Most towns possessed more than one court, each with its own unique name and practices, often administered by particular groups such as guilds or the officials of suburban manors that might be exempt from the jurisdiction of the borough. This volume intentionally adopts a broad definition of 'town court' in order to represent this complexity and variation in urban jurisdictions. This allows us to consider how different jurisdictions fitted together within individual towns. Each court and its procedures were unique to the context of the towns in which they existed, as we will see throughout the volume. But there were also differences that existed within towns, as legal practice developed and changed over time. Over the period studied in this volume, a court's jurisdiction, the type of plaints it heard, its procedures, records, meeting times and venues could all change, as did its officials. This is exemplified in Alan Kissane's chapter on Lincoln. A court in the late thirteenth century might look very different a century later, despite being the same court in the same place. However, survival of complete court rolls over such a long period is rare, thereby obscuring the process of change for historians.

The nature and setting of a town could also account for the lack of uniformity in boroughs and their courts. Not all towns were subject to 'town' courts. Christopher Dyer's chapter illustrates this through a case study of Shipston-on-Stour, a monastic town whose tenure mirrored that of most rural manorial settlements, where the burgesses attended their monastic lord's manorial court some two miles away. Other towns with royal charters were governed not by seigneurial lords but by groups of officials, often headed by a mayor, and it was these officials who determined practice and procedure in the town's court. The actions of plaintiffs and defendants could also influence the way courts dealt with justice, resulting in differences both between and within towns. As Teresa Phipps concludes, the negotiation or circumvention of formal court customs by the individuals attending them, and choices made by these individuals, all combined to create variable legal experiences for those using these courts. Only by examining the records of legal practice can we access these details. Therefore, whilst town courts often appear similar in terms of procedure, the nature of their records and their survival, on closer examination and comparison it becomes clear that their wide range of jurisdictions and privileges, the often unrecorded vagaries of time and the unpredictable actions of those who used them created considerable variability in the experience of justice for many in English medieval towns. This volume brings together just some of these wide-ranging practices and experiences.

The Jurisdiction of Town Courts

The collected essays exemplify many of the legal issues that town courts and local officials had the remit to deal with. These generally reflected the key characteristics of urban living: issues relating to trade, ties of credit and debt, interpersonal disputes and violence, urban property holding and the policing of misbehaviour. Each chapter details examples of some or all of these issues, amongst others. However, these concerns were generally not encapsulated under one single jurisdiction. Many urban centres, particularly larger towns, developed a system of multiple overlapping and sometimes competing jurisdictions. Again, the precise nature of these legal networks was specific to the context of each place. Port towns, for example, were home to courts dealing with maritime affairs, while many towns such as Chester and Winchester had exempt or suburban jurisdictions administered by other bodies, either within their boundaries or nearby. Centres that experienced a high volume of outside trade often operated piepowder courts[3] for those visiting traders of 'dusty foot' to settle their disputes during major fairs. This means that any study of town courts is often in fact a study of many courts, not one, in a particular place, as a single court cannot be examined in isolation. This is encapsulated in a number of the essays within this volume, which discuss the competition between courts within towns to attract business in the form of remunerative plaints.

3 A borough court held on the occasion of a market or fair. These courts had limited jurisdiction over personal actions that took place in the market, especially commercial disputes between merchants.

Samantha Sagui, discussing the leet court in Norwich, explains how the court attempted to ensure that residents attended this court rather than others in competing jurisdictions. Jane Laughton's study of the courts of later medieval Chester reveals the complexity of multi-layered jurisdictions that existed within large medieval towns, and the sometimes physical conflict that could erupt between these enclaves of independent jurisdictions within the city. Christopher Dyer highlights the potential for jurisdictional uncertainty in towns like Bromsgrove, where the lordship of the place was divided between two lords, meaning that townsfolk who might be neighbours were therefore required to attend the different courts run by their differing landlords. This competition for the dispensing of justice (and the profits that it offered) meant that officials and local governments sought to reinforce their authority by entering illustrative cases from borough courts into custumals. Esther Liberman Cuenca examines how some of these cases were used as legal precedent to legitimise local customary law and thereby clearly delineate the jurisdictional reach and authority of the court and its officers.

As well as exemplifying the complexities of urban jurisdictions, the chapters in this volume highlight how two particular areas of jurisdiction were of central importance and prominence in the business of town courts: disputes concerning land and commerce. These concerns were central to both townsfolk and local officials. In Lincoln, the 'writ of right' (*writ de recto*) dealt with disputes over land and property. As Kissane shows, these important disputes illuminate the social and judicial structures of the town, and they were recorded in the city's muniments because of the centrality of land to medieval perceptions of status. Likewise, pleas concerning business – especially pleas of debt, but also pleas of detinue, contract and account – were of utmost importance to residents and officials alike, and were the most common plaints brought before borough courts. These pleas served to regulate and enforce commercial obligations within the urban community; the ability to easily and efficiently resolve trading disputes enhanced trust within local trade networks and enhanced business confidence within a town more broadly. In mid-fifteenth-century Chester, Laughton reveals that pleas of debt comprised between 50 and 70 per cent of the plaints dealt with by the city's Pentice court. Cuenca's essay on borough custumals highlights the centrality of urban trade to Exeter's officials, who sought to secure their court's jurisdiction in order to reinforce their citizen merchants' privilege of retail trading without paying tolls.

Goddard's chapter demonstrates the centrality of commerce to urban jurisdictions, suggesting that the huge number of debt disputes heard in the borough court, involving many of the town's inhabitants, indicates the vigour of commercial activity in the town. In addition, the social networks revealed by debt complaints highlight the interconnected nature of urban commerce and the central role played by debt litigation in managing these ties and obligations. One of these Nottingham individuals was Agnes Halum, who Teresa Phipps has found to be involved in (at least) twenty-four pleas of debt and two of detinue over two decades – a figure that highlights the centrality of the local court to everyday life and trade. These characteristics of urban courts reflect the important commercial functions of towns more generally. A court that efficiently and cheaply resolved commercial disputes and disputes over land was seen as pivotal to the prosperity of any late medieval town.

The Practicalities of Going to Court

Through the wide-ranging subjects addressed throughout the volume, we also gain a detailed insight into how justice worked for litigants, the role that officials took and the nature of official procedure. These procedures were urban society's principal method for dealing with unmet obligations or misbehaviour, and thereby enforcing the role of justice in everyday life. While some of the issues that led people to court may have represented 'hatred' or a complete breakdown in relations, others were more ordinary and everyday – particularly in the case of business disputes.[4] Court rolls can therefore be understood to reflect something of the ordinariness of everyday urban living. We see, through a number of chapters, the various procedures used in a range of personal pleas such as debt, trespass and account, with justice being dispensed by both court officers and inquisition juries. As a result, we gain a sense of the practicalities involved in going to court: when court sessions were held, how a plea was initiated, the various stages of litigation and the potential outcomes. The dispensing of justice by town courts was aided by their central locations, public-facing attributes and wide attendance, as a number of chapters highlight. Sagui locates Norwich's widely-attended leet court at the Tollhus adjacent to the market square; Lincoln's Burwarmote court, Kissane shows, was located in the guildhall above the city's southern intramural gate; and Phipps likewise places Nottingham's borough court in the common hall (also used as the guildhall), which was also adjacent to the weekday market. All of these were geographically central, 'public' locations that also had symbolic and practical centrality within the urban community.

Court records allow us to gain an insight into litigants' experiences of justice and the choices that were available to them from a number of perspectives. In Nottingham, both Goddard and Phipps demonstrate the readiness of local residents to use the court in settling their disputes, including the

4 Daniel Lord Smail has argued that, in medieval Marseille, use of the law courts was motivated by either love or hatred: *The Consumption of Justice: Emotions, Publicity, and Legal Culture in Marseille, 1264–1423* (Ithaca, NY, 2013), pp. 90–2.

acknowledgement of debts. This was undoubtedly characteristic of litigants in courts elsewhere, too. In Lincoln, Kissane shows how community and neighbourhood connections informed litigants' choices in appointing electors in *writ de recto* cases prior to the Black Death, and how the later emergence of a local oligarchy was reflected in these pleas and the narrowing group from which electors were chosen. Litigation underpinned much of the business of seigneurial jurisdictions in smaller towns, too, though residents sometimes resisted the power of their lord and his court. Close attention to individual pleas allows us to examine how these complaints were constructed, sometimes strategically, as they passed through courts and were entered onto their records. Jeremy Goldberg's chapter draws attention to the decisions made by litigants in initiating legal action and narrating their complaints in the course of performing the 'drama' of the legal process.

The role, actions and attitudes of officials were central to the way that each court operated, motivated both by the provision of justice and by the financial perquisites of courts as sources of revenue for urban governments and lords. Sagui argues that the early-fourteenth-century standardisation of court proceedings in Norwich represents an attempt by officials to reinforce their control over the courts and the perquisites they realised. By doing so, this group strengthened their hegemony over local justice. Likewise, Cuenca concludes that the action of embedding borough court cases into town custumals as exemplars empowered officers to create customary law that was ultimately enforced by the courts over which they presided. The richness of Chester's surviving court records allows Laughton to examine the official administration of justice in detail, from eminent mayors and sheriffs to lowlier jurors, pledges and attorneys. Indeed, whilst these courts were controlled by a relatively small set of often wealthy and politically active individuals or officials, the volume of records allows changes over time to be perceived, as Susan Maddock's work on Lynn highlights. Sagui also detects changes in the administration of sub-leets, combined with a significant increase in court business – possibly prompted by concerned officials – in the decades following the Black Death.

Court fines generated important revenue for civic governments and urban lords. The range of fees and fines that town courts collected was large, arising from both the processes and outcomes of litigation, as well as punishment for misbehaviour and other offences. Whilst both Laughton and Sagui point out that court fines sometimes remained uncollected or were pardoned, Sagui further demonstrates that fines for trading while not being a member of the franchise were an attempt to safeguard members of the Norwich freedom from unrestricted competition. There was an increase in these types of fines, particularly at the end of the fourteenth century after the Black Death. For Dyer, fines and the courts themselves were instruments of lords' attempts to control, profit from and administer seigneurial boroughs. The extent of lords' seigneurial control over courts brings some limitations to the study of court records, and Dyer warns us that 'if we focus our attention on the evidence of the courts attended by townspeople, we are in danger of examining urban life through the narrow prism of the lord's documents'. This, along with Goldberg's description of the multiple stages involved in the construction of court records and our subsequent analysis of these documents, serves as a reminder that court records can never be considered a direct window onto urban society. Nevertheless, across all the chapters we see how town courts sought to meet the needs of litigants seeking dispute resolution or compensation for various wrongs, and of officials who closely guarded the privileges of justice and relied on its profits.

Court Records and the Study of Medieval Urban Society

The value of bringing together different studies and approaches in a volume such as this lies in exemplifying the various ways and approaches by which court rolls can be used in historical research. As well as making detailed use of the court records, many of the chapters examine court rolls in conjunction with other surviving documentary material. In others, one type of court record is examined in isolation. All of these studies are exercises in piecing together and reconstructing the past, though they do so using a variety of methodologies. For example, using Lynn's court and other administrative records, Maddock achieves both spatial and prosopographical reconstruction. The chapter excavates in detail the urban world and family connections of Lynn's most famous woman, Margery Kempe, allowing readers to widen their understanding of her life and book and to place it more fully within its historical context. It is even possible to locate some of the tenements owned by Kempe's family within the town of Lynn. Kissane uses the Lincoln court rolls to investigate attitudes to urban space as well as the community networks revealed by litigation, arguing that those who were chosen by litigants to represent them in court – known as 'electors' – were not only upstanding members of the local community, but also were commonly drawn from the litigant's own neighbourhood. The different types of plaint handled by the courts also allow the lives of ordinary, unexceptional people – like Nottingham's Agnes Halum – to be cast into sharp relief. Taking a different approach, Goddard borrows from the methodology of social network analysis to reveal the networks of Nottingham's business people who traded within, and occasionally beyond, the town. Court records reveal the face-to-face nature of medieval urban living, even in larger cities where, as Goddard's discussion of credit networks in Nottingham suggests, everybody seemed to know everybody else's business.

Court records can also elucidate the attitudes of officials and communities, of interest to social historians in particular. Several chapters discuss attitudes to groups that were marginalised within urban society and had limited rights within their local courts, such as foreigners or women. Whilst the term 'foreigners' in court records often refers to those who were not property holders or burgesses within the town, or those who had not acquired the freedom or liberty to trade within it, some chapters shed light on the interactions of those from outside the kingdom who were more generally known as 'aliens'. Sagui suggests that increasing alien immigration to Norwich, witnessed in the post-plague leet rolls, may well have been perceived as a threat to local traders, but is also evidence of increased long-distance mobility and immigration in the later fourteenth century. Likewise, Maddock discusses the increase in immigrant alien craftsmen – commonly from Flanders – resident in Lynn in the early fifteenth century, who can be located within the various wards of the town.

Women too were active members of the urban community, and their identities are also illuminated by court records. Their legal action was circumscribed by local customary applications of the common law principle of coverture, whereby married women ceased to have an independent legal identity and were instead 'covered' by their husbands. They were not invisible, however, and a number of chapters bring the lives of urban women into focus, thanks to the details contained in the court records. The legal drama and narratives involved in a number of cases featuring women as litigants or the subject of complaints take centre stage in Goldberg's discussion of the construction of court testimonies. Likewise, female litigants feature in Laughton's chapter on Chester, where women could also act as personal pledges, albeit generally restricted to pledging for family members and servants. A few wealthy Chester widows appointed attorneys to act on their behalf, perhaps as a form of legal strategy. However, it is Phipps's prosopographical essay on Nottingham's Agnes Halum which really demonstrates how court rolls can be used to recover the lives and experiences of individual women – in this case a businesswoman – and how these women used town courts to negotiate business and interpersonal relationships, even despite the supposed limits of coverture.

All of the studies in this volume have mined court records in search of detail on a range of subjects, but the different chapters reveal various means of interpretation. Some have looked to uncover historical details, taking the records at face value; some have surveyed records over extended periods, while others have focused on shorter time frames or even individual years; others have discussed overarching attitudes, narratives or conventions elucidated by town court records, paying attention to what this reveals of the contemporary values of those in charge of courts and their litigants. For Dyer, seigneurial boroughs and their courts were venues for feudal enforcement where the actions of tenants could be regulated and curbed. Goldberg offers an alternative, important perspective on the *mentalités* that might be accessed through a critical approach to reading town court rolls, encapsulated in the way in which particular events and disputes were processed, interpreted and recorded. This interpretation views the creation of the records themselves as distinct historical moments. In analysing the narrative strategies employed by litigants in court and their sometimes fictive or scripted nature, Goldberg argues that the crafting of these cases tells us much about the contemporary values and anxieties of the men and women who regularly used these institutions, and that 'what really happened' is in fact out of reach. These are important qualifiers to the more practical and procedural study of court records, reminding us to approach court records with caution, sensitivity and a critical eye.

We also consider further research possibilities that might make use of town court evidence, in the hope that this book might be a starting point for future studies. For example, it is worth remembering that town courts could not solve all disputes. Shipston-on-Stour's burgesses rejected and abandoned their lord's court when seeking self-government for the town; they turned instead to the king's courts, where they felt, no doubt, that they would receive a fairer hearing. This serves as a reminder of the need to place town courts within their wider English legal framework, as part of a network of both local and kingdom-wide jurisdictions.

Within this volume, limited attention has been paid to London – an exceptional case due to its size, status and unique combination of different jurisdictions. Its many courts need to be considered as components of an extensive city-wide jurisdictional apparatus, as well as being contrasted with other urban courts in the kingdom.[5] Furthermore, some excellent work has already been undertaken on London's courts, a reflection of the city's command over the historiography of medieval urban Britain, as well as the wealth of surviving records. Matthew Stevens has worked extensively on Londoners in the Court of Common Pleas, a common law court that heard pleas between crown subjects (or 'commoners'), often relating to trade and commercial disputes, or disputes over land.[6] Likewise, Goddard has studied the statute staple

5 We are excluding here royal courts such as chancery, exchequer and king's bench. Pleas were heard in both chancery and exchequer, but these might be more appropriately considered departments of government. However, by the late fourteenth century the chancery did serve two distinct purposes, primarily as a royal secretariat and secondly as a court of equitable jurisdiction.

6 Matthew Frank Stevens, 'London's married women, debt litigation and coverture in the Court of Common Pleas', in Cordelia Beattie and Matthew Frank Stevens (eds), *Married Women and the Law in Premodern Northwest Europe* (Woodbridge, 2013), pp. 115–32; Matthew Frank Stevens, 'Londoners and the Court of Common Pleas in the fifteenth century', in Matthew Davies and James A. Galloway (eds), *London and Beyond: Essays in Honour of Derek Keene* (London,

debt-registration courts, another royal prerogative, of London and Westminster.[7] However, it is London's Mayor's and Sheriff's courts, previously examined by Caroline Barron, that most closely resemble the town courts discussed in this volume.[8] Some of the most exhaustive work on these London courts has been undertaken by Penny Tucker in examining the lawyers and litigants who used them in the fifteenth century, as well as the competition that existed between the London and Westminster courts in their attempts to attract litigants.[9] This volume therefore intentionally turns our attention to some of England's less well-known medieval towns and courts. Future research might benefit from direct comparative examination of London and provincial courts in order to consider the similarities in processes and jurisdiction in the capital and elsewhere. There is also scope for further comparative research on the medieval courts of Wales, Scotland and Ireland – each country having its own unique legal traditions and political context – as well as comparative studies of British and continental courts and the urban societies they presided over.

Other evidence from court rolls might also bear interesting fruit. A study of the goods taken in amercements or in distraint would reveal much about defendants and their standards of living.[10] For example, in Nottingham in 1396, a hosier, William de Sutton, was attached by a Flanders chest (*flaundreskyst*), seized from de Sutton's house in order to compel him to come to court to answer the plea of debt made against him.[11] Concerted analysis of these details would tell us more about the material culture of urban life, the wealth and status of litigants, and the specific tools by which the court sought to deliver justice. Similarly, recent research has considered changes in the languages used in royal courts of equity, particularly parliament and chancery, in the

---

2012); Matthew Frank Stevens, 'Failed arbitrations before the Court of Common Pleas: cases relating to London and Londoners, 1400–1468', *Journal of Legal History*, 31 (2010), pp. 21–44. See also Derek Keene, 'Changes in London's economic hinterland as indicated by debt cases in the Court of Common Pleas', in James A. Galloway (ed.), *Trade, Urban Hinterlands and Market Integration c. 1300–1600*, Centre for Metropolitan History Working Papers, Series No. 3 (London, 2000), pp. 59–81; Margaret Hastings, *The Court of Common Pleas in Fifteenth-Century England: A Study of Legal Administration and Procedure* (Ithaca, NY, 1947).

7 Richard Goddard, *Credit and Trade in Later Medieval England* (Basingstoke, 2016), pp. 198–211.

8 Caroline Barron, *London in the Later Middle Ages: Government and the People, 1200–1500* (Oxford, 2004), pp. 121–46.

9 Penny Tucker, *Law Courts and Lawyers in the City of London, 1300–1530* (Cambridge, 2007); Penny Tucker, 'London courts of law in the fifteenth century: the litigants' perspective', in Christopher Brooks and Michael Lobban (eds), *Communities and Courts in Britain, 1150–1900* (London, 1997), pp. 25–42; Penny Tucker, 'Relationships between London's courts and the Westminster courts in the reign of Edward IV', in Diana E. S. Dunn (ed.), *Courts, Counties and the Capital in the Later Middle Ages* (New York, 1996), pp. 117–38.

10 See, for example, Daniel Lord Smail, *Legal Plunder: Households and Debt Collection in Late Medieval Europe* (London, 2016), p. 35.

11 Nottinghamshire Archives (hereafter NA), CA 1296/II, fol. 1.

fifteenth century.[12] Town court rolls were generally written in Latin by grammar-school trained scribes and clerks, but we know remarkably little about the language used by litigants, their attorneys and the court's officers during the proceedings. Occasionally, as Goldberg discusses in his chapter, litigants' words were recorded, though they may have been specially scripted to tell a story or convey emotion. In 1323, Ralph de Hockrock, a servant, came to Robert le Mareschal's house in Nottingham to pick up a horse for a job he had been asked to do by his master – but le Mareschal, who didn't seem to know anything about the arrangement, 'called Ralph a false man and a thief and said he came there in order to rob him'.[13] We assume this exchange took place in English outside Robert's house, was then reiterated in the court in some language – English, Anglo-Norman or possibly Latin – and this recapitulation was then recorded and rendered into formulaic court-roll Latin by the court's scribe. It is generally acknowledged that scribes in towns borrowed from formulae used in common law courts (such as trespass 'with force and arms'), but a concerted analysis of this would further enhance our understanding of the relationships between legal knowledge and practice in central and provincial courts, as well as the stages involved in the pursuit of dispute resolution. These briefly elucidated ideas, of course, only scratch the surface. As this book demonstrates, the urban court rolls that survive in considerable quantities in British archives and in print – exemplified by Kowaleski's appendix of edited court rolls – represent a still under-used and potentially very fruitful source for medieval historians studying urban societies.

12 Gwilym Dodd, 'The rise of English, the decline of French: supplications to the English crown, c. 1420–50', *Speculum*, 86 (2011), pp. 117–50.

13 NA CA 1258a, fol. 12.

JANE LAUGHTON: IN MEMORIAM

We wanted to express our sadness at the death of Jane Laughton during the preparation of this volume. Jane died on 15 October 2017 of melanoma cancer. Her chapter for this collection was her final publication. Her husband, Tony, wrote to us about her unwavering enthusiasm for the project during her illness and that, 'some ten days before her death I spent time with her on the subject [of her chapter] as her computer refused to obey her instructions! I went through much of the text with her and typed in some corrections for her.' This is testament to her commitment and contribution to the study of later medieval urban history, and particularly the history of Chester, over many decades. Jane had already published on a number of aspects of seventeenth-century Cheshire before she received her Ph.D. from the University of Cambridge in 1994 on the subject of the economy and society of later medieval Chester. She always had an interest in medieval Chester's women. In the 1990s she wrote on the city's alewives and women's experiences in court.[1] Jane also wrote on Chester's physical fabric, its port and its surviving medieval buildings; she contributed three co-authored chapters to the *Chester Rows Research Project* publication.[2] Later her interests expanded and, whilst working on the ESRC-funded project, 'Urban Hierarchy and Functions in the East Midlands in the Late Middle Ages' with Christopher Dyer, she was part of the team that made a number of important contributions to the study of urban hierarchies and patterns of trade in the English Midlands.[3] She also published

1 Jane Laughton, 'The alewives of later medieval Chester', in Rowena E. Archer (ed.), *Crown, Government and People in the Fifteenth Century* (Stroud, 1995), pp. 191–208; Jane Laughton, 'Women in court: some evidence from fifteenth-century Chester', in Nicholas Rogers (ed.), *England in the Fifteenth Century: Proceedings from the Harlaxton Symposium* (Stamford, 1994), pp. 89–99.

2 Jane Laughton, 'The port of Chester in the later Middle Ages', in Peter Carrington (ed.), *'Where Deva Spreads her Wizard Stream': Trade and the Port of Chester*, Chester Archaeology, Occasional Paper No. 3 (Chester, 1996), pp. 66–71; Andrew Brown (ed.), *The Rows of Chester: The Chester Rows Research Project*, English Heritage Archaeological Report, 16 (1999), pp. 63–75, 77–94, 151–5.

3 Christopher Dyer and Jane Laughton, 'Small towns in the East and West Midlands in the

interdisciplinary pieces on medieval Northampton, Catesby in Northamptonshire and Meols in the Wirral (but historically in Cheshire).[4] However, she never abandoned her interest in Chester. In 2003, Jane contributed to the *Victoria County History* of Cheshire with a chapter on the economy and society of the city of Chester.[5] Indeed, it was her 2008 book, *Life in a Late Medieval City*, that really cemented her reputation as the leading scholar of medieval Chester and its records.[6] This was a clear and lively exploration of the late medieval city, based primarily upon the evidence of its courts. Its high quality of scholarship and lucid and accessible writing style meant the book was to become the standard single-volume work on late medieval Chester. Jane continued to write on aspects of Chester's medieval social history. In 2010 she wrote a chapter for Christopher Dyer's *festschrift* on how Chester's courts attempted to contain – often unsuccessfully – the violence, dissention and squabbling that regularly broke out amongst its townsfolk.[7] Subsequently she wrote an important chapter on immigrants to medieval Chester who originated from Wales and the Isle of Man for the *Mapping the Medieval City* project, and an article for *Cheshire History* on the successful careers of a number of men from later medieval Cheshire.[8] It is an honour to include Jane's last publication in this volume, which we hope will provide a fitting legacy to Jane's many decades of important research.

---

later Middle Ages: a comparison', *Midland History*, 24 (1999), pp. 24–52; Christopher Dyer, Jane Laughton and Evan Jones, 'The urban hierarchy in the later Middle Ages: a study of the East Midlands', *Urban History*, 28 (2001), pp. 331–57; Christopher Dyer and Jane Laughton, 'Seasonal patterns of trade in the later Middle Ages: buying and selling at Melton Mowbray, Leicestershire, 1400–1520', *Nottingham Medieval Studies*, 46 (2002), pp. 162–84.

4 Evan T. Jones, Jane Laughton and Peter Clark, *Northampton in the Late Middle Ages: The Archaeology and History of a Midland Town*, Centre for Urban History, University of Leicester, Working Paper No. 10 (2000); Jane Laughton, 'Catesby in the Middle Ages: an interdisciplinary study' [Part 1], *Northamptonshire Past and Present*, 54 (2001), pp. 7–32; Brian L. Giggins and Jane Laughton, 'Catesby: an interdisciplinary study' [Part 2], *Northamptonshire Past and Present*, 56 (2003), pp. 52–5; Jane Laughton, 'Catesby Priory as consumer in the first half of the fifteenth century', in Sylvia Pinches, Margaret Whalley and David Postles (eds), *The Market Place and the Place of the Market*, Friends of the Centre for English Local History, Friends' Paper No. 9 (Leicester, 2004), pp. 35–43; David Griffiths, Robert A. Philpott and Geoff Egan, *Meols: The Archaeology of the North Wirral Coast*, Oxford University School of Archaeology, Monograph 68, Institute of Archaeology (Oxford, 2007), pp. 406–12, 412–22.

5 Jane Laughton, 'Economy and society, 1350–1500', in C. P. Lewis and A. T. Thacker (eds), *The Victoria County History of the County of Cheshire*, vol. 5, part 1, *The City of Chester* (London, 2003), pp. 64–78.

6 Jane Laughton, *Life in a Late Medieval City: Chester, 1275–1520* (Oxford, 2008).

7 Jane Laughton, 'The control of discord in fifteenth-century Chester', in Richard Goddard, John Langdon and Miriam Müller (eds), *Survival and Discord in Medieval Society: Essays in Honour of Christopher Dyer* (Turnhout, 2010), pp. 213–30.

8 Jane Laughton, 'Mapping the migrants: Welsh and Manx settlers in fifteenth-century Chester', in Catherine A. M. Clarke (ed.), *Mapping the Medieval City: Space, Place and Identity in Chester c. 1200–1500* (Cardiff, 2011); Jane Laughton, 'Successful careerists from south-east Cheshire in the years 1383–1403', *Cheshire History*, 57 (2017–18), pp. 8–29.

1

TOWN COURTS IN MEDIEVAL ENGLAND: AN INTRODUCTION

MARYANNE KOWALESKI

This chapter aims to provide a practical introduction to the jurisdictions, format, procedure and business of town courts, particularly for those seeking to employ this source to understand the economic, political and social life of medieval English towns. Scholars have paid more attention to manorial and common law courts than to town courts, and there have been few attempts to provide comparative studies that categorise their jurisdictions and business.[1] This failure is due in large part to the tremendous variety of town courts and their reliance on local customary law, which have made them more a focus of specialists writing about a particular town. There is also no consensus – indeed, little sustained discussion at all – about how to define a town or 'borough' court, although the contributions to this volume should go some way towards addressing this lacuna.

The difficulty in defining a borough court rests in part on scholarly debates about the term 'borough', which has often been narrowly and legally construed by medievalists to mean a community recognised as a 'free borough' by the crown. This identification usually came in the form of a charter, although other signs – such as a parliamentary summons, taxation at the urban rate, or burgage tenure – are also considered evidence of borough status.[2] Scholars

1 For example, a search on the index term 'courts, manorial' for the period 1200 to 1520 in the online 'Bibliography of British and Irish History', <https://www.history.ac.uk/projects/bbih> [accessed 19 March 2019] turns up 168 items. There is no equivalent index term for borough or town courts, but a search on 'courts' and 'borough' yields twenty-five items for 1200 to 1520, and that for 'courts' and 'town' yields 113 references. See also G. H. Martin, 'The English borough in the thirteenth century', *Transactions of the Royal Historical Society*, 5th series, 13 (1963), pp. 126–8 on scholarly failures to deal with borough courts.

2 The definitive list (numbering 640 boroughs in England before 1509) is in Maurice W.

continue to find it difficult to identify the specific characteristics that set boroughs apart from other communities, but most agree that the enjoyment of burgage tenure, whereby property could be freely bought, sold, leased and bequeathed, is considered the chief characteristic of borough status.[3] Even so, there were recognised boroughs whose chief court was manorial, and communities with no substantive claim to borough status that had courts whose business and procedures resemble what happened in borough courts. Another problem is that 'borough' can be used as a synonym for 'town' – that is, a settlement in which most residents were engaged in non-agricultural occupations, even if the settlement lacked a borough charter and was no larger than most villages.[4] This question of definition requires more systematic investigation, but in what follows, 'borough courts' (and 'town courts') denote legally-sanctioned meetings that included presentments of offences and/or personal pleas, and that were run under the authority (partial or complete) of officials acknowledged as representatives of an urban community. Included in this definition are urban fair courts, market courts, staple courts, maritime courts, coroner's courts and even guild merchant courts in which civic officials took an authoritative role. Excluded are courts run by and for smaller, specifically-defined groups such as guilds and urban sokes, fees, and suburban manors exempt from the jurisdiction of the borough.

Early Borough Courts

Anglo-Saxon law codes and the Domesday Book refer to courts in *burhs* (fortified settlements) and the doomsmen (judges) who presided over them, but some of these *burhs* were scarcely urban, and many of their courts were convened as much for a regional population as for *burh* residents.[5] Nevertheless,

---

Beresford and H. P. R. Finberg, *English Medieval Boroughs: A Handlist* (Newton Abbot, 1973); Maurice Beresford, 'English medieval boroughs: a handlist: revisions, 1973–1981', *Urban History Yearbook* (1981), pp. 59–65. For boroughs recognised by charter, see Adolphus Ballard, *British Borough Charters, 1042–1216* (Cambridge, 1913); Adolphus Ballard and James Tait, *British Borough Charters, 1216–1307* (Cambridge, 1923); Martin Weinbaum, *British Borough Charters, 1307–1660* (Cambridge, 1943).

3 Morley de Wolf Hemmeon, *Burgage Tenure in Medieval England* (Cambridge, MA, 1914); Ballard, *British Borough Charters, 1042–1216*, pp. xliv–xlvi, cxxxviii–cxlvii; Ballard and Tait, *British Borough Charters, 1216–1307*, pp. xlix–liv, xc–cii; James Tait, *The Medieval English Borough: Studies on its Origins and Constitutional History* (Manchester, 1936), pp. 96–108.

4 Susan Reynolds, *An Introduction to the History of Medieval English Towns* (Oxford, 1977), pp. 91–102, 112, 114. See also Christopher Dyer, 'Small places with large consequences: the importance of small towns in England, 1000–1540', *Historical Research*, 75 (2002), pp. 1–24, and Dyer, 'Courts and Urbanisation: Jurisdiction in Late Medieval Seigneurial Boroughs and Towns', in this volume.

5 For this and the following, see: Tait, *Medieval English Borough*, pp. 30–67; John Hudson, *The Oxford History of the Laws of England*, vol. 2 (Oxford, 2012), pp. 812–24; F. M. Stenton, 'Norman London: an essay', in William Fitz Stephen, *Norman London* (New York, 1934), pp. 10–13.

aspects of the jurisdiction that became central to later borough courts can be glimpsed in the tenth and eleventh centuries, such as references to town law (*burhriht*) as distinct from country law, specific legal privileges that allowed *burhs* to adjudicate a larger range of cases, and more frequent court meetings in towns. London had at least two courts (the Folkmoot and the Court of Hustings) by the eleventh century (and possibly the tenth), and at least ten other Anglo-Saxon towns had also developed their own courts.

Borough courts and legal customs, particularly the right of burgesses to be impleaded only in their own borough courts, emerge more clearly in the borough charters that proliferated in the twelfth and thirteenth centuries, indicating the value that townspeople placed on adjudicating their own affairs. Other privileges granted in charters include the right to exclude county and hundred officials from interfering in borough matters, the right to enjoy specific forms of proof such as compurgation, the right to avoid trial by battle and certain types of fines, and the right to confiscate goods from debtors within the borough to ensure repayment.[6] The jurisdictional reach of borough courts, as well as their special procedures and punishments, are especially evident in the borough customs that were sometimes included in these charters, but increasingly recorded separately in borough custumals or urban compendia.[7] These customs were jealously guarded and often invoked by burgesses, but more work needs to be done to determine the origin and rationale behind those customs that dealt with borough courts. We also need to consider why some borough customs stood the test of time, and others – such as several of the more unusual punishments meted out to offenders – were rarely if ever observed.

In many instances, the borough charter was granted to a guild merchant that represented the entire urban community, even though the guild tended to act mostly in the interests of the wealthier merchants who dominated its ranks.[8] The guild merchant had disappeared in many towns by the thirteenth century or earlier, but in some places it remained strong into the later Middle Ages or became the basis for the borough 'freedom' or 'liberty' that conferred all the burgess privileges recorded in borough charters and custumals. In towns where the guild merchant survived, its members held annual or semi-annual meetings, often accompanied by drinking and feasting, to admit new members, punish those who did not adhere to the guild's rules, and make

6 Ballard, *British Borough Charters, 1042–1216*, pp. liii–lxvi, cxxxviii–cxlvii, 112–67; Ballard and Tait, *British Borough Charters, 1217–1307*, pp. xc–cii, 145–238.

7 Mary Bateson (ed.), *Borough Customs*, 2 vols, Selden Society, 18 and 21 (London, 1904–21). See also Cuenca, 'Borough Court Cases as Legal Precedent in English Town Custumals', in this volume.

8 The seminal work here remains: Charles Gross, *The Gild Merchant: A Contribution to British Municipal History*, 2 vols (Oxford, 1890).

new ordinances.[9] The main business of these meetings was administrative, but they frequently labelled themselves as 'courts', judged members who infringed guild ordinances, and adjudicated personal pleas. These guild meetings can be considered a type of 'borough court' when litigants came from outside the guild, or when the guild court supervised civic elections, discussions of civic finances or enforcement of civic ordinances.[10]

The earliest court rolls for a guild merchant survive for Leicester from 1196 and Shrewsbury from 1209.[11] The first extant rolls for a borough court survive for Wallingford Burghmoot from 1229, Ipswich Portmanmote from 1256, Exeter's Mayor's court from 1264, and a roll of pleas for Winchester from 1270; the first enrolments of deeds in the London Hustings court begin in 1252.[12] Court rolls from another five boroughs (Barnstaple, Bridport, Chester, Oxford and Great Yarmouth) are extant between 1277 and 1298, and the numbers of extant court rolls from other boroughs increase substantially in the fourteenth and fifteenth centuries. There is no master list of extant borough court records to match that available for manorial courts, although researchers can start by looking at the Historical Manuscripts Commission Reports (HMCR) and the National Register of Archives (NRA) reports for individual boroughs.[13] It should be noted, however, that although many borough court rolls survive, only a few survive in good, relatively continuous runs of more than fifty years (notably Exeter and Nottingham). Many towns also had other courts whose records are extant only for later periods. There is considerable scholarly work that needs to be done to work out not only the jurisdictions and procedures of the different types of courts in towns, but also how they changed over time.[14]

9 Gross, *Gild Merchant*, vol. 1, pp. 32–4.

10 For examples, see the guild merchant courts in Aberdeen, Leicester and Stamford (Kowaleski, 'Annotated List', in this volume). Both Bateson and Gross emphasise the eventual integration of guild merchant and borough government, but neither really consider the legal business of the guild merchant on its own terms since they see the issue through the lens of institutional history; Mary Bateson, 'Introduction', in *Records of the Borough of Leicester: Being a Series of Extracts from the Archives of the Corporation of Leicester*, ed. Mary Bateson, revised by W. H. Stevenson and J. E. Stocks, 3 vols (London, 1899–1901), vol. 1, pp. xxviii–xlix; Gross, *Gild Merchant*, vol. 1, pp. 32–3, 90, 123–6. For guild merchant meetings that were restricted to admissions and other issues directly related to the guild, see Shrewsbury (below, n. 11).

11 Bateson (ed.), *Records of the Borough of Leicester*, vol. 1, pp. 12–34; C. H. Drinkwater (ed. and trans.), 'The merchants' gild of Shrewsbury: the two earliest rolls for 1209–10 and 1219–20', *Transactions of the Shropshire Archaeological and Natural History Society*, 2nd series, 2 (1890), pp. 21–43.

12 Martin, 'English borough', pp. 129–30 for this and the following.

13 For the HMCR reports on boroughs, see the list in Charles Gross, *A Bibliography of British Municipal History* (London, 1897), pp. 10–12, although only a small proportion of these reports actually contain more than short descriptions of which court rolls survive; see Kowaleski, 'Annotated List', in this volume. The NRA reports on borough records are mostly in typescript, available at The National Archives in Kew and at the University of London, Institute of Historical Research.

14 Exceptions include: G. H. Martin, *The Early Court Rolls of the Borough of Ipswich*, Depart-

The Format of Borough Court Records

Most boroughs recorded their court sessions on rolls of parchment membranes, laced together at the top, exchequer-style; but a few, such as the London Court of Hustings, recorded deeds and wills on membranes sewn together end-to-end in chancery-style.[15] Only occasionally were borough courts entered in book folios, and then only towards the end of the Middle Ages. The language of the court proceedings was always Latin, though Middle English was increasingly employed in the second half of the fifteenth century. Individual court sessions were signalled by a heading on the roll, usually in a large script that noted the name, day and date of the court, and the presiding officer(s). Dating relied on religious feasts, though by the end of the fifteenth century some towns were using the day of the month. The main borough courts in the larger towns tended to meet on the same day each week, but business could be carried over to other days if needed (Table 1.1).[16] Borough leet courts met less frequently, one to three times a year. Fair courts convened only during fair-time. In some towns such as Colchester, and to a lesser extent Great Yarmouth, all these courts were recorded on the same roll – but in most boroughs, each court had its own separate roll, emulating the practice of the courts of the central government.[17]

Town clerks used highly abbreviated marginal notations to mark stages in the progress of an action, plea or presentment. Although some are common, such as *Ess'* to mark essoins (which often appear towards the beginning of the court roll) or *Dis'* to indicate that one party should be distrained, many towns and their clerks developed their own systems of notation and legal terminology.[18] The types of legal business handled depended on the type of court, but within each court there was a tendency to follow the same order of business, so that leet court presentments of, for example, breaking the assize of ale or forestalling were usually recorded in the same order year after

ment of English Local History Occasional Papers, 5 (Leicester, 1954), and Richard H. Britnell, 'Colchester courts and court records, 1310–1525', *Essex Archaeology and History*, 17 (1986), pp. 133–40. For how confusing it can be to distinguish the different courts and their changes over time, see the example of Ipswich in the following section. For such changes, see also in this volume: Kissane, 'The Black Death and the Borough Court'; Laughton, 'Justice and Jurisdictions in Late Medieval Chester'; and Maddock, 'Society, Status and the Leet Court in Margery Kempe's Lynn'.

15 G. H. Martin, *The Hustings Rolls of Deeds and Wills, 1252–1485: Guide to the Microfilm Edition* (Cambridge, 1990), pp. 9–10. The earliest Petty Pleas roll of Ipswich was also tied chancery-style; Martin, *Early Court Rolls of Ipswich*, p. 26.

16 See also Kowaleski, 'Annotated List', in this volume.

17 Martin, *Early Court Rolls of Ipswich*, p. 17.

18 For examples of this legal terminology and abbreviations, see Richard Britnell (ed.), *Records of the Borough of Crossgate, Durham 1312–1531*, Surtees Society, 212 (Woodbridge, 2008), pp. xlvi–xlviii; *Sheriffs' Court Books of the City of York for the Fifteenth Century*, trans. P. M. Stell (York, 2000), pp. 469–79.

year. This orderliness reflects the conservative nature of borough courts, but it also allowed clerks to write out the business of the court in advance.[19] In some court rolls, it is clear that the clerks prepared a template, with space for assize presentments or pleas at different procedural stages, and then filled in the details during or after the court session itself. In other courts, clerks even wrote out in advance the details of cases that they knew would be coming before the court. The court roll served as a working record of the court's business, as can be seen in annotations inserted in a different ink or hand, in superscripts that add details of pleadings and verdicts, and in small pieces of parchment stitched onto the sides with lists of jurors or a copy of a writ, or notes on a particular case.[20]

Further attention to the codicology and diplomatic of borough court rolls can also enhance our understanding of the legal knowledge of the clerks who recorded them, and can bring to light changes in the jurisdiction, business and procedures of these courts.[21] By tracking formatting features of the Ipswich courts, for example, scholars have shown (Table 1.1) how the Petty court emerged out of the Portmanmote court in the late thirteenth century as a new jurisdiction for personal pleas (particularly debt cases), and how a third court, the Petty Court of Recognizances, was formed in the mid fourteenth century to handle land transactions (once recorded in the Petty court), along with burgess admissions and testaments (originally the province of the Portmanmote). Around the same time, pleas of abatement (Ipswich's version of assize of novel disseisin) began to be recorded in their own roll, but after twenty years the practice halted, so no separate court formed and these pleas eventually became part of the Petty Court of Recognizances. In the early fifteenth century, moreover, a General court (later called the Great court) split off from the Portmanmote to handle administrative functions such as burgess admissions, elections and new ordinances. Its records were kept in book form rather than rolls. The growing prestige and purview of the Petty court at the expense of the Portmanmote was evident in the headings to its sessions in the early 1420s, when it was being called 'the court of the lord king held at Ipswich', while a royal charter in 1463 confirmed its position as Ipswich's chief court. Ipswich's Maritime court survives in separate rolls from 1434 and most likely treated business once handled by the Portmanmote and

19 For this and the following, see Britnell, 'Colchester courts', and Devon Heritage Centre, Exeter City Archives [hereafter DHC, ECA], Mayor's court rolls, passim.

20 Such 'riders' are common on Exeter court rolls (DHC, ECA, Mayor's court rolls, passim) and in Ipswich; Martin, *Early Court Rolls of Ipswich*, p. 27.

21 Useful works on the codicology and diplomatic of borough court records include: G. H. Martin, 'Introduction', in G. H. Martin (ed.), *The Ipswich Recognizance Rolls 1294–1327: A Calendar*, Suffolk Records Society, 16 (Ipswich, 1973); Britnell, 'Colchester courts'. For town clerks, see Esther Liberman Cuenca, 'Town clerks and the authorship of custumals in medieval England', *Urban History* (2018), pp. 1–22, and the works cited there.

later the Petty court. These courts were all presided over by the town bailiffs, and from 1438 to about 1479 their proceedings were entered on a single roll, albeit distinguished by court. This complicated history of the courts of one well-studied borough illustrates the dynamic nature of legal jurisdictions and cautions against complacency about format and names: a court could retain its name and even its format while the substance of its business changed.

Borough Courts and Their Business

The sheer variety and number of borough courts (Table 1.1)[22] explain why they have more often been studied as part of one town's history than within an analytic and comparative framework. The spotty survival of borough courts presents other challenges, while our understanding is further complicated by changes over time in a court's jurisdiction, authority, format, meeting times and places, officers and suitors. With all these variables in play, exceptions can always be found – but some generalisations can be made in what follows.

The major borough courts were usually courts of record required to document their proceedings, which could be searched for precedents and evidence. The manicules (pointing fingers) in the margins of many court rolls to draw attention to a specific case or ruling is one reflection of this function. Although some court proceedings were initiated by jurors' presentments (especially of misdemeanours, nuisance and trading offences), most of their business was brought to the court as personal *querelae* in which a plaintiff made a complaint against a defendant involving debt, detinue, contract, account or trespass. The bulk of this private litigation was initiated by oral or written complaints, with written complaints more common in later centuries. By the later Middle Ages, bills of complaint (whereby a clerk wrote out on a separate paper the plaintiff's complaint before his or her appearance in court) were regularly used.[23] Because the bills were kept by the clerk, this practice reduced the need to keep a copy of the plea on the court roll, which is partly responsible for the shrinking size of the court rolls of boroughs like Colchester and Winchester during the fifteenth century.[24] Law suits could also be initiated by royal writs, since many of the larger boroughs acquired the franchise of return of writs.[25] Most of these suits involved property, but they represented only a small part

22 See also Kowaleski, 'Annotated List', in this volume.

23 In London, these bills appear from the 1360s onward and formed a separate class of documents; Caroline M. Barron, *London in the Later Middle Ages: Government and the People, 1200–1500* (Oxford, 2004), pp. 154–5.

24 Other factors were new efficiencies such as writing out instructions about essoins, arrests and distraints only once; recording all procedural steps, answers and verdicts with the original plea; and keeping new pleas in a separate roll; Britnell, 'Colchester courts', pp. 135, 137–8; Derek Keene, *Survey of Medieval Winchester*, vol. 1, Winchester Studies, 2 (Oxford, 1985), p. 20.

25 M. T. Clanchy, 'The franchise of return of writs', *Transactions of the Royal Historical Society*, 17 (1967), pp. 59–82.

of the cases before the borough courts, not least because writs were expensive.

The most common personal action in borough courts was debt, which accounted for over two-thirds of all pleas during the last three decades of the fourteenth century in the borough courts of Colchester, Exeter, Nottingham and Winchester.[26] Debts over £2 technically had to be heard in royal courts, but borough courts did not always abide by this restriction.[27] Even so, most of the debts in borough courts were for small sums. In Nottingham, 62 per cent of the debt pleas were under five shillings; in Exeter, 59 per cent of all debts whose amounts are stated concerned five shillings or less; and in Colchester in the same period, the figure was 31 per cent.[28] Trespass complaints about assault, property damage or minor theft constituted the second most common complaint, accounting for 24 per cent of the pleas in Exeter and 15 per cent of pleas in Colchester.[29] Not surprisingly, patterns in litigation changed over time. Litigation reached its height during the late fourteenth and early fifteenth century, even though the population of towns had shrunk considerably after the Black Death. In Colchester, the number of pleas increased by five times over the course of the late fourteenth century, fuelled in large part by a ten-fold rise in the number of debt pleas, a surge paralleled in the small-town courts of Clare and Sudbury.[30] This increase in debt pleas has been interpreted not as a sign of economic difficulties or monetary crisis, but as an indicator of commercial development and positive attitudes towards extending credit. More open to debate is the extent to which the fall in litigation in the fifteenth century, particularly in debt pleas, can be attributed to economic decline, or to procedural changes that speeded resolution of debts, or to other factors.[31]

Borough courts also wielded some jurisdiction over criminal matters,

26 Richard H. Britnell, *Growth and Decline in Colchester, 1300–1525* (Cambridge, 1986), p. 99 (74 per cent of 2,712 pleas in four years from the Hundred court and Court of Pleas); Maryanne Kowaleski, *Local Markets and Regional Trade in Medieval Exeter* (Cambridge, 1995), pp. 202, 337–8, 340 (36 per cent of 992 pleas in three years of the Mayor's court, and over 80 per cent of the pleas in the Provosts' court, for a total of 65 per cent of all pleas in these two courts in three years). For Nottingham courts from 1395 to 1401, see Richard Goddard, 'Surviving recession: English borough courts and commercial contraction 1350–1500', in Richard Goddard, John Langdon and Miriam Müller (eds), *Survival and Discord in Medieval Society: Essays in Honour of Christopher Dyer* (Turnhout, 2010), pp. 70, 81. For Winchester, see ibid., p. 81.

27 John S. Beckerman, 'The forty-shilling jurisdictional limit in medieval English personal actions', in Dafydd Jenkins (ed.), *Legal History Studies, 1972* (Cardiff, 1975), pp. 110–17; Britnell, *Colchester*, p. 108; Kowaleski, *Exeter*, pp. 203–4, 214.

28 Goddard, 'Surviving recession', p. 73; Kowaleski, *Exeter*, p. 203 (418 of 716 debts, 1378–88, in the Mayor's and Provosts' courts); Britnell, *Colchester*, pp. 107–8 (315 of 1,030 debts in 1387/8 and 1398/9). As Britnell notes, the majority of the debts for which no amount is specified were likely for smaller sums, which (if known) would raise the percentage of these smaller debts at Colchester closer to that for Exeter.

29 Based on the same sample as above, n. 26.

30 Britnell, *Colchester*, pp. 98–105, 206–8, for this and the following.

31 Ibid., pp. 206–8; Britnell, 'Colchester courts'; Keene, *Survey of Medieval Winchester*, p. 20. Goddard, 'Surviving recession' and R. Goddard, *Credit and Trade in Later Medieval England,*

although only the more ancient towns tended to enjoy any authority over felonious crime.[32] Borough courts could handle misdemeanour trespass, which included minor assaults and petty larceny, but felonies (homicide, burglary, robbery, grand larceny, counterfeiting, receiving, arson, treason and rape) were technically reserved for royal courts. The line between felonies and misdemeanours, however, was sometimes blurred. For example, courts and their juries could lessen the severity of a charge of felony, particularly in cases of grand larceny (absconding with goods worth over one shilling), by undervaluing the amount in order to qualify the case as a misdemeanour.[33] Either the victim or the court could also choose to prosecute a case as a misdemeanour trespass rather than a felony. The line between royal and borough criminal justice was further blurred because many of the royal boroughs had the right to make arrests and take sureties from those who committed felonies in the town, although trials to determine their guilt or innocence had to wait until the king's justices arrived, which could take months and even years.[34]

The right to arrest and take sureties from accused felons was only one type of criminal jurisdiction that towns acquired via royal charters. As early as 1200, towns began to secure the right to elect their own coroner, whose inquisitions into suspicious deaths could yield verdicts of murder.[35] In Lincoln, the coroner was the third most important civic official, presiding over the Burwarmote with the mayor and bailiffs.[36] Another crown criminal jurisdiction that often passed to towns was the right to hold sessions of the peace; from the fourteenth century onwards, the larger towns sought this prerogative, usually through incorporation, with mayors and other civic officials acting as justices of the peace. When Stamford was incorporated in 1465, the alderman (equivalent to a mayor elsewhere) and the First Twelve (the chief council) became justices of the peace, and the town was allowed to keep profits from the sessions and to exclude all of the county justices of the peace from interfering.[37] Ipswich's charter of incorporation in 1446 made the town bailiffs justices of the peace, aided by four of the twelve Chief Portmen

---

1353–1532 (London, 2016) sees the contraction of debt pleas as a sign of economic recession.

32 Bateson (ed.), *Borough Customs*, vol. 2, pp. xxi–xxii.

33 Karen Jones, *Gender and Petty Crime in Late Medieval England: The Local Courts in Kent, 1460–1560* (Woodbridge, 2006), p. 34.

34 Ballard and Tait, *British Borough Charters, 1217–1307*, p. lx.

35 Ballard, *British Borough Charters, 1042–1216*, pp. 246–7; Ballard and Tait, *British Borough Charters, 1217–1307*, pp. 357–60; Weinbaum, *British Borough Charters, 1307–1660*, pp. xxv–lxii.

36 Alan Kissane, *Civic Community in Late Medieval Lincoln: Urban Society and Economy in the Age of the Black Death, 1289–1409* (Woodbridge, 2017), pp. 132–4. In Lincoln and other towns, there could also be three to four coroners serving at one time, another indication of the wide business they handled. For coroners in other towns, see R. F. Hunnisett, *The Medieval Coroner* (Cambridge, 1961), pp. 139–46.

37 Alan Rogers (ed.), *William Browne's Town: The Stamford Hall Book, 1465–1492* (Stamford, 2005), pp. ii–vii, 1–3. Stamford was under the control of the duchess of Richmond at this time.

(representatives elected from each parish). Borough rights over gaol deliveries were less common, though Ipswich did obtain this privilege and often kept its records of gaol delivery and sessions of the peace together. We know less, however, about how the administration of crown justice by burgesses might have differed from the royal courts, though it is perhaps significant that many borough coroners had to swear an oath of fealty before the mayor before they could exercise their office.

Another important function of borough courts was to administer the privilege of devise and sale attached to burgage tenure. In this capacity, town courts enrolled and adjudicated land transactions, including bequests, final concords, deeds of title, charters, and actions begun by the possessory assizes. The oldest continuously kept court proceedings in London and Norwich were records of deeds and wills, and it has been plausibly argued that registration of land title lay at the heart of the development of the earliest borough courts.[38] The Church's zealous protection of its right to probate wills, however, precluded all but a few boroughs from supervising the post-mortem devolution of real property.[39] Practice varied widely. Towns like Ipswich and London recorded wills in separate registers or courts, while Colchester, Exeter, Norwich and Nottingham enrolled both conveyances and the sections of wills dealing with landed property on their court rolls.[40] In Bristol and Oxford, the process of probate followed multiple steps, first in ecclesiastical courts, then in a borough court, then a formal entry in a separate register. In Leicester, no record of deeds or wills was kept at all.

Borough courts adopted some common law procedures in property transfers but also developed their own distinctive customs. One innovation was the care taken to ensure that wives freely consented to the alienation of property that they held with their husbands or by dower. In Ipswich, this custom was a central feature of the Petty Court of Recognizances.[41] Another divergence from common law was the assize of fresh force, which (unlike the common law assize of *mort d'ancestor*) took into account burgesses' right to freely devise

38 G. H. Martin, 'The registration of deeds of title in the medieval borough', in D. A. Bullough and R. L. Storey (eds), *The Study of Medieval Records: Essays in Honour of Kathleen Major* (Oxford, 1971), pp. 151–73, for this and the following.

39 Reginald R. Sharpe (ed.), *Calendar of Wills Proved and Enrolled in the Court of Husting, London, 1258–1688*, 2 vols (London, 1889–90); David Postles, 'Record keeping in the medieval borough: proof of wills', *Archives: The Journal of the British Records Association,* 16 (1983), pp. 12–15.

40 Postles, 'Record keeping', for this and the following. For Exeter, see DHC, ECA, Mayor's court rolls, passim. Colchester enrolled the whole will in its court rolls for a short time, but stopped – perhaps because church officials objected to this practice; Henry Harrod, *Report on the Records of the Borough of Colchester* (Colchester, 1865), p. 14.

41 Martin (ed.), *Ipswich Recognizance Rolls*. See also Bateson (ed.), *Borough Customs*, vol. 2, pp. ci–ciiv, 115–19.

and sell rents and property.[42] Boroughs also had a variety of customs to help landlords recover rent arrears, a problem more common in towns than elsewhere. Landlords in Exeter, Ipswich, London, Northampton and other towns, for example, used a process called 'gavelok' to foreclose on free tenants who owed rent arrears. What is particularly interesting are hints that this borough custom may have had an influence on the development of the writ of *cessvit* used in common law to recover lands when the tenant failed to meet certain tenurial conditions, such as paying rent.[43]

In addition to handling personal pleas, some criminal matters and property transfers, borough courts also took on legislative and administrative functions. Because the courts' suitors and officers provided the authority needed to back up civic decisions, the courts show them witnessing the results of municipal elections, making ordinances and trade regulations, leasing city property and admitting freemen to the franchise. In some towns, admissions to the guild merchant were the most prominent feature of early courts, and from these the 'guild court' eventually developed into a full-fledged borough court.[44] In other towns, admissions to the guild merchant (even when later equivalent to burgess admissions) were always recorded in separate rolls that had no court proceedings.[45] The borough court's legislative and administrative functions in towns like Grimsby and Hull were so complete that it served as the governing authority in these towns.[46] In the case of Grimsby, its small size and the absence of rival authorities (such as merchant and craft guilds or wards) probably helped funnel civic government into the borough court.

A wide variety of ancillary town courts also developed for the use of urban residents, presided over by town officials, recorded and archived by town clerks, and yielding revenues that went into town coffers. These courts include piepowder (fair) courts, market courts, staple courts,[47] orphans'

42 Bateson (ed.), *Borough Customs*, vol. 1, pp. 231–45; vol. 2, pp. lxii–lxv; Alan Harding, *The Law Courts of Medieval England* (New York, 1973), p. 42.

43 Bateson (ed.), *Borough Customs*, vol. 2, pp. lxiv–lxv.

44 For example, at Totnes; see Kowaleski, 'Annotated List', in this volume.

45 For example, Drinkwater, 'The merchants' gild of Shrewsbury: the two earliest rolls'; C. H. Drinkwater, 'The merchants' gild of Shrewsbury', *Transactions of the Shropshire Archaeological and Natural History Society*, 2nd series, 2 (1890), pp. 29–59; C. H. Drinkwater, 'The merchants' gild of Shrewsbury: seven rolls of the thirteenth century', *Transactions of the Shropshire Archaeological and Natural History Society*, 2nd series, 12 (1900), pp. 229–82. Drinkwater continued to publish translations of the rolls into the sixteenth century: *Transactions of the Shropshire Archaeological and Natural History Society*, 3rd series, 5 (1914), pp. 101–8.

46 Stephen H. Rigby, *Medieval Grimsby: Growth and Decline* (Hull, 1993), pp. 82–3; Edward Gillett and Kenneth A. MacMahon, *A History of Hull*, 2nd edn (Hull, 1989), p. 90.

47 For market, piepowder and staple courts, see Charles Gross (ed.), *Select Cases Concerning the Law Merchant: Local Courts, A.D. 1270–1638*; Hubert Hall (ed.), *Select Cases Concerning the Law Merchant: Central Courts, A.D. 1239–1633*; Hubert Hall (ed.), *Select Cases Concerning the Law Merchant: Supplementary Central Courts, A.D. 1251–1779*, Selden Society, 23, 46, 49 (London, 1903–32). Some towns had 'piepowder' courts that adjudicated disputes in the local

courts,[48] maritime or admiralty courts,[49] and, as noted above, royal jurisdiction that devolved to boroughs, such as coroners' inquests, sessions of the peace and gaol deliveries. Some produced jurisdictional anomalies and tensions, particularly piepowder courts that were administered by a fair owner who was not the town (Table 1.1). In towns like Hereford, Westminster, Winchester and York, the borough courts were suppressed during fair-time in favour of the piepowder court run by an outsider, which could lead to significant conflict. The right of the Cinque Ports towns to control all jurisdiction in Great Yarmouth during the six weeks of the autumn herring fair was the source of riots and ongoing court battles for many years.[50]

There were fees attached to doing business in the borough courts, paid largely by plaintiffs, especially creditors, and shared by town officers who were involved in moving the plea through the court. Schedules of these fees appear in the borough regulations of Stamford and the custumal of the York Sheriffs' court, while a rare survival of sums owed by creditors and entered into an expenses section in the York Sheriffs' court proceedings offers concrete evidence of the fees paid to use the court (Table 1.2). Each stage of the legal process required a fee, on top of fines that plaintiffs paid for not pursuing or filing a false complaint, and that defendants paid for agreeing to settle out of court, failing to wage their law, or being found guilty.[51] These fees could mount up quickly, and – given the small sums involved in many borough court debts – must have occasionally (even regularly) outstripped what creditors could hope to recoup of their original debt. Nonetheless, the expense of pursuing litigation in the central courts was even more costly and much slower, which helps explain the popularity of local borough courts as a venue for dispute resolution.[52] Even within a town, however, plaintiffs often chose to place their business in the least costly court with faster procedure, as was the

market rather than the fair: see J. S. Furley (ed.), *Ancient Usages of Winchester, from the Anglo-French Version Preserved in Winchester College* (Oxford, 1927), pp. 19–20; Richard Goddard, 'Nottingham's borough court rolls: a user's guide', p. 3, at <https://www.nottingham.ac.uk/ucn/documents/online-sources/nottinghamsboroughcourtrolls-usersguide2.pdf>.

48 Charles Carlton, *The Court of Orphans* (Leicester, 1974), pp. 13–22; T. P. Wadley (ed.), *Notes or Abstracts of the Wills Contained in the Volume Entitled the Great Orphan Book and Book of Will: In the Council House at Bristol*, Bristol and Gloucestershire Society, 1 (Bristol, 1886).

49 Reginald G. Marsden (ed.), *Select Pleas in the Court of Admiralty*, vol. 1, Selden Society, 6 (London, 1894); Maryanne Kowaleski (ed.), *The Havener's Accounts of the Earldom and Duchy of Cornwall, 1287–1356*, Devon and Cornwall Record Society, new series, 44 (Exeter, 2001), pp. 41–3; David H. Allen (comp.), *Ipswich Borough Archives: A Catalogue*, Suffolk Records Society, 43 (Woodbridge, 2000), pp. 83–4.

50 Gross (ed.), *Select Cases Concerning the Law Merchant*, vol. 1, pp. xx–xxvi; K. M. E. Murray, *The Constitutional History of the Cinque Ports* (Manchester, 1935), pp. 146–50.

51 For these resolutions in the Exeter borough courts, see below, p. 35.

52 For the slow pace and expense of the central courts, see Margaret Hastings, *The Court of Common Pleas in Fifteenth-Century England: A Study of Legal Administration and Procedure* (Ithaca, NY, 1947), pp. 224–30.

case in Exeter, where creditors overwhelmingly favoured the Provosts' court over the Mayor's court.[53]

Leet Courts

Leet courts are easily distinguished from other borough courts because of the nature of their business (the keeping of the peace) and their procedure (presentment by jury). They are also not unique to urban jurisdictions. Although the term 'leet court' was not widely used outside East Anglia until the very late Middle Ages, the view of frankpledge at its heart can be traced back to the Anglo-Saxon period. In these views, male residents over age twelve were divided into tithings headed by a chief tithingman, later called a capital pledge.[54] In the absence of a paid police force, members of a tithing were collectively responsible for each other's behaviour, required to report violations of the law by fellow tithing members. If they failed to report a crime about which they had knowledge, or failed to bring one of their members to court to respond to charges, the entire tithing was fined. By the twelfth century, this reporting occurred at the view of frankpledge, held twice a year as part of a county-wide circuit made by the sheriff (the sheriff's tourn). Private hundreds, manors and boroughs could, however, be awarded their own view of frankpledge, exempting them from the sheriff's tourn.

The frankpledge system generally lasted longer in the countryside than in towns, where the size and mobility of the population made tithings difficult to enforce. But remnants of the tithing system and its associated view of frankpledge survived longer in some towns. In Norwich the names of tithing members were carefully listed at the beginning of several late-thirteenth- and early-fourteenth-century leet courts, and the jurors making presentments were the capital pledges.[55] Even in towns where frankpledge declined, the leet courts' jurisdiction over breaches of the peace remained remarkably unchanged, in some places well into the eighteenth and even nineteenth century. This jurisdiction can be seen in the articles of enquiry which, despite local variations in the number, order and content of the articles, covered the same general types of offences for centuries: minor assaults (but not felonies); infractions against the assizes of ale, bread and measures; market offences; and common nuisances.[56]

53 Kowaleski, *Exeter*, pp. 216–17.

54 The classic work is William Alfred Morris, *The Frankpledge System* (London, 1910).

55 William Hudson, 'Introduction', in William Hudson (ed.), *Leet Jurisdiction in the City of Norwich during the 13th and 14th Centuries*, Selden Society, 5 (London, 1892), pp. xlvi–liiii. See also Sagui, 'The Business of the Leet Courts in Medieval Norwich, 1288–1391', in this volume. The Ipswich leet presentments were also made by capital pledges, known as headboroughs; Allen (comp.), *Ipswich*, pp. 85–8.

56 F. J. C. Hearnshaw, *Leet Jurisdiction in England: Especially as Illustrated by the Records of the*

Leet courts relied on presentments made by jurors, usually numbering twelve. They generally met only one to three times a year, and their jurisdiction was territorial in focusing on a particular ward, leet or quarter in the town. The names of leet courts could vary widely, from the Mayor's Tourn in Exeter and the Mickeltorn in Nottingham, to the Lawhundred of Colchester, the Halmote of Durham and the Wardmotes of London. They all relied on presentments by sworn juries – men of the neighbourhood – whose indictments were usually considered guilty verdicts punishable by fines.[57]

The procedure prescribed for the London Wardmotes probably resembled what happened in most urban leet courts.[58] Each ward alderman asked his bedel to summon all male householders and servants in the ward to appear before him on a particular day, time and place. Before the meeting, the bedel entered their names in a roll according to whether they were freemen of the city (full burgesses) or non-freemen. When the ward residents convened at the appointed time and place, the clerk of the alderman read aloud their names so that the bedel could check if all were in attendance; absentees were fined. The bedel then presented the panel of jurors, who had been assembled by the constables of the ward from among the most reputable men of the ward. In some towns, these jurors could be capital pledges, but analyses of leet jurors in Exeter and the capital pledges in Norwich indicate that both came from the same social group of well-off residents, mostly artisans, but not usually the elite office-holders and not always freemen of the town.[59] The articles of the inquiry were then read to the jury, and another day appointed for the jurors to come and make their presentments or 'verdicts'. Other business at the Wardmote included the election of ward officials; the identification of innkeepers, brewers, bakers, cooks, victuallers and hucksters by the bedel; the certification of the stamps employed by each baker and the weights and

Court Leet of Southampton (Southampton, 1908), pp. 30–2, 43–64. For examples of articles of inquiry in urban leet courts, see Henry Thomas Riley (ed.), *Munimenta Gildhallæ Londoniensis: Liber Albus, Liber Custumarum, et Liber Horn*, vol. 1 (London, 1859), pp. 257–60, 337–8, translated in H. T. Riley (ed. and trans.), *Liber Albus: The White Book of the City of London. Comp. A. D. 1419, by John Carpenter, Common Clerk. Richard Whitington, Mayor* (London, 1862), pp. 226–8, 287–92.

57 J. H. Baker, *The Oxford History of the Laws of England: 1483–1558*, vol. 6 (Oxford, 2003), p. 302. In the Exeter Mayor's Tourn, however, some of those presented for offences such as breaking the assize of ale, scolding or minor assault could object and be found not guilty.

58 Riley (ed.), *Munimenta Gildhallæ Londoniensis*, vol. 1, pp. 36–9; Riley (ed.), *Liber Albus*, pp. 32–4. For procedures followed for view of frankpledge in a manorial court, see Frederic William Maitland and William Paley Baildon (eds), *The Court Baron: Being Precedents for Use in Seignorial and Other Local Courts, Together with Select Pleas from the Bishop of Ely's Court of Littleport*, Selden Society, 4 (London, 1891), pp. 93–106. See also Maddock, 'Society, Status and the Leet Court in Margery Kempe's Lynn', in this volume.

59 Sagui, 'Leet Courts in Medieval Norwich' in this volume; Maryanne Kowaleski, 'Social groupings and legal participation in a medieval English town', unpublished paper given at the American Society of Legal History Conference (October 1984).

measures used in the ward (for a fee that went to the alderman); and oaths of frankpledge sworn by non-freemen, a vestigial sign of the view of frankpledge. Finally, the alderman was required to 'correct' all the problems presented by the jurors, which in the vast majority of cases meant a fine. In many leet courts, special 'affeerors' were appointed to assess these fines.[60]

Leet courts in all boroughs were broadly similar in format and business, but a comparison of the leet courts of Exeter and Norwich shows how they could vary. For example, presentments at the Mayor's Tourn of Exeter were made once a year before the mayor by twelve jurors for each of the city's four quarters.[61] Early presentments were enrolled on the Mayor's court rolls, but by 1368 they were being recorded on their own roll. The Norwich leet courts also met annually before the town's highest officials (four bailiffs).[62] They too were organised territorially into ten (once eleven) administrative units or sub-leets, which followed parish boundaries; the sub-leets were in turn assigned to one of the city's four great leets, each with its own bailiff and constable. Like Exeter, presentments in Norwich were made by twelve jurors (called capital pledges) at each of the courts of the sub-leets. But Norwich leet courts were recorded in separate rolls of presentments and rolls of amercements. They also lasted into the nineteenth century, whereas the Exeter tourn petered out in the 1450s. And traces of the tithing system are more evident in Norwich, where fines for being out of tithing, failing to attend court, or raising the hue and cry comprised 9 per cent of all presentments (but are not found at all in Exeter).[63]

In the early 1380s, the Exeter tourn made about eight hundred presentments a year, 67 per cent of which were for economic infractions (such as brewing against the assize of ale or forestalling the market) or trading infractions (in order to protect the monopolies of freedom members). Nuisance and sanitation indictments (for straying pigs, muckheaps and other obstructions) made up another 25 per cent of presentments; and infringements of the peace (such as prostitution, scolding and minor thefts) comprised only 1 per cent of the court's business. The late-fourteenth-century leets of the larger city of Norwich made an average of 1,120 presentments each year, 66 per cent of which were economic infractions. Although both borough leets focused on economic violations, their emphasis differed; brewing infractions

60 For example, Allen (comp.), *Ipswich*, pp. 85–6; DHC, ECA, Mayor's Tourn, passim; Maddock, 'Society, Status and the Leet Court in Margery Kempe's Lynn', in this volume.

61 Kowaleski, *Exeter*, pp. 92, 338–9. The figures cited in the following paragraph come from an analysis of 2,429 presentments in the twelve tourns for 1381 to 1383, in DHC, ECA, Mayor's Tourn.

62 See Hudson, 'Introduction', *Leet Jurisdiction*, and Sagui, 'Leet Courts in Medieval Norwich', in this volume (especially Tables 6.1–6.3, which provide the figures in the following paragraph from the amercement rolls of 1375 and 1391).

63 See also Samantha Sagui, 'The hue and cry in medieval English towns', *Historical Research*, 87 (2014), pp. 179–93.

constituted a far larger proportion of Exeter's offences, while poor quality work, infringements of the freedom and forestalling caused more concern in Norwich. In both towns, the long lists of brewing infractions, year after year, reflect licensing fees rather than genuine wrong-doing.[64] Even greater differences, however, are evident in the fifteen leets in the suburban London ward of Portsoken from 1465 to 1483, where there were no assize or economic infractions at all. Instead, 70 per cent of the indictments focused on nuisances, particularly problems associated with life in a densely populated city, like the fire hazards posed by thatched roofs and wooden chimneys.[65] Most other presentments focused on disorder, primarily prostitution and brothel-keeping. The late-fifteenth-century London Wardmote's greater interest in sexual regulation might reflect what some scholars have argued was an increasing concern with morality and personal behaviour in the later Middle Ages and early modern period.[66]

Leet courts offer particularly useful measures of the changing economic, social and political circumstances of their towns, because their proceedings included a far greater range of urban residents than other town courts. Since leet jurors were generally well-off men who were not among the civic elite and who lived among the neighbours they reported, their presentments point to common issues of concern in their communities. Leet courts were clearly on the front lines in reacting to periods of significant demographic, social and economic change, and as a result they merit further study and comparison.[67] Such analyses should help us address legal questions as well. Why did the view of frankpledge and hue and cry disappear from some town leets but not others? Why did the criminal jurisdiction of early leet courts increasingly become the purview of the sessions of the justices of the peace in some towns? And why did leet courts in towns like Coventry make law as much as administer it?[68]

64 For a discussion of how leet court presentments regulated trade, see Kowaleski, *Exeter*, pp. 180–92, 338–9. For assizes as licensing fees, see ibid., pp. 132, 187, 339; Sagui, 'Leet Courts in Medieval Norwich', in this volume, and Britnell, *Colchester*, p. 89.

65 Christine L. Winter, 'The Portsoken presentments: an analysis of a London ward in the 15th century', *Transactions of the London and Middlesex Archaeological Society*, 56 (2005), pp. 97–161. I have reorganised her categories of indictments (pp. 148–9) to match the categories used for Exeter and Norwich. There were 1,312 presentments for the fifteen courts, making for an annual average of ninety-four; the numbers were probably far higher in the Wardmotes of central London. See also the Wardmote courts in A. H. Thomas (ed.), *Calendar of Plea and Memoranda Rolls Preserved among the Archives of the Corporation of the City of London at the Guild-hall, 1413–37* (Cambridge, 1943), pp. 115–41, 150–9.

66 For example, Marjorie Keniston McIntosh, *Controlling Misbehavior in England, 1370–1600* (Cambridge, 1998).

67 On this point, see Marjorie Keniston McIntosh, 'Local change and community control in England, 1465–1500', *Huntington Library Quarterly*, 49 (1986), pp. 230–4. For examples of how leet courts can be used to track economic changes in towns, see Britnell, *Colchester*, pp. 193–202, 269–76; Kowaleski, *Exeter*, pp. 89–92.

68 Mary Dormer Harris (ed.), *Coventry Leet Book: Or Mayor's Register, Containing the Records*

Procedure in the Borough Courts

Thanks to the pioneering work of Mary Bateson, we have considerable evidence about the development of procedure in borough courts and variations in local customary law from town to town.[69] The focus of much of the legal scholarship on procedure in town courts, however, has tended to concentrate on the influence and eventual triumph of common law in local town courts. This focus has yielded major dividends, as has the attention paid to the impact of the training in common law increasingly enjoyed by local lawyers, particularly town recorders.[70] But it has also diverted attention away from studying the customary content and implications of borough court procedures for their own sake. In the spirit of this chapter's aim to provide a practical introduction to town courts, the following discussion centres on the common procedural steps followed by litigants in borough courts, particularly in debt pleas, which represented by far the bulk of business before these courts.

Private litigation began when a plaintiff made a formal complaint to the town clerk or another officer of the court, though the process was often replaced by a written bill of complaint towards the end of the Middle Ages.[71] To ensure that plaintiffs would come to court and pursue the charge, they were required to name two pledges (*manucaptores*), local men of good reputation. Plaintiffs and defendants could also appoint attornies to represent them in court so that they did not have to show up in person.[72] These attornies need not be trained lawyers, though they usually were by the later Middle Ages. The majority of borough court procedure was directed at the defendant, and each of the processes noted below was carefully recorded in court proceedings; legal scholars refer to this as the mesne (or middle) process in between the filing of a complaint and the final resolution. To get the defendant into court to answer the plaintiff, a summons was issued, which basically meant the defendant was informed in person by an officer of the court that he or she must show up.[73]

---

of the City Court Leet or View of Frankpledge, A.D. 1420–1555 with Divers Other Matters, Early English Text Society, original series 134, 135, 138, 146 (London, 1907–13).

69 Bateson (ed.), *Borough Customs*, 2 vols; this section relies heavily on the evidence that she offers, only a small percentage of which is summarised here.

70 Baker, *History of the Laws of England*, vol. 6, pp. 291–319. His comment that material 'in local archives is, therefore, in general, less informative than the plea rolls of the central courts' (p. 304) reflects his greater interest in common law.

71 See above, p. 23. For overviews of procedure in personal debt actions, see Bateson (ed.), *Borough Customs*, vol. 1, pp. 89–210; vol. 2, pp. xxii–lix, 1–59; Britnell, 'Colchester courts'; Goddard, 'Nottingham's borough court rolls'.

72 In some borough court rolls, the initials of attornies appear in superscript above the plea; Stell (trans.), *Sheriffs' Court Books of York*, p. 7, and passim. In Winchester, *ponit loco suo*, followed by the initials of the attorney, is inserted in superscript; J. S. Furley, *Town Life in the XIV Century as seen in the Court Rolls of Winchester City* (Winchester, 1947), p. 41. In the Exeter Mayor's court, the attornies' names were usually written out in the body of the plea.

73 A summons was not usually sent to a non-resident defendant, who was immediately attached;

Defendants had a period of time to obey the summons (usually around three to seven days, shorter than the time required in common law). One of the privileges of citizenship was the right to receive three summons before appearing in court, though further excuses (called essoins) could be acknowledged for absence out of town (especially if serving the king) or illness. Essoins, however, could generate a fee (Table 1.2). The granting of endless essoins was a major cause of delay in many courts.[74] If the defendant continued to fail to show up, the court could then move to attachment, whereby a defendant had to find pledges (usually two) to ensure s/he appeared. This measure was favoured over attachment of the defendants' goods or imprisonment, though these options could be implemented if the defendant could not find sufficient pledges. If defendants remained recalcitrant, the court could pursue other remedies, including assessing fines on the defendant and his/her pledges and, as an ultimate remedy, ordering distraint (also called distress), which involved seizure of the defendant's property or goods to pay fines or ensure a court appearance, or to satisfy the creditor. The customs surrounding the timing and nature of attachment and distraint could vary from town to town. Only when all else failed was the defendant attached and imprisoned.

Once the litigants were both in court, there were various paths towards a resolution. They could, for example, decide to settle the matter between them out of court by paying for a licence of concord (which usually cost 2–3d) or seeking a love-day, which meant seeking arbitration to settle their dispute.[75] Plaintiffs who were simply satisfied to get the defendant's attention or who realised that their case was weak could opt not to prosecute the case, a resolution that cost a plaintiff 3d. If defendants chose to dispute the charge, they too had options. The first – especially typical in debt cases, though also used for other accusations – involved compurgation or wager of law (usually signified by the word *lex* in the margin of the court roll), in which the defendant secured a number of local men to vouch for his/her good character. These oath-helpers were not swearing to the facts of the case, just that the defendant was credible – the idea being that only trustworthy and reliable litigants could find the requisite number of oath-helpers. The court fixed the number, which (in addition to the defendant) could require as few as two and as many as twelve or even more oath-helpers, depending on the nature of the charge and the reputation of the defendant. Women could serve as oath-helpers, though in practice they did so mainly for other women.

Bateson (ed.), *Borough Customs*, vol. 2, p. xxiii.

74 For the slow process in borough courts, see, for example, Furley, *Winchester*, pp. 25–7, 30–3, 36.

75 For example, Carole Rawcliffe, '"That kindliness should be cherished more, and discord driven out": the settlement of commercial disputes by arbitration in later medieval England', in Jennifer I. Kermode (ed.), *Enterprise and Individuals in Fifteenth-Century England* (Gloucester, 1991), pp. 99–117.

Either plaintiffs or defendants could demand a jury to settle their dispute – a process pursued more often for trespass cases than for debt, for which compurgation was more common. Those asking for a jury 'put themselves on the country' (*ad patriam*), which emphasises, as oath-helpers do, the reliance of dispute resolution on the good will of neighbours. Jury panels were made up of twelve men, who had to be summoned and often distrained to show up in court, a cost presumably borne by the litigant who asked for a jury trial (Table 1.2). The failure of jurors to show up when summoned (despite being fined for non-appearance) led to endless adjournments in the borough court rolls, noted as *pro defectu iurate*. Juries of twelve were also used in making presentments (indictments treated as verdicts in most instances) in leet courts, but they rarely had to be distrained, probably because they were part of the view of frankpledge system and thus responsible for collecting information on offenders, and because the leet courts met infrequently on a predetermined schedule. Neither type of jury formally called witnesses to testify.[76] The final steps were the fines paid for the different resolutions and damages assessed on defendants who were found guilty. Imprisonment was a last option, used only for defendants who had no goods to distrain for restitution, or for egregious offences, although public-shaming punishments – a wider variety of which existed for towns than for any other communities – were favoured for particular offences, especially for recidivists.

An analysis of the court resolutions for over 4,500 debt disputes in Exeter from 1378 to 1388 shows that 37 per cent of the cases ended with the plaintiff not prosecuting, one-third concluded with the defendant being found guilty, 18 per cent terminated in a licence of concord, 8 per cent in a false query by the plaintiff, and 4 per cent in the failure of the defendant to wage law.[77] The larger debts (averaging more than twenty-four shillings) were those settled by licence of concord, suggesting that both litigants felt there was enough at stake to try to end their disagreement amicably. The lowest average debts were those which ended with the defendant's failure to find sufficient oath-helpers. Almost all of these defendants were Exeter residents, as opposed to quarrels ending in the plaintiff not prosecuting, in which almost half of the debtors and 41 per cent of the creditors were from outside the city – an indication of the greater difficulties facing litigants who did not enjoy the legal benefits of citizenship or residence in the city.

76 London, however, had a process that allowed witnesses to be called by one party; see A. H. Thomas, 'Introduction', *Calendar of Early Mayor's Court Rolls, 1298–1307* (London, 1924), pp. xxxvii–xxxix. For the use of evidence in London city courts (including witnesses), see Penny Tucker, *Law Courts and Lawyers in the City of London, 1300–1550* (Cambridge, 2007), pp. 189–93, 197–8.

77 Kowaleski, *Exeter*, p. 218 for this and the following. Note that 70 per cent of the information on debt amounts comes from guilty verdicts because clerks recorded more details for these cases.

Conclusion: Towards a Social History of Town Courts

Many questions remain to be addressed about the legal history of town or borough courts, including how and why different court jurisdictions developed within towns, why some components of borough customary law survived for so long, and how borough administration of crown pleas may have affected a town's criminal jurisdiction. Other legal issues also deserve more attention, such as what has been called 'the curious history of wardship in the boroughs', and how growing concern with morality and social control surfaced in urban leet and borough courts.[78] Recent work by economic historians has very usefully pointed the way towards how to exploit debt cases and leet courts to advance our understanding of urban economies, particularly in terms of commerce and credit. The administrative and legislative content of town courts has also been profitably drawn upon to illustrate the workings of civic government and regulation, as well as the intersection of political and economic institutions. But potentially the most fruitful avenues of inquiry focus on what might be called the social history of town courts. What was the balance of power of the magistrates of borough courts (mayors, bailiffs and others of the civic elite) as opposed to the different levels of jurors, many drawn from the middling groups of urban society? Who really ran the borough courts, and did this change over time? Could burgesses use a town court to construct an effective alternative to seigneurial power? How representative of the total population were the litigants in particular courts? What functions did borough courts play in maintaining social bonds or political authority in urban society? To what extent was the legal development of town courts reliant on litigants acting as consumers in deciding whether, when and where to litigate?[79] These and other questions await the attention of scholars interested in exploring the riches of town court proceedings in medieval England.

[78] Bateson (ed.), *Borough Customs*, vol. 1, p. xix; Baker, *History of the Laws of England*, vol. 6, p. 304; above, n. 66.

[79] On this question, see Daniel Lord Smail, *The Consumption of Justice: Emotions, Publicity, and Legal Culture in Marseille, 1264–1423* (Ithaca, NY, 2003).

TABLE 1.1. A COMPARISON OF THE VARIETY OF COURTS OPERATING IN FOUR MEDIEVAL BOROUGHS

Borough/Court	Who Presided?	Timing	Jurisdiction and Business	Notes
EXETER[a]				
Court of the city of Exeter (later the Mayor's court)	Mayor, assisted by the two stewards	Weekly on Mondays, though pleas could continue on other days	Personal pleas; real actions and return of writs; presentments of assaults, trespass, and nuisance by crown jurors and by aldermen for the suburbs	Dorses contain elections, testaments, final concords, recognizances, and freedom entries
Mayor's tourn (leet court)	Mayor, with 12 presentment jurors for each of four quarters	Annually (usually in Oct–Nov)	Presentments of assize of ale, market offenses, nuisance, prostitution, scolding, including some trespass presentments by aldermen for the suburbs	Business declined in the 15th century and the court had disappeared by 1460
Provosts' court	2 provosts (called bailiffs or stewards)	Daily if necessary (but not on Mondays)	Mostly personal debt pleas	
Piepowder courts	Steward/bailiff of owner of fairs (city, St Nicholas Priory, and Earl of Devon)	During fair times	Disputes occurring during the fair	Some extant for St Nicholas fair, Lammas (Crolleditch) fair; Whitsundtide fair; and Lenten fair, sometimes recorded in Mayor's court rolls
Staple court	Mayor and Constable of the Exeter Staple	As needed	Disputes concerning recognizances made at the Exeter staple	
Seigneurial courts	Stewards/bailiffs of seigneurial fees, aided by jurors	Rarely more than three times a year	Court barons and leet courts for: (1) Dean and Chapter's fee of St Sidwell; (2) St Nicholas Priory fee; (3) Bishop of Exeter's St Stephen's fee; (4) Exe Island fee of the Earl of Devon; (5) Duryard fee in the northern suburb (owned by the city)	Often included leet court business

IPSWICH[b]				
Leet court	Bailiffs, with 3 capital pledges or headboroughs from each of the four wards	Annually on Tuesday of Whitsun week	Included View of Frankpledge, assizes of bread and ale; trading offenses, nuisance, and assault	Jurisdiction over assault lost in 1461
Portmanmote	Bailiffs	Alternate Thursdays	Originally pleas begun by royal writ, crown pleas, transfers of property in recognizances, testaments, but by 1378 heard only pleas of land, tenement, and rent begun by writ	Abatement pleas recorded separately 1308-29. Lost its independence when the Great court formed
Petty court	Bailiffs	Twice weekly, but not Thursdays	Split from Portmanmote by 1285, heard personal pleas. By 1378 added possessory assizes; by 15th century, the town's most important court	By 1438 recorded in the Composite Enrolments and by 1486 in the Composite Court Books
Petty court of Recognizances	Bailiffs and two coroners		Sales of free tenements in borough, enrolled in Great court until c. 1295; by 1307 included testaments; by 1325 pleas of abatement recorded here	
Maritime court	Bailiffs	As needed (from tide to tide)	Pleas of debt, account, and covenant involving outsiders in the port	
Coroners' court	Town coroners and bailiffs	As needed	Inquests on suspicious deaths, felons' goods	
Admiralty court	Bailiffs	As needed	Disputes on piracy and other matters at sea	In 1446, a charter exempted the town from Crown Admiralty jurisdiction; in 1463, the bailiffs were given the powers of the admiralty

Sessions of the peace and gaol deliveries	Bailiffs and others	As needed; usually one to three sessions per year.	Jurors presented and ordered arrests for trespass and criminal cases in sessions; justices adjudicated trespass and less serious crown pleas. Gaol deliveries of those imprisoned for serious felonies	Given in 1446 charter. Until 1486, indictments usually made by two juries: one for the town and one for four nearby hamlets
LINCOLN[c]				
Court of the Bail (Court de la Haye)	Rep. of the constable of the castle for the earl of Lincoln (later the crown)	Weekly on Tuesdays	Court baron, including personal pleas; assizes of bread, ale, and measures within bounds of the Bail	
Galilee court	Rep. of the Dean and Chapter	Weekly and daily	Court baron and crown pleas, including personal pleas, presentments of trespass, assize of ale within the cathedral close and properties owned by the Dean and Chapter	
Burwarmote court	Mayor and bailiffs (and often the coroners)	Weekly on Mondays and Thursdays	Personal pleas; real property; presentments of market offences, nuisance, and debts to city; assizes of bread, ale, and weights; also had right to hang thieves and confiscate chattels of felons, waifs and strays	
Coroners' court			Inquests on suspicious deaths, felons' goods	
Sheriffs' court	Sheriffs of the county of the city	Monthly		Established in 1409
Statute merchant (later the staple court)	Mayor (there was also a mayor of the staple)		Credit contracts	Statute Merchant business enrolled in Burwarmote from c. 1283 to c. mid 15th century

SHREWSBURY [d]				
Curia generalis (General court)	Bailiffs	Twice yearly	Presentments by a jury of 12 of misdemeanors, assault, market offences, nuisance in the town, suburbs and liberties	Suit of court owed by 'streeters' who were male householders
Ward inquests	Sub-bailiffs (one for each of 3 wards)	Ad hoc meetings	Leet presentments of affrays	During 15th century to supplement General court
Curia Salop or (from 1392) *Curia parva*	Bailiffs	Fortnightly on Tuesdays	Personal pleas, land disputes	Record restricted to procedural amercements by late 15C, discontinued by c. 1530; actions entered in paper books from 1480s
Piepowder court		Fair time and irregularly during year	Supplemented civil litigation of the *Curia Salop* with speedier process, but little used	Defunct by 1495
Coroners' court	Town coroners	As needed	Inquests on suspicious deaths, felons' goods	
Sessions of the peace and gaol delivery (from 1445)	Bailiffs as JPs	As needed	Crimes and felonies	Rights granted by a charter of 1445

NOTES AND SOURCES:

[a] Kowaleski, *Exeter*, pp. 65–7, 337–40, 342; Gross (ed.), *Select Cases in Law Merchant*, vol. 1, pp. 116–17; DHC, ECA, Misc. Rolls 13, 14, 40. The 'stewards' or *seneschalli* were originally called 'provosts' (probably from 'port-reeve') and later 'bailiffs'.
[b] Allen (comp.), *Ipswich Borough Archives*, pp. 40–92.
[c] Kissane, *Civic Community in Late Medieval Lincoln*, pp. 11–12, 42-3, 88, 128, 130–1, 133.
[d] Alan Thacker and Dorothy Cromarty, 'Shrewsbury 1200–1340', in W. A. Champion and A. T. Thacker (eds), *The Victoria History of the County of Shropshire*, vol. 6, part 1, Shrewsbury General History and Topography, (London, 2014), pp. 41–6; W. A. Champion, 'Shrewsbury, 1340–1540', ibid, pp. 100–03.

TABLE 1.2: COURT FEES CHARGED IN SOME MEDIEVAL ENGLISH TOWNS

Town (Year)	**Charge**	**Fee**	**Note**
York custumal of the Sheriffs' court (c. 1415–33)	Entering name of attorney [in court roll], whether for individual or a man and wife	1d	To sheriffs' clerk
	Entering first essoin offered by plaintiff or defendant and warranty of this essoin	1d	To sheriffs' clerk
	Each essoin 'after the seasonable day'	1d	To sheriffs' clerk
	Each essoin after wager of law	1d	To sheriffs' clerk
	Entry for each plea that is delayed	2d	To sheriffs' clerk
	Issuing a record of a case from the [court] rolls	6d	To sheriffs' clerk
	Each entry of the king's protection	24d	To sheriffs' clerk
	Bond made to the sheriffs	2d	To sheriffs' clerk
	Entering [promise] to keep the peace	2d	To sheriffs' clerk
	Summons or attachment	1d	To sheriffs' sergeant
	Distraint	2d	To sheriffs' sergeant
	Summons of a [jury] panel	2d	To sheriffs' sergeant
	Distraint of this [jury] panel to attend court	2d	To sheriffs' sergeant
	Executing [verdict] in plea of debt or trespass for ≤ 20s (2d) and ≥ 20s (4d)	2–4d	To sheriffs' sergeant
Stamford borough regulations (1462)	For entering/writing a fine, a burgess entry, or any other entry	2d	To common clerk
	For every warrant written	4d	To common clerk
	Citizens arrested by writ	20d	8d to town bailiff
	Non-residents arrested by writ	24d	16d to town bailiff
	Citizens arrested by warrant of court	8d	4d to town bailiff
	Non-residents arrested for surety of peace	16d	4d to town bailiff
	Non-citizens and non-residents who commit trespass	8d	4d to town bailiff
	Non-citizens and non-residents who commit assault or affray on a citizen	3s4d	8d to town bailiff
	Non-citizens and non-residents who commit assault or affray on member of the First Twelve	6s8d	12d to town bailiff
	Fine on citizens convicted of offense by Alderman	6d	2d to town sergeant

Town (Year)	Charge	Fee	Note
York Sheriffs' court (1498–99)	Summons [to court]	1-2d	Owed by creditor
	Warrant of attorney	1-2d	Owed by creditor
	Entry of plaint	2d	Owed by creditor
	Entry of the plea	4–8d	Owed by creditor
	For distraint	2–4d	Owed by creditor
	Enrollment of judgement	8–12d	Owed by creditor
	For a capias ad satisfactionem [writ to place debtor under arrest until the claim is satisfied]	3–8d	Owed by creditor
	Attorney's fees	2–20d	Owed by creditor
	Essoin whereof law was waged	2d	Owed by creditor

SOURCES: Rogers (ed.), *William Browne's Town*, pp. 10–11; Stell (trans.), *Sheriffs' Court Books of the City of York*, pp. 351–54, 406–07, 450–52 (the original text is in Anglo-Norman in Maud Sellers (ed.), *York Memorandum Book: lettered A/Y in the Guildhall muniment room*, vol. 1, Surtees Society 120 (1911), pp. 137–39; vol. 2, Surtees Society 125 (1912), pp. 143–55).

2

BOROUGH COURT CASES AS LEGAL PRECEDENT IN ENGLISH TOWN CUSTUMALS

ESTHER LIBERMAN CUENCA

> Item, in the year of our Lord 1407, Robert Puttok, with others, broke the heads of gutters, called *clowses*, at Figham and Swinemoor and elsewhere, and he cast dirt from them. Therefore he placed himself at the mercy of the keepers, with Thomas Whyte, senior, as pledge, and put down 3*s*. 4*d*. because he was poor, and 16*d*. is returned to him as charity. And the penalty is imposed on him that he should no longer trespass under penalty of 20*s*.[1]

On the surface, the case of Robert Puttok may appear trivial, involving a penalty for property damage and nuisance, though such matters may have been particular concerns to civic officials entrusted with the maintenance of public health and sanitation, especially given the recurring outbreaks of plague, including one in 1407.[2] The keepers (also called governors) of early-fifteenth-century Beverley found Puttok guilty but reduced his fine on account of his poverty, with a warning that recidivism would incur a penalty of

1 Arthur F. Leach (ed.), *Beverley Town Documents*, Selden Society, 14 (London, 1900), p. 17: '*Item Anno Domini m*° *cccc*° *septimo Robertus Puttok cum aliis fregit capita gutturarum dicti clowses apud le Fegang et Swynemore et alibi et projecit lutum ab eis Ideo posuit se in gracia custodum, per plegium, Thomam Whyte seniorem, et exposuit iijs. iiijd., quia pauper, et xvjd. sibi caritative reliberantur Et pena eidem injuncta est ne amodo sic transgrediatur sub pena xxs.*'

2 J. F. D. Shrewsbury, *A History of Bubonic Plague in the British Isles* (Cambridge, 1970), p. 143.

twenty shillings.[3] This case was considered worthy of note in one of Beverley's custumals, the *Great Guild Book*. When it became enshrined in a custumal – which typically included laws on trade, property, disorder, morality, the operation of borough courts and other matters that fell under the jurisdiction of town officials – it served as a legal precedent for how other such offenders in Beverley could be policed for incidents of nuisance. When court cases were singled out for inclusion in the record of a town's customary law, the borough court became more than a venue for the administration of justice; it also played a role in preserving, shaping and even creating the legal precedents that governed such administration.

The town custumal reveals the rich world of prescriptive ideals that constituted borough customary law, which developed as towns grew larger and more autonomous over the central Middle Ages.[4] Customs first appeared in royal and seigneurial charters in the twelfth century, but by the late thirteenth and early fourteenth centuries, officials began preserving their laws in stand-alone custumals and compilations, which could also include other types of customs such as ordinances, memoranda and extracts from charters.[5] The very attributes that made these laws customary – for example, their appeals to antiquity or claims of their supposed origins in the eras of long-dead kings – also lent them their legitimacy.[6]

Examples of borough court cases, when embedded in custumals, provided legal justification for customs that informed the operation and jurisdiction of borough courts. Borough court cases were valuable because they provided concrete evidence and examples of customs in practice, from a particular moment in time as experienced by real people, as judged by civic authorities in the past. Because medieval jurists and lawmakers did not generate treatises about borough customary law in the same way they did for common or canon law, the idea of legal precedent was flexible and dependent largely on borough officials' interpretation of what qualified as past practice.[7] Tradition-

3 The power of the keepers of Beverley was, according to Leach, solidified in the early fourteenth century, though charters that appealed to antiquity retroactively confirmed the keepers' authority: Leach (ed.), *Beverley Town Documents*, pp. xxv–xxvii.

4 The best overview of this genre is Geoffrey Howard Martin, 'The diplomatic of English borough custumals', in Walter Prevenier and Thérèse de Hemptinne (eds), *La diplomatique urbaine en Europe au Moyen Age: Actes du congrès de la Commission internationale de diplomatique, Gand, 25–29 août 1998* (Leuven, 2000), pp. 307–20.

5 Adolphus Ballard (ed.), *British Borough Charters, 1042–1216* (Cambridge, 1913), pp. xiii–xvi; Martin, 'The diplomatic of English borough custumals', pp. 317–18.

6 Anthony Musson, 'Appealing to the past: perceptions of law in late-medieval England', in Anthony Musson (ed.), *Expectations of the Law in the Middle Ages* (Woodbridge, 2001), pp. 172–3.

7 Neil Duxbury argued that custom and precedent were not synonymous concepts and, at times, were opposed to one another: N. Duxbury, *The Nature and Authority of Precedent* (Cambridge, 2008), pp. 8–9.

ally, custom itself was based on the idea (though perhaps not actual fact) of past usage or practice that was local or particular to a region.[8] Legal scholars studying common or crown law have typically used the term 'precedent' to describe a legal decision, or case, whose underlying principles became exemplary for subsequent cases that were similar enough to be adjudged on the same merits.[9]

But with the exception of local studies and histories of individual towns, borough customary law as a whole has infrequently been the subject of sustained research and, as such, the use of precedent in customary law has not been systematically examined.[10] Even less attention has been paid to the diversity of forms that customs could take.[11] Transcriptions of borough court cases frequently appeared as memoranda, so-called because officials 'remembered' them for guidance on how they should conduct town business in future.[12] Borough court cases, however, were embedded within town custumals only occasionally, in less than a tenth of the 156 extant custumals identified and analysed for this research.[13] Their rarity suggests the existence of a contingent, *ad hoc* process through which officials (usually town clerks) incorporated them into custumals.[14] These cases, such as the one involving Robert Puttok, were embedded in custumals seemingly at the discretion of the various compilers responsible for deciding which regulations were to be considered customary.

Lawmakers and compilers used the authority of the borough court to provide examples of legal precedent and, in the process, construct and strengthen the customary law for their boroughs. Thus the court itself was

8 David Ibbetson, 'Custom in medieval law', in Amanda Perreau-Saussine and James Bernard Murphy (eds), *The Nature of Customary Law: Legal, Historical and Philosophical Perspectives* (Cambridge, 2007), pp. 155–7.

9 Duxbury, *Nature and Authority of Precedent*, pp. 7, 31–3.

10 The most comprehensive work on borough customary law is in two volumes: Mary Bateson (ed.), *Borough Customs*, Selden Society, no. 18 for vol. 1, no. 21 for vol. 2 (London, 1904–06). See also Justin Croft, 'The custumals of the Cinque Ports, c. 1290 – c. 1500: studies in the cultural production of the urban record' (unpublished doctoral thesis, University of Kent at Canterbury, 1997).

11 Bateson, in her introduction, briefly mentioned the diversity of documentary formats, though she was not particularly concerned with the variety of forms that customs could take: Bateson, *Borough Customs*, vol. 1, p. xv.

12 G. H. Martin, 'English town records, 1250–1350', in Richard Britnell (ed.), *Pragmatic Literacy, East and West: 1200–1330* (Woodbridge, 1997), p. 126. Memoranda can be found in about 80 per cent of compilations.

13 This sample size does not include charters, only stand-alone manuscripts and compilations. Many of these, dating to the period before 1600, are listed in Bateson (ed.), *Borough Customs*, vol. 1, pp. xviii–lvi, and are the basis of my doctoral thesis, 'The making of borough customary law in medieval Britain' (unpublished doctoral thesis, Fordham University, 2019).

14 John Baker explained that the systematic use of precedent was not common in the Middle Ages, and that citations from previous common law cases were done by memory: J. Baker, *The Oxford History of the Laws of England: 1483–1558*, vol. 6 (Oxford, 2003), pp. 486–9.

integral to the making and development of borough customary law. For evidence, this chapter draws on a sample of fifty court cases embedded in six custumals from five boroughs (Exeter, London, Beverley, Northampton and Ipswich), ranging from the thirteenth to the early sixteenth centuries.

TABLE 2.1: *TYPES OF COURT CASES EMBEDDED IN BOROUGH CUSTUMALS, C. 1240–1515*

Borough and custumal	**Property**	**Law & order**	**Trade**	**Morality and public disorder**	**Total**
Exeter (Anglo-Norman custumal, c. 1240–1282)	1		1		2
Beverley (*Great Guild Book*, c. 1306–1600)	7		3	2	12
Ipswich (*Little Domesday*, c. 1320)	5				5
London (*Liber Albus*, c. 1419)	6	5	2		13
London (*Liber Dunthorn*, c. 1464–1491)		4		11	15
Northampton (*Liber Custumarum*, c. 1414–1515)	3				3
Total	**22**	**9**	**6**	**13**	**50**
Percentage %	**44**	**18**	**12**	**26**	**100**

SOURCES: Exeter: J.W. Schopp (ed.), *The Anglo-Norman Custumal of Exeter* (Oxford, 1925), pp. 26-8; Beverley: Arthur F. Leach (ed.) *Beverley Town Documents*, Selden Society, no. 14 (London, 1900), pp. 17–18, 23–4, 27, 30, 36, 44–5, 48–50; Ipswich: Suffolk Record Office, Ipswich C/4/1/1 fol. 71r; London, *Liber Albus*: H.T. Riley (ed.), *Munimenta Gildhallae Londoniensis: Liber Albus, Liber Custumarum, et Liber Horn*, vol. 1 (London, 1859), pp. 332–3, 339–44, 349–51, 354–7, 369–71, 373–6, 402, 412–15, 419–21, 426–7; *Liber Dunthorn*: London Metropolitan Archives COL/CS/01/010, fols. 50v-51v, 122r, 122v, 123v, 126v-128r; Northampton: Christopher A. Markham (ed.), *The Records of the Borough of Northampton*, vol. 1 (Northampton, 1898), pp. 242–3, 267–8.

These five boroughs not only represent a wide cross-section of different population sizes and locations, but their surviving custumals illustrate a range of concerns and foci in the borough court precedents upon which officials drew. These cases – dealing with issues relating to property, law and order, trade, and morality and public disorder – reveal a broad spectrum of legal actions in the borough court that officials depended on to strengthen the legitimacy of their customs.

Borough court cases could serve as town customs in three ways. First, these cases helped to further define the customs of the courts by demonstrating the correct procedure or resolution to a legal problem in the borough. Secondly, they established a sense of custom that was rooted in a definitive past, rather than the indeterminate past from 'time immemorial' that officials so often referenced to give authority to borough customs. Lastly, these cases reinforced the authority of civic officials over the borough courts and as originators of customary law.

Property

Lawsuits concerning property, including disputes about inheritance claims, comprise almost 45 per cent of recorded cases (Table 2.1). As property was the main source of wealth and a marker of status for urban inhabitants, there was much at stake for the parties involved in disputes over the transfer and ownership of property, and for the officials who adjudicated these cases. While many custumals contained laws about holding, inheriting and maintaining property, the transcription of specific cases about property reinforced the borough courts' status as venues through which disputes affecting the fortunes of moneyed individuals were settled.[15] The property cases from London's famous custumal, the *Liber Albus*, show particular concern for the protection of individuals whose vulnerability made them useful pawns in corrupt practices, such as orphans of wealthy London freemen.[16] For example, a lengthy 1363 case in the *Liber Albus* cited Andrew Pykman, who had become stepfather to Alice Forneaux, still in her minority and the daughter of a deceased fishmonger.[17] Custom dictated that guardians such as Andrew first seek the approval of the mayor and aldermen before arranging a marriage for their wards, a measure designed to protect vulnerable orphans from forced or unsuitable marriages that could diminish their inheritances. Andrew had defied this custom in giving Alice in marriage to Robert Pykman (likely one of his kinsmen) without notifying civic authorities, an action that led to the sheriff empanelling a jury of twenty-four men from the wards closest to the tenements owned by Alice's deceased father.[18] The jurors then inquired after Alice's *maritagium* – that is, the value of her marriage based on the size of her inheritance – which they determined to be £44.[19] Andrew was imprisoned for breaking the law and was

15 See Bateson (ed.), *Borough Customs*, vol. 2, pp. 60–144, for customary law on property rights and inheritance.

16 Reginald R. Sharpe (ed.), *Calendar of the Letter-Books*, vols A–K (London, 1899–1912) catalogues more than a hundred such references to cases dealing with orphans.

17 H. T. Riley (ed.), *Munimenta Gildhallæ Londoniensis: Liber Albus, Liber Custumarum, et Liber Horn*, vol. 1 (London, 1859), pp. 488–90.

18 As Elaine Clark argued, men held the majority of wardships, but stepfathers had no implicit rights to their stepchildren's inheritances: E. Clark, 'City orphans and custody laws in medieval England', *The American Journal of Legal History*, 34 (1990), pp. 168–87, esp. 178–9.

19 Sue Sheridan Walker, 'Free consent and marriage of feudal wards in medieval England', *Journal of Medieval History*, 8 (1982), pp. 123–34. Traditionally, *maritagium* was the 'feudal' right of the king to control, or approve, the marriages of his most important vassals, to ensure that such

then ordered to pay the £44 to the chamberlain when he was released, thus forfeiting his stepdaughter's *maritagium* to the city.[20]

The placement of this 1363 case in the custumal demonstrates its multivalent function. Since the case was about sixty years old, it was likely a resolution to a pressing legal problem in the wake of the Black Death, when the pestilence left many children, still in their minority, orphaned.[21] It was also an addition to the city's voluminous customs that addressed the ongoing problems surrounding the guardianship of orphans and the protection of their wealth. And perhaps most importantly, this case was at once a demonstration of the city's custom and an embodiment of the process through which challenges to it were resolved. The marriage of wealthy orphans was a matter that demanded the attention of civic officials, since many such officials were both citizens and men of property who wanted sureties that their children would be protected in the event of their own deaths and the remarriage of their widows.[22] The case showed the procedure through which such cases were resolved, according to the city's long-standing custom that ensured the protection of orphans and their estates. It began with Andrew's citation by the common sergeant, the official assigned to keep track of orphans' inheritances, at the court before London's mayor and aldermen. The dispute ended before the sheriff, who acted on information from 'reputable and lawful' jurors likely familiar with the family and their property; this local expertise ultimately determined the value of Alice's *maritagium*.[23]

While the Andrew Pykman case had a clear outcome, other cases did not; many instead focused on how indictments and lawsuits should proceed in the borough courts. For example, five lawsuits from Ipswich (purposely embedded between the table of contents of a French custumal and the body of the customs itself) were excerpted, but their conclusions (if they were even recorded in the original plea rolls) were excised from the text. The outcomes

---

unions would not be hostile to his political interests. When many boroughs acquired 'feudal' rights and privileges, free *maritagium* was one of them. The authority to approve marriages, however, was transferred to the city, which, in London's case, claimed the value of the entire *maritagium* if approval of the marriage was not obtained.

20 Kate Kelsey Staples explained that the *maritagium* was given to a woman upon her marriage. The Pykman case, however, does not clarify if the *maritagium* would remain in the city's coffers or be given to Alice's husband at a later date: K. K. Staples, *Daughters of London: Inheriting Opportunity in the Late Middle Ages* (Leiden, 2011), p. 87.

21 This span of time is calculated by subtracting the date of the court case (1363) from the date that most scholars believe that John Carpenter compiled the *Liber Albus* (c. 1419). See also William Kellaway, 'John Carpenter's *Liber Albus*', *Guildhall Studies in London History*, 3 (1978), pp. 67–84.

22 Caroline Barron, *London in the Later Middle Ages: Government and the People, 1200–1500* (Oxford, 2004), pp. 181, 189.

23 Bracton discussed how *maritagium*, in a seigneurial context, should have been assessed: George E. Woodbine (ed.) and S. E. Thorne (trans.), *Bracton on the Laws and Customs of England*, vol. 2 (Cambridge, MA, 1968), p. 77.

of these suits were not as important as the borough court procedures they highlighted. Carefully rubricated and annotated with subject headings in the same clerical hand and style as the French customs that follow, these five cases also survive intact in a later recension.[24] They were transcribed specifically for the purpose of showing how pleas of waste and *rationabili parte,* both of which dealt with inherited property, could be initiated in Ipswich's borough court, the Portmanmote, without a writ. Their inclusion as customs illustrated the privileges that the town had enjoyed since at least the reign of Henry III.[25] The details of each case, including the names of the litigants, were significant in establishing the legitimacy and origins of these customs, as the identities of such individuals rooted the custom in a past case that established precedent for current practice. The second case listed, for example, is a short extract of a plea of waste first recorded in the Ipswich 'Roll of Pleas' in 1255. A certain John of St George initiated his suit without a writ against a widow called Levota in the Portmanmote.[26] Whether John had won his suit against Levota, or Levota successfully defended herself against it, had little bearing on the case's value for the officials who included it (and others like it) in Ipswich's custumal. The crucial information was that a plea of waste could be initiated in the local court without the expense of obtaining a writ – a practice that, at the time of this case, was valid according to Ipswich custom. Copying the case into the custumal reinforced this privilege as customary law and offered a precedent that officials could cite. Borough court rolls thus functioned as intermediary texts that brought customary law to light, facilitating the transition from practice in the court to prescriptive custom.[27]

Two of the three cases embedded in the late-fifteenth-century custumal of Northampton dealt with disputes about lands which the town held in common, showing that case precedents could be deployed to protect the interests of the commonalty as a whole. Two separate property disputes found a certain Richard Knyghtley and the abbot of the nearby monastery of St

24 Suffolk Record Office, Ipswich (hereafter SROI) C/4/1/1 fol. 71r is in an early-fourteenth-century court hand. A recension of the same cases is in SROI C/4/1/3 fol. 26v, in a neat, mid-fourteenth-century court hand.

25 A writ was needed to initiate a plea of waste for heirs to obtain restitution for any damages made to their inherited property; see Sue Sheridan Walker, 'The action of waste in the early common law', in J. H. Baker (ed.), *Legal Records and the Historian* (London, 1978), pp. 185–206. According to Britton, a writ of *rationabili parte* allowed heirs to initiate a plea to recover their fair share of any property left to them by an ancestor: Francis Morgan Nichols (ed.), *Britton: The French Text Carefully Revised with an English Translation*, vol. 2 (Oxford, 1865), pp. 80–5.

26 SROI C/4/1/1 fol. 71r: 'Item compertum est in Rotulo pl*acitorum* pred*ic*te ville de a*nno* R*egni* pred*ic*te Reg*is* xl^mo q*uod* q*uod* [*sic*] quoddam pl*ac*itum de vasto p*er* querelam sine bre*vi* motum fuit in Cur*iam* eiusdem ville int*er* Ioh*ann*em de Sa*nc*to Georgeo quer*elam*. Et leuotam que fuit uxor Osb*er*ti Lyuerd defend*it* s*ecundu*m consuetudinem ville etc.'

27 According to Duxbury, medieval litigants and advocates searched in plea rolls for precedents that could help their case: Duxbury, *Nature and Authority of Precedent*, p. 32.

James culpable for occupying a meadow 'to the prejudice of the town of Northampton'. The cases reveal the boundaries and location of the meadow, called 'Dustoun', emphasising that the guilty parties, at two different times, had occupied it unlawfully.[28] Such attention to detail – about the size, location and even the name of the property – reinforced the town's customary claims to holding common rights over this particular place.[29] The cases about 'Dustoun' occurred in two separate years and produced different guilty parties, suggesting that the town's rights to 'Dustoun' likely needed to be reinforced in the Northampton custumal in the face of opposition from the local abbey.[30]

Law and Order

The cases concerned with 'law and order', most of which are drawn from the *Liber Albus*, make up almost a fifth of the total; they generally dealt with how trespass and felonies should be adjudicated in London's courts (Table 2.1). The placement of these cases in the custumal served to highlight their function as precedents that reinforced the jurisdiction of the city's courts and its officials over trespasses and felonies. Compilers sometimes drew precedents from court cases recorded in older custumals or other town registers. The copying of material from older custumals was particularly widespread among London's clerkship. William Dunthorn, author of his own custumal, which he compiled during his tenure as London's common clerk from 1461 until 1490, borrowed liberally from John Carpenter's *Liber Albus*, including a case involving two London skinners dating to 1323.[31] Carpenter himself had drawn the case from Letter-Book E, one of many London registers containing legal memoranda for the city.[32] This case was adjudicated nearly a century before Carpenter began to compile the *Liber Albus* in c. 1419; it involved a Nicholas de Whittone, who brought a plea of force and arms at Westminster against John de Cotone, whom he accused of forcibly imprisoning him for eight weeks.[33] Despite the serious

28 Christopher A. Markham (ed.), *The Records of the Borough of Northampton*, vol. 1 (Northampton, 1898), pp. 242–3, 267–8.
29 Helen Cam, 'Northampton borough', in William Page (ed.), *The Victoria History of the County of Northampton*, vol. 3 (London, 1970), p. 21.
30 Markham (ed.), *Records of the Borough of Northampton*, vol. 2, p. 266.
31 Penny Tucker, 'Dunthorn, William (*d.* 1490)', in *Oxford Dictionary of National Biography* (Oxford, 2004). For London's custumals and their influences, see Neil R. Ker, 'Liber Custumarum, and other manuscripts formerly at the Guildhall', *The Guildhall Miscellany*, 1 (1959), pp. 37–45; Neil R. Ker, *Medieval Manuscripts in British Libraries*, vol. 1 (Oxford, 1969), pp. 20–42; and Debbie Cannon, 'London pride: citizenship and the fourteenth-century custumals of the City of London', in Sarah Rees Jones (ed.), *Learning and Literacy in Medieval England and Abroad* (Turnhout, 2003), pp. 179–98.
32 Reginald R. Sharpe (ed.), *Calendar of Letter-Books: Letter-Book E, circa A.D. 1314–1337* (London, 1903), pp. 188–9.
33 Riley (ed.), *Munimenta Gildhallæ Londoniensis*, pp. 433–6.

charge and damages (£100) that Nicholas sought for his pain and suffering, Carpenter's lengthy transcription of this case did not include the resolution between the two litigants. This case reinforced a custom which Henry III guaranteed by charter in 1227, prohibiting London citizens from suing one another outside the city's walls.[34]

For Carpenter, the worth of this court case lay neither in its prosecution nor its eventual outcome, but rather in what it confirmed about London's ancient customs and how it helped define the legal jurisdiction of London's courts. Carpenter made the decision to include citations of two previous pleas of trespass to which this custom had applied and, for additional reinforcement, a transcript of a confirmation issued by Edward II in 1324.[35] With customs and legal precedents seemingly confirmed and established as a matter of public record, and with an attorney intervening on behalf of the city's interests in court to furnish proof of these long-standing customs, it was decided that Whittone's suit against Cotone was to proceed before the mayor and aldermen at the court in London's Guildhall rather than at Westminster.[36]

Carpenter's placement of Whittone's case in the *Liber Albus* seemed out of place with the type of laws that directly preceded it; but when Dunthorn copied the case from the *Liber Albus*, he made a crucial editorial decision that accentuated Whittone's suit as an example of a customary right held by London's citizens. In Carpenter's *Liber Albus*, Whittone's suit, transcribed on the front and back of one folium, follows a proclamation claiming to confirm an old London custom that dictated where corn merchants were to sell their victuals, and the forfeiture of these merchants' goods if their corn were found to be of poor quality.[37] About a half-century later, when Dunthorn copied the same case into his custumal in the 1470s, he must have decided that context and further explanation for this precedent was needed, since he eschewed Carpenter's organisation and instead placed Whittone's case after a somewhat lengthy prologue, written in English, about the many notable privileges and 'free lib*er*tees' enjoyed by the citizens of London. According to this prologue, these privileges were confirmed by the mayor, John Norman, 'with the full assent of the comons' in August 1454 in London's Guildhall.[38] One of these customs was that 'no man*er* p*er*sone enfraunchised in the seid citee shuld onplete nor pursue ony accion ayenst ony other p*er*sone enfraunchised of the

34 Walter de Gray Birch (ed.), *The Historical Charters and Constitutional Documents of the City of London* (London, 1887), p. 28.

35 Riley (ed.), *Munimenta Gildhallæ Londoniensis*, pp. 435–6.

36 Again, the city court here was not specified, though it was likely not the Hustings court, as it was not empowered to hear pleas of the crown. See Barron, *London in the Later Middle Ages*, p. 128.

37 Riley (ed.), *Munimenta Gildhallæ Londoniensis*, pp. 432–3.

38 London Metropolitan Archives (hereafter LMA) COL/CS/01/010 fol. 50v.

same withoute the libertee thereof'.[39] In this instance, Dunthorn's addition of the prologue to his custumal in the 1470s helped foreground Whittone's suit of 1323 as a precedent relevant to existing civic privileges, which had been reconfirmed in 1454.

Dunthorn decided to keep Carpenter's organisation intact when it came to transcribing another case (also a plea of force and arms) that he, like Carpenter before him, decided to place after Whittone's case. Reaffirming the exclusive privileges of citizens seems to have been as important to Dunthorn as it had been to Carpenter when it came to highlighting trespass and felony cases. The case of the armourer Thomas of Cantebrugge and his wife, Alice, centred on the damages owed to Alice, who claimed the loss of £200 when men burgled her house and stole valuable goods.[40] Neither Carpenter nor Dunthorn included the outcome or the settlement of Alice's suit in their respective transcriptions, or what fate befell the accused burglars.[41] Much like Whittone's case, it concluded with the mayor and commonalty being ordered (it was unclear by whom) to ensure a fair, swift and just resolution to her suit, when an attorney representing the city's interests argued that her case needed to be adjudicated in the court at the Guildhall. The application of this privilege – that is, the exemption of citizens from being sued in courts outside the city's liberties – may have raised questions about the legal standing of a plaintiff bringing a suit against another citizen if the plaintiff were the wife of a citizen. The inclusion of Alice's suit clarified that this privilege was not to be interpreted differently in its application to lawsuits involving women married to citizens.[42]

Dunthorn also copied the case of Yoenet (Johanna) Cogenho, who was convicted of forging an indenture, from an undated entry in Letter-Book K.[43] This case was likely notable for a variety of reasons, not least because she attempted to defraud Henry Barton, a citizen skinner, out of a considerable £100.[44] She was required to stand in public with the forged contract around

39 LMA COL/CS/01/010 fol. 50r.

40 Kay E. Lacey implied that Alice too was an armourer, though this is not entirely clear from the text: K. E. Lacey, 'Women and work in fourteenth and fifteenth century London', in Lindsey Charles and Lorna Duffin (eds), *Women and Work in Pre-Industrial England* (London, 1985), p. 52.

41 LMA COL/CS/01/010 fol. 51r; Riley (ed.), *Munimenta Gildhallæ Londoniensis*, p. 417.

42 Alice's possible status as a *femme sole* trader, or as a woman with a distinct legal status separate from that of her husband, could also have prompted the recording of this case for posterity. See Marjorie K. McIntosh, 'The benefits and drawbacks of *femme sole* status in England, 1300–1630', *Journal of British Studies*, 44 (2005), pp. 410–38, esp. 414–15.

43 Reginald R. Sharpe (ed.), *Calendar of Letter-Books of the City of London: K, Henry VI* (London, 1911), pp. 16–17.

44 The case does not indicate in which city court the accused appeared, but the inquest into the matter (found in Sharpe, *Letter-Book K*, p. 24) says that it was taken in the Guildhall on 12 December 1423, according to the custom of the city and before the mayor and aldermen.

her neck, though the rest of her punishment was later cancelled, at Barton's request, on account of her 'womanhode'.[45] Though the punishment reflected her infamy as a common 'disseyuer and begyler of the people', the case established a precedent for demonstrating leniency towards women in particular circumstances, especially those who might have been considered too old or frail to withstand the full punishment for their crime as custom demanded.[46]

Trade

The cases on trade constitute only about a tenth of the total, but their inclusion in the custumals of Beverley, London and Exeter indicates how officials consciously chose them to reinforce their jurisdiction to either tax or punish tradespeople in breach of custom (Table 2.1). The one trade case in Exeter's thirteenth-century custumal ostensibly centred on butchers, but it was actually focused on the rights of the city to tax the retail trade of non-citizens.[47] As a final 'judgement' handed down in the Mayor's court, it noted that all butchers who were not citizens of Exeter were to pay customs, or tolls, to sell meat in Exeter.[48] The case also clarified that citizen butchers, who were usually exempt

---

The case itself does not adequately convey how important Barton was to London politics; he had been a mayor (twice), an MP, a sheriff and a yeoman of the royal household. See Carole Rawcliffe, 'Barton, Henry (*d.* 1435), of London', in J. S. Roskell, L. Clark and C. Rawcliffe (eds), *The History of Parliament: The House of Commons, 1386–1421* (Woodbridge, 1993).

45 LMA COL/CS/01/010 fol. 121r: 'For so mochell as Yoenet Cogenho that here stonte is openly convycte and atteynt before the mair & aldermen of this Citee that she with anothir of hir covine whiche is not yet taken the xii day of decembir last passed forged and countrefeted a fals obligacion conteyneng that Henry Barton citizen and skynner of London shuld haue be bounde to Henry Chaterton and John Tetenale in c li to pay at witsontyde next comyng Therfore and for as mychel as the seid yhonet is knowen and by com*en* voyse and fame publysshed for a comyn disseyu*er* and begyler of the people. It is awarded by the seid mair and aldermen that the same Yonet in chastisment of other that myght catche enboldisshement in excercise of suche falsnesse if she scaped vnpunysshed shall stond this day answere in this open place to be seen and knowen with the seid fals obligation aboute her neke And the remenaunt of the punysshement that she hath deserued to be for yeue atte reu*er*ence of womanhode and instance of the same Henr*y* Barton.'

46 Barbara Hanawalt cites the case as it appeared in A. H. Thomas (ed.), *Calendar of Plea and Memoranda Rolls, A.D. 1413–1437*, vol. 4 (Cambridge, 1943), pp. 189–90. Here it was mentioned that Johanna was ordered to stand next to the pillory because she was feeble. If she were the widow Johanna who appeared in the 1383 will of a certain Nicholas de Cogenho (found in Reginald Sharpe (ed.), *Calendar of Wills, A.D. 1358–1688*, vol. 2 (London, 1890), pp. 237–8), she would have likely been considered elderly in 1423. B. Hanawalt, *The Wealth of Wives: Women, Law, and Economy in Late Medieval London* (Oxford, 2007), p. 205.

47 Maryanne Kowaleski, *Local Markets and Regional Trade in Medieval Exeter* (Cambridge, 1995), p. 96.

48 Jacob Wilhelm Schopp (ed.), *The Anglo-Norman Custumal of Exeter* (Oxford, 1925), p. 26. The case likely appeared in the Mayor's court, as this seemed to be the only extant borough court in the thirteenth century, though the proceedings of the Provosts' court were entered into the mayoral court rolls up until the late fourteenth century. This case also pre-dated the existence of the city's other court, the Mayor's Tourn, which first appeared in Exeter in 1302

from these taxes, were also to pay them if they were in partnership with unenfranchised butchers.[49] This case set a precedent for the types of merchants taxed in Exeter – be they non-free (non-enfranchised individuals in the city), foreign (those from outside the liberty of the city and subject to a different jurisdiction), or citizens whose status did not shield them from paying customs under certain circumstances.[50] That the original case was about butchers was incidental, as its placement in the custumal reinforced the privilege that citizen merchants could sell goods or victuals at retail without charge.[51]

This 'judgement' (seemingly transcribed from a court roll in its original Latin, and placed within a custumal that was written predominantly in Anglo-Norman French) stands out from the text preceding it through contrast in language, format and subject. Its placement, however, is clearly deliberate rather than haphazard. It follows a list of tolls placed on goods that were going to Exeter's market, and a list of distinct groups of residents or tenants of jurisdictions exempt from paying tolls.[52] Thus the 'judgement' reinforced a lengthy series of clauses about tolls paid on specific items in Exeter.

In London's *Liber Albus*, two trade cases demonstrate how Carpenter's selections from chronicles and other custumals could be used not only to reaffirm the city's jurisdiction over the Thames, but also to provide precedent for enhancing the status and power of certain merchant guilds over other trades. One of these was a lengthy undated case that came before the mayor and aldermen, involving individuals who used fishing nets made of mesh deemed too small in size.[53] These fishers were indicted for overfishing the Thames, though in general the use of nets was regulated because they could obstruct waterways.[54] The owners of the fishing nets brought them to be inspected at the Guildhall and, after another memoranda book was consulted, the court confirmed that the mesh needed to be two inches in width.[55] A panel of jurors made up of fishmongers, who belonged to one of the wealthiest groups of

---

(the proceedings of this leet court were also enrolled in the Mayor's court rolls until 1368); see Kowaleski, *Exeter*, pp. 337–40.

49 According to Kowaleski, problems arose in Exeter when unenfranchised traders falsely claimed they held the freedom, and when franchised merchants claimed non-citizen traders' transactions as theirs to avoid paying tolls: Kowaleski, *Exeter*, pp. 196–7.

50 Schopp (ed.), *The Anglo-Norman Custumal of Exeter*, p. 19 n. 2.

51 This was a privilege that was first extended to Exeter's citizens in royal charters to the borough, dating back to the reign of Henry II; see George Oliver, *The History of the City of Exeter* (Exeter, 1861), pp. 279–80.

52 Schopp (ed.), *The Anglo-Norman Custumal of Exeter*, pp. 24–6.

53 Riley (ed.), *Munimenta Gildhallæ Londoniensis*, pp. 385–6.

54 As Barron noted, the jurisdiction of the city over the Thames and, in particular, the dismantling of unauthorised fishing weirs was guaranteed by royal charters dating back to Magna Carta: Barron, *London in the Later Middle Ages*, p. 40.

55 Riley noted that the *Minori Nigro Libro* consulted in this instance was no longer in the possession of the city: Riley (ed.), *Munimenta Gildhallæ Londoniensis*, p. 385 n. 1.

merchants in London, inspected the nets; these fishmongers had a vested interest in the Thames not being depleted of its fish, but also in situating themselves as arbiters and overseers over other occupations that supplied fish to the city.[56] The fishmongers decided that half the nets were not up to standard and should be burned. The case concluded with Carpenter providing a short commentary on how it came to influence London custom; mayors and aldermen, from that day forward, burned substandard nets whenever they were discovered in the Thames.[57]

This case of the fishing nets may have spoken to larger political concerns about the policing of the Thames and enforcing the city's water rights; in the *Liber Albus*, however, it formed part of a series of ordinances on the fish trade, as fish was an important staple that city authorities felt they needed to manage to prevent food shortages. Additionally, these ordinances reflected how the mercantile interests of the fishmongers, many of whom held prestigious civic offices in London, likely influenced the inclusion of customs which were established in London's courts that were favourable to their trade.[58] This case followed, for example, ordinances on how individuals were to catch fish, the tolls levied on certain types of fish brought to market, penalties for forestalling and regrating, how to ensure the quality of the catch, restrictions on selling oysters and mussels, the sheriffs' jurisdiction over the court of fishmongers, and the conditions by which apprentices could be taken into the trade.[59] Carpenter likely included this case as part of these ordinances to underscore that there was legal precedent, as well as a rich historical tradition mined from chronicles and other custumals, allowing civic officials and fishmongers to regulate and intervene in the fish trade.

Morality and Public Disorder

The 'morality and public disorder' cases, making up about a quarter of the total, reflected the anxieties borough officials harboured when they drafted ordinances to quash what they perceived to be social disorder (Table 2.1).[60] Officials typically framed such ordinances as renewals of customs that had fallen out of practice, or as correctives to 'bad' customs they were now obli-

56 George Unwin, *The Gilds and Companies of London* (London, 1908), pp. 38–42; Sylvia Thrupp, *The Merchant Class of Medieval London, 1300–1500* (Ann Arbor, 1948), pp. 60–97.

57 Derek Keene mentioned that the practice of burning nets was done periodically: D. Keene, 'Issues of water in medieval London to c. 1300', *Urban History*, 28 (2001), p. 168. For incidents in 1236 and 1263, see H. T. Riley (ed.), *Chronicles of the Mayors and Sheriffs of London* (London, 1863), pp. 7–8, 22.

58 Barron, *London in the Later Middle Ages*, p. 41.

59 Riley (ed.), *Munimenta Gildhallæ Londoniensis*, pp. 373–85.

60 Marjorie Keniston McIntosh, *Controlling Misbehavior in England, 1370–1600* (Cambridge, 1998), pp. 186–208.

gated to enforce.[61] These cases date mostly from the fifteenth century and come from two custumals, though primarily from the wardmote cases found in the *Liber Dunthorn*. The wardmote was the local court of London wards over which aldermen presided, usually over lawsuits and indictments that touched on neighbourly relations and all manner of perceived disorderly conduct.[62] The wardmote cases in the *Liber Dunthorn* feature guilty individuals, whose convictions in the wardmote demonstrated how ordinances should be enforced to police misbehaviour, including prostitution.

The wardmote cases served primarily to demonstrate the ways in which malefactors were to be punished, thus providing direction and examples for borough officials as they enforced new ordinances aimed at eliminating immorality, public disorder and peace-breaking. One of the cases embedded in these ordinances dates to the reign of Richard II, nearly a hundred years before Dunthorn's late-fifteenth-century transcription.[63] John Thaine was cited in a London wardmote by his alderman, Thomas atte Noket, for instigating affrays and disturbing the peace with several barking dogs that annoyed his neighbours at night-time. Perhaps more importantly, Thaine had consistently disobeyed his alderman, the constables and other civic officials. A jury of twelve men investigated the matter and, although Thaine had sworn he was innocent, the jury found him guilty and sent him to prison. These wardmote cases show how Dunthorn was drawing from specific examples, and even duplicating them, to outline the legal processes through which neighbourhood nuisance and disobedience were to be addressed. This case demonstrated how the authority of aldermen and the ward's *probi homines* ('good men') manifested itself on a local level when enforcing the law.[64]

Rebellion against civic officials also cropped up in two cases embedded in Beverley's custumal, and they too reflected growing anxieties about challenges to civic authority during the later Middle Ages. Both of these cases date to

61 For example, LMA COL/CS/01/010 fol. 121v: 'It is considered and ordeyned by the mair and aldermen by the advyce of the comyns that from this day forward the olde ordenaunce of punysshementis of suche mysdoers shall be vtterly executed and p*ro*clamyd to be kept in eschewyng of suche mysdoers above seid in tyme comyng.'

62 Barron, *London in the Later Middle Ages*, p. 123.

63 LMA COL/CS/01/010 fols 123v, 128r: 'Alias coram Thoma atte Noket Aldermanno warde de langebo*rne* in wardemoto suo tento in festo S*an*cti Iacobi anno Ric*ardi* Regis p*re*dict*o* p*er* inquisic*ionem* ib*idem* captam p*re*sentat fuit q*uo*d Ioh*ann*es Thaine Barbour est comunis p*er*turbator pacis et affraia plurima fac*tor* int*er* vicinos ib*id*em etc. Et etiam q*uo*d est inobediens Aldermanno Constabularis et alijs Ministris Ciuitatis vnde pluies antea ind*ic*tatus extiterat etc. Et etiam q*uo*d tenet diu*er*sos canes in domo sua nocte latrantes quod p*ro*pt*er* eor*um* vicini ib*id*em requiem suam noctant*er* h*ab*ere non possunt etc. Vnde ad p*re*s*en*tic*ion*em eiusdem Ioh*ann*is hic allocutus pon*it* se sup*er* iurat*um* q*uo*d non est culpabilis etc. Postea xxvij die Octob*ris* Iura*tores* videl*icet* Thomas Rose Ioh*ann*es Beuerage [...] ven*iunt* et Iur*ant* etc. Om*nes* dicunt sup*er* sacr*amentu*m suu*m* q*uo*d d*ic*tus Ioh*ann*es Thaine culpabilis est de om*n*ib*us* punctis p*re*dictis etc. Io*hannes* comittit*ur* prisone quousq*ue* etc.'

64 Frank Rexroth, *Deviance and Power in Late Medieval London* (Cambridge, 2007), pp. 195–6.

1412 and involve men who had defamed the keepers of Beverley. These cases were precedents that elevated the keepers' positions of authority, just as that position had become increasingly exclusionary towards outsiders, even other burgesses.[65] In one of these cases, the twelve keepers sued a burgess, John Howell, in a plea of debt, claiming that he owed them forty shillings because the customs of Beverley dictated that burgesses should be fined that amount when they engaged in any kind of resistance against the keepers' authority. Howell had been fined for spreading a malicious rumour that the keepers had infringed purposefully on the jurisdiction of the archbishop of York. Despite their numerous demands, Howell refused to pay the fine, and the keepers claimed damages of twenty shillings on account of Howell's obstinacy.[66] The case as it was transcribed has no resolution, and neither did the second case, which levied the same fine for a similar transgression.[67] Lawmakers likely cited these court cases in Beverley's custumal for three reasons: first, to show the amount of damages (twenty shillings) the keepers could claim as a result of burgesses disobeying or defaming them; secondly, to record the amount (forty shillings) according to custom that the keepers could fine burgesses for disrespecting their authority; and lastly, to show that the keepers as a corporate body could sue individual burgesses for breaching the customs of the city.

Cases about morality and public disorder also reveal the law in action from the top down and the bottom up – that is, the agents of the law and members of the community working in tandem to ensure the punishment of transgressors. This dynamic is evident in the seven prostitution cases in the *Liber Dunthorn*, as they not only established the punishments officials should dole out for both women and men involved in the sex trade, but also illustrated how transgressors should suffer for their crimes in public and in full view of their neighbourhood.[68] Written in English and ranging between 1473 and 1476, they were contemporary with Dunthorn and could feature an unusually harsh punishment for female offenders that combined public humiliation, a long imprisonment and, in some cases, the possibility of exile from the city.[69] The cases featured individuals who had already confessed to

65 Leach (ed.), *Beverley Town Documents*, pp. 48–50; Rosemary E. Horrox, 'Medieval Beverley', in K. J. Allison (ed.), *A History of the County of York: East Riding*, vol. 6 (London, 1989), p. 22.

66 Leach (ed.), *Beverley Town Documents*, pp. 48–9.

67 Leach (ed.), *Beverley Town Documents*, pp. 49–50.

68 LMA COL/CS/01/010 fols 126v–128r. See also Ruth Mazo Karras, *Common Women: Prostitution and Sexuality in Medieval England* (Oxford, 1998), pp. 14–18, 35–8.

69 For example, see LMA COL/CS/01/010 fol. 126v: 'For asmoche as Emme Straunge Jane Cotton [...] that here stonden been endited afore the Aldreman of the warde of Portsoken somme for comune baudes and sume for comyn Strumpetes and thereof been laufully atteynt. It is considered by the Mair and Aldremen after the custume and lawes of this citee that the said woomen be led with mynstralcy and Ray hoodes on their heedes and white roddes in their handes from prison to Algate and from Algate to this pillorye and heere the causes to be proclaymed and from hens to be conueyed unto Neugate and there to be voyded out of

being common 'bawds' or 'strumpets'.[70] They were then sentenced in a court before the mayor and aldermen, according to the directives outlined in a set of ordinances that preceded these cases.[71] Their punishment, which was nearly identical across all these cases, was a shaming ritual that began with the transgressors being compelled to process with minstrels, wear a striped hood and hold a white rod in their hands as they walked to the pillory in Cornhill. If they relapsed into prostitution after their release, they could be placed on the pillory again, sent to prison for a year and a day, and even ordered to abjure the city.[72] The threat of such public shaming could have been enough to discourage unregulated prostitution. As Ruth Mazo Karras has observed, the aim of such threats was to eliminate 'casual' or 'part-time' prostitution or brothel-keeping, as 'professional' women involved in the sex trade had little to lose from a public loss of reputation.[73] The ordinances attempting to curb prostitution were thus given life, as Dunthorn's custumal contained several examples of prostitutes 'performing' the consequences of violating city ordinances, which themselves were imagined to be renewals of customs meant to eliminate such transgressions in the city.

Conclusion

These cases reveal that civic officials saw the connections between customary law (as recorded in the town custumal) and practice in the borough court as mutually reaffirming. Embedding cases into custumals drawn from older sources, such as court rolls, not only reinforced their authority as officers of the court, but also as lawmakers empowered to create customary law by sourcing cases from the borough court, which itself was an institution that helped

the fraunchises of this Citee for euer. And if here after the seyd woomen or eny of them may befounde within this Citee or the suburbes of the same they than to be sette vppon the pillory in kornhill in market dayes eny day by the space of an houre. And also to haue enprisonment of a yeere and a day [...]'.

70 A bawd was (usually, a female) procurer; that is, a woman in charge of a brothel. A strumpet was a prostitute. See also Judith M. Bennett and Shannon McSheffrey, 'Early, erotic and alien: women dressed as men in late medieval London', *History Workshop Journal*, 77 (2014), pp. 1–25, at p. 22, which briefly discusses Trude Garard, a cross-dressing prostitute whose case was copied into the *Liber Dunthorn*.

71 For example, see LMA COL/CS/01/010 fol. 122r: 'Also every comyn strompet thereof atteynt shall be ledde from prison to Algate with a hode of Ray on her hede sengle and a white yerde in her hand with mynstrelcy and thens to the pillorye and there the cause shall be proclaymed and from thens thorowe chepe and Neugate and voyded oute of the ffraunchise of this Citee.'

72 That is, the prostitutes would be forced to leave the city, in a type of 'self-exile'. See William Chester Jordan, *From England to France: Felony and Exile in the High Middle Ages* (Princeton, 2015), pp. 7–32, and T. B. Lambert, 'The evolution of sanctuary in medieval England', in Paul Dresch and Hannah Skoda (eds), *Legalism: Anthropology and History* (Oxford, 2012), pp. 115–44.

73 Karras, *Common Women*, p. 15.

enforce town regulations. One might imagine these officials, most likely the town's clerks, searching the plea rolls and other court books for past cases to help their current legal arguments and supply material for their custumals.

In such custumals, borough court cases could function as legal precedent, and thus the cases were integrated as customary law in several ways: as examples of 'case law' for how certain conflicts should be resolved, as guides to pleading in the borough courts and, perhaps most importantly, as delineations of the borough court's jurisdictional reach and the authority of its officials. Ultimately, the act of embedding cases in custumals paralleled the various strategies officials employed to establish precedents for customary law, including claims to antiquity, the sworn testimonies of elders and *probi homines*, and citations to laws or practices sanctioned by or under certain English kings. By providing examples of the law in practice, local officials made significant contributions to their corpus of customs and to our understanding of legal precedents as they were deployed in borough customs.

3

THE PRIEST OF NOTTINGHAM AND THE HOLY HOUSEHOLD OF OUSEGATE: TELLING TALES IN COURT

JEREMY GOLDBERG

Court records have conventionally been analysed from the perspective of what they tell us about people's engagement with law, or to generate information about the local economy, social networks and the like.[1] This chapter proposes instead to focus on the fictive nature of court records, including depositions from Church courts, and to explore issues of narrative and narrative structure. The concern is less with what we can learn from the information recorded, such as the nature and value of goods in debt cases or patterns of litigation by status or gender, but rather to ask what the narrative strategies adopted by litigants or by those charged with recording cases tell us about contemporary values and anxieties. Realising and trying to understand this may help us better comprehend the underlying information recorded; it is also of value in its own right as a window into the cultural values and *mentalité* of civic magistrates or of canon lawyers, and of the bourgeois men and women who were the primary users of the urban courts. The chapter will draw upon a small number of case studies chosen from different kinds of court record and

1 E.g. Matthew Frank Stevens, 'London's married women, debt litigation and coverture in the Court of Common Pleas', in Cordelia Beattie and Matthew Frank Stevens (eds), *Married Women and the Law in Premodern Northwest Europe* (Woodbridge, 2013), pp. 115–31; Shannon McSheffrey, 'Men and masculinity in late medieval London civic culture: governance, patriarchy and reputation', in Jacqueline Murray (ed.), *Conflicted Identities and Multiple Masculinities: Men in the Medieval West* (New York, 1999), pp. 243–78.

different urban communities, but all from the last years of the fourteenth and early years of the fifteenth century, to make its arguments.

We can think about court records in terms of three distinct stages or historical moments, where the third stage is the use by modern scholars of the extant records. The first stage is represented by the historic event or events that generate the litigation in the first place. So, in a disputed marriage case, for example, a couple exchange loving words signifying that they desire to be married to one another. Or maybe – as the defendant in the subsequent court action will claim – they do not, because the man (it usually is the man) was someone else at the time. What actually happened – history '*wie es eigentlich gewesen*' (how it really was), as von Ranke famously put it – is fixed, but also always beyond our reach. We can access evidence for that history only in the form of documents that by their nature dispute these past events.

The second stage is the process of litigation from which evidence is generated in the form of court records. Of course, these vary considerably according to the nature of the jurisdiction and type of law, but also accident of survival. Records of borough courts, for example, can be relatively bald and devoid of any clue as to why a particular judgement was reached, if at all. Instance litigation in the Church courts, in contrast, can at times generate voluminous documentation, including numbers of depositions or written accounts of the responses of witnesses to sets of tame questions drawn up in advance of the examination. This last observation alerts us to the fact that the second stage ought perhaps itself to be subdivided. Though the creation of the documentation that litigation generates, and upon the survival of which the historian is so dependent, is in itself an integral part of the legal process, it is only one part. The more substantial part – namely the flesh and blood interactions, the actual words exchanged, even the thoughts and emotions of all those in some way involved in the business the court records necessarily imperfectly record – is either entirely hidden from modern scholars or is glimpsed only through the distorting lenses of the court records which, as Shannon McSheffrey argues, often record what should have happened rather than what may have happened.[2]

As social and economic historians, we tend to be interested in the first stage. The events alleged in litigation records serve as a proxy for what actually happened, and can thus be used as evidence for social relations and social practice. Disputes about trade, labour or debt may inform economic analysis. For example, borough court records form the basis of important scholarly monographs on Colchester and Exeter, and more recently court records have been used to explore trade and commercial networks in later

2 Shannon McSheffrey, 'Detective fiction in the archives: court records and the uses of law in late medieval England', *History Workshop Journal*, 65 (2008), p. 66.

medieval Nottingham.[3] Marjorie McIntosh has systematically sampled small town court records to explore patterns of what she terms 'misconduct' and its regulation through presentments.[4] Similarly, questions about the construction of gender may be asked. For example, it has been argued from the evidence of defamation litigation that women's reputation was tied to sexual honour, since women were more likely to be defamed as 'whore', but men's was more tied to their honesty.[5]

The second stage has in the past tended to be of most interest to scholars concerned with how the courts worked and how the law was applied. There has been some attention given to canon law and its application in the Church courts. For example, Richard Helmholz's brilliantly lucid study of English medieval marriage cases is concerned 'to describe the practice of the Church courts in dealing with ... marriage litigation'.[6] Several studies have debated the social standing of people using the Church courts, or the propensity of males or females to be involved either as litigants or deponents.[7] There appears, however, to have been comparatively little recent scholarship on borough custom and its application in borough courts, though there are of course earlier editions of material that offer some preliminary discussion, including Mary Bateson's important two-volume collection of borough law for the Selden Society.[8]

Modern scholarship demands that some attention is given to the second stage of the three-stage model just outlined, in the attempt to recover or reconstruct stage one, or at least to make observations about social practice or economic trends. Knowledge of the law and of court procedure is indeed

3 Richard Britnell, *Growth and Decline in Colchester, 1300–1525* (Cambridge, 1986); Maryanne Kowaleski, *Local Markets and Regional Trade in Medieval Exeter* (Cambridge, 1995); Richard Goddard, 'Surviving recession: English borough courts and commercial contraction, 1350–1500', in Richard Goddard, John Langdon and Miriam Müller (eds), *Survival and Discord in Medieval Society: Essays in Honour of Christopher Dyer* (Turnhout, 2010), pp. 69–87; Richard Goddard, 'Medieval business networks: St Mary's guild and the borough court in later medieval Nottingham', *Urban History*, 40 (2013), pp. 3–27.

4 Marjorie Keniston McIntosh, *Controlling Misbehavior in England, 1370–1600* (Cambridge, 1998).

5 This has been commented on by a number of scholars; see, for example, Sandy Bardsley, *Venomous Tongues: Speech and Gender in Late Medieval England* (Philadelphia, 2006), pp. 77–8, and Derek G. Neal, *The Masculine Self in Late Medieval England* (Chicago, 2008), pp. 31–2.

6 R. H. Helmholz, *Marriage Litigation in Medieval England* (Cambridge, 1974), p. 2.

7 Frederik Pedersen, 'Demography in the archives: social and geographical factors in fourteenth-century York cause paper marriage litigation', *Continuity and Change*, 10 (1995), pp. 405–36; P. J. P. Goldberg, 'Fiction in the archives: the York cause papers as a source for later medieval social history', *Continuity and Change*, 12:3 (1997), pp. 425–45; Charles Donahue, Jr., 'Female plaintiffs in marriage cases in the Court of York in the later Middle Ages: what can we learn from the numbers?', in Sue Sheridan Walker (ed.), *Wife and Widow in Medieval England* (Ann Arbor, 1993), pp. 183–213.

8 Mary Bateson (ed.), *Borough Customs*, Selden Society, 18 and 21 (London, 1906). Recent scholarship tends to discuss custom in relation to specific groups such as women, orphans, the insane etc., rather than more generally.

seen as an essential prerequisite to better understanding the significance of what the records say and do not say. For example, canon law required that insulting words had to impute a crime that might be punishable in law before they might be deemed actually defamatory.[9] It follows that the defamatory words reported in actions from the Church courts are exclusively those that conform to this legal yardstick, and insults that did not meet this yardstick may consequently have gone unreported. The words recorded are thus likely to be selective, rather than a verbatim record of what was said. Thus, when in 1422 Emma Lylle allegedly shouted at Agnes Popilton as she crossed a churchyard in the centre of York, where a substantial congregation were coming out of church after Sunday vespers, that she was an 'ald munkhore and ald frerehor' and 'ald rank tayntydthefe', she may well have said much more besides. Ralph Amcotes, the parochial chaplain who testified in support of Agnes, indeed deposed that Emma 'had a tongue flexible and vigorous for articulating her talkativeness', suggesting that her utterances were somewhat more fulsome.[10] For the purposes of the action in the ecclesiastical Court of York (*Curia Eboracensis*), however, the legal counsel whom Agnes instructed homed in on the specific words that met the canonical yardstick for defamation.

In like vein we may notice how a contract dispute litigated in the Nottingham borough courts in 1355 is recorded as between William Barbour and one Robert le Waterleder, for supply of water to the man's house. Upon closer inspection it becomes apparent that the agreement to supply water for brewing purposes was actually – or allegedly – made between Robert and William's wife, Maud, who likely had charge of the household brewing business. The court record reads, '*convenit cum Roberto per Matilldam uxorem eius*' ('he agreed with Robert by Maud his wife'). For the purposes of litigation, however, it fell to the husband to initiate the action, since his wife's married and hence dependent status militated against her acting in her own right. The court record consequently all but effaces the (likely) social reality that Maud ran a brewing business and entered into agreements associated with the business without directly involving her husband. On the other hand, because Robert denied that any such contract had ever been made, the court asked for an inquest to determine the truth of the matter. The inquest found for Robert, concluding that '*nullum conventionem fecit*' ('he made no agreement').[11] Do we surmise that, because the alleged agreement was made with a married woman

9 Debora Shuger, *Censorship and Cultural Sensibility: The Regulation of Language in Tudor-Stuart England* (Philadelphia, 2006), pp. 70–1.

10 York, Borthwick Institute for Archives, CP.F.153. One of the pertinent depositions from which these words are taken is translated in my *Women in England, c. 1275–1525: Documentary Sources* (Manchester, 1995), p. 230.

11 W. H. Stevenson (ed.), *Records of the Borough of Nottingham*, vol. 1 (London, 1882), pp. 158–9.

and not in person with her husband, the inquest jurors were disinclined to accept its validity in the perennial and unequal contest of her word against his?

Such close attention to the way in which the documents generated by court action are influenced by the law and legal conventions takes us towards a more profound reconsideration of court records as fictive, but not necessarily fictional (in the sense of purely invented) texts.[12] The seminal work for the historian here is Natalie Davis' *Fiction in the Archives*. Davis' study of sixteenth-century letters of remission seeking royal pardon for capital offences demonstrates the way in which professional lawyers played a key role in shaping the petitioner's account of events in ways calculated to win a sympathetic audience. In Davis' interpretation, the involvement of literate and cultured lawyers ensured that the essential quality of the resultant narrative as story was integral to their work.[13] Davis' work *inter alia* has come to have had a marked impact on more recent historical scholarship that explores the essentially fictive nature of narrative sources. Shannon McSheffrey, for example, discusses a London consistory court case where evidence from outwith the extant court record, comprised exclusively of depositions, might suggest that the alleged plaintiff was actually absent and the case was instead contrived by the supposed defendant.[14] Tom Johnson has also used litigation from the London consistory to argue that participants – litigants and witnesses alike – were well able to manipulate the law to further their own agenda.[15] I have also contributed to this debate, arguing *inter alia* for the way depositions are the product of a process of negotiation between a number of players, including the witnesses themselves, the canon lawyers who might 'prepare' them to answer questions, and the clerks who set the verbal testimony down as Latin depositions.[16]

My particular interest here is to draw attention to this second stage of a three-stage process relating to the production and use of court records, namely the court action from which records of proceedings are generated, as process. Indeed, as we have just observed, the second stage is itself comprised of two elements: the historical events of the court process, and the documentation that records – or purports to record – that process. The documents themselves are our window to this process, though the formulation and writing of

12 Natalie Davis uses 'fictional' where I use 'fictive', but 'fictional' carries too many resonances of invention and falseness, whereas 'fictive' references the process of crafting narrative: Natalie Zemon Davis, *Fiction in the Archives: Pardon Tales and their Tellers in Sixteenth-Century France* (Stanford, 1987), p. 3.

13 Davis, *Fiction in the Archives*, especially pp. 17–18.

14 McSheffrey, 'Detective fiction in the archives'.

15 Tom Johnson, 'The preconstruction of witness testimony: law and social discourse in England before the Reformation', *Law and History Review*, 32 (2014), pp. 127–47.

16 Jeremy Goldberg, *Communal Discord, Child Abduction, and Rape in the Later Middle Ages* (New York, 2008), ch. 2.

them was itself an integral part of that process. Because the process followed patterns and structures determined by the conventions of the law and court procedure, it is more akin to drama: it is scripted, though this need not presuppose a guiding author, since many parties may contribute to the process; it follows narrative conventions; and the participants have well-defined parts to play. The analysis that follows will explore all three of these characteristics.

A telling illustration of the scripted nature of court proceedings comes from a disputed marriage case in the Court of York. We will discuss the case in more detail at a later stage, but briefly the court was asked to decide between the claims of two different men for the hand of Agnes Grantham, a wealthy York widow. Agnes herself was attempting to extricate herself from an alleged contract with one John Dale, which she claimed she had entered into entirely against her will and under great duress. One day, as she was travelling with her son and her maid to Acomb Grange, a couple of miles outside York, in response to a dinner invitation from the then master of St Leonard's Hospital, she and her party were attacked. Whilst her son and her maid were scared off, Agnes was thrown over the back of a horse and ridden off into the woods by her assailants.[17] According to the documentary evidence – and here I follow Richard Helmholz's transcription and translation – as Agnes was ridden away by her abductors, she cried out:

> Oh, men! What do you mean to do with me? Alas that I left the city of York today! Alas that I rose from my bed today, or that my father begot me, or that my mother brought me into the world.[18]

The voluminous surviving records of the case include a large number of depositions, which derive from the verbal responses of witnesses to set questions, but also a considerable number of associated legal documents, including libel, positions and articles. The words that Agnes reportedly uttered are from these last, rather than from an actual deposition. Her rhetoric is just that. It is a record not of what Agnes was heard to have cried out, and it is highly unlikely that it reflects anything of what Agnes might actually have said at the time. Rather, it represents what a lawyer considered effective rhetoric to convince the personnel of the court, and the presiding officer in particular, that Agnes was abducted entirely against her will and that she feared for her personal safety – 'what do you mean to do with me?'

17 I have discussed the case in my *Communal Discord, Child Abduction*, ch. 8, and more recently in 'St Richard Scrope, the devout widow, and the feast of Corpus Christi: exploring emotions, gender, and governance in early-fifteenth-century York', in Susan Broomhall (ed.), *Authority, Gender and Emotions in Late Medieval and Early Modern England* (Basingstoke, 2015), pp. 66–83. The case is also discussed in Charles Donahue, Jr., *Law, Marriage, and Society in the Later Middle Ages: Arguments about Marriage in Five Courts* (Cambridge, 2007), pp. 172–5.

18 York, Borthwick Institute for Archives, CP.F.36, transcribed and translated in Helmholz, *Marriage Litigation*, p. 7.

The point is reinforced by the observation that Agnes' supposed lament was not recorded in the vernacular, but in Latin. The text as recorded reads:

> *O homines, quid mecum proponitis facere? Heu quod hodie de civitate Ebor' exivi. Heu quod hodie de meo lecto surrexi, aut quod pater me genuit, seu mater in mundum me produxit.*[19]

The rhetorical force of the words has far greater impact in Latin. Besides the rhetorical '*o*' and '*heu*', we may note the use of alliteration – '*mater in mundum me*' and the repetitive '*heu quod hodie*' – and the use of sound – the plosive 'p' and 't' of '*proponitis*', the 'd' and 't' of '*hodie de civitate*', '*hodie de meo lecto*', and '*pater me genuit, seu mater in mundum me produxit*', or the sibilant '*civitate ... exivi*' and '*surrexi*'. There is also the rhyming pairing of '*quod pater me genuit, seu mater in mundum*'. To some extent these sounds are characteristic of Latin, but there is too much artifice here to suggest that the patterns observed are simply a product of accident. This then is text that purports to represent the lament of a wronged widow, but which in fact exists only on parchment as a text to be read. Written in the abbreviated Latin of the court records, it was accessible and comprehensible only to the audience for whom it was created, namely the personnel of the ecclesiastical court. What we can be sure of is that, whatever Agnes may have cried out when, as she claimed, she was abducted, rhetorical Latin never passed her lips.

Our next example concerns borough court litigation between a Nottingham burgess and a local priest. The case reads in W. Henry Stevenson's very precise translation:

> John de Bilby makes plaint of Roger de Mampton, chaplain, on a plea of trespass, and he makes plaint that whereas the said John, at the feast of Saint Peter ad Vincula, in the 11th year of the reign of King Richard the Second [1 August 1387], was at Ratcliff attending to his affairs, the said Roger, at the said feast, broke his close, and entered his chamber here at Nottingham in the Brydilsmythgate, in contempt of the said John, and was found under a curtain of the bed of the aforesaid John, and the said John interrogated the said Roger as to what he was doing there, and he made answer to him that he was not nor came there in any evil way, and then afterwards the said John warned the aforesaid Roger that he must not be found by him with his wife, nor in his houses, in any manner, neither by day nor night, and afterwards the said Roger, after the aforesaid promise, in the week next after the feast of Saint Alban, in the 13th year of the reign of King Richard the Second [22x27 June 1389], came by night to the house of the aforesaid John in

19 Helmholz, *Marriage Litigation*, p. 7.

> the Stonstrete here at Nottingham, and there broke the wall of the aforesaid John, and leaped over it to the houses of the aforesaid John de Bilby where his secret places were, which he entered with the wife of the aforesaid John, and was there with the wife of the aforesaid John for a long time, without the permission and consent of the aforesaid John, and so he was there continually for a whole year after the aforesaid warning, so that through the coming of the aforesaid Roger the goods and chattels of the aforesaid John were and are expended and wasted in evil ways, to wit, two pairs of sheets, table-cloths, towels, and one brass pot, of the value of 13s. and 4d., are wasted and destroyed, and the whole profit of 10 quarters of malt was spent and wasted of the money of the said John, by the aforesaid Roger and the wife of the aforesaid John, and especially through the coming of the said Roger, to the damage of the aforesaid John of a hundred pounds, wherefore he enters suit, etc. And the aforesaid Roger comes in his own person, and defends the force and injury and damages, etc., and says that he, as is the custom for the parish clerk [*mos est clerico parochiali*] to go through their parish with the holy water, went to the house of the aforesaid John with the aforesaid water in good manner, and not in any evil manner, and as to the breaking of the wall or the wasting of the goods or chattels of the aforesaid John or the entering of the house of the said John, he says he is in nothing guilty, and he seeks that this may be inquired into; and the other likewise.[20]

The case has been explored to some effect by Sarah McLoughlin.[21] My own discussion will try not to trespass too much on hers.

The abbreviated Latin court record distils John de Bilby's case against Roger de Mampton (which is essentially an action for illegal entry and for damages for the loss of household goods and malt) and Roger's response. The narrative purports to be an objective record of proceedings, compiled by a clerk working for the Nottingham court. Certainly it records all pertinent information – names, dates, the evidence of illegal entry, the specific goods allegedly 'wasted' and their valuation, the damages claimed, and finally the substance of the defendant's response. The record ends by noting that the parties agreed that an inquest be conducted to determine the validity of the respective claims.

20 Stevenson (ed.), *Records of the Borough of Nottingham*, vol. 1, pp. 241, 243. I have made one change to Stevenson's translation. The phrase in italics is rendered by Stevenson as 'with parochial clergy', but this does not fit the Latin. See also Urban Culture Network, 'Nottingham borough court rolls 1303–1457', PDF file for 1378–97 (extracts), no. 18, published electronically at <http://www.nottingham.ac.uk/ucn/onlinesources/index.aspx>. This also renders *clerico parochiali* as parish clerk.

21 Sarah McLoughlin, 'Gender and transgression in the late medieval English household' (unpublished doctoral thesis, University of York, 2011), pp. 15–23.

As McLoughlin points out, the jurors of inquest subsequently reported their findings, namely that Roger was 'guilty of entering by night John's ... chamber and house and defrauding John's wall (*defraud' muri*)'. No mention is made of the damages to the sheets, towels, malt etc., but Roger was nevertheless ordered to pay substantial damages of ten marks (£6 13s 4d) and to be held in prison until he satisfied John.[22]

Although, as noted, the clerk's narrative follows the usual conventions, using precise dates that combine feast days with regnal years, and deploying elements of legal discourse, including the use of doublings – Roger '*fregit* (broke)' John's wall, he acted '*sine licentia et voluntate*' of John, he left John's goods '*expendita et alienata*' and his money '*expenditum et devastatum*' – this is more than just a formal record of court proceedings. The clerk has skilfully organised his material to comic effect. His narrative of illicit entry and the despoiling of goods serves as a metaphor for Roger de Mampton's affair with John Bilby's unnamed wife. Roger is described as having penetrated John's close, chamber and the very curtains of his marital bed, but it is implicit that this act of penetration went further.[23] The description resonates with that of Langland's contemporary creation, Sire Penetrans-domos (aka Friar Flatterer), a name which itself references a passage in Timothy's second epistle: 'For of these sort are they who creep into houses and lead captive silly women laden with sins, who are led away with divers desires.'[24] Roger was accused of having, over the course of a year living in John's Stoney Street house with John's wife, wasted 'two pairs of sheets, table-cloths, towels, and one brass pot ... and the whole profit of 10 quarters of malt'. It is not difficult to read the table-cloths, the brass pot and the malt (for brewing ale – a task regularly assigned to wives in a domestic context) as symbolic of sharing food, just as the sheets symbolise the sharing of a bed. They signify the bed and board that a man and a wife commit themselves to share. The wasted goods thus represent the *de facto* breakdown of John's marriage to his unnamed wife.

In the clerk's account of the case, the cuckolded John becomes a ridiculous figure. Discovering the priest in his bed, implicitly with his wife (or at least

22 'Nottingham borough court rolls 1303–1457', PDF file for 1378–97 (extracts), no. 83; McLoughlin, 'Gender and transgression', pp. 21–2 and n. 59. John de Bilby appears a number of times in the court rolls in various capacities, including on several occasions as an appraiser of goods. In 1394/5 he came into conflict with the mayor and burgesses by refusing to serve as an inquest juror. He was imprisoned for a while, but was subsequently reconciled on payment of a fine: 'Nottingham borough court rolls 1303–1457', PDF file for 1378–97 (extracts), nos 170, 275.

23 Cf. Shannon McSheffrey, 'Whoring priests and godly citizens: law, morality, and clerical sexual misconduct in late medieval London', in Norman L. Jones and Daniel Woolf (eds), *Local Identities in Late Medieval and Early Modern England* (Basingstoke, 2007), pp. 50–70.

24 Douay-Rheims Bible, II Tim 3:6; A. V. C. Schmidt, '*Lele Wordes* and *Bele Paroles*: some aspects of Langland's word-play', *Review of English Studies*, 34, no. 134 (1983), pp. 141–5.

in circumstances that implied an affair, even if not actually caught in the act), John impotently – I use the adverb advisedly – warned him that he should not be so discovered again. Roger thereupon engaged upon a year-long affair with John's wife – 'and so he was there continually for a whole year after the aforesaid warning'. In the meantime, John apparently did nothing to confront the incontinent priest who had so contemptuously ignored his warning, and nothing to restore his wayward wife to obedience. Only after a whole year does the clerk's narrative suggest that John was moved to action. Where other men would have exercised righteous anger to teach the priest a lesson and to oblige the erring wife to submit to her husband and return to the marital bed, John launched an action for damages in the borough court. His action details item by item the goods supposedly wasted, beginning with two pairs of sheets. This is a very public airing of John's dirty linen. John is presented as publicly drawing attention to his status as a cuckold. But the clerk's narrative does not end there. The punchline has still to come.

Roger was given an opportunity to respond to the claims made against him and to refute them. He explained that he was merely carrying out his duty as a parish clerk 'to go through their parish with the holy water', a statement that in any other context would appear entirely reasonable. At the church of St Nicholas, Bristol, in 1481, for example, the clerk's duty to take holy water round the parish, and apparently to sprinkle (asperge) the same, was recorded. He was 'to bere his holy water to euery howse Abuding soo convenient a space that every man may receive hys Holy water'.[25] Distributing holy water was indeed a duty incumbent on the clerk, though it hardly explained or justified illicit entry into parishioners' homes. Within a subgenre of seduced maidens' lyrics that McLoughlin has also written about, however, the holy water clerk has very different resonances. Here were young men in minor orders, sometimes specifically identified (as, for example, Jak in 'A Midsummer's Day's Dance') as holy water clerks, and whose singular intent was the seduction of young women.[26] Chaucer's Absolon, who similarly lusted after Alisoun, the carpenter's wife in 'The Miller's Tale', was also a holy water clerk. Both Roger himself and the Latin-literate clerk of the court were likely familiar with this genre and hence these resonances.

Roger's defiant – even brazen – response that he was merely fulfilling his duty to take water blessed by the parish priest round the parish of a Sunday – and perhaps also on major feast days such as St Peter in Chains – knowingly gestured towards sexual impropriety. Indeed, even for an era prior to

25 P. H. Ditchfield, *The Parish Clerk* (London, 1907), pp. 27–9; Eamon Duffy, *The Voices of Morebath: Reformation and Rebellion in an English Village* (New Haven, 2001), pp. 54–5.
26 McLoughlin's analysis of the subgenre is substantive and important: McLoughlin, 'Gender and transgression', ch. 1.

Freud, it is very likely that the water that Roger claimed to sprinkle round the parish would, as McLoughlin suggests, have been understood as the 'water of sperme'.[27] Roger's response was tantamount – literally – to saying 'fuck you'. Certainly by saying that he had taken the water to John's house, he is presented as in effect acknowledging his affair with John's wife – and hence that John was a cuckold. Of course, this may not be a full account of what Roger told the court. The content and precise ordering of what is recorded is the work of the clerk of the court. He, not Roger nor John, is the master storyteller.

The final case I wish to discuss is that of Agnes Grantham, who was (as noted earlier) a prosperous widow of York. I have explored this case on two previous occasions, but my focus initially was on making sense of the case from a social history perspective. More recently I have considered the narrative construction of the case, and it is this that I develop further here.[28]

Agnes was the recent widow of the mason Hugh Grantham, whose work included the choir of St Andrew's, York, and (to judge from his probate inventory) also the York churches of St Giles, All Saints in North Street, the church of the Dominicans, the Minster, and Pocklington church. He seems also to have had business interests involving *inter alia* trading in grain.[29] Agnes was herself the manager of a substantial brewing business. The case in the Court of York concerning a recently widowed Agnes is relatively substantial, but incomplete. In particular, depositions for one John Dale (the employee of the then master of St Leonard's Hospital, whose household Agnes supplied with ale) are lacking. Dale claimed to have entered into a binding contract of marriage with Agnes. This Agnes vehemently denied, offering a defence of force and fear that, as we have already seen, alleged the assault in which she was bundled over the back of a horse. According to this narrative, Agnes was ridden off into the woods and in time into the Forest of Knaresborough. Dale then forced her to enter into words of matrimony with him under threat of rape, and made her repeat those words before witnesses when they arrived in Healaugh.[30] Some two weeks later Agnes then contracted marriage to John Thornton, a widowed York draper.

27 McLoughlin, 'Gender and transgression', p. 21.

28 See n. 17 above.

29 James Raine (ed.), *The Fabric Rolls of York Minster*, Surtees Society, 35 (1859), p. 129; James Raine (ed.), *Testamenta Eboracensia*, vol. 3, Surtees Society, 45 (1865), pp. 47–55.

30 Sara Butler states that Dale raped her. This may or may not in fact have happened, but the testimony is very specific that Agnes agreed to enter into a contract of marriage because she was threatened with rape. Agnes' case relied heavily on representing her as a devout widow for whom guarding her chastity was more important than making a contract against her will; Sara M. Butler, '"I will never consent to be wedded with you": coerced marriage in the courts of medieval England', *Canadian Journal of History*, 39 (2004), p. 258; Goldberg, *Communal Discord, Child Abduction*, p. 206 n. 17; Donahue, *Law, Marriage, and Society*, p. 173.

That Agnes had entered into a contract of marriage is not denied. The issue was that, whereas Dale seems to have argued that the two went riding together on the day in question and subsequently contracted by mutual consent, Agnes claimed she was thrown over a horse, threatened with physical and sexual violence, and uttered words of matrimony only out of fear. Charles Donahue, Jr. argues that Dale's petition should be taken seriously – not least because, when judgement went against him in the Court of York, he was granted permission to appeal to Rome.[31] There is much, however, that militates against the plausibility of Dale's case, even though we lack the depositions that might have given greater credibility to it. The most significant obstacle, overlooked by Donahue, is that Agnes was a widow still in mourning. Her husband had died less than four months earlier and custom frowned upon remarriage before a year's mourning had been observed – which is precisely why so many widows who took vows of chastity did so as the anniversary of their husband's deaths approached.[32] Even had Agnes wished to marry John Dale, she would not have done so at that time. But Agnes had other good reasons for not wanting Dale. Certainly she had no need of a husband since she was financially secure, indeed wealthy, and she managed a successful brewing business. Dale was on the household staff of William Feryby, the master of St Leonard's Hospital, and so a mere employee. He was also perhaps a couple of decades younger than Agnes, though we do not know their precise ages.[33] Dale had much more to gain from marrying a wealthy widow. Agnes had little to gain, but she would have stood to lose her reputation and her business were she to have agreed.

Agnes contracted John Thornton in a hurry after the abduction and forced marriage – which Agnes had publicly renounced as soon as she had been released from Dale's company. It was a marriage contracted not out of desire – Agnes did not even go to live with her new husband – but out of fear.[34] It offered Agnes protection. It also offered spiritual solace. Agnes, we learn, moved to live in the home of William Pountfret, where she shared a room and a bed with Pountfret's kinswoman, the vowess Dame Christiana. Pountfret was the neighbour, business partner and spiritual friend of Thornton. Similar ties of friendship had bound the late wives of Pountfret and Thornton. My argument is that Agnes joined a *de facto* extended holy household in which

31 Donahue, *Law, Marriage, and Society*, p. 174.

32 P. H. Cullum, 'Vowesses and female lay piety in the province of York, 1300–1530', *Northern History*, 32 (1996), pp. 21–41.

33 Donahue, *Law, Marriage, and Society*, p. 172; Goldberg, *Communal Discord, Child Abduction*, pp. 129, 204 n. 3.

34 Dale's legal challenge to the validity of Agnes' marriage to John Thornton cannot explain why she went immediately to live in Pountfret's house, even if it did become an obstacle once litigation was initiated.

the parties were bound in spiritual friendship, piety and chastity. I have also argued for a shared devotion to the recently executed Archbishop Richard Scrope, whose cult closely identified with the virtue of chastity. Three years after Scrope's public execution just outside the walls of his own cathedral city, following a summary trial for rebellion against Henry IV in 1405, a new confraternity was established in York dedicated to the Corpus Christi. Primarily in the first instance a clerical guild under clerical leadership, it nevertheless numbered thirty-three lay founder-members, symbolic of the thirty-three years Christ lived in this world before his own sacrifice. Pountfret and his vowess kinswoman were two of that founding group. Nothing explicitly tied the Guild of Corpus Christi to the then illicit cult of the local martyr, but just as the narrative of Scrope's death specifically references and echoes the Passion, there is good reason to believe the guild was initially a vehicle for the cult.[35]

There is much artifice about the way testimony for Agnes was shaped. As Donahue observes, Agnes' claim that she was forcefully abducted is key to her claim against John Dale.[36] For this reason, perhaps, the testimony given mirrors cultural expectations. Narratives of abduction were well known and readily lent themselves to be adapted here. The trope of Agnes being thrown over the back of a horse is particularly resonant. When a century earlier Isabella, the wife of Walter Gacelyn, had been seized by a gang from her home at night, she was allegedly 'placed ... across a horse'. Half a century later, Joan de Fletewyk was likewise abducted at night and placed against her will on a horse from which she subsequently fell.[37] In a later case, Joan Boys was supposedly tied to a horse when snatched from her home. The location of Agnes' abduction by woodland and close to forest mirrors both rapes in romance literature, notably *Sir Gowther*, but also the high-profile abduction of Eleanor West whilst riding in the New Forest in 1382.[38] Agnes' consensual nuptials with Thornton, made before witnesses in the arbour of a city garden, pointedly contrast with her earlier forced nuptials in the forest; the ordered nature of the garden is metaphorically juxtaposed with the wild forest. My particular concern with the present case is, however, not with the crafting of the narrative of Agnes' account of the events of the last Thursday of June 1410, but with the metanarrative to which it contributes.

35 Goldberg, 'St Richard Scrope', pp. 71, 75.

36 Donahue, *Law, Marriage, and Society*, p. 174.

37 Maud Fullere was likewise put on a horse when taken by force from her home in 1383: *Calendar of Patent Rolls for the Reign of Edward II: 1317–1321*, vol. 3 (London, 1908), p. 485; *Calendar of Patent Rolls for the Reign of Edward III: 1358–1361*, vol. 11 (London, 1911), p. 83; *Calendar of Patent Rolls for the Reign of Richard II: 1381–1385*, vol. 2 (London, 1897), p. 453.

38 Caroline Dunn, *Stolen Women in Medieval England: Rape, Abduction, and Adultery, 1100–1500* (Cambridge, 2013), pp. 100, 103.

When litigation was initiated a month after the disputed contract between Agnes Grantham and John Dale, it was little more than five years since Richard Scrope, archbishop of York, had been executed in June of 1405. The execution was part of a ruthless assertion of authority over the city by Henry IV. He confiscated all properties associated with rebels and suspended the city's constitution, imposing a warden to govern the city in much the same way as Richard II had done in London in 1392.[39] He took advantage of the vacancy of archbishop to ensure that men favourable to the crown were appointed to the chapter where vacancies occurred. Over the course of the following year or so of the vacancy, the Minster acquired a new dean and several new canons.[40] The city was already divided before the 1405 revolt, and the roots of those divisions may have gone back at least to the time of the Peasants' Revolt, which saw significant rioting in York. Following the events of 1405, however, those who were willing – or opportunistic – supporters of Henry IV dominated city government, whereas those who identified with their martyred archbishop were marginalised. The early members of the Guild of Corpus Christi, both clerical and lay, were perhaps particularly committed in their desire to sustain the memory of their 'saint'.

Agnes' narrative can be read within this larger political context. The division between those who owed their authority to Henry IV and those who cherished the memory of their martyred archbishop is here played out symbolically. If we first consider the *dramatis personae*, there are two camps. On the one hand, there is John Dale and his two accomplices, who attacked Agnes as she journeyed from York through Acomb towards Acomb Grange. Dale was a *famulus* (or household employee) of William Feryby. Then there is William Feryby himself. Agnes, in her narrative, was headed for Acomb Grange because Feryby had invited her to dine with him. When Agnes was abducted, her servant Alice ran to the Grange to solicit help, but was rebuffed. We also learn that whilst Agnes was captive, there was communication between her captors and William Feryby. As an historical figure, Feryby is comparatively unknown, but what is pertinent here is that he was the master of St Leonard's Hospital, a position in the royal gift. Feryby himself was appointed to the office by royal mandate in July 1409, only a year before the case was initiated.[41] He was thus Henry IV's man, and Dale was his man.

39 His appointee as warden, William Frost, was elected mayor some months later in February 1406, thus restoring something of the *status quo ante*, since Frost had served as mayor for several years prior to the 1405 revolt before losing the mayoral election in the year of the revolt: Christian D. Liddy, 'William Frost, the city of York and Scrope's rebellion of 1405', in P. J. P. Goldberg (ed.), *Richard Scrope: Archbishop, Rebel, Martyr* (Donington, 2007), pp. 74–7.

40 Goldberg, 'St Richard Scrope', p. 70.

41 The grant was issued at Westminster on 13 July 1409 by the king: *Calendar of Patent Rolls for the Reign of Henry IV: 1408–1413*, vol. 4 (London, 1909), p. 88.

If John Dale is identified with the party of the king, then Agnes is very much identified with the party of St Richard. Agnes is presented as an honest, industrious and singularly devout widow. Her son Thomas, with whom she journeyed towards Acomb Grange, was a man of God in deacon's orders. (The prospect of William Feryby providing Thomas with a living was an inducement towards Agnes' acceptance of the dinner invitation.) William Pountfret and John Thornton were devout widowers who were to be buried in adjacent graves, just as they had lived in adjacent houses in life and worked as business partners. William lived with his kinswoman, Dame Christiana, a devout widow vowed to chastity. Both William and Dame Christiana were founder members of the Guild of Corpus Christi, created two years earlier. It was in the Pountfret house (standing in the shadow of the parish church of All Saints, Pavement, where Agnes was regularly to be found at her devotions) that Agnes, fearful that Dale would again attack her, sought sanctuary.

Agnes' account of her journey toward Acomb Grange has resonances with the narrative of Scrope's own fateful journey to Shipton Moor, likewise close to woods but a few miles outside the city. Scrope had taken his band of armed citizens, clergy and peasantry out from the city of York and halted them at Shipton Moor, hard by the Forest of Galtres, to await the arrival of the earl of Northumberland. After three days of futile waiting, Scrope encountered the earl of Westmorland and his army, sent to suppress the rebellion. Scrope and Westmorland parleyed. Scrope claimed that he desired reform not rebellion, peace not war. Westmorland replied in seeming good faith that he would ensure that the king received Scrope's petition, and persuaded Scrope to stand down his troops. Thus deceived, a defenceless Scrope was promptly arrested and made the subject of a hasty treason trial, at which he was condemned in short order. The resonances of this betrayal with the Passion narrative, together with Scrope's subsequent trial and execution as related in Clement Maidstone's hagiographical narrative, would have served as a mnemonic frame for the saint's devotees.

The deception and violence meted out to Agnes Grantham fits within the same mnemonic framework. Dale, her immediate attacker, is presented as an instrument of Feryby, who is himself a proxy for Henry IV. The devout and chaste widow Agnes, who yielded to a forced marriage so as to protect herself against rape, stands in for the martyr, Archbishop Richard Scrope, a man with a reputation for virginity. Through her close association with Scrope devotees, we may assume that Agnes was herself a devotee. The action played out in the Court of York (where we have reason to believe much sympathy for their late archbishop might have been found) was one that allowed the struggle between a saintly archbishop and the monarch who made him a martyr to be reimagined, and where justice in this world might perhaps be achieved. But the judicial re-enactment was also an act of piety that memorialised the martyr, whose own trial was such a travesty of justice that the then chief justice removed himself, allegedly warning the king, 'according to the laws of the kingdom, neither you, my Lord King, nor any of your subjects acting in your name, can legally condemn any bishop to death'.[42]

Conclusion

This chapter offers a modest contribution to the ways in which modern scholars interrogate medieval court records. Drawing attention to their fictive nature is hardly new, but through close readings I have attempted to show that it is not merely individual testimonies that were crafted. In the case of Bilby *v.* Mampton, the clerk of the court consummately retells an otherwise mundane action for unlawful entry and damages into a comic drama peopled with characters rooted in contemporary literary culture, viz. the cuckolded husband and incontinent holy water clerk. In so doing, the clerk draws attention to the wife's affair that the husband singularly fails to mention. The catalogue of supposedly spoiled household possessions, the outward markers of Bilby's bourgeois identity, stands as a metaphor for Bilby's failure as a husband and *paterfamilias*. Bilby is thus held up for ridicule, because his failure strikes at the core of what held urban society together.[43] (Mampton's subsequent punitive fine recognises his own culpability in undermining these same patriarchal values.)

I have noticed *en passant*, in regard to Agnes Grantham's matrimonial dispute with John Dale, the way in which her narrative similarly engages with wider cultural understandings, including those reflected in romances, in respect of her abduction and also her marriage in a garden arbour – but my main concern here has been to reveal the metanarrative that underpins the particular narrative. I have elsewhere made a similar argument in relation to the supposed record of the appearance of John Rykener before the mayor of London's court a generation earlier. There I argued that the court record serves as a parody of Richard II's rule, with Rykener standing in for the king.[44] The metanarrative here of devotion to a martyred archbishop, and hence of resistance to the monarch who ensured his execution, is not much less loaded because also politically highly subversive. On the one hand, this would explain why there is nothing in the testimonies offered on Agnes' behalf that makes

42 Clement Maidstone, 'The martyrdom of Archbishop Richard Scrope', ed. and trans. S. K. Wright, published electronically at <http://english.cua.edu/faculty/wright/maidston.cfm> [accessed 3 December 2017].

43 For discussion of the importance of the ideology of the orderly household to the governance of towns see, for example, P. J. P. Goldberg, 'Masters and men in later medieval England', in Dawn Hadley (ed.), *Masculinity in Medieval Europe* (London, 1999), pp. 56–70; McSheffrey, 'Men and masculinity in late medieval London'.

44 Jeremy Goldberg, 'John Rykener, Richard II, and the governance of London', *Leeds Studies in English*, 45 (2016), pp. 49–70.

the narrative explicit; but on the other, it may explain why the presiding officer, having determined in Agnes' favour, then granted Dale the right to appeal to Rome. Donahue justifiably argues that the presiding officer considered Dale's case to have sufficient merit to justify an appeal, even though the extant evidence is skewed so heavily in favour of Agnes Grantham.[45] The case was heard not by the official of the Court of York, but by the only recently appointed commissary general, Richard Arnall, who was also to be appointed auditor general for the Capitular court of York the following year.[46] Arnall, we may presume, was a man favourable to Archbishop Henry Bowet and implicitly to Henry IV. My suggestion is that he was willing to allow the case to be appealed to Rome, not necessarily because he felt the arguments were especially finely balanced, but rather because he realised the sensitivities that the case raised. Arnall perhaps realised the power of storytelling.

45 Donahue, *Law, Marriage, and Society*, p. 174.

46 Sandra Brown, *The Medieval Courts of the York Minster Peculiar*, Borthwick Papers, 66 (1984), pp. 6–7.

4

FEMALE LITIGANTS AND THE BOROUGH COURT: STATUS AND STRATEGY IN THE CASE OF AGNES HALUM OF NOTTINGHAM

TERESA PHIPPS

Agnes Halum lived in Nottingham at the end of the fourteenth century. She was a businesswoman of middling status, just one of hundreds of individuals who lived, worked and traded in the town and used its borough court to resolve interpersonal complaints and disputes. There are many things we cannot know about her, as is true of many other ordinary medieval women: we do not know her age nor when she was born or died, her precise social status or level of wealth, what family she had, where she lived, whether she was an immigrant or born in Nottingham.[1] However, we do know that she was a rather litigious person, and her frequent court appearances help to create a detailed profile of other aspects of her life. Through tracing her legal action over several decades, we can identify many of the individuals she traded with, the goods and services she bought and sold, and the scale at which she operated, creating a picture of her work and commercial life. We can also glimpse some of her personal and social connections and interactions. This does not make her an unusual or singular woman, though the extent to which her life

1 The 'Halum' surname probably relates to one of 'the Hallams', the villages of West, Kirk and Little Hallam approximately eight miles west of Nottingham, but it is impossible to know if Agnes migrated to Nottingham from here, inherited the surname, or acquired it through marriage. Place name and surname spellings varied, as was typical of late medieval records, including Hallam, Hallum, Halom and Halum. Here, Agnes's surname has been standardised as Halum, the most common spelling, for the sake of consistency.

can be reconstructed or reimagined using the town's court records is somewhat more exceptional.

This chapter focuses on the experience of the female litigant in the borough court at the micro level, examining the legal 'life' or 'career' of Agnes Halum in Nottingham during the late fourteenth century. This approach, which Amy Stanley has recently termed archival 'excavation', allows us to recover the lives of ordinary, individual women like Agnes within their own social and economic landscapes, highlighting individual choices, actions and identities, and paying attention to agency.[2] Through these details, we can situate individuals within the broader narratives of urban and legal history that often obscure or ignore the histories of relatively unimportant people, particularly women. This type of analysis does not always yield complete, factual answers or uninterrupted biographies, necessitating some interpretation on the part of the historian, but the value of this approach extends beyond the potential for storytelling that comes with such a specific focus.[3] Individual case studies allow for the 'peopling' of medieval legal systems, moving beyond abstract discussions of jurisdiction or custom to examine practice at the most personal level.[4] After all, people were (and are) intrinsic to the law and litigation; it centred on their relationships, actions, agreements, expectations and complaints, so looking at the law through individuals enables us to better understand how these legal systems worked. By exploring how Agnes engaged with the law within her local environment, this chapter considers how individuals, and particularly women, accessed and experienced the jurisdiction of borough courts, and how these courts understood the status of women more generally. The study of Agnes also provides an insight into why women litigated, the aspects of their lives that drew them into court, how this litigation worked, and in what ways their sex played a part in how they accessed justice. For Agnes, this particularly involves thinking about women's legal knowledge and strategy.

2 See Amy Stanley, 'Maidservants' tales: narrative domestic and global history in Eurasia, 1600–1900', *American Historical Review*, 121 (2016), pp. 438–41.

3 See Joan W. Scott, 'Storytelling', *History and Theory*, 50 (2011), pp. 203–9. The potential for storytelling using court records is more fragmented than sources used in other studies of individual women, such as Laurel Thatcher Ulrich's study of Martha Ballard in *A Midwife's Tale* (New York, 1991). See also Katherine L. French, 'Well-behaved women can make history: women's friendships in late medieval Westminster', in Charlotte Newman Goldy and Amy Livingstone (eds), *Writing Medieval Women's Lives* (Basingstoke, 2012), pp. 247–65; Shannon McSheffrey, 'A remarrying widow: law and legal records in late medieval London', in Kim Kippen and Lori Woods (eds), *Worth and Repute: Valuing Gender in Late Medieval and Early Modern Europe: Essays in Honour of Barbara Todd* (Toronto, 2011), pp. 231–52; Briony McDonagh, 'Fragments from a medieval archive: the life and death of Sir Robert Constable', *Journal of Historical Geography*, 42 (2013), pp. 50–61; David Gary Shaw, 'Social selves in medieval England: the worshipful Ferrour and Kempe', in Nancy Partner (ed.), *Writing Medieval History* (London, 2005), pp. 3–21.

4 McDonagh has similarly suggested that a focus on individuals can serve to 'people' the histories of landscapes: 'Fragments from a medieval archive', p. 51.

Another key consideration is the way that women were documented in court records, and the role that marital status played in classifying women and their legal status. This chapter reassesses some of the categories and assumptions that exist surrounding the legal actions of medieval women, highlighting the need to pay attention to the specifics of each court's customs and practices, and the details of each legal complaint. These are issues that can be somewhat obscured in larger analyses that survey or quantify the actions of many women or seek to identify patterns in women's legal action, but which can come to the fore through qualitative studies.

Late Medieval Nottingham and its Court

Late medieval Nottingham was a medium-sized provincial town with a population of around two to three thousand in the 1370s, ranking as England's twenty-sixth wealthiest town, according to the Lay Subsidy of 1334.[5] Situated just north of the River Trent, it had a castle, three large parish churches, a large Saturday marketplace and a smaller weekday market. The common hall or guildhall where the borough court met was adjacent to the weekday market, its spatial centrality reflecting its fundamental role in the administration of town government and the overseeing of business and interpersonal relationships within the town. Nottingham might therefore be considered a typical provincial medieval borough. A number of borough charters granted by the crown from the mid twelfth century onwards gave the burgesses of the town various liberties and rights of self-governance. The first was granted by Henry II between 1155 and 1165, with further charters confirming and extending the town's rights from John, Henry III, Edward I and Edward II.[6] The town's borough court met fortnightly on Wednesdays from the early fourteenth century, hearing civil complaints between residents and enrolling land transfers in the town before its two bailiffs. It is among the voluminous rolls of the borough court that we find evidence of the life and litigation of Agnes Halum. Complaints heard by the court mainly concerned issues of debt and the detention of goods (detinue), but a significant proportion of litigation also related to complaints of trespass.[7] Trespass encompassed a wide range of

5 Alan Dyer, 'Ranking lists of English medieval towns', in D. M. Palliser (ed.), *The Cambridge Urban History of Britain: 600–1540*, vol. 1 (Cambridge, 2000), pp. 747–70; Trevor Foulds, 'The medieval town', in John Beckett (ed.), *A Centenary History of Nottingham* (Manchester, 1997), p. 56.

6 See borough charters in W. H. Stevenson (ed.), *Records of the Borough of Nottingham*, vol. 1 (London, 1882), pp. 2–80.

7 On debt litigation in Nottingham, see Richard Goddard, 'Surviving recession: English borough courts and commercial contraction, 1350–1500', in Richard Goddard, John Langdon and Miriam Müller (eds), *Survival and Discord in Medieval Society: Essays in Honour of Christopher Dyer* (Turnhout, 2010), pp. 69–87.

offences concerning misbehaviour and wrong-doing, including physical and verbal assault, theft and damage to property. Central to these complaints were the claims for damages sought as compensation for wrong-doing. The town's other court, the Mayor's court, met twice a year and heard presentments for trading offences, affrays and common nuisances.

Going to court was a relatively normal part of urban life in this period of increasing legal consciousness and knowledge among ordinary people, in part derived from court attendance. Litigation was not necessarily indicative of crisis or complete breakdown in relationships, but could be a useful tool for dispute settlement and reconciliation, or the enforcement of obligations.[8] It was therefore a key part of the management of relationships within the urban community. The outcome of a case was nearly always a small fine (often 2–3d), lower than the daily wage (3–4d) for skilled labourers such as carpenters and around double the cost of a gallon of ale.[9] In the later Middle Ages, as well as the early modern period, levels of litigation were high, drawing many individuals into court. At Nottingham in the late fourteenth century, around 400 to 450 different individuals appeared as litigants each year – a figure that represented perhaps 15 to 20 per cent of the total population, or approximately a third of those assessed under the various late-fourteenth-century poll taxes.[10] The jurisdiction and decisions of the borough court therefore encompassed significant numbers of the urban population. Its business was recorded in rolls and later in books which survive in considerable volume for much of the fourteenth and fifteenth centuries, making the tracing of individual legal careers possible. Most litigation was recorded in a relatively brief, formulaic fashion. Complaints were dealt with over the course of several court sessions, meaning that details sometimes need to be pieced together from several court rolls. While some pleas can be followed from the initial complaint to resolution, others disappear from the records part way through. They may have been abandoned or settled out of court, or the records may simply have been lost. Ascertaining the 'truth' of each complaint may not, therefore, be a viable or

8 See Craig Muldrew, 'The culture of reconciliation: community and the settlement of economic disputes in early modern England', *The Historical Journal*, 39 (1996), pp. 915–42.

9 Christopher Dyer, *Making a Living in the Middle Ages* (London, 2002), p. 293. Henry Phelps Brown and Sheila Hopkins similarly calculated that the daily wage of a skilled building worker had risen from 3d to 5d per day between the 1340s and 1390s, while daily wages for unskilled workers rose from 1½d to 3d: H. Phelps Brown and S. V. Hopkins, *A Perspective of Wages and Prices* (London, 1981), pp. 13–59. London brewers were ordered to sell their best ale at 1½d in 1356: see Judith M. Bennett, *Ale, Beer and Brewsters in England: Women's Work in a Changing World, 1300–1600* (Oxford, 1996), p. 44.

10 Number of litigants across three samples: 395 to 469; number of people eligible for the Poll Tax: 1,477 in 1377 (4d per head over age fourteen), 1,266 in 1381 (variable rate, over age fifteen). See Alan Dyer, 'Ranking of towns by taxpaying population: the 1377 poll tax', in Palliser (ed.), *Cambridge Urban History of Britain*, vol. 1, p. 758.

particularly useful endeavour.[11] The court records are nevertheless a valuable source through which we can understand how justice operated at the local level and the negotiation of individual agendas via litigation.

Agnes Halum and the Borough Court

Agnes Halum was just one of many economically and legally active women who used the court to resolve disputes and enforce obligations, though the scale of her litigation was notable in comparison to her peers. Agnes's total legal career spanned more than twenty-seven years, from June 1372 to August 1399, and though we do not know when she was born, we can speculate that she was around forty-five by 1399.[12] She was involved in at least thirty-five disputes involving thirty-one different parties, most being men, though some involved other women or married couples. The description of a 'legal career' here is particularly apt, as going to court (especially this frequently) constituted a type of work, and her litigation often resulted from ties of work and trade. She first appeared in the Nottingham court in June 1372 when John Tropwell and his wife brought a complaint of trespass against her.[13] In the same year, she acknowledged owing a debt of 15d to Nicholas Wyndesor.[14] Her last suit, in August 1399, related to five shillings that she owed to John Danyell.[15] An overview of her litigation is given in Table 4.1. As well as pleas of debt, detinue and trespass, she was party to one plea of covenant, a category that concerned broken contracts or agreements.

The year 1375–6 was a particularly busy one for Agnes, as she appeared in court against nine different parties over the course of the year. In 1381–2, she was the subject of five different debt complaints. Again, this was not an exceptional pattern for either men or women. Many people were repeat litigants over the course of a year or extended period. In 1375–6, when a total of

11 See McSheffrey, 'A remarrying widow', p. 248; Shannon McSheffrey, 'Detective fiction in the archives: court records and the uses of law in late medieval England', *History Workshop Journal*, 65 (2008), p. 73.

12 The age of legal majority in boroughs varied, though Kim Phillips has suggested this may have been age twelve or sixteen, so Agnes must have reached this status in order to litigate in the borough court. See K. M. Phillips, *Medieval Maidens: Young Women and Gender in England, c. 1270 – c. 1540* (Manchester, 2003), pp. 32–5. However, we might approximate that Agnes was at least eighteen to twenty in 1372, in order to be of working age with sufficient economic and social credit to accrue debts and enter into contracts (and litigation). She may well have been older than this, particularly if she had worked in service for some time as an adolescent or young woman, as many women did. Of course, servants could also be involved in debt pleas, though at no point is there any suggestion that Agnes Halum was a servant when she appeared in court. On work and women's life cycle, see P. J. P. Goldberg, *Women, Work and Life Cycle in a Medieval Economy: Women in York and Yorkshire c. 1300–1520* (Oxford, 1992), p. 172.

13 Nottinghamshire Archives (hereafter NA) CA1277a/18, 2 June 1372.

14 NA CA1277a/23.

15 NA CA1297/23.

TABLE 4.1: AGNES HALUM IN THE BOROUGH COURT, 1372–1399

Plea type	Number of suits	Plaintiff	Defendant
Debt	24	1	23
Detinue	2	0	2
Covenant	1	0	1
Trespass	8	4	4
Total	35	5	30

ninety-two different women litigated in the borough court, Margery Tapster was involved in four different suits.[16] John Samon, mayor of Nottingham, featured in ten different complaints (though always as plaintiff), while John Plumptre, a future mayor of the town, appeared in three. Agnes was not the only woman to be a regular in court, but her presence was particularly frequent and extended, making her visibility an issue of scale rather than marking her out as an exceptional woman. Elsewhere, too, women controlled their own businesses and were therefore more visible in local records – such as Exeter's Emma Hosiere, who made stockings for a living.[17]

As Table 4.1 shows, Agnes was repeatedly sued for debt, demonstrating that her economic activity was the main cause for her litigation. This was not unusual: the extension of credit was central to the medieval economy, meaning that probably everyone was in debt, giving borough courts a central role in the management of credit relationships.[18] Katherine French has suggested that women show up in legal records only when they broke the law, hiding ordinary 'well-behaved' women from view.[19] However, the commercial complaints heard in borough courts should not be interpreted as instances of law-breaking. Instead, they represent the interactions, transactions and networks of ordinary women and men, who may or may not have been 'well-behaved'. Agnes's litigation usually came about through the complaints of others, which might suggest that she repeatedly failed to fulfil agreements and repay her debts. But this can also be interpreted as evidence of her overall engagement and integration in the commercial networks of the town: the simple fact of

16 Ninety-two women from a total of 469 litigants.

17 See Maryanne Kowaleski, 'Women's work in a market town: Exeter in the late fourteenth century', in Barbara A. Hanawalt (ed.), *Women and Work in Preindustrial Europe* (Bloomington, 1986), pp. 153, 157. Emma Hosiere was listed as the head of her household in 1377.

18 On the ubiquity of credit and debt, see Pamela Nightingale, 'Money and credit in the economy of late medieval England', in D. Wood (ed.), *Medieval Money Matters* (Oxford, 2004), p. 51–71; James Davis, *Medieval Market Morality: Life, Law and Ethics in the English Marketplace* (Cambridge, 2012), pp. 348–68; J. L. Bolton, *Money in the Medieval English Economy: 973–1489* (Manchester, 2012), pp. 71–4.

19 French, 'Well-behaved women can make history', p. 248.

being in debt indicates that she was deemed worthy of credit in the first place.[20] She frequently acknowledged her debts when she came to court, suggesting that these were not always contentious disputes, but rather the final stage in a chain of credit.[21] As a regular litigant, Agnes would probably have gained considerable legal knowledge and competency from her repeated attendance at court.[22] She may have been aware that it was more prudent to recognise her debts and pay up quickly rather than be caught up in weeks of litigation, and this suggests she could afford to pay straight away.

Agnes's involvement in brewing dominated her appearances at court, with debt pleas revealing numerous transactions relating to the purchase or hire of equipment or ingredients, and the sale of the ale that she produced. Several complaints related to debts owed for raw materials (particularly malt) involved in the brewing process.[23] In January 1395, Henry Plumtree sued Agnes Halum for 9s 6d owed for malt bought from him six years before. Agnes acknowledged the debt.[24] Plumtree was a prosperous wool merchant from a wealthy family and was mayor of Nottingham from 1387 to 1388, having been a bailiff from 1384 to 1385.[25] Adam Clerk also sued her for ten shillings owed for malt in 1381.[26] These considerable volumes of malt suggest that Agnes was brewing on a large scale to sell to others in the town, and also demonstrate her ability to secure considerable credit in the form of deferred payment – sometimes from the town's political elite. Her customers may have included other women like Margery Tapster, whom Agnes sued in December 1375 for a debt of 16d.[27] The byname 'tapster' was frequently attached to women who sold ale, and Agnes was also called a tapster in some pleas, indicating that

20 On women's creditworthiness, see Teresa Phipps, 'Creditworthy women and town courts in late medieval England', in Elise Dermineur (ed.), *Women and Credit in Preindustrial Europe* (Turnhout, 2018), pp. 73–94.

21 Chris Briggs has suggested that being in debt was indicative of full participation in commerce, and debtors were 'sued not because they were in dire economic straits … but because it made sense to them to wait until the last possible moment before meeting their obligations': Chris Briggs, *Credit and Village Society in Fourteenth-Century England* (Oxford, 2008), p. 152.

22 Anthony Musson, *Medieval Law in Context: The Growth of Legal Consciousness from Magna Carta to the Peasants' Revolt* (Manchester, 2001), pp. 95–7.

23 On malt and the ingredients used for brewing, see R. W. Unger, *Beer in the Middle Ages and the Renaissance* (Philadelphia, 2011), p. 4; Bennett, *Ale*, p. 17.

24 Agnes paid 4d in damages and a fine of 3d to the court: NA CA1294/7 and 8.

25 Henry Plumtree was part of a wealthy family of Nottingham merchants, and was mayor of Nottingham in 1387–88. For Nottingham mayors, see Stevenson, *Records of the Borough of Nottingham*, vol. 1, pp. 422–6. Henry's brother (also mayor), John de Plumptre, founded the Hospital of the Blessed Mary in Nottingham around 1390. See M. W. Barley and I. F. Straw, 'Nottingham', in M. D. Lobel (ed.), *Historic Towns: Maps and Plans of Towns and Cities in the British Isles*, vol. 1 (London, 1969), p. 4; Stevenson, *Records of the Borough of Nottingham*, vol. 1, pp. 248–52.

26 NA CA1282/4.

27 NA CA1279/7 and 8.

she was known for selling ale as well as making it.[28]

Other suits point to the equipment that Agnes may have used to brew her ale, again suggesting that she was doing so on a large scale. Two different complaints brought in 1372 and 1376 by Nicholas Wyndesor and William Cotyler respectively concerned debts and contracts relating to Agnes's borrowing of lead dishes.[29] These may have been the sort frequently found in lists of the possessions of brewers, loaned to Agnes by other local brewers.[30] In both instances, Agnes was alleged to have damaged the dishes she had borrowed, though the jury reported that she was not guilty.[31] These complaints nevertheless present Agnes as someone known for brewing using this type of equipment. Perhaps she had indeed borrowed the dishes from the two men but had returned them in good condition, or at least had convinced the jury that this was the case. In a trespass plea (probably from 1378), Agnes complained that Adam Panyer had assaulted her, beating her and breaking a vase while drinking in her house where she ran a tavern. Agnes claimed ten shillings in damages, though the decision of the jury is not known.[32] This complaint indicates that Agnes ran an alehouse or tavern from her home, the location of Panyer's alleged misbehaviour, from where she sold some of the ale she brewed. Various studies have suggested that alehouses run out of domestic spaces, often managed by women, carried particular risks; these women, like Agnes, could be the targets of drink-induced violence.[33]

By piecing together these fragments, we can therefore create a picture of Agnes's commercial activity all the way from procurement of ingredients to the sale of the finished product. She was not just intermittently brewing, but this was instead more of a 'professional' or long-term occupation in a field typically dominated by women.[34] Kowaleski has argued for 'vigorous female

28 December 1392, NA CA1292/4. The amount and cause of the debt was not recorded; November 1396, NA CA1296/4.

29 In August 1372, Nicholas Wyndesor complained that Agnes owed him a debt of 15d. She acknowledged the debt and paid a fine of 3d to the court, plus 1d in damages to Nicholas. Two weeks later, Nicholas accused Agnes of breaking a contract concerning the lending of five leaden vessels. Nicholas was fined 3d for bringing an unjust suit, suggesting the jury's decision fell in Agnes's favour: NA CA1277a/23, 11 August 1372. In 1376 a complaint of William Cotyler also alleged that she had broken and damaged two lead dishes that he had loaned to her, as well as owing a debt of six shillings. Agnes was found not to be guilty of the detinue and broken vessels, and she acknowledged only 40d (3s 4d) of the six-shilling debt: NA CA1279/17.

30 Bennett, *Ale*, pp. 14, 49, 116.

31 '*non est culpabilis*'. On juries, see Musson, *Medieval Law in Context*, pp. 109–20.

32 NA CA1280a: '*cum sedisset in domo sua ad bibdend [sic] tabernam suam*'.

33 For example, Barbara A. Hanawalt, 'Medieval English women in rural and urban domestic space', *Dumbarton Oaks Papers*, 52 (1998), p. 19; Amanda Flather, *Gender and Space in Early Modern England* (Woodbridge, 2007), pp. 45, 53.

34 See Bennett, *Ale*, pp. 18–24; Elizabeth Ewan, '"For whatever ales ye": women as consumers and producers in late medieval Scottish towns', in Elizabeth Ewan and Maureen Meikle (eds), *Women in Scotland c. 1100 – c. 1750* (East Linton, 1999), pp. 129–30.

involvement' in brewing in Exeter, though the women often became fully visible only after their husband's death.[35] Nottingham's Mayor's court rolls feature presentments and fines for individuals deemed to have broken the assize of ale, which regulated the quality of ale and the measures and prices at which it was sold.[36] The extant roll from 1395 does not name Agnes among the list of individual brewers, but it included blanket fines for all brewers (*omnes braciatores*) and all innkeepers (*omnes hospitatores*), among other occupational groups.[37] If Agnes was a 'professional' brewer, as the borough court records suggest, then this presentment, likely to have served as licensing rather than punishment, may have included her among those well known to be engaged in brewing.[38]

In all of the pleas discussed so far, and in various others, Agnes used the court alone, bringing and answering complaints independently and in her own person.[39] She was recorded by her full name, with no other status or descriptor affixed. This is often interpreted as evidence of unmarried status, as the legal identity of wives is said to have been defined (and subsumed) by their husbands under common law. This doctrine, known as coverture, limited the legal actions of married women as they were said to be 'covered' by the guardianship of their husband.[40] However, Agnes's legal career serves to complicate our understanding of marriage and the recording of marital status in the litigation of individual women.[41] A number of cases show that she was married for at least part of her legal career. Several complaints from the late 1380s record Agnes's joint litigation with her husband, John Halum. John worked in the cloth trade, sometimes being described as a tailor, and we already know that Agnes was involved in brewing.[42] These details of the

35 Kowaleski, 'Women's work', p. 151.

36 On the assize of ale, see Bennett, *Ale*, pp. 21–2, 158.

37 NA CA3942/3d: '*qui dicunt quod omnes braciatores sunt culpabiles quia braciant contra Assisam etc et vendunt cum ciphis et discis contra Assisam etc.*' NA CA3942/4: '*Item dicunt quod omnes hospitatores Notingham hospitant contra Assisam et quilibet eorum vendunt infra domum faenum praebendarium et alia victualia tam humana quam equina sine assisa inde capta ad deceptionem populi etc.*'

38 On assizes as licensing, see Bennett, *Ale*, p. 100.

39 Sometimes recorded specifically as '*in propria person*' – i.e. without representation by an attorney.

40 See G. D. G. Hall (ed.), *The Treatise on the Laws and Customs of the Realm of England Commonly Called Glanvill* (London, 1965), p. 60; George E. Woodbine (ed.) and S. E. Thorne (trans.), *Bracton on the Laws and Customs of England*, vol. 2 (Cambridge, MA, 1968), pp. 287, 335.

41 Miriam Müller has also warned against making such assumptions about the marital status of women based on how they were recorded in manor court rolls. See M. Müller, 'Peasant women, agency and status in late thirteenth and early fourteenth century England: some reconsiderations', in Cordelia Beattie and Matthew Frank Stevens (eds), *Married Women and the Law in Premodern Northwest Europe* (Woodbridge, 2013), pp. 104–5.

42 See for example John Halom, tailor, complaint against William Cupper for 4s 2d owed for altering cloth: NA CA1281 (1380x81).

pair's working activities help to explain both their individual and joint litigation, indicative of their independent work as well as their economic and legal partnership as a married couple. The occasions when they used the court together concerned debts relating to these two trades. In January 1389, John Walker successfully sued John and Agnes Halum for a debt of 12d owed for fulling cloth.[43] In either 1389 or 1390, John Cook and Margery his wife complained that John Halum and Agnes owed 10s 7½d for malt, which they acknowledged.[44] Another complaint of 1390 concerned 6s 8d loaned to John and Agnes to buy barley, probably also for brewing.[45]

Both John and Agnes appeared separately in court before and after these pleas, demonstrating that both were living and working in the town before and after the evidence for their marriage appears. This joint litigation cannot therefore be explained by a short marriage, after which Agnes became a widow and again a sole litigant. John Halum can be found in rolls from as early as 1364, in complaints relating to clothing and the repairing of cloth.[46] He also continued to litigate into the early 1390s, and was a member of the jury that was responsible for presenting offences against the assize of bread in 1395.[47] Agnes was also in court alone again from December 1392 until her last appearance in 1399. Knowing that she had a husband who worked with cloth also helps to account for some of Agnes's individual litigation that did not relate to brewing, instead revealing instances where she may have acted as her husband's agent. In 1374 she sued Adam Roche for trespass after he had damaged cloth worth forty shillings that she had delivered to him for fulling, and in 1386 she settled a debt of 8d owed to William Aspley for washing woollen cloth.[48] In this complaint she was initially recorded as 'Halum', her forename being added only in the later details of the plea. Perhaps she was so well known that this was all that was needed.[49] The consistency in their

43 NA CA1288. The exact date of plea is not known.

44 NA CA1290 (1389x90). In this plea John was called a clerk, though this was a mistake confusing him with John of Hallam, rector of the church of West Hallam. Court scribes often confused individuals' names and the spelling of these names, sometimes making corrections on the rolls.

45 NA CA1280a. Numerous similar pleas demonstrate married women's involvement in brewing through litigation that also involved their husbands, such as various pleas involving John de Beeston and his wife Agnes. For example, NA CA1291/16, 17, 19 and 20d.

46 John Hallam was sued by Ralph Tollerton for 12d owed for silk and muslin bought from him in March 1364. John acknowledged only 4d of the debt. NA CA1273/12d. See also similar pleas from 1364–66: NA CA1274/11, CA1275/4, 4d and 5d.

47 The Mickletorn presentments are recorded in the rolls of the Mayor's court (NA CA3942/3 and 5). He was also part of an inquisition jury – called John Halum, tailor (NA CA1292/1), was summoned for a trespass plea in October 1392 (NA CA1292/8d) and was the subject of an unsuccessful plea for detinue of a tunic (NA CA1292/8).

48 NA CA1278/11, 12 and 14.

49 NA CA1296/4. No gap was left for the addition of her forename, suggesting that it was not simply that the court clerk did not know her name or was planning to insert this later. The

occupations and the nature of their litigation also helps to verify, as far as possible, that these were the same individuals. The fact that Agnes was interchangeably recorded by only her full name and as wife of John Halum reveals the danger in classifying individual women as unmarried on the basis of their naming in the court records. Recorded by her full name only, Agnes was able to take responsibility for her own transactions, independently of her husband. When they did appear jointly, there is no evidence that he attempted to decline responsibility, suggesting that these pleas represented their joint transactions and business partnership. This contrasts with several instances in Exeter's borough court, where husbands successfully declined legal responsibility for their wives' trading debts.[50]

A final complaint further complicates this pattern. In 1390, William de Wyrsop complained that Agnes Halum had assaulted Agnes, daughter of Adam Mathewson (probably William's servant). Agnes Halum refused to answer the plea as her husband had not been named alongside her. The case was dropped and William was fined for bringing an unjust suit.[51] Here, Agnes strategically highlighted the departure from proper legal practice, following the doctrine of coverture; it was this that vindicated her, rather than any question of her actual culpability. A handful of other Nottingham women used the same tactic in other trespass pleas. Katherine, wife of Richard Fyssher, was the subject of a trespass complaint brought by Roger Doket in 1395, when she appeared in court but refused to answer the suit without her husband, and it appears that it was dropped.[52] Similarly, in 1327, Richard le Taverner brought a plea of trespass against William Derby and his wife Petronella. Though Petronella came to court, William did not, and she claimed she was unable to reply without her husband. When William did appear, the parties came to an agreement and William and Petronella were amerced 4d.[53] When Stephen le Taverner complained of Peter of Bakewell and Coletta, his wife, Peter repeatedly failed to appear, and Coletta refused to answer the plea alone.[54] It is not clear whether the dispute was ever fully heard in court, or whether Stephen just gave up. The same happened in a complaint against Henry Cornwall and his wife Agnes in 1354.[55] These women understood how the laws of coverture should have functioned in the different complaints heard by the borough court, and they used this knowledge to contest unlawful litigation.

---

entry later refers to '*dicta Agnes*', confirming that this was Agnes Halum.

50 Kowaleski, 'Women's work', p. 146.

51 NA CA1290/25: '*dicit quod non interdit ei respondere unde petit indictum etc*'.

52 NA CA1295/I/4d. An annotation declares the plea as void and no further record of the dispute can be found within the subsequent court rolls.

53 NA CA1260/6 and 8.

54 NA CA1260/8, 9, 10, 10d, 12, 13, 14 and 15.

55 NA CA1265/13d and14.

The fact that these contestations occurred repeatedly suggests that this was a well-known practice among the women of the town.

This pattern reflects a distinction between the nature of coverture in debt and trespass pleas, and the way that women could (or chose to) appropriate this to their advantage. As an experienced litigant, Agnes Halum knew how to work her way around the law, performing her marital status to her own advantage in this instance, but choosing not to do so in other cases.[56] Agnes Halum was not the only married woman to act in this way. Agnes Pys appeared in the Nottingham court rolls in a debt plea against John Lenton in December 1371, where she complained that he owed 8d for weaving. However, a few months later, Agnes and her husband John complained together of an alleged violent assault (trespass and bloodshed) committed by John Dekonson and his wife.[57] Both of these married women were able to litigate alone in complaints relating to their business matters, but when it came to some trespass complaints (apparently those involving interpersonal violence), custom appears to have held that wives should plead with their husbands.

The fact that Agnes acted alone in many debt suits but was a co-litigant with her husband in this trespass plea may have been down to a distinction between women's status in debt and trespass pleas, though there is no evidence that this was a clear-cut set of rules. Instead, the precise nature of an alleged trespass may have been the subject of distinction, as those cases where the marital dependence of Agnes Halum (as for Agnes Pys) was called upon involved interpersonal violence. It was not the simple fact that this was a trespass suit that necessitated the involvement of her husband, as other trespass pleas were brought or answered by Agnes alone, including two concerning pigs that she owned.[58] She also did not appropriate her coverture in the complaint against Adam Panyer for disorder in her tavern, perhaps warranted by the fact that it related to her own business affairs. Her avoidance of litigation due to coverture in the complaint of William de Wyrsop was therefore a tactic that involved choice on the part of Agnes to perform her marital status in some pleas, but not in others. It also reflected an expectation that instances of personal violence should be dealt with by husband and wife together. The understanding of women's legal status was thus contingent upon the type and nature of the complaints that they were involved in, highlighting the flexibility of coverture in practice. As Tim Stretton and Krista Kesselring have highlighted, coverture only became an issue when it was contested or questioned, often

56 Marjorie Keniston McIntosh, 'The benefits and drawbacks of *femme sole* status in England, 1300–1630', *Journal of British Studies*, 44 (2005), pp. 427–8.

57 NA CA1277a/5 and 22.

58 NA CA1286: trespass plea *v.* Joan Cook, servant of Richard of Bradmore; NA CA1280a: trespass plea *v.* Nicholas Somur.

in times of crisis.[59] Rather than following a strict set of rules, the court and other litigants instead acknowledged the differing contexts of various pleas in determining the appropriate course of action.

If we compare the patterns identified for Nottingham with the customs of other English towns and cities, we see how the laws of coverture were interpreted and applied differently according to urban custom. In London, married women who were registered as *femmes soles* were expected to plead alone, as though single, in debt complaints relating to their trade and work where they were involved in business that was separate from their husbands.[60] However, the *Liber Albus* specified that, while pleas of trespass could be brought against husband and wife for trespass committed by the wife only, she could answer the plaint alone if her husband did not appear.[61] In Lincoln, which borrowed many of London's customs, wives accused of trespass were to be arrested and their husbands were expected to appear in court. If they did not, the plea would continue as if the wife were single.[62] Similarly, Ipswich's customs set out that a married woman (*femme covert*) should answer by herself in pleas of trespass, though not those relating to property. However, husbands were to answer for their wives' debts, contracted before or after marriage.[63] Kowaleski has suggested that the Exeter courts upheld the 'juristic distinction' of *femme sole*, by allowing husbands to decline responsibility for their wives' debts.[64] In Nottingham, there is no evidence that *femme sole* customs were adopted, yet Agnes Halum (and Agnes Pys – and probably others) were able to plead alone in relation to debt and with no reference to their marital status. The relatively normative nature of debt litigation, arising from ordinary commercial interactions, allowed some independent married women to deal with these issues

59 Tim Stretton and Krista J. Kesselring, 'Introduction: coverture and continuity', in T. Stretton and K. J. Kesselring (eds), *Married Women and the Law: Coverture in England and the Common Law World* (Montreal, 2013), pp. 8–9.

60 See McIntosh, '*Femme sole* status', pp. 410–38; Cordelia Beattie, '"Living as a single person": marital status, performance and the law in late medieval England', *Women's History Review*, 17 (2008), pp. 334–7.

61 See Cordelia Beattie, *Medieval Single Women: The Politics of Social Classification in Late Medieval England* (Oxford, 2007), pp. 27–8.

62 Mary Bateson, *Borough Customs*, vol. 1, Selden Society, 18 (London, 1904), p. 226: 'sche schall be putte to answere and haf hyr plee os a sole woman'.

63 'Usages and customs of Ipswich', cap. 55–6, in William H. Richardson (ed.), *The Annalls of Ipswche: The lawes customes and governmt of the same, collected out of ye records books and writings of that towne by Nathll Bacon serving as recorder and town clark in that towne. Anno Dom. 1654* (Ipswich, 1884), pp. 34–5. An early case (1290) recorded in Bacon's *Annals of Ipswich* demonstrates that this custom was indeed followed. Letis, wife of Edward le Ken, brought a complaint of defamation against Letis, wife of Alexander Burchier. The latter pleaded that she was a married woman and could not answer without her husband, though the plaintiff successfully alleged the customs of the town that married women were liable to answer personal actions, and judgement passed in favour of the plaintiff. See Richardson, *Annalls of Ipswche*, p. 17. See also pleas of 1306 (p. 46) and 1482 (p. 145).

64 Kowaleski, 'Women's work', p. 146.

alone. Women like Agnes did not use coverture as a 'get out' in relation to debt complaints, indicating that they were not able to appropriate the disabilities of their marital status in this way, and suggesting a recognition by them and the court that these debt pleas were a necessary means by which to manage trading relationships and issues that needed to be resolved for the continuity of business dealings. But in trespass pleas, Agnes and others sometimes chose to draw on the expectation that both husband and wife should answer the plea – seemingly in contrast to the customs of London and elsewhere. These alleged trespasses, particularly assaults, represented a more exceptional departure from codes of appropriate behaviour, with implications for the honour of both husband and wife.

This complicated pattern of litigation forces us to reconsider our assumptions about women's legal status and blurs the lines often drawn between married and single women, *femme covert* and *femme sole*. Agnes's use of the court suggests that possibilities for the negotiation of coverture extended beyond the *femme sole* framework that is often cited as the main explanation for wives' legal action and as the exception to the invisible, covered wife. However, there is no evidence that formal registration as *femme sole* was an option available to Nottingham women. Instead, if we accept that Agnes was probably married for much or all of her legal career, it becomes apparent that there may have existed in Nottingham a set of informal *femme sole* customs that validated wives' legal actions in certain situations. Matthew Stevens has also suggested that there were possibilities for women beyond *femme sole*, arguing that, in the Court of Common Pleas, 'the convention of coverture left ample scope for married women to appear before the court as party to litigation of an overtly economic nature'.[65] In London's Sheriff's court, too, there was a 'permissive attitude' towards married women's participation in debt litigation.[66] In Nottingham, this 'ample scope' went beyond wives joining with their husbands in litigation (as many did) to include independent action in debt complaints where these arose from their individual commercial activity, allowing for the practical management of obligations through the borough court. Without the formal system of registration that existed elsewhere, Agnes's neighbours and local officials nevertheless recognised her actions as a 'sole trader', engaged in work that was separate to her husband's. She was able to enter into commercial agreements independently and was held to account in any subsequent litigation. Cordelia Beattie has suggested that wives' independent economic activity may have been understood as an extension of

65 Matthew Frank Stevens, 'London's married women, debt litigation and coverture in the Court of Common Pleas', in Beattie and Stevens (eds), *Married Women and the Law*, p. 131.

66 Stevens, 'London women, the courts and the "golden age": a quantitative analysis of female litigants in the fourteenth and fifteenth centuries', *The London Journal*, 37 (2012), p. 75.

the 'law of agency', enabling them to make contracts in relation to their own occupations and not just the buying of household necessities.[67] This helps to account for Agnes's independent transactions and subsequent litigation. However, we also see evidence of the marital partnership transcending separate trades, revealing fluidity in both legal practice and commercial identity.

Conclusion

The history of medieval courts is not just one of institutions, officials and legal doctrine, but of those people – like Agnes – who used and were subject to these systems. The visibility of Agnes Halum in court can help us to understand the experiences of other, less visible, urban women who used the borough court to negotiate relationships and enforce agreements. Her story also demonstrates the potential to identify the legal and economic actions of some married women – often assumed to be hidden from view – beyond the limited scope of *femme sole* customs. As an independent businesswoman, Agnes was able to use the court to settle and manage her own trading relationships, as well as negotiating the interests of the marital partnership in tandem with her husband. However, her status as a female litigant was not constant. The story of Agnes demonstrates, through the litigation of one woman, the flexibility of coverture and the potential for women to act as independent litigants when custom and circumstance dictated, aside from the possibilities of *femme sole* status. These nuances tell us about how individuals experienced the law, not revealed by large-scale surveys or quantification of court records, but instead lying in the intricacies and stories of ordinary people like Agnes Halum.

This is the story of one woman, though its significance does not stop with Agnes Halum, or with Nottingham's borough court. Though specific to the context and conditions in which Agnes lived, as well as her own life story, the issues that this microhistory raises can be applied more widely to the study of women's legal status under various jurisdictions. We have seen how women's legal action was tied to their economic identity, how the flexible nature of coverture determined their action in different types of complaints, and how the nature of the records influences what we know about these women and the power of the assumptions we make about them. These issues of classification, record-keeping conventions, the existence of formal customs and their negotiation, and the agency of individuals, all combined to create a specific legal experience. The traditions that governed the nature of borough court litigation in Nottingham involved a nuanced, somewhat flexible set of understandings about the legal status of women as it applied in different legal scenarios.

67 Cordelia Beattie, 'Married women, contracts and coverture in late medieval England', in Beattie and Stevens (eds), *Married Women and the Law*, p. 153.

This sometimes allowed women to negotiate the restrictions that came with marriage in facilitating efficient, effective and accessible dispute resolution.

Despite this 'excavation' of Agnes's legal career, there are still many things we can never know about her. However, her active role as a litigant in her local court shows us that she was worthy of considerable credit and allows us to piece together details about her work and her wide range of trading contacts, as well as her marriage and economic partnership with her husband. It has also demonstrated that women could be knowledgeable and competent in using local justice to manage and negotiate both their commercial and interpersonal relationships. For Agnes, this often meant acknowledging her debts as part of the management of her commercial ties and transactions, but occasionally she strategically appropriated her own coverture as a married woman and used this to her advantage, reminding us that women could have agency and options, despite the restrictions imposed on them by the law.

5

COURTS AND URBANISATION: JURISDICTION IN LATE MEDIEVAL SEIGNEURIAL BOROUGHS AND TOWNS

CHRISTOPHER DYER

This chapter will begin with a consideration of the variety of courts and procedures which regulated medieval urban societies. The different courts reflect the absence of uniformity among the towns themselves, which sometimes gives rise to uncertainties in defining towns and boroughs. Close attention will then be given to a series of court records documenting two towns belonging to a single lord, Worcester Cathedral Priory, with a view to answering the question, did the institutional framework of lordship reflected in the courts help or hinder urban development?

Historians should keep in mind ideal types of towns and boroughs, as long as these do not become rigid models: the exceptions and varieties of forms must be recognised. In the case of towns, specific legal privileges, walls, or a large population (five thousand, for example) are no longer regarded as defining characteristics. The essence of a town has become the existence of a permanent and dense settlement in which a majority of the inhabitants gained their living from a variety of non-agricultural occupations.[1] Such places often had a sense of a separate identity, a distinctive plan with a marketplace, streets

1 Susan Reynolds, *An Introduction to the History of English Medieval Towns* (Oxford, 1977), pp. ix–x; Rodney H. Hilton, 'Small town society in England before the Black Death', *Past and Present*, 105 (1984), pp. 53–78, at pp. 56–7. I am grateful for the help of archivists, especially in Worcester Cathedral Library. Paul Hargreaves and Simon Penn helped with their transcripts of the Bromsgrove court rolls. Mr A.T. Foley kindly gave me permission to consult his Kinver archives.

and narrow building plots, or an association with an institution such as a hospital or religious fraternity.[2] But these additional characteristics were not essential. Doubts arise when we find a place with many crafts and trades, but with a majority of households occupied by peasants living from agrarian production. And though the size of the settlement ought not to be of crucial importance, can we really describe as a town a place with a population of two hundred, at a time when villages could have been three times as large?[3] We are dealing with complex and inconsistent past societies, and we cannot impose on them precise and dogmatic modern schemes.

An ideal type of borough should have more certain and straightforward characteristics, because its privileges were defined in law. Even if the inhabitants had not received a borough charter, they would have understood that they held their plots by burgage tenure. The burgage plots would have been liable to pay a fixed annual money rent (often between 6d and 12d per annum), and the land would have been held freely, without any of the disadvantages of servility such as heavy labour services, tallage or restrictions on movement. The plots could be sold, sublet, divided or mortgaged without needing the lord's permission. The burgesses had free access to the market and would attend a borough court to settle disputes, define customs and deal with trading offences.[4] Boroughs came in many forms, however, and burgages could be held by customary tenure with the appropriate dues, such as entry fines on first taking the holding. In many cases there was no separate borough court, but the burgesses attended a manor court.

In a world of ideal types, the borough and town should have neatly coincided. The borough was supposed to provide the institutional framework for urban development. The burgage plots gave their tenants a practical basis for conducting business, as the front of the plot faced on to the street or marketplace, and space behind the houses could be used for workshops and storage sheds. The tenants' legal rights over their burgages meant that land could be used to raise capital, by negotiating a loan or dividing the plot and selling part of it. The privileges of boroughs encouraged urban growth because they would attract migrants who could bring skills, connections and capital into the community.[5]

In the real world, the towns and boroughs were not aligned so neatly. Many towns had no claim to be counted as boroughs, and their tenants were

[2] T. Slater, 'Understanding the landscape of towns', in Della Hooke (ed.), *Landscape: The Richest Historical Record*, Society for Landscape Studies, supplementary ser., 1 (2000), pp. 97–108.

[3] H. S. A. Fox, 'Medieval urban development', in Roger J. P. Kain and William L. D. Ravenhill (eds), *An Historical Atlas of South-West England* (Exeter, 1999), pp. 424–31.

[4] Reynolds, *English Medieval Towns*, p. 93; Maurice W. Beresford, *New Towns of the Middle Ages: Town Plantations in England, Wales and Gascony*, 2nd edn (London, 1988), pp. 198–219.

[5] Peter McClure, 'Patterns of migration in the late Middle Ages: the evidence of English place-name surnames', *Economic History Review*, 2nd ser., 32 (1979), pp. 167–82.

not always easily distinguished from those occupying land on manors. In the eastern counties of England, towns which lacked borough status were especially common: late medieval Norfolk had six boroughs but at least twenty-four towns.[6] To the west, in counties such as Warwickshire and Staffordshire, the non-urban borough is more likely to be encountered. Here a lord would have granted burgage tenure to villagers, expecting to change their way of life; or perhaps the borough was planned on a greenfield site, and migrants were expected to flow in to take up the burgage plots. They had either trickled in so gradually as not to form the critical mass necessary for a functioning town, or they had arrived but then departed.[7] The result would be that the borough's few inhabitants made their living from farming. Lords sometimes introduced burgage tenure gradually but were not encouraged to continue the process, and we find settlements with no more than ten to twenty burgage plots, associated with rural tenements, which cannot be rated confidently as either boroughs or towns.[8]

Courts for Towns

Did the courts held in towns or boroughs provide a framework of law helpful for the growth of an urban community? The generalisations made so far were based mainly on surveys and rentals, which list the tenants, indicate their tenure and state the rent owed. The terms of tenure and the privileges of the tenants are known mainly from the borough charters issued by lords. The charters, rentals and surveys can all be regarded as providing an unreal picture of early towns, as the charters offer ideal privileges and the surveys give orderly lists of tenants paying rents, who may have sublet their holdings. The court records seem to contain the best insights into the government of the towns, and the economy and daily life of the townspeople. That does not mean that they convey an objective picture of a real world. The court rolls are full of formulae and conventions relating to legal procedures, using technical language which distances the court processes from the practices of the real inhabitants. For example, in reporting assaults, of which there might be six in a year in some towns, the lawyers needed to know if blood was shed, and to decide which of the parties should be amerced. The reason for the outbreak of violence, which could have arisen from a property or trade dispute, or simply as a result of a spontaneous outburst, is never explained.

6 Christopher Dyer, 'Small towns, 1270–1540', in David Palliser (ed.), *The Cambridge Urban History of Britain: 600–1540*, vol. 1 (Cambridge, 2000), pp. 507–10.
7 Beresford, *New Towns*, pp. 290–307.
8 Richard Goddard, 'Small boroughs and the manorial economy: enterprise zones or urban failures?', *Past and Present*, 210 (2011), pp. 3–31, at pp. 12–14.

This analysis of court records derives from twenty-two towns for which adequate numbers of court rolls survive.[9] The focus is on seigneurial towns and the sample is biased towards smaller towns, though the populations of a few may have edged over two thousand. Fifteen of the towns are from the Midlands, four from the south-west, one in the north and the rest from the south and east. The majority had ecclesiastical lords, most of them monastic, but ten of them belonged to laymen. The clerks observed no uniform convention when they chose the title of the court. Only three of them employed the term that we expect, 'court of the borough of…', but the majority preferred to use 'court' for routine sessions, with a 'view of frankpledge' (sometimes called the court leet) once or twice each year. The view at Leek (Staffordshire) was called a 'great court', and in 1424 at the same place a court was headed 'the court of the town (*ville*)'.[10] The view could be called the 'hundred', and the term *curia legalis* or legal court occurred at Shaftesbury (Dorset), Tiverton (Devon) and Thornbury (Gloucestershire).[11] The court equivalent to the court leet at the borough of Crossgates, which formed part of the complex of boroughs that made up the city of Durham, was called the *capitalis curia* or head court.[12] Courts in four places were known by the distinctive English title of portmoot.[13]

Seventeen of the towns or boroughs were served by a distinct and separate court, but that leaves a significant minority in which a manorial court covered both the town and its rural surroundings. Some boroughs looked like very small elements within a large manor. The borough of Brewood (Staffordshire) formed one of the nine tithings in the major rural manor of the same name, on the estate of the bishops of Coventry and Lichfield.[14] However, the Brewood tithing stands out with its distinctive business, such as forestalling and various offences committed by those selling meat and fish or keeping inns. The tanners were brought before the court for polluting the water course with their efflu-

9 The sample: Alcester (Warwickshire), Alton (Hants.), Bretford (Warwickshire), Brewood (Staffordshire), Bromsgrove (Worcestershire), Crossgates (Durham), Eynsham (Oxfordshire), Halesowen (Shropshire, now Worcestershire), Henley-on-Thames (Oxfordshire), Highworth (Wiltshire), Kinver (Staffordshire), Leek (Staffordshire), Orford (Suffolk), Pershore in two parts (Worcestershire), Shaftesbury (Dorset), Shipston-on-Stour (Worcestershire, now Warwickshire), Stratford-upon-Avon (Warwickshire), Tiverton (Devon), Thornbury (Gloucestershire), Uttoxeter (Staffordshire), Wimborne (Dorset).

10 Staffordshire Record Office (hereafter SRO), D1333/1, D1333/2, D1337/3.

11 Dorset Record Office, DC/SYB/B1, B2; Devon Record Office, CR 227; SRO, D641/1/4E/2.

12 Richard H. Britnell (ed.), *Records of the Borough of Crossgate, Durham 1312–1531*, Surtees Society, 212 (2008), pp. xix–xxv.

13 Eynsham: British Library (hereafter BL), Harleian Roll F21; Highworth: R. B. Pugh (ed.), *Court Rolls of the Wiltshire Manors of Adam de Stratton*, Wiltshire Record Society, 24 (1970), pp. 111–63; Pershore (Westminster part): Westminster Abbey Muniments (hereafter WAM), 21937, 21938, 21939; Tutbury: TNA, DL30 109/1615.

14 SRO, D590/4331, 2, 3. The court of the other lord, the dean of Lichfield, was also distinctive: SRO, D590/434.

ents. There was also a larger number of 'hue and cry' cases and assaults with bloodshed than in the other tithings. The best generic term for these courts, whether held just for the urban settlement or for the urban tithing within a larger manor, is the title used at Leek: the 'town court'. In some places, the business of the town is almost hidden from view; for example, at Winslow (Buckinghamshire), where we know of a group of burgages and a marketplace, but in the manor court the tiny borough was given no special space at all.[15]

Many town courts differed from manor courts because much of the tenant land was held by burgage tenure. Burgages were only mentioned occasionally as they were transferable without reference to the court, except in special circumstances such as an escheat resulting from a break in the line of inheritance, or a forfeiture when a tenant had been convicted of a felony. A dispute over inheritance might bring a burgage under the scrutiny of the court. A not uncommon situation was for a town to have holdings in different tenures. For example, shops and selds at Uttoxeter (Staffordshire), or cottages at Kinver (Staffordshire), were not held in burgage tenure.[16] Sometimes the original core of the town consisted of burgages, but later additions were held under another tenure.

In some towns a vocabulary was applied to tenant holdings that seems more appropriate for a rural manor, such as the 'tenements' at Orford in Suffolk, and the 'messuages' and 'cottages' that appear in the records of the two jurisdictions at Pershore (which was divided between Pershore Abbey and Westminster Abbey). Pershore holdings were not very privileged, leading to an entry fine of one hundred shillings being paid in 1337 for 'a messuage and a curtilage' in Westminster's part of the town, while Pershore Abbey's tenants could be required (like any customary tenant) to build on their plots.[17] Naming a holding 'burgage' did not necessarily mean that it enjoyed the normal advantageous terms. At Brewood, it was said that burgages were held 'according to the form of this tenure of the manor of Brewood, by services and customs owed', which could include paying an entry fine of five shillings.[18] Though burgage tenants generally enjoyed the usual privileges, the lord still wished to maintain a record of those who came into the borough by inheritance, gift or purchase, so new tenants were expected to present themselves to the court, acknowledge the lord, do fealty, show a charter if one had been granted, and pay at least a small token relief of 4d, which was the custom

15 David Noy (ed.), *Winslow Manor Court Book*, Buckinghamshire Record Society, 35 (2011), part 1, pp. x, xiv, 5, 17.

16 BL, Add MS 46460; Herefordshire Record Office (hereafter HRO), E12, FS/I/3, 4.

17 Suffolk Record Office (Ipswich branch), HD64/1/2, 28, 29; WAM 21942; TNA, SC2/210/71, 72.

18 SRO, D590/433/6.

at Kinver in Staffordshire.[19] The new tenants' names therefore appear in the court roll, but their reluctance to go through the formalities is apparent on occasion, from the interval between their acquisition of their holding and appearance in court.

Litigation appears prominently in the records of town courts. The cases followed the familiar pattern, beginning with a plaint by an individual alleging that a debt had not been paid, a trespass had been committed, or goods had not been returned. The other party would often not attend court, and a pledge would be required to secure a response. Eventually the defendant would accept an obligation, or a judgement came from a jury, and payment was enforced by the court. Often the parties would obtain a 'licence to agree' and arrive at a compromise. These procedures meant that each case came before the court a number of times.[20]

Statistical comparisons between town courts and manor courts are difficult to make, because the populations varied so much, because the number of cases coming before the court depended on the state of the economy, and even because courts were deemed to have varied effectiveness in dealing with unpaid debts.[21] Nonetheless, we gain the impression that town courts dealt with a greater volume of litigation, and this reflected the complexity and pressure of the urban way of life. Townspeople frequently made contracts with partners and customers, and in the urban economy there were more payments in money for goods and services, and habitual use of credit to enable transactions to proceed in a period when actual coin was in short supply. Traders and artisans who made up a high proportion of the town's population operated in a commercial world in which raw materials, transport, equipment and labour were obtained without immediate payment, and in which customers acquired manufactures or services on the basis of a promise to pay the full amount at an agreed date in the future.[22] This network of obligations could only work if the various parties trusted one another, or if they could have recourse to a legal system that would enable them to recover the money owed. Townspeople needed a court strong enough to enforce its decisions, but it ought to be fair and reasonable so that its judgements were respected, and the parties to the disputes could settle their differences and return to normal relationships.

The town court could attract litigants because it was run by its suitors, who acted as jurors and tithing men or chief pledges. These officials of the court

19 HRO, E12, F/S/I/4, 5.

20 John Baker, *The Oxford History of the Laws of England: 1483–1558*, vol. 6 (Oxford, 2003), pp. 308–9.

21 Chris Briggs, 'Manor court procedures, debt litigation levels, and rural credit provision in England, c. 1290 – c. 1380', *Law and History Review*, 24 (2006), pp. 519–58.

22 James Bolton, 'Was there a crisis of credit in fifteenth-century England?', *British Numismatic Journal*, 81 (2011), pp. 144–64.

had the technical knowledge to deal with the cases that were put before it. To take an example from the court of Pershore in 1388, John Stoke pleaded against William Colyns in a plea of broken contract. John had delivered to William 7lbs of linen yarn, and William (a weaver) agreed to make fourteen ells (16.8 yards) of cloth by a given date. As William failed to keep to his contract, John claimed damages of 6s 8d. The jury of townspeople would know if the yarn was sufficient to make the cloth and could judge whether the damages claim was reasonable – to a modern observer the sum seems to be too high, and the jurors probably made the same judgement.[23]

In the manor courts, the number of pleas diminished drastically in the fifteenth century. Town courts differed in that they continued to hear cases, though there was a tendency for numbers to fall in the long term, and in particular to dip in the early years of the sixteenth century.[24] This meant that those seeking to settle disputes went to other courts, such as the Westminster courts (which tended to attract major cases involving larger sums of money) or the church courts. More often the parties entered into private arbitrations which were sometimes organised by religious fraternities, but might sometimes have been promoted by neighbourly pressure.

Finally, the important specific needs of town dwellers were served by the views of frankpledge, as is apparent from the business recorded. The views in rural manors heard the presentments of the tithing men, which included agrarian offences such as the maintenance of hedges and ditches, enclosures, and offences in the harvest field. The assize of ale was enforced, by which brewers and ale-sellers were amerced for breaking the regulations and, in particular, for charging too high a price. The brewers also appear in views held in town courts, but more often than in the manor courts bakers were also presented for breaking the assize of bread (that is, for selling loaves below the weight fixed by the authorities). Views held for towns often heard of offences by butchers, fishmongers, and occasionally sellers of candles, oats, hay or leather goods, sometimes for selling low quality goods, but often for taking too much profit. Commercial offences might also include forestalling and regrating (that is, intervening in the market to buy goods before they went on sale, in order to dispose of them for a higher price). Huxters were also subject to regulation.[25] The suspicion must be that these 'rogue traders' were not thought to be serious offenders, especially as 'taking excessive profit' must have been difficult to define, but that the lord was using the opportunity to take a few pence for himself when he saw money changing hands. In the same spirit,

23 TNA, SC2/210/72.

24 Baker, *History of the Laws*, p. 311; Britnell (ed.), *Borough of Crossgate*, pp. xxvi–xxvii.

25 James Davis, *Medieval Market Morality: Life, Law and Ethics in the English Marketplace, 1200–1500* (Cambridge, 2012), pp. 274–409.

the offenders accepted the payments as necessary overheads. Occasionally, habitual brewers, instead of paying 2d, 3d or 4d every time a brew was sold, would buy a licence to trade for a year, untroubled by repeated amercements. In the mid fifteenth century at Eynsham in Oxfordshire, brewers (many of them women) paid an amercement of 2d for breaking the assize when each brew was sold. Some brewed often, one of them fifteen times in a year, but it can be suspected that they were not always observed and amerced. In 1475 and 1476, seven brewers each paid a 12d fine to brew for a year, while others who brewed occasionally continued to pay 2d for each offence.[26]

Regulation could have been important for the well-being of the town, because on occasion the presentment was not just a means of collecting a routine tax, but dealt with a serious infringement such as selling bad ale, burnt or seriously underweight loaves, measly pork or rotten fish. This meaningful element of consumer protection made the jurors and other officials willing to play their part in identifying and punishing wrong-doers. Internal social relations within the town would be damaged if consumers, especially of foodstuffs, believed that they were being cheated and exploited, and a town's external reputation for honesty and fairness also needed to be protected. One persistent group of offenders, for example, were the innkeepers, who – according to the presentments – sold fodder (oats, hay, horsebread) at high prices, and took excessive profits from food sold to their customers. Inns made an important contribution to a town's economy by attracting visitors, and they helped some places to become 'thoroughfare towns' where a stream of travellers visited and stayed overnight. It was important that outsiders should be able to trust these establishments.[27]

Like their manorial counterparts, town courts issued by-laws. They were often just repeating well-known rules to keep them in the mind of those charged with presenting and punishing the offenders. They would seek to regulate trade and were concerned with the improvement of the urban environment, such as removing dunghills from the streets and mending roads. Both manorial and town authorities show a growing concern in the fifteenth century with various types of anti-social behaviour, such as the playing of illicit games. At Tutbury (Staffordshire) in 1424, 'no-one henceforth should tell dishonest stories or spread scandalous talk about their neighbours', which carried a potential penalty of twenty shillings, the same as could be incurred by taking geese, ducks, capons, hens and pullets from neighbours.[28] There were also prohibitions on residents receiving suspicious strangers and harbour-

26 Judith M. Bennett, *Ale, Beer, and Brewsters in England: Women's Work in a Changing World, 1300–1600* (New York, 1996), pp. 99, 100, 106–7; BL, Harleian Roll F21, F35.

27 John Hare, 'Inns, innkeepers and the society of late medieval England, 1350–1600', *Journal of Medieval History*, 39 (2013), pp. 477–97.

28 TNA, DL30/111/1662.

ing prostitutes. These attempts to reform manners (to use a phrase from the eighteenth century) seem to have been more frequent in courts dealing with towns than those held in rural manors.[29] Town courts could be concerned with agricultural matters – not just dealing with wandering pigs, which was an urban problem, but also the regulation of common grazing. They are a reminder of the agricultural dimension in every town, not just those that were embedded within a rural manor.

By-laws reflect the different interest groups contributing to the court and its proceedings. The lord and his officials had the authority to make laws and often chose the subjects of legislation. For example, one reason for the restrictions on games such as cards and dice was the threat that they posed to public order. Another was the widespread anxiety about idleness, which connected with problems of vagrancy and migrations of strangers of dubious character. The underworld of indolence, mendicancy and petty criminality was linked in the minds of those in authority with the shortage of labour. Royal proclamations and parliamentary statutes show that these were regarded as problems on a national scale. In the local context, the jurors and other leading townsmen were making recommendations to the court for measures both to control behaviour and to improve the urban environment. The reputation of the town was again at issue, and the worthies of a town like Alcester in 1469 and 1475 did not wish it to be known in its locality for its potholed streets and flooding gutters, with steaming piles of dung at every corner, inhabited by disorderly youths liable to become involved in fights, and traders who sold rotten fish and substandard leather.[30]

This brief survey suggests that, although the urban societies of the Middle Ages cannot always be easily disentangled from their rural environments, the townspeople seem to have had their own concerns. In devising the jurisdictions for their estates and in operating their court system, lords and their officials had to adapt to economic and social circumstances and take some account of the needs and preferences of their subordinates. They must all have been aware of the widespread customs associated with towns and boroughs, but they did not apply a standard legal and institutional template. The traders, artisans and other inhabitants, who no doubt would have preferred a stronger involvement in the government of their town, attempted to make the courts work in their interests. Any series of town records reveals many people who failed to observe the rules, by selling underweight loaves or dumping rubbish in public places, but harmony seems to prevail, in which lord and leading townspeople had a common purpose. If there

29 Marjorie Keniston McIntosh, *Controlling Misbehavior in England, 1370–1600* (Cambridge, 1998) – though this lacks a clear sense of an urban/rural divide.

30 Warwickshire County Record Office, CR1886/172, 173D.

were serious discontents, the lord's court was not the place to air them, as the court would decide in favour of the lord, and did not in any case have the power to make fundamental changes.

Worcester Cathedral Priory and its Towns

Worcester Cathedral Priory, a major Benedictine monastery worth more than £1,400 per annum in the later Middle Ages, has left a rich archive, especially of court rolls. Most of its income derived from twenty-six rural manors, many of them large, distributed over all parts of Worcestershire with one in adjoining Warwickshire.[31]

The monks of the priory became involved in urban development in the mid thirteenth century because new sources of income were becoming harder to acquire, yet the institution was costly to manage and the cathedral was being embellished with a new and elaborate east end and choir between about 1224 and 1260.[32] Its last major endowment, the very lucrative rectory of Bromsgrove, came in 1232 to 1237 as a result of King John's choice of Worcester Cathedral as his burial place.[33] New income also came from the pilgrims attracted by the cult of St Wulfstan, who was canonised in 1203 and translated into an ornate shrine in 1218.[34] Land was being assarted in the woodlands, but eventually only limited areas were left for clearing new land.[35] During the first half of the thirteenth century, the demesnes were taken back from the farmers who had previously paid a fixed rent, and the land was brought under the management of estate officials, giving the priory the opportunity to profit from the higher prices of grain, wool and livestock.[36] As peasants were selling more produce, they could make increased rent payments – including of course the cash obtained through the courts, from amercements and from entry fines when holdings changed hands. New mills could be built to generate income, including four new fulling mills recorded for the first time in 1240, three of them within reach of a town where cloth was made.[37] Increased income from demesnes, rents and mills needed much hard administrative work and some investment.

31 Rodney H. Hilton, *A Medieval Society: The West Midlands at the End of the Thirteenth Century* (London, 1966), pp. 26, 33, 77, 79.

32 Alan Brooks and Nicholas Pevsner, *The Buildings of England: Worcestershire* (New Haven and London, 2007), p. 683.

33 Reginald R. Darlington (ed.), *The Cartulary of Worcester Cathedral Priory*, Pipe Roll Society, new ser., 38 (1968), pp. 176–8.

34 Reginald R. Darlington (ed.), *The Vita Wulfstani of William of Malmesbury*, Camden Society, 40 (1928), p. xlviii.

35 William H. Hale (ed.), *Registrum Sive Liber Irrotularius … Prioratus Beatae Mariae Wigorniensis*, Camden Society, 91 (1865), pp. 12a, 17a, 17b, 18a, 42b, 49a, 51a.

36 Hilton, *A Medieval Society*, pp. 78–9.

37 Hilton, *A Medieval Society*, pp. 207–12.

The monks had experience of urban tenants from their portfolio of properties in the city of Worcester. From the mid thirteenth century onwards, they pursued a successful policy of enhancing their income from houses and land in the city. They disposed of houses which produced only a small fixed rent income and acquired new properties which could be rented profitably. As donations diminished, monks made purchases to acquire houses around the cathedral itself and in the suburbs.[38] At the end of the Middle Ages they were drawing an income of more than £100 from Worcester tenants, many of them leaseholders. Through the Guestenhall court, they exercised lordship over their Worcester city tenants.[39]

New towns offered a chance to raise income from rent for houses, market tolls, mill revenues and court profits. Manorial lords of all kinds saw benefits in urban development, because their peasant tenants could pay rents in cash more easily if they had ready access to an active market. The lords' motives were not entirely and narrowly economic. The town plans, with their long main streets or grids, impressed visitors who realised they were entering a special place with an important lord.[40]

Some monastic lords were reluctant to embark on town foundations. They were aware that granting advantageous terms to tenants could be seen as alienating a monastery's assets, and gave the tenants ideas above their station. Worcester Cathedral Priory made a very small beginning by allowing the development of the hamlet of Bridgetown on the manor of Alveston in the early thirteenth century, as an unofficial suburb of the new borough of Stratford-upon-Avon, founded by the bishops of Worcester in 1196.[41] They hesitated to go further, and then founded two towns in about 1260 at Shipston-on-Stour and Bromsgrove. The prior at that time, Richard de Dumbleton, enjoyed a good reputation subsequently, so perhaps the monks were persuaded that he had made a wise move.[42]

Shipston-on-Stour and its Court

The town of Shipston was laid out on a site designed to catch trade on two main roads: that from Chipping Campden to Banbury, which crossed the River Stour by a bridge, and the route from Stratford-upon-Avon to Oxford. Around 1260, Worcester Cathedral Priory established a new town with a planned

38 Nigel Baker and Richard Holt, *Urban Growth and the Medieval Church: Gloucester and Worcester* (Aldershot, 2004), pp. 267–77.

39 Baker and Holt, *Urban Growth*, pp. 297–301.

40 Keith D. Lilley, *City and Cosmos: The Medieval World in Urban Form* (London, 2009), pp. 77–85.

41 Hale (ed.), *Registrum ... Prioratus*, p. 83a.

42 Joan Greatrex, *Biographical Register of the English Cathedral Priories of the Province of Canterbury, c. 1066–1540* (Oxford, 1997), p. 801.

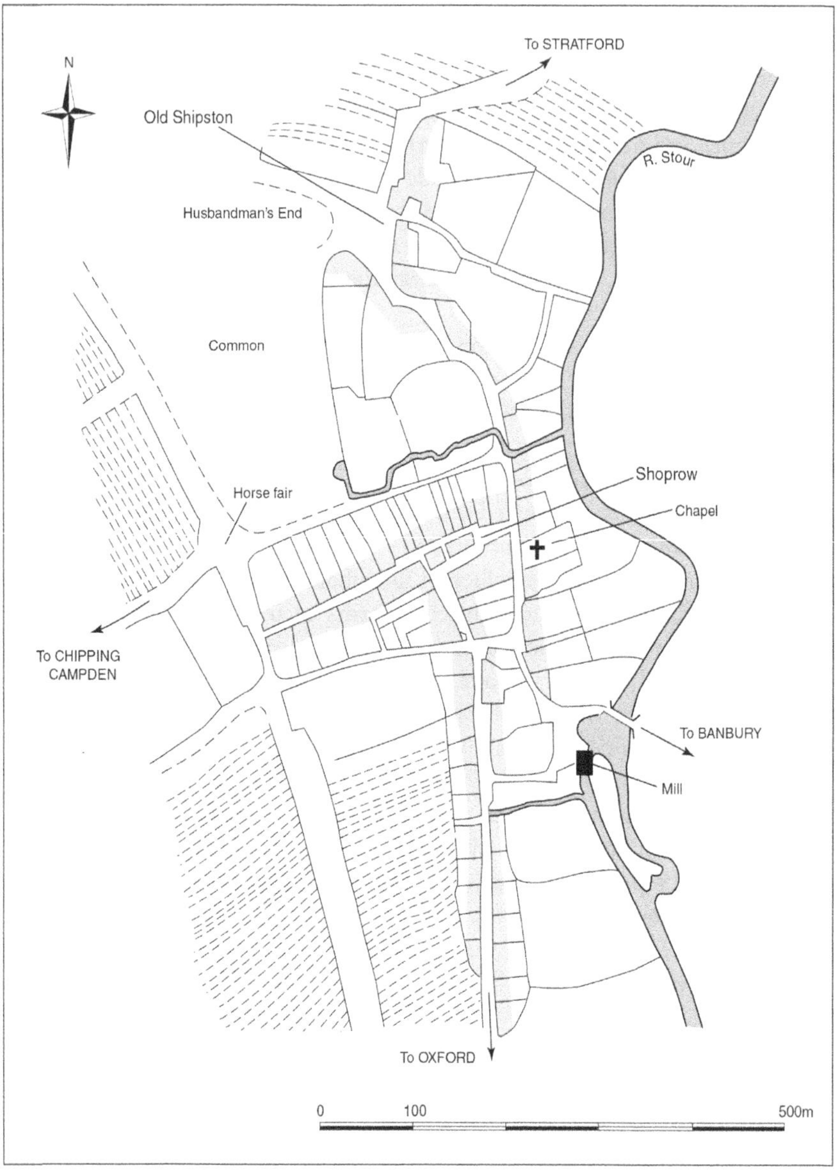

MAP 5.1: MEDIEVAL SHIPSTON-ON-STOUR

grid of streets and burgage plots, sometimes called New Shipston, alongside a village with an entirely agricultural economy, henceforth called Old Shipston (though it appears on later maps as Husbandman's End). People from both Old and New Shipston attended the manor court at Blackwell, another manor of the priory.[43] This arrangement went back before 1260 and was entirely for the administrative convenience of the priory's officials, who could deal with the business of two manors in a single court session. For the inhabitants of both Old and New Shipston, this was peculiarly inconvenient as they had to travel two miles to reach Blackwell. The priory's court records were headed 'Blackwell'. Sometimes 'Shipston' appears as a subheading, and sometimes Blackwell and Shipston were entered separately, as if on occasion a court was actually held in Shipston. The impression must be that, for most court sessions, dozens of Shipston tenants had to make the journey to Blackwell. The larger number of people living at Shipston, and the existence of two settlements at Shipston, was acknowledged in 1325 when a jury of twelve in the Blackwell court contained four representatives of Blackwell and eight for Shipston, presumably with four from Old Shipston and four from New Shipston.[44] Much of the business of the court was dealing with agrarian matters and the transfer of customary holdings, and one can imagine the frustration of the Shipston townsmen, sitting (or more likely standing) through time-consuming business which had little relevance for them. The modern reader of the court records can speculate about the prevailing mood and atmosphere, because the clerks provided more detail than is usually encountered: they even reported speech and offered explanatory words such as 'voluntarily' or 'maliciously'.

The priory's two manors of Blackwell and Shipston were in turn embedded in the large parish of Tredington, which had its own church court, and in secular jurisdiction they were subject to the bishop of Worcester's private hundred court of Winburntree.[45] Between 1315 and 1325, Shipston tenants were amerced for incurring financial penalties for moral offences in the church court, and the Blackwell court also dealt with defamation cases which overlapped with the concerns of the church court.[46] Such rivalries were not uncommon.

Some institutions were exclusively for the use of Shipston people, notably their chapel, which in 1319 had a cemetery – though properly Tredington church retained burial rights, and the priory was suspicious of the chapel's independence.[47] The town also had a separate court for the market and fair, revealed in 1314 when it was farmed out to two New Shipston tenants, Richard Baret and Robert le Taylor, together with a row of new shops, for forty shillings. They were to profit from 'all the small amercements of the

43 Christopher Dyer, 'Small-town conflict in the later Middle Ages: events at Shipston-on-Stour', *Urban History*, 19 (1992), pp. 184–210.
44 Worcester Cathedral Library (hereafter WCL), E10.
45 Worcestershire Archives, ref. 009:1 BA 2636 177/92504, 92508, record proceedings of the hundred court in the early sixteenth century.
46 WCL, E7, E8, E9, E10.
47 Dyer, 'Small-town conflict', pp. 196–7.

market of Shipston from the piepowder pleadings (*placitis pepoudrose*) and from the weighing of bread, saving to the lord all the great profits of the same market'. The implication must be that the two tenants would hold the piepowder court for a limited range of matters, perhaps with the participation of the priory's local reeve or bailiff, but without a visiting steward or official from Worcester – nor, unfortunately, with any written record of the proceedings.[48] The lord's court held at Blackwell seems to have recognised Shipston's separate institutional identity when it referred to urban tenants holding land 'according to the custom of the manor of Shipston'. A difficult problem of customary law arose in 1341, when Isabell Robynes asked for a judgement concerning a half burgage held by Geoffrey Robynes. 'The whole homage of New Shipston', in accordance with 'the custom of New Shipston', said that she had no right because John Robynes, Isabell's deceased husband, had sold the property by the lord's licence. The whole vill could also act as a pledge on behalf of a tenant – as, for example, when it was decided on the death of Isabell Rondewy in 1333 that her heir would not be her son John, who had departed from the lordship for a long time, but her daughter Joan.[49]

It was entirely appropriate that, in dealing with property in the Blackwell court, burgages in New Shipston were transferred alongside rural customary holdings. Burgages in the town were held by customary tenure, with the usual financial liabilities and restrictions. In 1315 John Campion acquired a burgage from the lord, and the entry in the court roll tells us that it was 'to him and his heirs', 'for service and customs due' (phrases used in relation to customary holdings), for which he paid an entry fine of 16s 8d.[50] In 1321 it was said in court that two burgages were held 'in bondage', and in 1337 the same phrase was used again for a burgage and to describe the tenure of a shop.[51] Shipston tenants, like customary tenants on most manors, were not allowed to sell their burgages without the lord's permission. The same conditions governed their ability to sublet land. If they neglected their buildings, the court could order them to carry out repairs. Some of the terms applied to New Shipston customary tenants seem to have been devised to meet their special circumstances. In 1333, Thomas le Gurdeler took on a cottage holding 'by the custom the new vill'.[52] This seems to have changed when William de Mongwode took a burgage holding in 1341 and the court used the phrases normally employed for customary tenants: that he would hold 'to him and his brood (*sequele*)' 'of the lord in bondage for services owed according to the custom of the manor of Shipston', and subsequently 'the custom of the

48 WCL, E7.
49 WCL, E1, E11a.
50 WCL, E7.
51 WCL, E9, E13.
52 WCL, E11a.

manor' was habitually used, as if the priory had decided not to give the town's customs special recognition.[53] Occasionally we are told that a tenant, such as Richard Baret in 1321, was a *nativus* (also known as a *neif* or born serf), showing that, for Worcester Cathedral Priory, 'town air' did not 'make free'.[54]

The monastic lord attempted to enforce the traditional seigneurial monopolies, perhaps because of their value in an urban context, or perhaps in pursuit of a principle. Campaigns in the court were mounted occasionally against those who failed to do suit of mill – for example, by taking their corn to the bishop of Worcester's mill at Tredington. When a new tenant took over the Shipston mill in 1377, the court roll record of the grant mentioned the suit of mill of both free and *neifs*, evidently as an asset to the miller.[55] The oven monopoly was taken seriously, and attempts were made to enforce it in the court. In 1325, 'all men and their tenants' (presumably including sub-tenants) were said to be liable to suit of oven, and in 1334 three people were amerced for 'baking elsewhere'. As late as 1518 and 1519, two Shipston innkeepers (one of whom kept the Swan) applied to the court to pay a rent for permission to bake bread in their own oven for their guests, on condition that the loaves were not offered for general sale.[56] The idea that chartered markets in England exercised some form of monopoly on trade was sometimes voiced, but not much enforced. It was typical of Worcester Cathedral Priory's ambition that it attempted in 1342 through the court to force those selling cattle to do so in Shipston market: 'None of the lord's tenants should sell avers nor any other cattle before they were offered in Shipston market', though no cases are recorded as being brought against offenders.[57]

Many borough courts gave limited financial benefits for the lord, but the manor court of Blackwell (which the townspeople of New Shipston had to attend) was helping to enforce rent payments, because the inheritance and transfers of burgages were administered by the court. The original rents of 16d per annum for a burgage seemed rather low to priory officials by the fourteenth century, and when three new cottage holdings were granted out through the court in 1333 their rents were near to the market rate, at 3s 6d, 4s 6d and 5s 6d per annum.[58] The entry fines levied by the court when holdings were acquired by new tenants again reflected the rising land values of an active urban centre, leading to a burgage being granted for £6 13s 4d in 1401.[59]

53 WCL, E1.
54 WCL, E9.
55 WCL, E9, E27.
56 WCL, E10, E11a, E95.
57 Adolphus Ballard and James Tait (eds), *British Borough Charters: 1216–1307* (Cambridge, 1923), pp. 241–6, 285–9; WCL, E2.
58 WCL, E11a.
59 WCL, E14, E41.

Heriots (death duties) were demanded from burgage tenants, as happened in some other boroughs, and the item taken and its value were entered in the court roll. On the death of a tenant who was entirely dependent on petty trade or work as an artisan, the heriot would be a kitchen utensil or article of clothing of modest value, but in 1343 a valuable ox was paid when the tenant of a burgage died, and another for the same tenant's shop. A tenant with a messuage, and a number of cottages and stalls, yielded in heriots in 1367 an ox and three horses worth more than £2.[60]

The priory's instinct to enforce strict discipline led to its imposition through the court of high collective penalties of ten, twenty and even one hundred shillings for such serious offences as concealment of trespasses, appointing a priest to the chapel without permission, and attacks on the lord's officials.[61] These sums of money were scarcely affordable, as one hundred shillings represented more than five years' wages for a labourer, and were to some extent symbolic. They were designed to threaten the tenants and were not actually collected.

The inhabitants of small towns should not be regarded merely as low status artisans and petty traders. Some Shipston people could obtain at least a minimal education locally, presuming that the surname 'Scolemaster' (which appears in the court records around 1400) tells us his occupation.[62] The courts refer occasionally to apprenticeship, and young people who did not receive a formal training will have gained experience by working in the households of established traders and craftsmen. Leading townspeople were expected to take on demanding administrative tasks, like John Lomberd, who was 'elected' in the court in 1347 to be reeve of the tolls and aletaster, so he collected market tolls and regulated the town's many brewers. In the same year, he was appointed with three others to 'supervise all the stalls and customs of the market'.[63] The administrative talents and powers of persuasion needed in public office were presumably acquired from running private businesses. Among the tenants there was much worldly experience, which would influence the way that they approached their lord and his courts.

The Shipston tenants knew that their court, based in Blackwell, with their lord's steward in charge, was very different from the arrangements at nearby Stratford-upon-Avon. There the borough court was separated from the manorial court for Old Stratford, and the free burgesses could transfer land by charter.[64] In spite of their disadvantages, however, the Shipston townspeople

60 WCL, E14, E22.

61 WCL, E9, E10, E14.

62 WCL, E45: John Scolemaster appears in 1406.

63 WCL, E15.

64 Centre for Kentish Studies, Maidstone, Sackville of Knole U269 M73; Shakespeare Centre Library and Archives, Stratford-upon-Avon, DR 75/4, 7, 8.

were drawn into the whole system of seigneurial courts which worked by cooperation with the assembled suitors, who provided information, made declarations about custom and sometimes influenced decisions. They presumably valued the facilities that the court provided to pursue pleas of debt and trespass, though the courts met only four times each year, which limited the speed with which problems could be resolved.

Perhaps the town dwellers of Shipston derived some benefit from the courts, but they were fundamentally distrustful of the lord and his supervision of their affairs, as was demonstrated when suitors persistently concealed matters from the court. In the 1360s and 1370s, the townspeople were transferring burgages outside the court without obtaining the lord's permission, and much trouble ensued in 1376 when this evasion was discovered.[65] As well as practising their own conveyancing of property, the townspeople were also evading the high fines and heriots levied on burgages, which were imposed because the lord's officials realised that the tenants had the capacity to pay. Of course, townspeople in places where the lord could not demand large entry fines were able to keep more of their profits to fund consumption and investment.

Occasionally, overt discontent was expressed – for example, when Robert Gervays in 1320 accused the steward of falsehood (*falcitatem*), or when the reeve was assaulted in 1325.[66] Grumbling frictions were probably seething below the surface, but when the Shipston tenants turned to rebellious agitations they were voiced not in the manor court at Blackwell, but in the royal court of King's Bench in 1398. The tenants brought a case in which they put forward a coherent alternative to the priory's version of Shipston's legal status. They argued that Shipston was an ancient royal borough held at fee farm by the priory. They believed that they should have a degree of self-government, by having two catchpolls. They had gained ideas (and no doubt advice) from contacts with other towns such as Cirencester, which was held by its monastic lord at fee farm, and Stratford, which had two catchpolls (under bailiffs). Their plea to King's Bench included a complaint about the narrowing of a road caused by the building of market stalls, which went back to 1382 and shows that they had been nursing grievances for many years before 1395. Their claim to be a royal borough, though it gained only small plausibility from a charter of King Edgar of 964, was crucial for their legal argument, because it entitled them to royal protection and proved that they were free men. Otherwise, the monastery could reassert that it alone had jurisdiction over the bondsmen of Shipston, and as they had no right to plead before the king's judges, the priory's court of Blackwell should reign unchallenged.[67]

65 WCL, E27. Nine offenders had their burgages seized and were excluded from any claim to them.

66 WCL, E9, E10.

67 Dyer, 'Small-town conflict', pp. 202–7.

The Shipston rebels' claims to borough status had been encouraged by the rector of Tredington, who would gain more valuable mortuary payments if the tenants were judged to be exempt from heriots as burgesses. The Blackwell court became an issue in the conflict when, in 1399 to 1400, the townspeople did not pay brewing fines and mill tolls, setting up their own malt mills, and in 1403 the priory complained that they prevented the view of frankpledge at Blackwell from being held.[68] Agitations continued, but were resolved with a one-sided arbitration and the release (after a period of imprisonment) of some of the leading rebels. The priory hoped that it would resolve the problems by withdrawing all reference to burgages in Shipston in the manor court, after which the standard tenant holding was called 'a messuage and a curtilage'.

Bromsgrove and its Courts

In the 1260s, the town of Bromsgrove was established near the prominent parish church as the most important settlement in the extensive royal lordship of Bromsgrove and King's Norton (covering in excess of 23,000 acres). Worcester Cathedral Priory had acquired control of the rectory of Bromsgrove in the 1230s as a gift from the crown. It was a valuable asset with a large revenue from tithes, but its territory was small and its tenants few. In the 1260s the priory embarked on its town-planning scheme, perhaps in coordination with the estate managers of the royal manor, and by 1311 forty priory tenants occupied a row of messuages and cottages on the west side of the High Street, standing on plots running down to the stream (the Spadebourne) that ran parallel to the street. The court for the rectory manor of Bromsgrove was presumably held at the priory manor house near the church, as the priory had now taken over the role of rector. Its records are quite brief, and mainly consist of records of non-attendance and short records of changes of tenancy of holdings situated along the High Street.

The High Street was originally a Roman road, and in the Middle Ages it was the main route from Worcester to Lichfield. Around the time that the priory manor was setting up its new tenants along the west side of this important highway, the authorities in charge of the royal manor (probably local administrators rather than Henry III himself) were recruiting tenants to build their houses in plots arranged along the eastern side of the street, resulting in a conventional town plan with two rows of houses facing one another, with all the appearance of a single community under a unified authority. The route of the road from west to east, from Kidderminster to Coventry, was manipulated so that travellers would have to use a section of the main street and provide

68 WCL, Reg. A IV, fols 427–428.

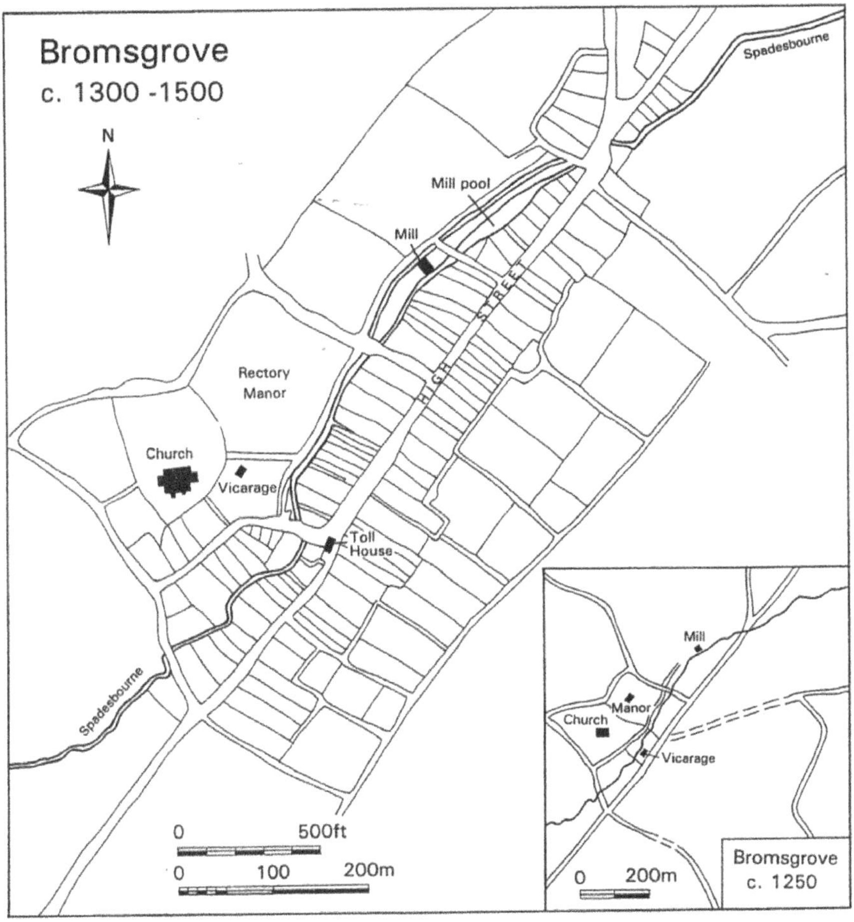

MAP 5.1: MEDIEVAL BROMSGROVE

the town's retailers with opportunities for sales.[69] For the royal manor the court was held on a remote hill at Lickey, and the separate and distinct character of the town was only apparent at the view of frankpledge. Among the ten or more tithings making their presentments, the Bromsgrove tithing stands out for the quantity of business, and especially the concentration of sellers of ale, bread, meat and fish. Its importance as a centre of industry is suggested by the complaints that tanners were polluting the Spadebourne.[70]

69 Christopher Dyer, *Bromsgrove: A Small Town in Worcestershire in the Middle Ages*, Worcestershire Historical Society Occasional Publication, 9 (2000), pp. 12–27.

70 A. F. C. Baber (ed.), *The Court Rolls of the Manor of Bromsgrove and King's Norton 1494–1504*, Worcestershire Historical Society, new ser., 2 (1963).

By about 1300 Bromsgrove was a single, quite prosperous town, under two lords, and each lordship dealt with business arising from its tenants in the town in its own courts. Neither of these two courts was a borough court, and indeed Bromsgrove in surviving documents was only once (by accident) called a borough. The royal tenants from the town attended the Bromsgrove manor court at Lickey. This had a greater authority than the Worcester Cathedral Priory court because, after some disputes in the early days of the town, the royal court held the view of frankpledge, so that, for example, offences under the assize of bread and ale committed on both sides of the High Street were reported to the royal court. We are primarily concerned with the manor court for the rectory manor, held by the priory, as it offers a comparison with the court of Blackwell attended by the townspeople of Shipston. In contrast with the full and detailed writing of the Blackwell and Shipston court records, the Bromsgrove rolls contained relatively terse entries reflecting the priory's limited powers of jurisdiction over a place acquired at a late date and overshadowed by the royal manor. There were no serfs among the priory's Bromsgrove tenants, and customary tenure is not mentioned. However, the new holdings were not called burgages, but were described as 'a messuage', 'a messuage and curtilage', 'a messuage and appurtenances', 'a cottage' or 'a cottage and curtilage'. The record does not describe them as free, but they have some of the characteristics of freeholdings as they paid a cash rent and were only rarely expected to do labour service. New tenants did not pay entry fines. There was no standard rent, as found in a borough, but apparently as holdings were granted in the late thirteenth century varied rents were agreed, mostly between 21d and 2s 8d per annum, and they remained fixed at that level for the next two centuries. Heriots were due at the end of a tenancy; most of these reflected the urban nature of the economy, because they were paid in cash or the lord took an article of clothing or a chattel. Of fifty recorded heriots, nine cattle were levied and eight horses. The lord expected in the early fourteenth century to be involved in transfers of land, and complained in 1342 that a tenant had sold a holding 'against the custom of the manor'.[71]

Eventually a procedure developed that holdings could be inherited or transferred outside the court, but the lord should be informed and the new tenants should attend the court and do fealty. The court made decisions about tenancy in complicated cases of inheritance, as (for example) when it was found in 1374 that a tenant had been a bastard and there were doubts about who should succeed him. The succession to a holding was disputed in the following year, in which a 'sealed indenture' was quoted as evidence that Richard Noreyse had a life interest in a messuage and curtilage.[72] The court heard about enfeoffments,

71 WCL, E2.
72 WCL, E26.

subdivisions between heirs, and what appears to be a mortgage arrangement leading to repossession of a holding in 1396.[73] The priory was anxious to be kept informed of changes, and insisted that its tenants should acknowledge the monks' lordship and pay their rents and dues. The nightmare of all lords was the disappearance of a holding, as happened to the Bromsgrove guildhall. After it was converted into dwellings, its tenants ceased to pay rent, and it took some time for the responsible person to be discovered.[74] From the point of view of seigneurial revenues, Bromsgrove generated an income of a few pounds in rents and a gradual trickle of heriots, but the profits of justice were negligible, as the royal manor gained most of the income from enforcing the assize of bread and ale, and (apart from a period in the early fourteenth century when the priory court dealt with pleas between tenants) received most of the litigation.

The court business reflects a certain amount of friction between the priory and its tenants. The most serious episode of antagonism was recorded in 1342, when Walter le Fleshewer (whose surname suggests that he was a butcher by trade) sold a holding, concealed the horse that should have been paid as heriot, and beat and ill-treated the miller. Five members of the jury were amerced in the same court for quarrelling among themselves.[75] In 1364, tenants appear to have boycotted the court and only two suitors attended. They arrived late.[76] The tenants perhaps expressed alienation – or at least indifference – by regularly defaulting (that is, they did not attend the court), or were essoined (sending an excuse for absence). The priory had to pursue tenants for heriot payments and to compel them to do fealty. In all, the priory did not exercise a close control over its Bromsgrove tenants, and to some extent it was an observer of their activities rather than being an assertive lord. As the court did not have the range of functions and powers practised in other towns, the tenants had no strong motive to assert themselves, and the lord could be indifferent to their low level of attendance and activity.

The tenants of the priory's manor were not just surly avoiders of obligations, as they belonged to an urban community in which they lived and traded alongside their counterparts across the main street. Some conflicts broke out between the two manors, especially over matters of jurisdiction, such as the obligation of the priory tenants to attend the view of frankpledge held by the royal manor. In 1307, the priory won the right to hold the assize of bread and ale for its own tenants, but this seems to have been a temporary vic tory.[77] These disputes were resolved and did not have major consequences for

73 WCL, E38.
74 WCL, E17, E32, E38, C897.
75 WCL, E2.
76 WCL, E21.
77 Dyer, *Bromsgrove*, pp. 15–16.

the inhabitants. They lacked urban institutions after the guildhall had fallen into decay by 1352, and no 'guild' appears in the documents.[78] The leading townspeople from both sides of the High Street probably met in advance of the view of frankpledge to decide the town's presentments, and could have used this unofficial and undocumented 'town meeting' outside the court to discuss matters of common interest. All of those living in the town were parishioners of the church of St John the Baptist, but it could not be regarded as an expression of civic unity because it also served the very large rural population, rather as the Lickey court was attended by the whole population of the royal manor. A chantry (the priest of which would have said his masses in the parish church) was endowed with rents and managed by local worthies (called feoffees); though not recorded until 1548, it probably had much earlier origins. It funded a school, paid for useful local causes such as repairing roads and bridges, and may have been involved in other matters of town business. We do not know how the paving of the High Street and the building of the High Cross were organised, but the building that stood in the marketplace, called a prison and seld (for market stalls) in 1427 and a tollhouse in 1467, was the responsibility of the royal manor.[79]

Conclusion

Was lordship as expressed in the jurisdiction of seigneurial courts a help or a hindrance for the development of towns? Lords, even conservative monasteries, appreciated the advantages of having towns on their estates. Worcester Cathedral Priory gained about a tenth of its income from urban rents, and it was able to expand its revenues from urban sources at times when other types of growth had slowed. Medieval lords, however, were not just rent collectors, but sought to extend their authority over their subordinates – partly to protect their incomes, but also because they regarded lordship as a positive good. Their courts were instruments of government, not just sources of profit or means of disciplining tenants. To some extent, they received support from those attending their courts. The institutions worked with an element of consent – the court could only operate if it was receiving information from the suitors, and the decisions made and penalties levied needed cooperation. It was in the interests of the townspeople to have access to a body that could legislate for the good of the community, and which could help to maintain law and order. They made use of facilities for solving disputes and recovering debts. Individuals played a prominent role as officials – partly, no doubt, because they were helping to improve their communities, but also because they gained in status

78 WCL, E17.

79 Dyer, *Bromsgrove*, pp. 43–4.

and even in material terms from their association with authority. Seigneurial towns encouraged the growth of oligarchy through such institutions as the jury at the view of frankpledge, even if the employers and landholders who made up the oligarchy would have preferred more independence.

The adverse consequences of the rule of lords are readily apparent from the examples given. The reluctance of some lords to establish a separate court for the townspeople must have caused many inconveniences, not least the time spent travelling to distant venues, and more seriously the lack of time and expertise enabling the court to deal with the complexities of urban business. Lords also jealously guarded their imagined monopoly of jurisdiction and sought to prevent townspeople taking cases to alternative tribunals, which must sometimes have included the royal courts as well as local church and hundred courts.

Lords imposed the rule of their courts, partly because it enabled them to raise revenue. Entry fines, collective financial penalties, heriots, and amercements enforcing the assizes of ale and bread could add pounds each year to the income collected through the lord's court, and in turn reduced the incomes of the townspeople. Other obligations were not very costly, but servile status, customary tenure and seigneurial monopolies were constant humiliations for those who were subject to them. In most villages the lord's oven had ceased to trouble the inhabitants by 1400, but at Shipston-on-Stour bread was still being taken to the lord's baker well into the reign of Henry VIII. A much more serious example of the exercise of lordly power was the withdrawal of the use of the term 'burgage' at Shipston – in effect, the cancellation of burgage tenure.

The lords could exercise a strong influence over the urban property market. After the initial planning of the urban space, the creation of new plots or permanent market stalls needed action by the lord, with or without advice or requests from the townspeople. The transfer of holdings, if conducted in the court, was subject to the lord's approval and could involve payments for entry or for the heriot of a predecessor. The normal urban devices of investment in property to secure income, or the use of land as security for a loan, had to take into account the lord's role. Access to land was linked with migration, as new tenants often came in from outside; though little is said about selection, we suspect that occasionally the lord chose new tenants or discouraged those he regarded as undesirable.

The frictions that developed between lords and townspeople often resulted in minor acts of protest, but they could also flare into serious rebellion. Insurrections were most likely in the larger seigneurial towns, such as Bury St Edmunds, but at Shipston and also Abingdon (Berkshire), small towns could launch stout resistance, and similar issues were raised in both large and small towns. Rebellious towns commonly demanded more say in the appointment of officials, such as bailiffs. They protested about aspects of the conduct of the courts, such as the administration of the assize of bread and ale, and the view of frankpledge. They wished to form associations (that is, guilds and fraternities). They complained about levies in cash and kind, including milling tolls and heriots. There was also controversy about the use of space, such as the location of marketplaces, and the use of waste land, pastures and woods.[80] They demanded reforms and modifications of lords' powers, rather than planning the abolition of unjust lordship, as if they accepted the validity of the seigneurial regime.

If we focus our attention on the evidence of the courts attended by townspeople, we are in danger of examining urban life through the narrow prism of the lord's documents. Towns of all kinds could organise themselves with minimal involvement by lords or courts. Bromsgrove was a single town, though divided between two lords, and there are other examples of towns with three or more lords forming a single community. Bromsgrove could organise the space and buildings for a dignified marketplace,[81] and such small-scale town planning did not always require the intervention of a lord. When a fraternity developed into an alternative means of government, the lord sometimes resisted, but more often accepted the new institution and allowed it to run parallel with his administration.[82] Higher authorities expected the inhabitants of towns and villages alike to take on complex administrative roles outside the framework of seigneurial power, such as tax-gathering for the state or managing the parish church fabric for the ecclesiastical hierarchy. In devising their own methods of government and social cooperation, the inhabitants were not acting subversively. They were by-passing the lord and his court, rather than confronting or undermining seigneurial institutions.

80 Samuel K. Cohn, *Popular Protest in Late Medieval English Towns* (Cambridge, 2013), pp. 203–62.

81 Lucy Toulmin Smith (ed.), *Leland's Itinerary in England and Wales* (London, 1906), p. 95.

82 Gervase Rosser, *The Art of Solidarity in the Middle Ages: Guilds in England 1250–1550* (Oxford, 2015), pp. 187–213.

6

THE BUSINESS OF THE LEET COURTS IN MEDIEVAL NORWICH, 1288–1391

SAMANTHA SAGUI

Norwich was one of medieval England's most populous and wealthiest towns.[1] Located in the east of England, where the frankpledge system is thought to have originated and where it endured longest, Norwich has the earliest surviving borough leet rolls and provides an ideal case study of how early leet courts functioned.[2] The Norwich leet court met annually to hear and punish misdemeanours (minor crimes punishable by fines) that affected the urban community. As with the equivalent courts in other towns, it did not have jurisdiction over felonies (serious offences which could lead to a death sentence), nor did it hear private suits.[3] The city coroners dealt with

1 Alan Dyer, 'Ranking lists of English medieval towns', in David M. Palliser (ed.), *The Cambridge Urban History of Britain: 600–1540*, vol. 1 (Cambridge, 2000), pp. 752, 755, 758, 761, 765; James Campbell, 'Norwich before 1300', in Carole Rawcliffe and Richard Wilson (eds), *Medieval Norwich* (London, 2004), p. 29.

2 William A. Morris, *The Frankpledge System* (London, 1910), p. 25; Frederick Pollock and Frederic W. Maitland, *The History of English Law before the Time of Edward I*, 2nd edn, vol. 1 (Cambridge, 1968), p. 580; Bruce Campbell, 'Hundreds and leets: a survey with suggestions', in Christopher Harper-Bill (ed.), *Medieval East Anglia* (Woodbridge, 2005), pp. 157–60; F. J. C. Hearnshaw, *Leet Jurisdiction in England: Especially as Illustrated by the Records of the Court Leet of Southampton* (Southampton, 1908), pp. 12–13; L. R. Poos, *A Rural Society after the Black Death: Essex 1350–1525* (Cambridge, 1991), p. 92.

3 Hearnshaw, *Leet Jurisdiction*, p. 140; James Davis, *Medieval Market Morality: Life, Law and Ethics in the English Marketplace, 1200–1500* (Cambridge, 2012), p. 147; Gervase Rosser, *Medieval Westminster, 1200–1540* (Oxford, 1989), p. 232; Maryanne Kowaleski, *Local Markets and Regional Trade in Medieval Exeter* (Cambridge, 1995), p. 339; Richard H. Britnell, *Growth and Decline in Colchester, 1300–1525* (Cambridge, 1986), p. 27; John Hudson, *The Oxford History of the Laws of England: 871–1216*, vol. 2 (Oxford, 2012), p. 823.

suspicious deaths, while the justices of the gaol delivery courts heard reports of felonious crimes.[4] Individual pleas, largely consisting of property disputes and civil pleas, were heard at the city court (*curia civitatis*), over which the town bailiffs presided.[5]

Because the leet court heard cases that affected the well-being of the community, its records furnish a unique insight into the shifting values and needs of the urban community and to the concerns of middling level men.[6] This chapter uses the Norwich leet rolls to provide a case study answering several questions about urban leet courts: how did the leet court work? What punishments could the court dispense and how effective were these penalties? What can the records reveal about the concerns of Norwich residents and how they changed over the course of the fourteenth century?

In order to address these questions, this chapter draws upon eleven surviving leet rolls from Norwich. The first seven rolls record the business of the court between 1288 and 1300. There is also a fragment from a roll created around 1307 and three rolls from 1313, 1375 and 1391.[7] The rolls from 1288, 1290 and 1307 are presentment rolls, which means that they record the names of the capital pledges (who served as presentment jurors) along with the accusations they made. They do not, however, contain any information about the penalties assessed. Of these three, only the 1288 roll survives in its entirety. The eight remaining rolls take the form of amercement rolls, which list the charges along with the fines assessed, although the 1289 roll is the only one that indicates the amounts actually collected. In total the rolls contain reports of 6,908 offences, all of which have been recorded in a database.[8] The original rolls form the basis of the following discussion, whereas many previous studies of Norwich have relied upon William Hudson's edition of the leet rolls published for the Selden Society in 1892.[9] Although Hudson's edition provides excellent transcriptions and translations, it contains only selected excerpts from the rolls and should not be used for quantitative analysis.

[4] Barbara Hanawalt, *Crime in East Anglia in the Fourteenth Century: Norfolk Gaol Delivery Rolls 1307–1316*, Norfolk Record Society (1976); Philippa Maddern, *Violence and Social Order: East Anglia 1422–1444* (Oxford, 1992), pp. 48–63.

[5] Norfolk Record Office (hereafter NRO), NCR Case 8A; NRO, NCR Case 8D/1–7; William Hudson and John Cottingham Tingey (eds), *The Records of the City of Norwich*, 2 vols (Norwich, 1906–10), vol. 1, pp. cxxiii–cxxviii.

[6] Marjorie McIntosh, *Controlling Misbehavior in England, 1370–1600* (Cambridge, 1998), p. 37.

[7] NRO, NCR Case 5B/1–11.

[8] *Norwich Leet Rolls Database*. This database is based on the original rolls (NRO, NCR Case 5B/1–11).

[9] William Hudson (ed.), *Leet Jurisdiction in the City of Norwich during the 13th and 14th Centuries, with a Short Notice of its Later History and Decline from the Rolls in the Possession of the Corporation*, Selden Society, 5, (London, 1892).

The Mechanics of the Court

The leet court in Norwich was held once annually in the Lenten season from at least the thirteenth century through to the nineteenth century. It is not clear when the city of Norwich received the right to hold its own leet court, but by 1288, when the earliest records appear, the city was responsible for administering the court and retained the proceeds from it. The 1375 roll explicitly states that the court was held before the four bailiffs, who likely presided for the entire period before 1404.[10]

The 1288 roll shows that the city was, at that time, divided into eleven administrative units, called sub-leets. These sub-leets were uneven in size, containing between one and ten parishes. They were invariably drawn along parish boundaries, which allowed the leet court to utilise an existing community. The subdivisions were consistent in the early rolls, but by 1375 two of the Conesford leets were collapsed into one, leaving a total of ten sub-leets. The combination of these leets likely represents an attempt to reinforce the frankpledge system by increasing the size of the tithing groups (which consisted of ten or more men who had lived in the city for at least a year and who were mutually responsible for the good conduct of each man enrolled in the group) and ensuring that each sub-leet would have at least twelve capital pledges. This procedure of combining or reorganising tithing groups was common in the late fourteenth century.[11] Throughout the medieval period, the sub-leets adhered to the boundaries of the city's four great leets, each of which had its own bailiff and constables. Hudson has argued convincingly that the sub-leets in the 1288 leet roll were entirely pragmatic. Parishes were grouped together based on the number of tithings they contained, so that each presentment jury would have at least twelve capital pledges to represent each sub-leet.[12]

Each of the eleven sub-leets was represented by at least twelve capital pledges responsible for making presentments to the court. Functioning as spokesmen for their sub-leets, the jurors seem to have reported minor misdemeanours reliably. Their transgressions and those of their wives appear in the rolls, and they were rarely cited for concealing offences or for making false accusations.[13] Indeed, among the 6,908 offences contained in the leet

10 NRO, NCR Case 5B/10 m. 1.

11 Hudson, *Leet Jurisdiction*, p. xix; Phillipp R. Schofield, 'The late medieval view of frankpledge and the tithing system: an Essex case study', in Zvi Razi and Richard M. Smith (eds), *Medieval Society and the Manor Court* (Oxford, 1996), p. 417.

12 Hudson, *Leet Jurisdiction*, p. xviii.

13 Samantha Sagui, 'A prosopography of the capital pledges of medieval Norwich', *Medieval Prosopography*, 31 (2016), pp. 107–8; Anne Reiber DeWindt, 'Local government in a small town: a medieval leet jury and its constituents', *Albion*, 23 (1991), p. 632; Daniel Klerman, 'Was the jury ever self-informing?', in Maureen Mulholland and Brian Pulman (eds), *Judicial Tribunals in England and Europe, 1200–1700: The Trial in History*, vol. 1 (Manchester, 2003), p. 127.

courts, only 104 were citations for concealing offences. The identifiable capital pledges lived in the parishes they represented.[14] They typically served for an extended period of time – based on the evidence of the Mancroft tithing roll (which lists all of the men enrolled in tithing groups in one quarter of the city c. 1311), probably averaging about seven years – a practice that facilitated the process of making presentments.[15] Because the residents of Norwich likely knew who would be representing them in the leet court, they could lodge their complaints with the jurors.[16] Caroline Barron argues that in London it was equally important for the jurors to be well known so that they could hear reports from their neighbours; in that city, however, public knowledge was achieved by selecting the jurors openly in court, rather than through repeat service, which was less common in London than in Norwich.[17] In the end, the choice of what to present lay with the capital pledges, and their identities must have influenced their judgements.[18] A comparison between the Mancroft tithing roll (c. 1311) and the 1332 lay subsidy suggests that, as a whole, the Norwich capital pledges were slightly better off than their neighbours. They were about twice as likely to be included in the roll, and they paid about a shilling more than the other tithingmen listed in the roll.[19] Only three of the 274 identifiable capital pledges, however, can be considered members of the elite, using office-holding as a proxy for social status and defining those who held the position of bailiff (or later mayor) as elite.[20] The capital pledges also participated in a wide variety of occupations.[21] The concerns of the Norwich leet jurors, as reflected in their presentments, might therefore serve as a proxy for the fears and concerns of moderately well-to-do residents.

14 Hudson, *Leet Jurisdiction*, pp. 59–61; Elizabeth Rutledge, 'Immigration and population growth in early fourteenth-century Norwich: evidence from the tithing roll', *Urban History Yearbook* (1988), p. 24.

15 NRO, NCR Case 5C/1.

16 Sagui, 'A prosopography', pp. 102, 108–110.

17 Caroline Barron, 'Lay solidarities: the wards of medieval London', in Pauline Stafford, Janet L. Nelson and Jane Martindale (eds), *Law, Laity and Solidarities: Essays in Honour of Susan Reynolds* (Manchester, 2001), p. 224; Christine Winter, 'The Portsoken presentments: an analysis of a London ward in the fifteenth century', *Transactions of the London and Middlesex Archaeological Society*, 56 (2005), p. 100.

18 Davis, *Medieval Market Morality*, p. 297; Rodney H. Hilton, 'Small town society in England before the Black Death', *Past and Present*, 105 (1984), p. 68; Sara Butler, 'Local concerns: suicide and jury behavior in medieval England', *History Compass*, 4 (2006), p. 823.

19 Sagui, 'A prosopography', p. 105.

20 Ben McRee, 'Peacemaking and its limits in late medieval Norwich', *The English Historical Review*, 109 (1994), p. 836; Ruth Frost, 'The urban elite', in Rawcliffe and Wilson (eds), *Medieval Norwich*, pp. 235–54; Britnell, *Growth and Decline in Colchester*, p. 128; Kowaleski, *Exeter*, p. 102; Stephen H. Rigby and Elizabeth Ewan, 'Government, power and authority 1300–1540', in Palliser (ed.), *The Cambridge Urban History of Britain*, vol. 1, p. 301.

21 Sagui, 'A prosopography', pp. 103–7; Rosser, *Medieval Westminster*, p. 234.

Unlike the procedure in criminal courts, presentment before the leets was tantamount to conviction and was usually followed by the imposition of a fine. There are eleven instances – all located in the 1289 roll – in which a fine was pardoned because the accusation was not true.[22] There are also two instances in the 1291 roll in which women cited for breaking the assize of ale were exonerated because they did not brew. Another woman in that roll was excused because she kept the assize.[23] It appears, therefore, that there may have been some form of appeals process whereby individuals accused of a misdeed in the leet courts could clear their name. This process, however, was not common. Fines could also be pardoned because the accused were poor, because they served the city in an official capacity, or because they had a patron intercede in their favour.[24] In the 1289 roll, the bailiffs were responsible for excusing most crimes. In addition, there are twenty-five instances in which amercements were dismissed at the request of a named individual. These people were most often elite citizens – those who had served as bailiff or who would hold the position at a later time. One person was pardoned at the request of Isabella de Tudenham, who was the wife of Roger de Tudenham, one of the city's four bailiffs.[25]

The 1289 roll – the only one that lists both the amounts assessed and those collected – demonstrates that the leet court did not have an effective mechanism to impose punishments.[26] Each great leet had two collectors, who were probably permanent officers of the bailiffs because they served for multiple years.[27] After the meeting of the leet, they collected the fines and returned the sums to the court. There is no indication that unpaid fines elicited any additional penalty. According to the 1289 roll, while amercements for the city totalled £72 18s 10d, only £17 2d – slightly less than a quarter of the total – was collected.[28] Although some of these fines were formally pardoned, many were simply not paid or were not paid in full, though it is possible further collections were taken at a later time, as was common practice in Exeter.[29]

The amounts assessed for various crimes cannot be used as a gauge to determine which crimes were most concerning for the people of Norwich, because there is no discernible relationship between the offence and the amount

22 NRO, NCR Case 5B/2; Hudson, *Leet Jurisdiction*, p. xliii.

23 NRO, NCR Case 5B/4 m. 2r.

24 NRO, NCR Case 5B/2.

25 NRO, NCR Case 5B/2 m. 4r.

26 Hudson, *Leet Jurisdiction*, p. lxxiii; David Gary Shaw, *The Creation of a Community: The City of Wells in the Middle Ages* (Oxford, 1993), p. 206.

27 Hudson, *Leet Jurisdiction*, p. xxxiii; P. Maddern, 'Order and disorder', in Rawcliffe and Wilson (eds), *Medieval Norwich*, p. 192.

28 Hudson, *Leet Jurisdiction*, p. xl; Campbell, 'Norwich before 1300', p. 35.

29 Margery Rowe and John Draisey (eds), *The Receivers' Accounts of the City of Exeter, 1304–1353*, Devon and Cornwall Record Society, 32 (1989), pp. 74, 81.

amerced. It is possible that assessments were made based on the ability of the suspect to pay, or on the severity of the offence, or some combination thereof.[30] Because most of the people being fined cannot be identified beyond their inclusion in the leet rolls, it is difficult to determine which of these possibilities is most accurate. The references to people about whom little is known substantially increases the value of these records for historians, by furnishing source material for prosopographical studies which could potentially shed light on the question of amercements and social status, among other things. In the meantime, the discrepancy between the amounts assessed and those collected suggests that the court was not very effective at determining a suspect's ability to pay – if that was, indeed, the mechanism being used. Given that the capital pledges were entrenched in the community and that they often served as affeerers (the officials who assessed fines), it is unlikely that the suspect's ability to pay was the only factor in determining an amercement.[31] It is equally difficult to determine the severity of a transgression, though it seems likely that persistent or severe crimes may have been assessed at a higher rate. For example, in 1313 Roger de Pelham was fined two shillings for forestalling, while Robert Bewyne was fined only 12d. It is possible that Bewyne was an occasional offender, while Pelham was guilty on a regular basis.[32] Similarly, Richard de Hemenhale was fined two shillings for assault in the same year that Nicholas de Taverham was fined only 12d for the same crime (though in the end both men ended up paying 12d).[33] The difference in assessments might indicate that Hemenhale caused more harm than Taverham.

In spite of the court's apparent inability to collect fines, the proceedings of the leet played an important social role by bringing misdeeds to light. Although the rolls do not specify where the court was held, they do imply that it was overseen by the bailiffs; it seems likely, therefore, that the leet took place in the same location as the bailiff's court, the Tolhus.[34] The Tolhus was just off the main market square in the site that would later house the guildhall; as such, it was very much within the public view. Moreover, the leet court was presumably widely attended. In addition to the bailiffs and capital pledges (who on their own accounted for 155 attendees), people who had business before the leet and an unknown number of the better sort of residents would have been in attendance (probably including the patrons who we can see interceding in the 1289 roll). Being brought before the court, therefore, would not only have been time-consuming; it would also have had a significant

30 Hudson, *Leet Jurisdiction*, p. xxxviii.
31 NRO, NCR Case 5B/3 m. 1r.
32 NRO, NCR Case 5B/9 m. 1.
33 NRO, NCR Case 5B/2 m. 2.
34 Hudson, *Leet Jurisdiction*, p. xxiii.

impact on one's reputation or *fama*.[35] It could also have been detrimental to one's business. Who, after all, would choose to patronise a butcher accused of selling bad meat if there were other butchers nearby? Not all of the misdeeds presented before the leet, however, would have had an appreciable impact on one's reputation. In Norwich, the wives of respected men were often fined for brewing counter to the assize. It is unlikely, therefore, that this offence carried any stigma; the fine may have functioned instead as a form of licensing. The tendency to fine otherwise respectable people for brewing has also been demonstrated in other cities, notably Colchester.[36]

In addition to issuing fines and bringing misbehaviour into the glare of the public assembly, the bailiffs issued orders for miscreants to be arrested in 203 instances (about 3 per cent of cases). These included the few times when the capital pledges reported felonies – presumably in these instances the suspects were held to await gaol delivery. In most other cases, the order for an arrest came in addition to a fine. The majority of arrests (138 cases, roughly two-thirds of the total) followed accusations of assault. Arrests were also made for wandering outside at night, theft, receiving stolen goods, unjustly raising the hue, and hamsoken. There was one arrest ordered for not attending the leet court. There are no arrests recorded for crimes that were purely economic in nature, or for public nuisances. Violent crimes forced the bailiffs to take action, perhaps because the perpetrators were perceived to present an immediate danger to the community, or because they were more likely to default on their fines.

The Business of the Courts

As in many towns, the volume of business coming before the Norwich leet courts was significantly greater at the end of the fourteenth century than at the beginning of it.[37] Excluding the presentment rolls, which (as will be discussed below) may not include all of the fines assessed, the number of citations ranged from 552 amercements in 1291 to 954 amercements in 1313. The 1375 and 1391 rolls included 1,014 and 1,231 cases respectively (Table 6.1). This increase is particularly dramatic in the context of population change. The population of Norwich declined by as much as 68 per cent between the 1330s and the 1370s, suggesting that *per capita* presentments more than doubled between

35 Frank Rexroth, *Deviance and Power in Late Medieval London*, trans. Pamela Selwyn (Cambridge, 2007), p. 221; Thelma Fenster and Daniel Smail, 'Introduction', in Thelma Fenster and Daniel Smail (eds), *Fama: The Politics of Talk and Reputation in Medieval Europe* (Ithaca, NY, 2003), pp. 3–5.

36 Britnell, *Growth and Decline in Colchester*, p. 90.

37 Kowaleski, *Exeter*, p. 188; Britnell, *Growth and Decline in Colchester*, pp. 98, 115, 135.

1313 and 1375.[38] This increased business demonstrates that the leet court was still an active part of the civic administration during this period. It is difficult to know why the business of the court increased so much. Were the bailiffs driving the increase? Did the capital pledges perceive more disorder in the city? The increase in regulation of economic transactions might be explained by increased trade; as the amount of business taking place in Norwich swelled, so too did regulation of the economy (Table 6.1). Maryanne Kowaleski and Richard Britnell have suggested that increased commerce resulted in more court business in Exeter and Colchester.[39]

Prior to 1313 the capital pledges recited crimes haphazardly, but thereafter they listed transgressions in the same order – a shift that might reflect a change in record-keeping. The 1313 roll witnessed a marked rise in the number of crimes presented, but the indictments that defy classification (which were probably listed purely at the discretion of the jurors) remained consistent with previous years (Table 6.1). This pattern suggests that the new ordering of presentments signifies an attempt by borough officials to bolster their control over the courts by dictating how presentments were made. Such a shift might have been motivated by a desire to increase the profits realised by the courts, by ensuring that more crimes were reported.[40] It could also have been a reaction to an influx of poor migrants into the city, which, Elizabeth Rutledge has argued, began to undermine social cohesion in Norwich in the first half of the fourteenth century.[41] Regardless of the reasoning, there was a concerted effort to regularise court proceedings. In 1313 and later, we see the capital pledges for each sub-leet reporting first on instances of assault, theft, hamsoken and uses of the hue. Next, they reported common nuisances and assorted market offences, before listing those who broke the assize of ale. At the end of each jury's statement is a list of men who were not enrolled in tithing groups or who did not come to court. This order may reflect the perceived severity of the crimes, with the most dangerous misdeeds being listed first. The Norwich jurors also related seemingly random offences that varied widely: 108 crimes do not fall into one of the regularly reported categories. In 1288, for example, the jurors reported that Emma de Ashwell and Martin Whiteside's

38 Rutledge, 'Immigration and population growth', p. 27; Carole Rawcliffe, 'Sickness and health', in Rawcliffe and Wilson (eds), *Medieval Norwich*, pp. 317–18.

39 Kowaleski, *Exeter*, p. 186; Britnell, *Growth and Decline in Colchester*, p. 135; Penelope Dunn, 'Trade', in Rawcliffe and Wilson (eds), *Medieval Norwich*, p. 214.

40 Miriam Müller, 'Social control and the hue and cry in two fourteenth-century villages', *Journal of Medieval History*, 31 (2005), p. 32; Sandy Bardsley, *Venomous Tongues: Speech and Gender in Late Medieval England* (Philadelphia, 2006), p. 40; Edward Britton, *The Community of the Vill: A Study in the History of the Family and Village Life in Fourteenth-Century England* (Toronto, 1977), p. 40.

41 Rutledge, 'Immigration and population growth', p. 28.

wife commonly declined bare measures of corn and malt.[42] In 1375 the jurors reported that Thomas Tytel and Richard Jobbe were lepers and must abjure the city.[43] These sporadic insertions suggest that the capital pledges wielded discretionary power to determine what to present before the courts.[44]

Given that the marketplace was the nerve centre of the city, it is hardly surprising that economic infractions feature prominently in the rolls. Moreover, the capital pledges, who were often merchants and artisans, had a vested interest in creating an atmosphere where commerce could thrive.[45] Regulating trade could reduce transaction costs by providing consistent conditions for trade – though the volume of business brought before the courts may also indicate that this endeavour was not entirely successful.[46] Approximately 63 per cent of the business of the Norwich leet courts involved breaking the assize, forestalling the market, bad workmanship, perpetrating fraud, or selling without being in the freedom of the city (Table 6.2).

Fines for breaking the assize of ale were, by volume, the most common offence, accounting for about 30 per cent of all presentments. Although the leet courts could theoretically deal with the assize of bread, in Norwich bread sales were regulated separately and do not appear in the leet rolls (alternative policing mechanisms likely account for the lack of presentments for baking or brewing in the London Portsoken presentments as well).[47] Offences related to the assize of ale were reported far less often in the surviving presentment roll than in the amercement rolls. In the presentment roll from 1288, the assize accounts for only 13 per cent of presentments – significantly less than the average of 37 per cent in the amercement rolls from 1313 and earlier. Fines for breaking the assize in the amercement rolls are listed together (even in the rolls prior to 1313), and the names of the brewers often appear in the same order across multiple rolls. The repetition suggests that the names were copied (though it is possible that there was another ordering principle – brewers may, for example, have been entered geographically). It seems likely, therefore, that the jurors did not report all of the brewers; instead, the names of the people who brewed the previous year were entered into the list when the amercement rolls were composed. Alternatively, as in Colchester, it is possible that

42 NRO, NCR Case 5B/1 m. 1r.

43 NRO, NCR Case 5B/9 m. 2d.

44 McIntosh, *Controlling Misbehavior*, p. 8; Maddern, 'Order and disorder', p. 195; Rosser, *Medieval Westminster*, p. 234; Butler, 'Local concerns', p. 827; Anthony Musson, 'Lay participation: the paradox of the jury', *Comparative Legal History*, 3 (2015), p. 251; Klerman, 'Was the jury ever self-informing?', p. 127.

45 Sagui, 'A prosopography', pp. 106–7; Frost, 'The urban elite', p. 243; Hilton, 'Small town society', p. 68.

46 Kowaleski, *Exeter*, p. 191.

47 Hudson and Tingey, *Records of the City of Norwich*, vol. 1, pp. 174–6; Winter, 'The Portsoken presentments', p. 102.

assessors were selected to compile a list of brewers who were then recorded in the amercement rolls.[48] In the Norwich leet rolls, fines for breaking the assize were sometimes excused because they were not true, and the juries incurred no fines in these cases. We also see both capital pledges and their wives included frequently among those amerced for breaking the assize. The assize of ale, it seems, took on the character of a *de facto* tax for brewing.[49]

Some other market offences contained in the leet rolls may also have taken on the character of a tax, allowing offenders to repeat offences year after year. Take, for example, forestalling, which generally involved purchasing goods *en route* to the market and then reselling them. This definition of forestalling was comparatively new in the late thirteenth century, and it was not uniformly applied in English cities or even in Norwich.[50] Nevertheless, one might expect jurors to be concerned with this offence because it could have a serious impact on the market, by allowing sellers to manipulate market prices. Forestallers could also evade tolls on goods brought to market. Indeed, the Norwich custumal (c. 1308) treats forestalling as a serious offence. It dictates that on the first instance an offender should be heavily fined. On the second, according to the custumal, forestallers should have their merchandise confiscated and the offenders could be sent to the pillory. On the third offence, they should be punished as before and be forced to abjure the city. The custumal expressly states that, because forestalling 'is against the whole community', the bailiffs may not commute the punishment to a fine.[51] Judging by the number of reports of forestalling – about 16 per cent of the misdeeds reported before the leet courts involved forestalling – leet jurors were concerned with the practice. Perpetrators were, however, treated more leniently than the custumal would lead us to expect. Forestallers were fined before the leet courts repeatedly without any additional penalties. Ranulph le Pessuner, for example, was fined two shillings for forestalling in 1289. He was fined four shillings for the same offence in 1291, one mark in 1296, and half a mark in 1300. Each time, Ranulph was the first in a list of several men accused of forestalling – and in each instance the lists were similar.[52] Thus it appears that, as with the assize, fines for forestalling might have been copied over from one roll to the next. In essence, certain individuals may have effectively been allowed to continue this activity in exchange for filling the city coffers at

48 Britnell, *Growth and Decline in Colchester*, p. 89.

49 Hudson, *Leet Jurisdiction*, p. xxxviii; Judith M. Bennett, *Ale, Beer, and Brewsters in England: Women's Work in a Changing World, 1300–1600* (New York, 1996), pp. 4, 162; Kowaleski, *Exeter*, p. 39; Derek Keene, *Survey of Medieval Winchester*, vol. 1 (Oxford, 1985), p. 256; Britnell, *Growth and Decline in Colchester*, p. 89.

50 Richard H. Britnell, 'Forstall, forestalling and the Statute of Forestallers', *The English Historical Review*, 102 (1987), pp. 99, 102.

51 Hudson and Tingey, *Records of the City of Norwich*, vol. 1, pp. 181–3.

52 Hudson, *Leet Jurisdiction*, p. lxxiv.

the annual leet court. Norwich was not exceptional in its treatment of forestallers. Observing the same leniency in Exeter, Kowaleski suggested that the civic officials might have recognised that it would be impossible to effectively restrict forestalling. She also theorised that increasing penalties for repeat offenders may indicate an attempt to force men to join the freedom of the city.[53] In his study of Colchester, Britnell noted that, although the custumal dictated that forestallers should be expelled from the city, they were usually fined instead. Amercements were a more palatable punishment because they furnished more profit for the city.[54]

Fines for selling without being in the liberty of the city protected the rights of members of the freedom (including most of the capital pledges) by penalising those who sold in the market illicitly, and thereby limiting the competition. Whereas the frequency of fines for other economic offences remained roughly the same before and after the Black Death, fines for selling without being in the liberty of the city increased dramatically. In nine rolls from before the advent of plague, 5 per cent of cases dealt with selling without being in the freedom. This increased to nearly 30 per cent of indictments at the end of the fourteenth century (Table 6.2). The increased volume of fines for selling without being in the freedom was likely connected to a concerted effort by the Norwich elite to minimise competition and to enlarge the franchise of the city. This effort is also evidenced by a set of local regulations introduced in 1378, which increased the local bureaucracy's control over trade. As a result, the number of craftsmen and merchants who joined the franchise of the city tripled.[55] The attempt to limit competition suggests that economic regulation after the Black Death was directed at outside commerce. Fines for breaking the assize, which most often impacted local women, though still a sizeable portion of court business at the end of the fourteenth century, occupied a smaller portion of the business of the leets than in the pre-plague rolls. Fines for breaking the assize fell from nearly 40 per cent of presentments to just over 20 per cent.[56]

The two rolls from the latter half of the fourteenth century also include the first references to aliens and *Duchemen*. Although aliens and strangers in this context could refer to anyone who was not a member of the freedom of the city, the use of the term *Duchemen* suggests that there was increasing

53 Kowaleski, *Exeter*, p. 186.

54 Britnell, 'Forstall, forestalling', p. 102.

55 McRee, 'Peacemaking', p. 842; 'Richard II: October 1378', in Chris Given-Wilson, Paul Brand, Seymour Phillips, Mark Ormrod, Geoffrey Martin, Anne Curry and Rosemary Horrox (eds), *Parliament Rolls of Medieval England* (Woodbridge, 2005), British History Online at <http://www.british-history.ac.uk/no-series/parliament-rolls-medieval/october-1378> [accessed 1 June 2017]; Hudson and Tingey, *Records of the City of Norwich*, vol. 2, pp. xxxii, xxxix.

56 Kowaleski, *Exeter*, p. 132.

concern with people who were not from England. This anxiety about foreigners threatening trade can also be found in other English cities, especially London.[57] Although xenophobia became more pronounced in the fifteenth century, the shift in language in late fourteenth century Norwich suggests that, in the era after the Black Death, as mobility increased and the city faced increasing immigration, the capital pledges were concerned with protecting their place in the market.

Fines for selling bad goods (roughly 6 per cent of offences) constituted one final mechanism to regulate the marketplace. A wide range of offences fell into this category, including making fraudulent sales (selling the wrong hides, for example), selling spoiled meat, and the use of false weights and measures. Prosecutions for all of these crimes promoted a prosperous marketplace that protected residents of Norwich from the risk of purchasing tainted products. Although the courts continued to regulate these behaviours after the Black Death, the number of offences reported remained roughly consistent with the earlier rolls.

After economic offences, the next most frequent infractions in the leet rolls were common nuisances, which account for roughly 10 per cent of the total presentments (Table 6.1). Nuisances were a broad category of minor offences, including both environmental and social pollution.[58] Some actions, like blocking the river or digging up the street, could interrupt trade. Others, such as dumping muck into the street or owning a noisome dunghill, had a negative impact on public sanitation. The cases that came before the leet court were, in theory, those that had an impact on public welfare. For private disputes, neighbours could bring complaints to the bailiff's court.[59] The presentments before the Norwich leet court suggest that residents had a duty to care for the environment.[60] Urban dwellers were increasingly concerned with sanitation in the wake of the Black Death, as evidenced by increasing presentments for environmental offences.[61] In Norwich, fines increased from roughly 8 per

57 J. L. Bolton (ed.), *The Alien Communities of London in the Fifteenth Century: The Subsidy Rolls of 1440 and 1483–84* (Stamford, 1998), p. 2.

58 Sarah Rees Jones, 'The regulation of "nuisance": civic government and the built environment in the medieval city', in Maria do Carmo Ribeiro and Arnaldo Sousa Melo (eds), *Evoluçâi da Pausagen Urbana: Sociedade e Economia* (Braga, 2012), p. 284.

59 Helena Chew and William Kellaway (eds), *London Assize of Nuisance, 1301–1431: A Calendar* (London, 1973), p. xxiv.

60 Isla Fay, 'Health and disease in medieval and Tudor Norwich' (unpublished doctoral thesis, University of East Anglia, 2008), p. 286.

61 Carole Rawcliffe, *Urban Bodies: Communal Health in Late Medieval English Towns and Cities* (Woodbridge, 2013), pp. 7–9; Isla Fay, *Health and the City: Disease, Environment and Government in Norwich, 1200–1575* (York, 2015), p. 145; Fay, 'Health and disease', p. 292; Rees Jones, 'Regulation of "nuisance"', p. 286; Carole Rawcliffe, 'Sources for the study of public health in the medieval city', in Joel Rosenthal (ed.), *Understanding Primary Sources* (London, 2014), pp. 183–4; Dolly Jørgensen, '"All Good Rule of the Citee" and civic government in England, 1400–1600',

cent of cases in the early-fourteenth-century rolls to 14 per cent in the rolls following the Black Death, and *per capita* indictments increased by more than a factor of six. A similar pattern can be detected in other cities. In London, for example, orders for keeping the streets clean increased four-fold in the same period.[62] It is difficult to say whether the overriding concern in Norwich and elsewhere was health and sanitation, or if it was protection of trade – regulating nuisance could be inspired by either – but we clearly see the capital pledges taking an increasing interest in their physical and social environment at the end of the fourteenth century.

The fourteenth century also witnessed increased citations for violations against the court itself: being out of tithing and failure to attend court (Table 6.3). Taken together, these offences account for about 9 per cent of cases. The capital pledges functioned as representatives of their tithing groups when they presented offences at the leet court. In order to maintain this system, any man who had lived in the city for a year and a day (or who came of age having grown up in the city) was supposed to take an oath and join a tithing group.[63] While the function and decline of the frankpledge system is a matter for debate, it is clear that the capital pledges of Norwich sought to maintain the system by fining those who did not participate in it.[64] Their efforts might explain why the frankpledge system seems to have survived longer in Norwich than in many other towns.[65] Unlike many of the other offences previously discussed, there are no surviving examples in which an individual was fined for being out of tithing more than once. This evidence suggests that after someone was fined, he was either enrolled in a tithing or asked to leave the city. It is possible that these fines functioned as an entry fee to the tithing for certain individuals. Given the relatively small number of fines compared to the large number of people enrolled in the Mancroft tithing roll, not everyone was subjected to such fines. Nor were fines for entry reserved for immigrants;

Journal of Urban History, 36 (2010), p. 302; Ernest Sabine, 'City cleaning in mediaeval London', *Speculum*, 12 (1937), p. 30.

62 Rawcliffe, *Urban Bodies*, p. 34.

63 Rutledge, 'Immigration and population growth', p. 19.

64 Morris, *Frankpledge*; Schofield, 'The late medieval view of frankpledge'; D. A. Crowley, 'The later history of frankpledge', *Bulletin of the Institute of Historical Research*, 48 (1975), pp. 11–14; Kenneth C. Newton and Marjorie Keniston McIntosh, 'Leet jurisdiction in Essex manor courts during the Elizabethan period', *Essex Archaeology and History: Transactions of the Essex Archaeological Society*, 3rd ser., 13 (1981), p. 3; William Stubbs, *The Constitutional History of England in its Origin and Development*, 5th edn, vol. 1 (Oxford, 1891), pp. 94–5; William Holdsworth, *A History of English Law*, 7th edn (London, 1956), vol. 1, pp. 76–8, vol. 2, p. 104; Frederic W. Maitland, 'Leet and tourn', in Helen Cam (ed.), *Selected Historical Essays of F. W. Maitland* (Cambridge, 1957), pp. 41–51; Frederick Pollock and Frederic W. Maitland, *The History of English Law before the Time of Edward I*, 2nd edn, vol. 1 (Cambridge, 1968), pp. 568–71; Paul Hyams, *Rancor and Reconciliation in Medieval England* (Ithaca, NY, 2003), pp. 115–16.

65 Hudson, *Leet Jurisdiction*, pp. x–xi; Morris, *Frankpledge*, p. 25.

there are examples of sons of Norwich residents being fined for failure to enrol in tithings, even while they still lived with their fathers.[66]

The end of the fourteenth century witnessed a dramatic increase in fines for not attending court (Table 6.3). As with fines for being out of tithing and the changes in record-keeping discussed above, this shift indicates an active attempt to bolster the leet court. All of those fined were men, and approximately one-fifth of those amerced for failure to appear were also cited for being out of tithing. Whereas fines for being out of tithing represent an attempt to preserve the leets as a system for law enforcement, however, increased fines for failure to attend court might indicate that attendance had declined and had to be enforced, or that the people of Norwich were pursuing their interests in competing courts. If, as Daniel Smail has suggested, medieval people used the courts to enhance their control over their lives, they also had the power as consumers of justice to determine where to bring their complaints.[67] Any decline in the leet courts could, therefore, be explained by the increasing popularity of another court. However, given the public nature of justice, the leet courts had to be well attended to be fully effective. Therefore, penalties for absences from court may have been intended to increase attendance, thereby legitimising the court and augmenting its impact. Alternatively, the shift might indicate that, because of increased immigration after the Black Death, there were more people who had not been in the city very long and who had to be conditioned to use the leet court. The latter explanation would also, perhaps, reflect a concern with regulating foreigners. Either way, at the end of the fourteenth century there are indications that the people of Norwich perceived enough value in the leet courts to maintain them – which is hardly surprising since the leets were a significant source of income for the town, even if only a quarter of the fines were being collected. The civic authorities also attempted to preserve the authority of the leet courts by preventing residents from using the ecclesiastical courts for matters unrelated to marriage or wills. Although indictments for bringing cases before ecclesiastical courts were limited, there were at least two cases in each complete roll and twenty indictments in 1313 (which also supports the thesis that the civic authorities were actively concerned with strengthening the leet court and increasing the business it handled in that year).

Criminal misdemeanours (including assault, hamsoken and theft) also appear frequently in the rolls, accounting for roughly 9 per cent of indictments (Table 6.1). Both assault and theft are likely under-reported, because

66 Sarah Rees Jones, 'Household, work and the problem of mobile labour: the regulation of labour in medieval English towns', in James Bothwell, P. J. P. Goldberg and W. Mark Ormrod (eds), *The Problem of Labour in Fourteenth-Century England* (York, 2000), pp. 143–5.

67 Daniel Lord Smail, *The Consumption of Justice: Emotions, Publicity, and Legal Culture in Marseille, 1264–1423* (Ithaca, NY, 2013), pp. 18–20.

the leet courts would not have been the only way such infractions could be handled. Theft of goods over a specified value constituted a felony rather than a misdemeanour, and fell under the jurisdiction of the gaol delivery courts. Likewise, if anyone died from injuries inflicted during an assault, the case would be referred to justices of the gaol delivery. It was also possible for victims to bring a private suit against their assailants. Given the jurisdiction of the leet court and its focus on crimes against the common good, it is surprising that criminal misdemeanours appear as frequently as they do. Their inclusion in the rolls indicates that these crimes were perceived to be a threat to the community. Nevertheless, the evidence suggests that, with the exception of 1313 (when there was an unusually high number of assault and hamsoken indictments), violent crimes were never the primary concern of the leet court. It is unclear why there was a spike in presentments of assault in 1313; there is no record of a riot or other noteworthy turmoil in that year. The grain prices in Norfolk did, however, experience inflation in that year, which may have increased criminal activity – or at least, concern about crime.[68]

One final category of crime that received significant attention in the rolls was misuse of the hue and cry, accounting for about 2 per cent of indictments. As early as 1313, the leet rolls indicate that there was increased regulation of the hue; the rolls begin to report justified usage of the hue in addition to misuse in that year.[69] By 1375 there are signs of decline of the hue, which likely indicates an attempt by civic authorities to maintain peacekeeping mechanisms within their own hands.[70] As with several of the other changes discussed, the desire to crack down on the hue might have been inspired by the influx of poor, migrant labourers. Such workers, especially women, were disproportionately likely to use the hue because they lacked other mechanisms to get their grievances heard.[71]

Conclusion

The Norwich leet courts functioned fairly consistently throughout this period. Between 1288 and 1391 the court met once annually and heard presentments made by groups of capital pledges, who represented a few named parishes.

68 Hanawalt, *Crime in East Anglia*, p. 15.

69 Samantha Sagui, 'The hue and cry in medieval English towns', *Historical Research*, 87 (2014), pp. 189–90.

70 Sagui, 'The hue and cry', pp. 192–3; Judith Bennett, *Women in the Medieval English Countryside: Gender and Household in Brigstock before the Plague* (Oxford, 1987), p. 41; Bardsley, *Venomous Tongues*, p. 40; Müller, 'Social control', p. 30.

71 Rutledge, 'Immigration and population growth', p. 28; Sagui, 'The hue and cry', pp. 192–3; P. J. P. Goldberg, *Women, Work and Life Cycle in a Medieval Economy: Women in York and Yorkshire c. 1300–1520* (Oxford, 1992), pp. 225–32, 290–1; P. J. P. Goldberg, 'Urban identity and the poll taxes of 1377, 1379, and 1381', *Economic History Review*, new ser., 43 (1990), pp. 197, 212.

The organisation of the records changed between 1307 and 1313, at which time presentments began to be recorded in the same order for each sub-leet, which suggests an increase in oversight. At this time the number of indictments soared. Two of the sub-leets were combined sometime between 1313 and 1375, likely in an attempt to decrease the total number of capital pledges required to make presentments as each sub-leet needed a minimum of twelve. This change helped ensure the continued viability of the system in the wake of the Black Death. Both the reorganisation of the presentments and the shifting boundaries of the sub-leets suggest an active attempt to bolster the leet court and to maximise the profits it could generate for the town.

The punishments dispensed by the court remained consistent; it could issue fines and, occasionally, order an arrest. However, it could not adjudicate felonious crimes, nor did it deal with interpersonal disputes. Instead, it was concerned with crimes affecting the entire community. Although the amercements it assigned could be significant, it appears that the court did not collect the fines effectively. Instead, its power lay primarily in making misbehaviour public and thereby tarnishing the reputation of offenders.

Throughout the period under consideration, the leet courts were predominantly concerned with economic transgressions, but the focus of the presentments shifted in a few noteworthy ways. Although the number of presentments for breaking the assize of ale, for forestalling and for bad workmanship remained fairly consistent, there was a significant increase in the number of presentments made for selling without being in the freedom of the city. This change, along with the emergence of language about foreigners, suggests increasing xenophobia and protectionism. It may also represent an attempt to force men to join the freedom by penalising them for failure to do so. After the Black Death, there was also an increase in fines punishing public nuisances; this helped to protect and augment trade, but may also have been a response to the pestilence and the concomitant heightened concern about public sanitation. A third change – the increase in fines for failure to attend the leet court – demonstrates an official attempt to bolster the leet court and to increase the profits it could command. This effort, it seems, was successful, as the Norwich leet courts were still performing a critical role in policing the borough at the end of the fourteenth century.

TABLE 6.1: SUMMARY OF INFRACTIONS HEARD BY THE NORWICH LEET COURTS, 1288–1391

Year	Economic		Nuisances		Court Violations		Violent		Other		Total
	No.	%	No.	%	No.	%	No.	%	No.	%	No.
1288	91	35	32	12	36	14	49	19	54	21	262
1289	512	72	53	7	48	7	27	4	75	10	715
1290	23	30	18	24	9	12	9	12	17	22	76
1291	341	62	61	11	69	13	26	5	55	10	552
1293	483	83	31	5	23	4	27	5	20	3	584
1296	392	64	31	5	38	6	23	4	131	21	615
1300	506	60	98	12	98	12	78	9	64	8	844
c.1307	33	54	4	7	9	15	14	23	1	2	61
1313	553	58	79	8	38	4	217	23	67	7	954
1375	624	62	154	15	101	10	84	8	51	5	1014
1391	827	67	161	13	130	11	70	6	43	3	1231
Total	4385	63	722	10	599	9	624	9	578	8	6908

SOURCE: Norwich Leet Rolls Database (from NRO NCR Case 5B/1-11)

NOTES: The 1288, 1291 and 1307 rolls are presentment rolls; all of the others are amercement rolls. Also note that the 1291 and 1307 rolls are incomplete.

TABLE 6.2: ECONOMIC INFRACTIONS IN NORWICH LEET COURTS, 1288–1391

Year	Assize		Forestalling		Bad Work		Not in freedom	
	No.	%	No.	%	No.	%	No.	%
1288	35	13	35	13	21	8	0	0
1289	311	43	122	17	55	8	24	3
1290	5	7	17	22	0	0	1	1
1291	177	32	74	13	83	15	7	1
1293	298	51	113	19	50	9	22	4
1296	255	41	127	21	81	13	29	5
1300	277	33	183	22	10	1	36	4
c.1307	2	3	22	36	0	0	9	15
1313	257	27	131	14	62	6	103	11
1375	218	21	136	13	6	1	262	26
1391	276	22	130	11	37	3	381	31
Total	2111	31	1090	16	405	6	874	13

SOURCE: Norwich Leet Rolls Database (from NRO NCR Case 5B/1–11)

NOTE: Indictments that listed multiple infractions are counted twice in this chart. For example, if a single indictment listed both fraudulent work and forestalling it is listed twice.

TABLE 6.3: COURT VIOLATIONS IN NORWICH LEET COURTS, 1288–1391

Year	**Out of Tithing**		**Not coming to court**	
	No.	%	No.	%
1288	36	14	0	0
1289	48	7	0	0
1290	9	12	0	0
1291	69	13	0	0
1293	23	4	0	0
1296	21	3	17	3
1300	98	12	0	0
c.1307	3	5	6	10
1313	32	3	6	1
1375	21	2	100	10
1391	66	5	84	7
Total	426	6	173	3

SOURCE: Norwich Leet Rolls Database (from NRO NCR Case 5B/1–11)

NOTE: There were twenty men in 1375 and another twenty men in 1391 who were fined for being out of tithing and for failure to attend court. They are counted twice (once in each column).

7

THE BLACK DEATH AND THE BOROUGH COURT: THE CHANGING PATTERN OF SOCIAL AND JUDICIAL REPRESENTATION IN LATE MEDIEVAL LINCOLN

ALAN KISSANE

The impact of the Black Death upon urban communities is, and has been for many years, a subject of much scholarly debate. In the past fifty years alone, consideration has been given over to the issues of demography,[1] urban decline,[2] social and economic policy,[3] labour legislation,[4] developments in

1 John Hatcher, 'England in the aftermath of the Black Death', *Past and Present*, 144 (1994), pp. 3–35; Maryanne Kowaleski, 'The demography of maritime communities in late medieval England', in Mark Bailey and Stephen Rigby (eds), *Town and Countryside in the Age of the Black Death: Essays in Honour of John Hatcher* (Turnhout, 2012), pp. 87–118; Jens Röhrkasten, 'Trends of mortality in late-medieval London (1348–1400)', *Nottingham Medieval Studies*, 45 (2001), pp. 172–209.

2 Alan Dyer, *Decline and Growth in English Towns 1400–1640* (Cambridge, 1991); Richard Britnell, 'The Black Death in English towns', *Urban History*, 21:2 (1994), pp. 195–210; Keith Lilley, 'Urban planning after the Black Death: townscape transformation in later medieval England (1350–1530)', *Urban History*, 42:1 (2015), pp. 22–42. For a recent discussion of the 'urban decline' debate, see Alan Kissane, *Civic Community in Late Medieval Lincoln: Urban Society and Economy in the Age of the Black Death, 1289–1409* (Woodbridge, 2017), pp. 93–123.

3 Jim Bolton, '"The world upside down": plague as agent of economic and social change', in W. Mark Ormrod and Phillip G. Lindley (eds), *The Black Death in England* (Stamford, 1996), pp. 17–78; James Davis, 'Selling food and drink in the aftermath of the Black Death', in Bailey and Rigby, *Town and Countryside*, pp. 351–406.

4 Robert Braid, 'Behind the Ordinance of Labourers: economic regulation and market control in London before the Black Death', *Journal of Legal History*, 34:1 (2013), pp. 3–30; Robert C.

building and architecture,[5] shifting religious and pious trends,[6] burials,[7] urban sanitation and health,[8] the role and status of women,[9] even extents of debt,[10] all of which complement general studies of the pestilence,[11] which touch upon the urban experience at various junctures. One area hitherto neglected, however, is that of the borough court. Certainly, few studies have systematically tackled the extent to which the Black Death influenced the various procedures, customs and practices of urban courts.[12]

This chapter seeks to redress this lacuna by demonstrating how records of urban property disputes can effectively be used to illuminate changes to the social and judicial landscape of towns in the pre- and post-Black Death periods in new ways. More specifically, it is argued here that such records not only remain important for identifying the process by which the borough court played an increasingly central role in the ordinary lives of local inhabitants in the years immediately following the Black Death, but also that they demonstrate how shifting patterns of representation at a local level reveal a pragmatic response by survivors to existing practices.

Focus throughout this discussion will be placed on a single, albeit common, type of judicial plea known as *writ de recto* (writ of right), which dealt with disputes over lands and property. Containing various details, including the names of litigants and their representatives (identified here as 'electors'), these records can be used as a basis to reconstruct local judicial relationships by considering how they shifted during a period of demographic upheaval.

Palmer, *English Law in the Ages of the Black Death, 1348–1381* (London, 1993); W. Mark Ormrod, 'The politics of pestilence', in Ormrod and Lindley, *The Black Death in England*, pp. 147–81; Anthony Musson, 'New labour laws, new remedies? Legal reaction to the Black Death "crisis"', in N. Saul (ed.), *Fourteenth Century England*, I (Woodbridge, 2000), pp. 73–88.

5 Phillip Lindley, 'The Black Death and English art: a debate and some assumptions', in Ormrod and Lindley, *The Black Death in England*, pp. 125–46.

6 Christopher Maklin, 'Stability and change in the composition of a "plague Mass" in the wake of the Black Death', *Plainsong and Medieval Music*, 25:2 (2016), pp. 167–89; Christopher Harper-Bill, 'The English church and English religion after the Black Death', in Ormrod and Lindley, *The Black Death in England*, pp. 79–123.

7 Barney Sloane, *The Black Death in London* (London, 2011).

8 Carole Rawcliffe, *Urban Bodies: Communal Health in Late Medieval English Towns and Cities* (Woodbridge, 2013).

9 Caroline Barron, 'The "golden age" of women in medieval London', *Reading Medieval Studies*, 15 (1989), pp. 35–58; P. J. P. Goldberg, *Women, Work and Life Cycle in a Medieval Economy: Women in York and Yorkshire c. 1300–1520* (Oxford, 1992); Matthew Frank Stevens, 'London women, the courts and the "golden age": a quantitative analysis of female litigants in the fourteenth and fifteenth centuries', *London Journal*, 37:2 (2012), pp. 67–88.

10 Richard Britnell, *Growth and Decline in Colchester, 1300–1525* (Cambridge, 1986), pp. 98–114.

11 Ole J. Benedictow, *The Black Death, 1346–1353: The Complete History* (Woodbridge, 2008), pp. 123–45, 342–79; Philip Ziegler, *The Black Death* (Stroud, 1969); Colin Platt, *King Death: The Black Death and its Aftermath in Late Medieval England* (London, 1996), pp. 19–32.

12 One exception being Matthew Stevens, who, through an analysis of the city's court records, identifies an enhancement in female economic opportunities in post-Black Death London: Stevens, 'London women'.

Evidence of these pleas is drawn from Lincoln's Burwarmote Book, a register kept by the local borough or Burwarmote court, which recorded issues relating to lands and properties held within the civic jurisdiction.[13] In all, these cover a period of fifty-three years (from 1323 to 1376), thus enabling pre- and post-Black Death comparisons to be made.[14]

Whilst in many cases the evidence presented here is brief or formulaic – there being few details relating to the exact location of disputed properties or lands, or indeed to the exact street locations of those involved in disputes – it is nevertheless possible (by cross-referencing these pleas against other surviving records, including lay subsidies, charters and wills) to identify the parish of residence of many of those named, as well as some indication of their status and wealth. From a methodological point of view, this approach favours wealthier townspeople, in particular those owning or holding lands and property. However, in no way does this negate the conclusions put forward here, as it serves to demonstrate how judicial representation became increasingly centralised after the Black Death, as electors began to be chosen for their links to the borough court, not the parish, as was the custom prior to the disaster. Whilst for many towns the absence of precise residential markers might otherwise preclude spatial analysis,[15] Lincoln's forty-six small intra- and extramural parishes provide a useful framework through which individual locations might be identified (Map 7.1).

During this period Lincoln was the largest town in the Midlands, housing a population of approximately 12,300 on the eve of the Black Death, and it ranked as one of the top five urban centres in England after London (Map 7.1).[16] As a provincial capital, it had well-established links to the wool and cloth trades, both at home and abroad, and it maintained a large and wealthy mercantile class, many of whom served the local civic government. Through the cathedral and castle, the city was also the spiritual and judicial point of focus for many of the county's inhabitants, thus marking Lincoln out as one of the leading English towns during the late medieval period.[17]

13 Burwarmote Book, Lincoln Cathedral Library, MS 169 (hereafter BB). For Lincoln's jurisdictions, see Kissane, *Civic Community*, pp. 10–13 and table 1.

14 For details of the register, see Reginald M. Thomson, *Catalogue of the Manuscripts of Lincoln Cathedral Chapter Library* (Cambridge, 1989), pp. 135–6, and F. W. Brooks, *Calendar of the Rolls of the Lincoln Court of Burghmanmote*, L[incoln] A[rchive] O[ffice], FL/TRANSCRIPTS/U/28.

15 For example, such an approach would be impossible in towns such as Boston or Lynn, which had only one parish each, or Beverley, Bury St Edmunds and Coventry, which had only two parishes in c. 1300: Jennifer Kermode, 'The greater towns, 1300–1540', in David M. Palliser (ed.), *Cambridge Urban History of Britain: 600–1540*, vol. 1 (Cambridge, 2000), pp. 442–3.

16 Bruce M. S. Campbell, 'Benchmarking medieval economic development: England, Wales, Scotland, and Ireland, c. 1290', *Economic History Review*, 61:4 (2008), pp. 896–945, at p. 908, table 4; Alan Dyer, 'Ranking of towns by taxpaying population: the 1377 poll tax', in Palliser, *Cambridge Urban History*, vol. 1, pp. 758–60.

17 For Lincoln's civic records, see Kissane, *Civic Community*, pp. 7–10, 126–9. For Lincoln more

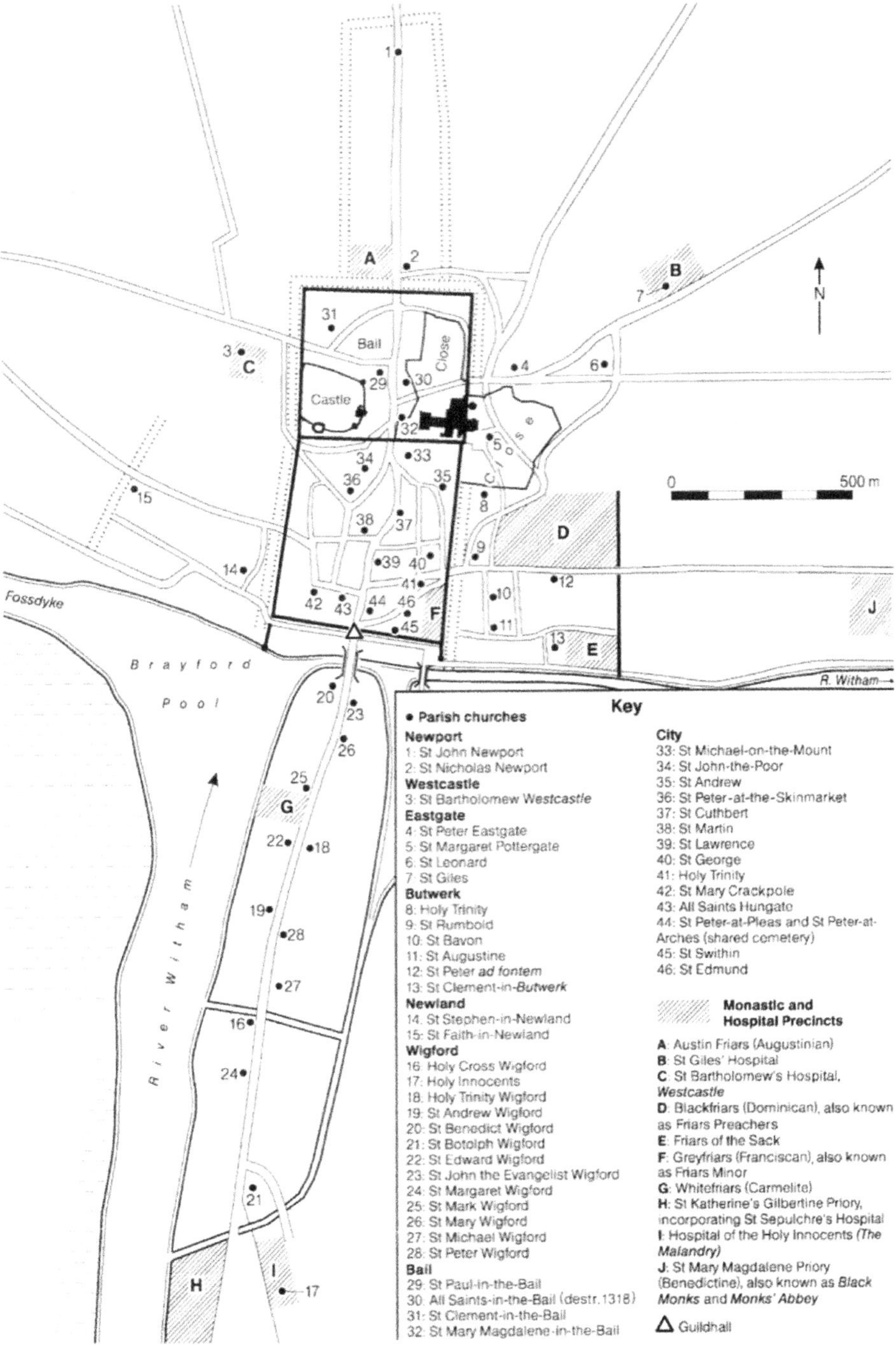

MAP 7.1: LINCOLN C. 1350

Pleas of *Writ de Recto*

Pleas of *writ de recto* were extremely common throughout the later Middle Ages, and were invoked when customary or hereditary rights to lands and property were disputed. This included challenges to rents, the right of pasturage and habitation, and (less frequently) hereditary transfers.[18] Whilst these pleas were most commonly placed before a grand assize or inquest, which decided who held the greater right to the disputed lands or properties,[19] this practice differed from manor and leet courts which, after 1300, looked to a presentment jury to judge disputes over land.[20] Although lists of names of men serving on juries and assizes remain instructive for understanding local structures of power and status in both urban and agrarian settings,[21] the main concern here is the relationship between litigants and 'electors' – men otherwise chosen directly by litigants, who were tasked with appointing suitable jurors to serve on the assize. By analysing these relationships, it becomes possible to identify, at least in broad outline, the type of men who had access to the levers of power in the city and how this changed over time, in particular in the post-Black Death period.

Yet before considering these relationships, it is first important to outline the two main approaches to establishing the grand assize. Take, for example, the custom of Beverley, where the community played a central role, it being stated in the fourteenth century that:

> If after any one's death certain persons claim to have right in his tenement, and intrude upon his tenement, we will that the serjeant of the town and the community shall enter with them on behalf of the community to keep the peace till the next court, and then inquest shall be made by the community and the bailiff as to who has the nearest right, and the tenement shall be restored to him.[22]

This differs significantly from the recorded custom of Winchester, dating from c. 1280, where the community played no such role. There the accused

generally: Kissane, *Civic Community*, passim; James W. F. Hill, *Medieval Lincoln* (Cambridge, 1948; reprint Stamford, 1990), pp. 239–69; David Stocker (ed.), *The City by the Pool: Assessing the Archaeology of the City of Lincoln* (Oxford, 2003), pp. 159–317.

18 Frederick Pollock and Frederic W. Maitland, *The History of English Law Before the Time of Edward I*, 2 vols (Cambridge, 1898), vol. 2, pp. 62–3.

19 Before the fourteenth century, trial by battle was seen as a viable alternative for settling such disputes: Pollock and Maitland, *History of English Law*, vol. 2, p. 62. For the issue of 'greater right', see also pp. 75–8.

20 Mark Bailey, *The English Manor, c. 1200 – c. 1500* (Manchester, 2002), pp. 172–5.

21 See, for example, John B. Post, 'Jury lists and juries in the late fourteenth century', in J. S. Cockburn and T. A. Green (eds), *Twelve Good Men and True: The Criminal Trial Jury in England, 1200–1800* (Princeton, 1988), pp. 65–77.

22 Mary Bateson (ed.), *Borough Customs*, 2 vols (London, 1904), vol. 1, pp. xix, 237–8.

were granted forty days to answer a summons, at which point they were to be judged by twelve learned men (*prud'hommes*), all of whom were chosen by the local court.[23] Whilst it is unnecessary to read too much into this procedural distinction, it is nevertheless possible that at Beverley the involvement of local inhabitants in the judicial process may have been seen as a source of pride, whereas at Winchester it may have been seen as an imposition by the civic authorities.

Turning to Lincoln, it is possible to identify how, at the beginning of the fourteenth century, the process of establishing an assize in a plea of *writ de recto* was identical to that of Winchester.[24] However, a change occurred in 1323 which served to transfer the decision-making process from the court to the litigants themselves, as at Beverley.[25] The first recorded plea to do so was that involving John and Margaret Jowel, querents, and Christina, wife of Hamo de la Dale, deforciant, enrolled in February of that year before the Burwarmote court, which was located in the guildhall above the city's southern intramural gate, the Stonebow (Map 7.1).[26] In this dispute over one messuage and appurtenances (location not cited), it was stated that both parties were free to place themselves on an inquest of twenty-four men in the 'form of the great assize' (*forma magnus assisa*), and that both parties were to elect (*elegerunt*) four men (two individuals each), who were to choose from themselves and others (*de ipsus et alii*) twenty-four proved and lawful men who would speak their will (*dicere voluntatum*).[27] In other words, the four men (or electors) were selected by the litigants to choose twenty-four individuals to make up the great assize, which may or may not have included the electors themselves, and which collectively decided the outcome of the case.[28] Whilst the exact reasons behind this change are unknown, it is likely that it formed part of the wider municipal reforms of the early fourteenth century following the restitution of Lincoln's civic liberties, including, for example, new mayoral terms of office, innovative methods of recording civic business (the newly instituted Burwarmote Book being one example of this), and new civic ordinances (known as the 'Provisions of Lincoln').[29] This marked the

23 Bateson (ed.), *Borough Customs*, vol. 1, p. 253. See also the similar processes recorded for Cork and Kilkenny, pp. 256–7, 262.

24 For example, BB, fols 86–87, 88.

25 For two known cases dating after 1323 employing the method of Winchester: BB, fols 218 (1352) and 261–261v (1366).

26 For details of this court, see Kissane, *Civic Community*, pp. 12, 79, 148–9.

27 BB, fol. 94. For earlier disputes between these litigants, see BB, fols 85, 88, 90v.

28 It is impossible to say whether electors confirmed their right to take their place on the assize, as no accompanying lists of the assize are ever given. Lists of jurors are given in cases of fresh force and novel disseisin: for example, BB, fols 89, 112v, 133. For the differences between these cases and *writ de recto*, see Pollock and Maitland, *History of English Law*, vol. 2, pp. 47–53, 614, 621 n. 1.

29 Kissane, *Civic Community*, pp. 126–9.

end of eleven years of direct rule (from 1289 to 1300) by the king's representative, known as the *custos* or keeper, following fiscal abuses by several leading citizens in the 1280s.[30] It is thus useful to identify this development as part of the sweeping changes to civic procedures at this time, which sought anew to legitimate and consolidate authority with the blessing and consent of the wider body politic.

The significance of this shift is two-fold. First, it helps identify how associates and neighbours were provided with a platform from which they might become more involved in judicial practices, as they were the ones most likely to be *chosen* by litigants; and secondly, it provides a tangible means through which to understand how urban networks were constituted during a period of unprecedented demographic upheaval. Of course, the involvement of neighbours in judicial affairs was by no means innovative, and evidence of this exists for other towns prior to the 1320s. For example, at Leicester in 1277 it was said in cases of thwartnay that 'if the parties by consent wish to put themselves on an inquest of neighbours who know the truth of this thing, let the inquest be taken'.[31] In 1291 at Ipswich, too, cases of fresh force saw an assize of twelve neighbours summoned to try the case.[32] Throughout much of the Middle Ages, such intervention was regarded as good practice, legitimating and justifying the methods by which the civic government ruled, whilst benefiting litigants themselves.[33]

In analysing the evidence of pleas (Figure 7.1), it is first important to qualify that, of the seventy-three cases employing this new system of dispute resolution between 1323 and 1376, only seventy can be used, as three pleas dating from 1370/1 omit the names of electors.[34] Of the remaining seventy, however, all can effectively be used to establish a spatial framework to explore the types of relationship which existed between litigants and electors. The following analysis (Figure 7.1) is divided into three categories according to the involvement of the individuals and their parish of residence, where known.

30 For the indictment of 1290, see *Calendar of Patent Rolls for the Reign of Edward I: 1281–1292*, vol. 2 (London, 1893), p. 404.

31 'Thwartnay' was the denial by the deforciants of all the querent's assertions during a plea: Pollock and Maitland, *History of English Law*, vol. 2, p. 615; Bateson (ed.), *Borough Customs*, vol. 1, p. 163.

32 'Fresh force' was the illegal seizure of another's lands or property: Bateson (ed.), *Borough Customs*, vol. 1, pp. 233–4.

33 For example, Benjamin McRee, 'Peacemaking and its limits in late medieval Norwich', *The English Historical Review*, 109 (1994), pp. 831–66; Carole Rawcliffe, '"That kindliness should be cherished more, and discord driven out": the settlement of commercial disputes by arbitration in later medieval England', in Jennifer Kermode (ed.), *Enterprise and Individuals in Fifteenth-Century England* (Stroud, 1991), pp. 99–117.

34 BB, fols 270v, 273v.

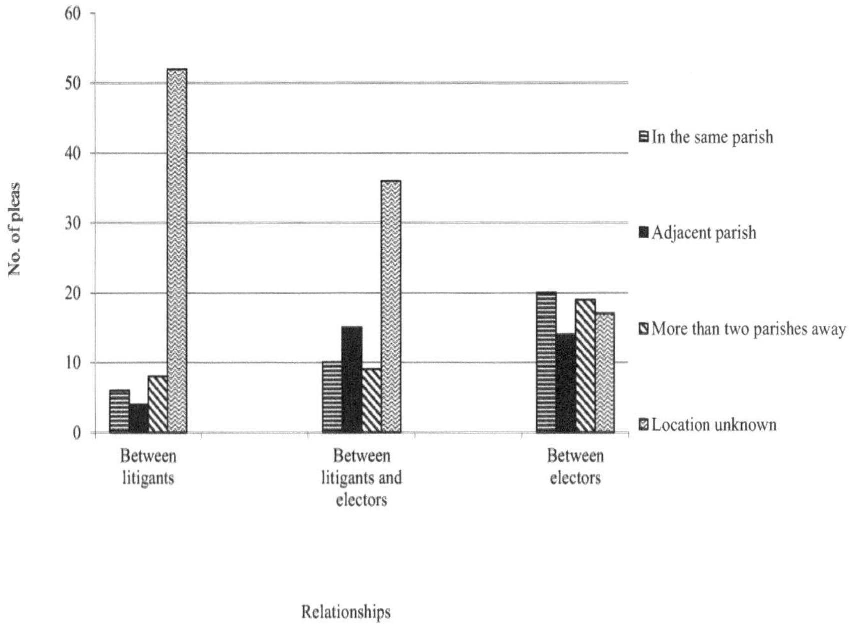

FIGURE 7.1: RELATIONSHIPS HIGHLIGHTED BY PLEAS OF *WRIT DE RECTO*

These categories record the residential pattern between litigants, litigants and electors, and electors, respectively. Each category is divided according to whether individuals were drawn from the same parish, from an adjacent parish or from further away. Whilst the residential pattern of litigants is relatively straightforward to establish, given that only two parishes need to be identified, it is less clear-cut for electors. For example, in a 1329 case involving John Morekok of Lincoln and his wife, Matilda, querents, against William de Welingoure, deforciant, only three of the four electors' locations are known: two lived in St Augustine (Alan de Hodelston and Henry de Humberston), whilst another lived in St Rumbold (Geoffrey de Welton).[35] In such cases, it is the *most* frequently recorded location of the electors, and not each separate location, that is used here. Where no predominant parish emerges from the evidence, as in the case of Dymmok versus Laundeby, Laun and Banbury in 1343, where three separate parish locations can be identified for the four electors,[36] the category 'more than two parishes away' has been chosen, as

35 BB, fol. 116v; TNA E 179/135/12, 16. The residence of the fourth elector, John de Carum, is unknown. For a more straightforward example, see the case dating from 1336 between Eudo Costard of Lincoln and his wife, Catherine, querents, against John de Thorp, deforciant; three of the four electors named (John le Mareschall, Henry atte Sudeness and Robert de Appilby) lived in St Peter, Eastgate; BB, fol. 131; TNA E 179/135/12.

36 BB, fol. 162: Simon de Graham lived in St Mary Crackpole, John de Thragilthorp in St

this typically represented a more disparate residential pattern for electors.

Disregarding pleas where the locations of the participants are unknown, of the 102 relationships identified here, thirty-three cases involved individuals from the same parish, thirty-three from adjacent parishes, and thirty-six from further afield (two parishes away or further). Such evidence demonstrates that two thirds of all pleas of *writ de recto* involved individuals from the same or an adjacent parish, highlighting that disputes were typically local matters which relied on local men for resolution, many of whom would have had first-hand knowledge of the locale and properties under dispute.[37]

Looking more closely at the evidence, it is clear from a case enrolled in 1347 between Robert de Drax of Lincoln and his wife, Isabel, against William Belle of Lincoln that this was indeed the case, with each living within the general vicinity of the guildhall in the parishes of St Edmund and St Benedict, respectively (Map 7.1).[38] Considering the general findings here, it is unsurprising to learn that all four electors – John de Fenton and Alan Faukes (for Robert and Isabel), and Stephen Russell and William de Braytoft (for William) – also lived in St Benedict, again emphasising that the land under dispute was possibly in St Benedict.[39]

A second case comes from June 1343, which saw John, son of John Yole of Lincoln, and his wife, Edusa, raise a plea against Simon Underwode de Derby, all of whom lived in Holy Trinity.[40] Three of the four electors were men from the local area, with Geoffrey de Welton and Henry de Edelyngton living in the adjacent parish of St Rumbold, whilst Henry de Brune lived slightly further away in St Augustine.[41]

In cases where the locations of both the querent and the deforciant remain unknown, evidence regarding electors is still illuminating. Take as a case in point the plea of William de Drayton and his wife, Isolde, who, along with William Durem and his wife, Emma, made a claim against John, son of Alan le Tannur, over a plot in the 'suburbs' in 1345.[42] Although the location of their domiciles is unknown, the combination of the reference to the suburbs and the fact that all four electors lived in parishes adjacent to one another in Wigford, Lincoln's southernmost suburb, suggests that the litigants lived

Edmund, and William de Thornhagh and John de Brunne both resided somewhere in the eastern suburb of Neuland. BB, fol. 155v; TNA E 179/135/12.

37 Despite this conclusion, the diversity of recorded locations for electors demonstrates that they were not local minor officials, such as tithing men. For more on this, see Pollock and Maitland, *History of English Law*, vol. 1, pp. 657–8; vol. 2, pp. 634–5.

38 BB, fols 178–178v, 191.

39 BB, fols 196, 197; TNA E 179/135/12, 16.

40 Underwode also held considerable lands there: Lincoln Archives Office (hereafter LAO) Dij 77/1/12, 16, 28–29, 31, 35, 42.

41 TNA E 179/135/12, 16.

42 BB, fol. 172v.

in close proximity to one another and that the property under dispute was also probably local.[43]

A final illustration comes from the plea involving John, son of Roger Ermyn, and his wife, Joan, against John de Northampton of Lincoln in 1360.[44] According to the short entry, the dispute (which related to a messuage held in a 'suburb') was heard at Westminster on 1 May 1360 and enrolled in Lincoln's records in June later that year, where a decision was made in favour of the querents. Fortunately, two charters dating from February 1359 and April 1360 highlight how both John and Joan, and John, all lived in the parish of St Augustine, thereby most likely placing the messuage in that parish.[45] Both charters record how John and Joan granted a messuage with a garden in *Wedensty* in St Augustine's called *Godelovehous* to John in 1356, suggesting that this may in fact have been the land under dispute. Furthermore, two of the three electors for which there is evidence also lived in St Augustine.[46]

Despite these obvious parochial ties, it would be wrong to suggest that in all pleas of *writ de recto* (especially in cases for which less detailed evidence survives) there was a direct link between the locations of the individuals named and the locations of the lands in dispute. For example, some of the disputes may have included lands outside the city, perhaps in the common fields; certainly no exact locations are ever recorded in any pleas, with entries typically noting only how the dispute related to 'one bovate of land in the suburb' or was 'concerning a shop'.[47] In addition to this, not all evidence points to relationships between individuals in single or even adjacent parishes, highlighting more disparate ties. Take as a case in point the 1359 plea between Adam de Leek and his wife, Agnes, querents, against Antony de Goldesburgh, canon of the cathedral, deforciant, over a messuage in the suburbs.[48] In this case the electors were drawn from all across the city: John Baret from St Michael in Wigford, John Brotherson from St Botolph in Wigford, John de Torkesay from St Mary Magdalene in the Bail, and William de Torkesay, possibly a relative of John, from St Peter in Eastgate (Map 7.1).[49] This raises two questions: firstly, where was the land held? And secondly, in pleas where electors had no obvious links, at least in terms of proximity to the litigants, why were they chosen? Whilst the first question has been discussed above,

43 For the deforciants, John de Whiten (St Margaret) and John de Hibaldstowe (St Margaret); for the querent, Thomas Frere (Holy Cross) and William Page (St Michael): TNA E 179/135/12.

44 BB, fol. 242.

45 LAO Dij 74/1/8, 18.

46 John de Barton and William Groo: BB, fol. 248; LAO Dij 74/2/6, 10. The third elector, Eudo Cooke, resided in St Botolph, Wigford: TNA E 179/135/12. The whereabouts of the fourth elector, Robert Haynton, is unknown.

47 BB, fols 143–143v, 155.

48 BB, fol. 241.

49 BB, fol. 253; TNA E 179/135/12, 16.

the second seemingly points to the fact that they were probably friends or extended kin, though more informal associations of trade and guild should not be discounted. As David Shaw has shown for Wells, 'friendship in the rich and proper sense that a medieval audience would have acknowledged, was often a contextual relationship', one based upon 'shared antipathy [and] shared circumstance'.[50] Put another way, these relationships might easily be described as 'structured friendships'.[51] To what extent can the relationships identified in pleas of *writ de recto* be characterised in this way?

One of the easiest methods of testing these relationships is to consider the frequency of reciprocity, as recorded in surviving court rolls. Of the 420 individuals named in the seventy pleas of *writ de recto* at Lincoln, only twenty (4.7 per cent) appeared as both litigant (querent or deforciant) and elector.[52] Of this group, not one person can be said to have acted reciprocally towards another, even when the opportunity arose. For example, although Robert de Misen acted as elector for Richard Kele in 1366, when the opportunity presented itself later that same year for him to return the favour, he was not chosen, or perhaps declined.[53] While such evidence remains anecdotal at best, it seems to suggest that, in pleas of *writ de recto*, electors were most frequently chosen for reasons other than friendship – namely, for their standing within the local community – and the majority were drawn from the litigant's neighbourhood.

Participants in Pleas of *Writ de Recto*

Of the seventy querents recorded in pleas of *writ de recto*, only eleven ever held one of the three leading civic positions in local government (mayor, bailiff and coroner), all of whom appeared alongside their spouse (Table 7.1). Even when the former sheriff (Gilbert de Ledered) and under-sheriff (Thomas de Carleton) are added to this group, it is clear that less than one fifth of all querents ever held official status.[54] No clergymen ever appeared as a querent. When this is compared to the status of deforciants, an altogether different picture emerges, with more than half (forty-three) holding civic office or serving as clergy – a point emphasising the well-established links between wealth, office and property-holding on the one hand, and the church and urban landholding

50 David G. Shaw, *Necessary Conjunctions: The Social Self in Medieval England* (Basingstoke, 2005), pp. 97–103, quote at p. 99.

51 Shaw, *Necessary Conjunctions*, p. 106.

52 This figure has been capped at 420 (seventy querents, seventy deforciants, 280 electors), despite there being multiple entrants in the former two categories. In these cases the male alone is considered, as no woman ever appeared as an elector. It is worth noting, however, that in the few cases made by or against groups, the principal (i.e. first) name is considered: for example, BB, fols 247, 253.

53 BB, fols 240v, 261–261v.

54 BB, fols 144, 224; TNA SC 8/57/2819; *Calendar of Close Rolls for the Reign of Edward III: 1330–1333*, vol. 2 (London, 1898), pp. 270, 382.

on the other.[55] Even so, it is important to recognise that, despite there being such a high proportion of deforciants coming from these two groups, they should not be seen as more litigious or aggressive than other landholders in defending or pursuing their rights; it is only that they were, on the whole, more likely to hold lands and properties due to their wealth.

TABLE 7.1: STATUS OF LITIGANTS APPEARING IN PLEAS OF *WRIT DE RECTO*

	Married couple (inc. officials)	**Lay group ∞**	**Single man (inc. officials)**	**Single woman**	**Clergy**	**Father & Daughter**	**Total**
Qu.	65 (13*)	3	1	1	0	0	70
De.	7 (4)	1	42 (22)	2	17	1	70

Key: * = includes one former sheriff and one former under-sheriff; ∞ = two or more couples; Qu.= querent; De. = deforciant.

Aside from those holding office, it is clear that there was a divide between the general status of querents and deforciants. In particular, although most pleas were brought before the borough court by married couples (sixty-five), they were primarily brought against men individually (forty-two), despite many of those men being married.[56] According to the doctrine of coverture, the husband's legal identity covered that of the woman he married.[57] However, these pleas demonstrate that, in practice, wives had the capacity to act alongside their husbands in litigation, apparently playing an important role in bringing these complaints.[58] Certainly, in a handful of cases – such as that of Robert de Waltham of Lincoln and Alice, his wife, against Thomas de Lokton and Beatrice, his wife, in 1342, or of John de Adynet and Rose,

55 For example, Gervase Rosser, 'The essence of medieval urban communities: the vill of Westminster, 1200–1540', in Richard Holt and Gervase Rosser (eds), *The Medieval Town in England, 1200–1540* (London, 1990), pp. 216–37; Richard Goddard, 'Church lords and English urban investment in the later Middle Ages', *Past and Present*, Supplement 2 (2007), pp. 148–65; Sarah Rees Jones, *York: The Making of a City, 1068–1350* (Oxford, 2013), pp. 138–234.

56 For example, Robert de Dalderby, who appeared on multiple occasions as a deforciant, was married twice – though in these cases he was noted alone. For his will, dated January 1363, see BB, fols 255v–260.

57 Tim Stretton and Krista J. Kesselring, 'Introduction: coverture and continuity', in Tim Stretton and Krista J. Kesselring (eds), *Married Women and the Law: Coverture in England and the Common Law World* (Montreal, 2013), p. 7.

58 For similar suggestions, see Cordelia Beattie, 'Living as a single person: marital status, performance and the law in late medieval England', *Women's History Review*, 17 (2008), pp. 327–40, at p. 334; Margot Finn, 'Women, consumption and coverture in England, c. 1760–1860', *The Historical Journal*, 39 (1996), pp. 703–22; Barbara Hanawalt, *The Wealth of Wives: Women, Law, and Economy in Late Medieval London* (Oxford, 2007), pp. 116–18; Cordelia Beattie and Matthew Frank Stevens (eds), *Married Women and the Law in Premodern Northwest Europe* (Woodbridge, 2013).

his wife, versus Peter de Bylughton and Elizabeth, his wife[59] – both man and wife were cited as deforciants, demonstrating that wives could also be named in the complaints of others. Quite why there is such a disparity between the status of named deforciants and querents is unclear, though it is possible that many pleas related to lands originally held or claimed by wives, suggesting that inherited or dower land was a key factor behind many of these disputes. Further research in this area would help to elucidate the role of husbands and wives in these joint pleas in Lincoln.

TABLE 7.2: FREQUENCY OF ELECTORS APPEARING IN PLEAS OF *WRIT DE RECTO*

	No. appearances by individuals (percentage of all appearances)				
Unique individuals	**One**	**Two-three**	**Four-five**	**Six-nine**	**Ten+**
170	122 (43.6%)	37 (28.9%)	5 (8.2%)	3 (6.4%)	3 (12.9%)

In terms of the electors, 170 men undertook this role on a total of 280 occasions (seventy cases, with four electors per case) (Table 7.2). Of these individuals, by far the most numerous were those appearing once (122). The sheer number of individuals involved in these cases supports the idea put forward at the outset that, by the 1320s, Lincoln's civic government sought to integrate the wider community in judicial practices wherever possible, underscoring how access to justice was not simply the preserve of the minority or elite. This was undoubtedly a symptom of and a reaction to the broader judicial developments of the thirteenth century, which saw an increasing number of ordinary people gain knowledge of the 'legal experience'.[60] Yet who were these people? The following table (Table 7.3) considers this question by identifying their taxable wealth, civic status and kinship ties.

TABLE 7.3: WEALTH AND STATUS OF ELECTORS APPEARING IN PLEAS OF *WRIT DE RECTO*

Independent actors	No. appearing in 1327, 1332 and 1340 subsidies	No. holding office	Relatives of officials
170	71 (41.2%)	49 (28.8%)	17 (10.0%)

SOURCE: TNA E 179/135/12, 16, 26)
NOTE: these figures are not cumulative, there being considerable overlap between categories.

59 BB, fols 157v–158, 231v.
60 Anthony Musson, *Medieval Law in Context: The Growth of Legal Consciousness from Magna Carta to the Peasants' Revolt* (Manchester, 2001), pp. 83–134.

More than 40 per cent of all individuals named as electors were recorded in the subsidies of 1327, 1332 and 1340 (taxes paid on movable goods at various rates),[61] which explains why there are more residences known for this group than for litigants (Figure 7.1). Even so, the majority of electors (roughly 60 per cent) were still those with no taxable wealth.[62] Despite this, the point here is not so much the overall figure (whatever that might be) – rather that, in pleas of *writ de recto*, the relative wealth of an individual was not necessarily a defining factor in his ability to effectively organise the assize on a litigant's behalf. A similar observation might also be made with regard to the status of electors, with a little over a quarter holding one of three main civic posts at one stage or another. Even when factoring in a further tenth of electors who can be identified as the relatives of officials, the overall picture alters little. Hence – much like wealth – office and social standing were not defining characteristics of electors, again underscoring the link between the communal knowledge and understanding of legal processes. When placed alongside the evidence of residential status previously identified, it is thus clear that electors were most frequently locally respected individuals drawn from their own neighbourhood. This was, of course, not without significance, as it increased the standing of the individual whilst simultaneously lending credence to the fairness and integrity of local judicial practices and customs.

However, despite these conclusions, this reading of the evidence is in many ways over-simplistic, as it ignores several important nuances of the data. In an attempt to redress this issue, the pleas heard at Lincoln have been reorganised into two distinct periods, before and after the Black Death (Table 7.4).

TABLE 7.4: THE IMPACT OF THE BLACK DEATH ON THOSE NAMED AS ELECTORS IN PLEAS OF *WRIT DE RECTO*

		Appearances (percentage of all cases)				
Dates	**Electors (Total named)**	**One**	**Two-three**	**four-five**	**six-nine**	**ten+**
1323–49	86 (108)	70 (64.8%)	15 (30.6%)	1 (4.6%)	0	0
1350–76	88 (172)	57 (33.7%)	21 (26.7%)	5 (12.8%)	2 (7%)	3 (19.8%)

61 Work on lay subsidies is extensive, but see John F. Hadwin, 'The medieval lay subsidies and economic history', *Economic History Review*, 36:2 (1983), pp. 200–17 and James F. Willard, *Parliamentary Taxes on Personal Property, 1290–1334* (Cambridge, MA, 1934).

62 This figure would undoubtedly have been higher had the returns of 1377 been complete.

The period after 1350 saw a marked drop in the proportion of electors appearing in pleas only once, with the figure falling by almost half. There was, however, a significant rise in the number of electors appearing four times or more, with five individuals appearing six times or more – something unheard of in the earlier period. More significant still is the fact that, whilst the overall number of pleas rose from only twenty-seven (1323–49) to forty-three (1350–76), this was actually a more dramatic rise than first appears, due to the loss of life inflicted by the Black Death and subsequent bouts of pestilence.[63] For the twenty-seven years after the pestilence, there were (pro rata) roughly three times as many pleas of *writ de recto* enrolled before the borough court, compared to the twenty-six years prior to the disaster,[64] demonstrating a sharp rise in landed disputes during this period. This was a common feature of English and European towns during this period, and it has been attributed to a combination of factors – including an increase in personal wealth (which brought with it the ability to buy up vacant holdings) and the dislocation of urban lands and properties, following the deaths of so many property holders in the plague (a problem exacerbated by issues over inheritance).[65] Yet who were these men appearing time and again as electors, and what was their status within Lincoln's civic society (Table 7.5)?

Of the eleven figures who appeared at least four times, ten (with the exception of John de Brune) made the majority of their appearances after 1350. Eight of the eleven men held civic office, with the remaining three (Richard de Dyke, John de Brune and Thomas Felissone) maintaining a strong presence in the surviving records, suggesting that they were well known and respected individuals.[66] This evidence marks a shift away from electors being drawn from a litigant's own parish of residence, towards those with a strong relationship to the borough court. This is illustrated most clearly by the fact that at least one of these men acted in thirty-five of the forty-three surviving pleas dating from after 1350. For the period before 1349, this number stood at a much more modest eight (out of twenty-seven). An illustration of the

63 The Black Death arrived in Lincoln in April 1349, finally subsiding by November. For the impact of the Black Death on the city, see Kissane, *Civic Community*, passim; and Anthony H. Thompson, 'The registers of John Gynewell, bishop of Lincoln, for the years 1347–1350', *Archaeological Journal*, 68 (1911), pp. 300–60.

64 For the period from 1323 to 1349, there was one plea per 455 inhabitants (pre-Black Death population of 12,300 people divided by twenty-seven), whereas between 1350 and 1376 there was one plea per 174 inhabitants (post-Black Death population of 7,500 people divided by forty-three). For these figures, see main text above.

65 For this issue see, for example, Richard Britnell, 'Town life', in Palliser, *Cambridge Urban History of Britain*, vol. 1, pp. 134–79; P. J. P. Goldberg, *Medieval England: A Social History, 1250–1550* (London, 2004), pp. 29–51; Christopher Dyer, *Standards of Living in the Later Middle Ages: Social Change in England, c. 1200–1520* (Cambridge, 1998), pp. 304–6.

66 For example, for Dyke, BB, fols 224v, 246v, 250–250v, 260–260v, 263, 272; for Brune, fols 146v, 154, 184, 214v–215, 218v; for Felissone, fols 213, 214v, 218v, 224v, 225v, 240v, 242, 247.

TABLE 7.5: STATUS OF ELECTORS RECORDED IN PLEAS OF *WRIT DE RECTO* FOUR TIMES OR MORE

Name	Profession/Official Status	Appearances (before 1350)
William de Thornhagh	merchant, mayor (1362/63)	15 (2)
Walter de Ouresby	merchant, mayor (1356/57)	11
Richard de Thorp	merchant, mayor (1367/68)	10
Peter Belasis	spicer, mayor (1358/59)	6 (2)
Richard de Dyke	merchant, mem. of civic council (1352/53, 1367/68)	6
Thomas de Banham	merchant, coroner (1363–69)	6
John de Brune	unknown, none	5 (5)
Thomas Felissone	unknown, none	5
Walter de Kelby	merchant, mayor of the staple; mayor (1350/51)	5
Roger de Tatersale	baker, mayor (1360/61)	4
William de Fynchingfeld	unknown, bailiff (1352/53)	4

increasing monopoly by these men can be seen from pleas involving William de Thornhagh, a resident of St Rumbold. Over a period of twenty-five years, Thornhagh dealt with litigants (where known) from the parishes of St Augustine, St Edmund, St Mary Crackpole (1343), St Bavon (1353), Peter at Pleas (1362), Newport and St Michael on the Mount (1366) – parishes spread throughout the city (Map 7.1).[67] The same can be said of Richard de Dyke, a resident of St Swithun, who had dealings with individuals from Newport, St Peter in Eastgate (1352), St Michael on the Mount, St Rumbold (1366) and St Augustine (1366).[68] Hence, where litigants had traditionally chosen the majority of electors from their own or adjacent parishes, following the Black Death they began to look to more established public figures with links to the borough court; in turn, this led to an increasing professionalisation

67 Duplicate locations not noted: BB, fols 158v, 162, 224, 224v, 226, 238, 248v, 250, 253, 259, 259v, 260, 261, 261v, 262.

68 Duplicate locations not noted: BB, fols 250, 253, 261, 262, 263, 263v.

of electors, as the networks of a small elite group of office holders expanded beyond traditional roles.

The catalyst for this shift was almost certainly the loss of life inflicted by the outbreak of plague, which would have seen many locally respected individuals perish in parishes across the city. The significance of this was that it quickly eroded the rights of wider communal involvement in judicial affairs, by shifting the suitability of electors away from the parish towards the borough court. It is possible – even likely – that this was influenced further by immigration, with many of the city's newer inhabitants not knowing who to turn to in matters of dispute, suggesting that the growing dependency on the borough court actually became something of a necessity after 1349.[69] The deaths of at least a dozen former officials in the plague was undoubtedly an additional blow to local customs, as many men remained actively involved in civic business right up until their deaths.[70] This would have left something of a power vacuum in the city, and it is possible that a number of those named as elector saw the role as an opportunity to promote and maintain their own status within a society recently devastated by pestilence, all the while performing a vital civic duty. This would explain why the same men were named as electors time and again.

In many ways the changes at Lincoln mirrored those elsewhere, only at an earlier date. For example, David Shaw has shown that at Wells by the end of the fourteenth century, the development of 'confraternal structures such as arbitration and commensality' were being used primarily to weld the town's burgesses 'into an effective political unit'.[71] This was, he argues, significant; not only did it enhance the prominence of this group through their continued involvement in judicial processes, but it also created a situation whereby those of lesser status were able to interact with individuals of greater wealth and social standing to achieve their goals.[72] Similarly, Maryanne Kowaleski has shown that at Exeter in the 1370s and 1380s, judicial practices were becoming increasingly monopolised by the leading townspeople – so much so that judgements were frequently given by the court in favour of their own members. The impact of this was that it discouraged litigants from pressing claims against what came to be seen as a corrupt group.[73] Carole Rawcliffe, too, demonstrates how in London by the early fifteenth century litigants in

69 Kissane, *Civic Community*, pp. 38, 61–2.

70 For example, John Fenton worked until at least May 1349 (his will was enrolled in June), whilst Robert Maunsfeld worked until July 1349 (his will was enrolled later that month): BB, fols 191, 199v; Kissane, *Civic Community*, p. 3.

71 David G. Shaw, 'Social networks and the foundations of oligarchy in medieval towns', *Urban History*, 32:2 (2005), p. 220.

72 Shaw, 'Social networks', pp. 215–21.

73 Maryanne Kowaleski, *Local Markets and Regional Trade in Medieval Exeter* (Cambridge, 1995), pp. 113–14.

cases of commercial disputes were free to choose their own arbitrators, many of whom were local and held related interests. More important still was the fact that many arbitrators were chosen primarily because their 'standing in the community lent further weight to their findings'.[74] Finally, Sarah Rees Jones has identified how the power of the mayor and aldermen at York notably increased during the 1370s after their institution as justices of the peace, a development which coincided with the growing centralisation of urban policing. The result was that powers for resolving craft disputes shifted the guilds themselves to civic government.[75]

It is thus clear that many of the developments identified in other towns were replicated to some extent in recorded pleas of *writ de recto*. In particular it is clear that, following the Black Death, several leading townspeople sought to consolidate their own social status (both in the borough court and in the urban hierarchy more generally) through increased participation in pleas, whilst simultaneously providing support and representation to their social inferiors, a development mirroring to some extent changes at York. The evidence also echoes the arbitration process at both London and Wells, where individuals were chosen for their standing in the community and for their familiarity with judicial practices. Whilst at Wells this process worked 'because it preserved the fraternal nature of the city without undermining the possibility of individuals of due stature from emerging into civic leadership',[76] such a conclusion should not be projected onto Lincoln; Shaw's evidence is not only drawn from a later period, but also remains representative of the tensions that existed between the town and its ecclesiastical lord, issues otherwise not evident at Lincoln. Nonetheless, as at Exeter, there was undoubtedly an element of bias at Lincoln in pleas of *writ de recto*, especially in cases pitting civic officials against those of lower social standing: of twenty-one such pleas, civic officials were successful on fourteen occasions, with a further two non-verdicts.

Conclusion

Through the use of a single type of plea, this analysis has provided a glimpse into the judicial practices of Lincoln's borough court during the fourteenth century, and it has identified how customary practices were influenced significantly by time and circumstance. It has shown how, after 1323 (following the introduction of wider municipal reforms), procedural changes to pleas of *writ*

[74] Rawcliffe, 'Settlement of commercial disputes', p. 102.

[75] Sarah Rees Jones, 'York's civic administration, 1354–1464', in Sarah Rees Jones (ed.), *The Government of Medieval York: Essays in Commemoration of the 1396 Royal Charter* (York, 1997), pp. 121–5.

[76] Shaw, 'Social networks', p. 220.

de recto allowed those seeking justice in the courts to call upon local men of standing as their electors, the majority of whom typically lived within a stone's throw of their own domicile. Until the Black Death, these parochial relationships were characterised by modest wealth and status and a large degree of choice, thereby extending the judicial franchise to individuals otherwise unable or unsuitable for civic office. Shaw's observation of Wells in the fifteenth century – that 'respect, if not great influence, was available without great wealth or high office'77 – was also true of Lincoln at this time, and the process identified here afforded a platform for litigants whereby local issues could be organised and settled upon by local people.

After 1349 the situation changed rapidly, as electors began to be drawn from across much of the city, with many of those being identified as extremely wealthy men with well-established links to the borough court. Whether this shift in judicial representation was made at a grass-roots level or was a measure imposed by those at the top of the social ladder is unknown, though it undoubtedly provided opportunities for a number of leading townspeople to make a name for themselves, all the while providing a much-needed civic duty. This was particularly important given the power vacuum created by the deaths of so many former civic officials in 1349. Whether these opportunities were accompanied by any form of remuneration, as in some cases of pledging, is not known,[78] though it seems unlikely that financial gain was the driving force behind the upsurge in individuals undertaking the role on multiple occasions.

In spite of the localised nature of the *writ de recto* evidence drawn upon here, the significance of these findings goes far beyond Lincoln itself. In particular, it points towards the Black Death as a catalysing force in the emergence of oligarchy, a political development which saw the customs, procedures and practices of civic government become concentrated into fewer hands by the beginning of the fifteenth century at the latest.[79] While further research on the daily business of borough courts is undoubtedly needed to confirm this hypothesis, it is perhaps no coincidence that, in the immediate aftermath of the Black Death at Lincoln, both the city's MPs and those named as executors in wills enrolled before the borough court began to be chosen from a small pool of citizens, many of whom were, as in pleas

77 Shaw, 'Social networks', p. 205.

78 David Postles, 'Personal pledging in manorial courts in the later Middle Ages,' *Bulletin of the John Rylands Library*, 75:1 (1993), pp. 65–78.

79 For example, Stephen H. Rigby and Elizabeth Ewan, 'Government, power and authority, 1300–1540', in Palliser, *Cambridge Urban History of Britain*, vol. 1, pp. 291–312; Stephen H. Rigby, 'Urban "oligarchy" in late medieval England', in John A. F. Thomson (ed.), *Towns and Townspeople in the Fifteenth Century* (Gloucester, 1988), pp. 62–86; Jennifer Kermode, 'Obvious observations in the formation of oligarchies in late medieval English towns', in Thomson, *Towns and Townspeople*, pp. 87–106.

of *writ de recto*, present or future civic officials.[80] Whilst from the outside looking in, the business of civic government appeared to continue with a minimum of disruption throughout much of 1349, despite the arrival of plague,[81] fundamental changes to the practices of the borough court saw official and unofficial roles begin to be monopolised in new ways, thus paving the way for later political developments.

80 Kissane, *Civic Community*, pp. 141–2; Alan Kissane, 'Lay urban identities in late medieval Lincoln, 1290–1400' (unpublished doctoral thesis, University of Nottingham, 2013), pp. 93–102.

81 The business of the borough court halted for approximately two months between March and June: BB, fols 183v–185.

8

JUSTICE AND JURISDICTIONS IN LATE MEDIEVAL CHESTER

JANE LAUGHTON

Chester's medieval court rolls survive in large numbers, meaning that historians can therefore address the key themes of jurisdiction and the operation of justice in the city with some confidence. There are gaps in the record and many rolls are more or less illegible, but we must be grateful for the wealth of material at our disposal, albeit sometimes daunted by its profusion. The rolls of the mayor's Portmote begin in 1295, those of the sheriffs' Pentice court in 1297, those of the Crownmote in 1316; the first two continue relentlessly until the sixteenth century, and other sources shed more light on the third. It is clearly impossible to cover the entire late medieval period in a short chapter; this study will therefore begin in the 1390s, when new sources document changes in Chester's governmental framework, and conclude in 1506, when the structure of its courts was amended by the Great Charter. It presents a detailed study of two fundamental issues, beginning with an account of how the city's three courts functioned, an analysis of the contrasting attitudes of the officers and litigants to their experiences, and a presentation of reasons for dissatisfaction. This is followed by an enquiry into the conflicts which arose between Chester's civic authorities and the jurisdictions over which they had no control: the county court, the manorial courts held by the bishop, prioress and abbot, the court of the archdeaconry and the court of Dee Mills. The emphasis throughout is on what the court records can tell us about the city and its people – and, although the focus is on Chester, the findings reveal much about attitudes to and structures of justice across many medieval and early modern towns.

The Organisation and Experience of Justice in Late Medieval Chester

Chester's pre-Conquest hundredal court with its twelve judges (*iudices*) was recorded in Domesday Book. The probable successor to this court was the Portmote, in existence by 1200; doomsmen (*judices* or *judicatores*) provided by particular urban properties were appointed to pronounce on laws and customs.[1] As was true of many medieval towns, an intricate network of courts and officials, each responsible for different aspects of local justice, developed in the city over time. The Pentice court emerged in the mid thirteenth century and was fully established by 1288; sessions were held in the lean-to structure built against St Peter's church from which it took its name. Edward I's charter of 1300 granted crown pleas to the citizens, a unique privilege for the period. Initially, crown pleas seem to have been heard in the Portmote; but a separate court, the Crownmote, appeared in the later fourteenth century. Over the years, presiding officers changed and court business and procedures gradually evolved.[2] By the 1390s a new civic institution, the Assembly, had been established, attended by a body of aldermen known as the Forty-Eight. They routinely witnessed property transactions at the Portmote and served as jurors at the assize of wine.[3]

Chester was divided into four quarters for administrative purposes, based on the original Roman lay-out and named after the four main streets. Receipts from fines were listed by street in the first Mayors' Book in 1392; the collectors for each street were named from c. 1399, and the names of those fined at the 'great indictments' (*magna indictamenti*) of 1410 survive for Eastgate Street and Bridge Street.[4] From about 1450, constables who were required to attend the mayor's 'full' Portmote were regularly listed by street, as too those who were fined. A few years later, a body of councilmen known as the Twenty-Four was established and their names were recorded by street in the Mayors' Books from 1459. Constables and councillors were routinely listed together until the early sixteenth century.[5] Fines paid were listed by street in the Sheriffs' Books from 1451 to 1452, with a pronounced emphasis on the

1 B. E. Harris (ed.), *The Victoria County History of the County of Cheshire* (hereafter *VCH Cheshire*), vol. 1 (London, 1987), pp. 342–3; C. P. Lewis and A. T. Thacker (eds), *VCH Cheshire*, vol. 5, part 1 (London, 2003) pp. 24, 27–8.

2 *VCH Cheshire*, vol. 5, part 1, pp. 39, 43; *VCH Cheshire*, vol. 5, part 2 (London, 2005), pp. 21–4.

3 Jane Laughton, *Life in a Late Medieval City: Chester 1275–1520* (Oxford, 2008), pp. 109–10.

4 Cheshire Archives and Local Studies (hereafter CALS), ZMB 1, fols 45, 46; ZMB 2, fols 59, 67–67v, 92v.

5 CALS, ZMB 4, fols 9, 21, 29, 45; ZMB 5, fols 41, 69v, 85v, 129v, 180v; ZMB 6, fols 3v, 4v, 34v, 83v; ZMB 8, fols 59v, 60–60v; ZSB 1, fols 60–63, 115–118, 134v–135v, 137–139, 158, 162v; ZSB 2, fols 2–6v, 63–65; ZSB 3, fols 41–46, 99–100.

fines paid by non-citizens to trade within the franchise.[6] These topographical details make Chester's judicial records a priceless treasure trove of information about the lives and relationships of the townspeople, both rich and poor, and also about the distinctive character of each quarter.[7]

Among the first civic ordinances approved *viva voce* at an assembly held in May 1390 was one urging neighbours to settle disputes between their fellows. If they failed, the matter could be brought before the mayor – and only if his intervention proved unsuccessful could the parties resort to the antagonistic process of the law.[8] Townspeople nevertheless regularly turned to Chester's courts to obtain justice, and the civic authorities guarded their judicial privileges jealously, reacting forcibly to any infringements. The Pentice Cartulary, a collection of documents recording the city's rights and customs and examples of procedures, was available in the Pentice for consultation. Among the documents are notes on a case of novel disseisin brought to the Portmote in 1405, which was challenged by writs of *recordari, alias* and *pluries* delivered to the mayor by Cheshire's deputy sheriff. When mayor and sheriffs refused to comply, they were threatened with attachment for contempt. The mayor wrote 'in right grett hast' to the eminent palatinate lawyer Sir Hugh Holes, justice of the King's Bench, who responded immediately giving the 'Right hon'able Sir and my well beloved frynds' the assurance they required. No pleas could be removed outside their franchise except by writ of error. Sir Hugh's opinion was reinforced by the command of Henry, Prince of Wales (as earl of Chester) to the same effect. This example of the mayor and sheriffs risking arrest to defend the city's jurisdiction provides telling evidence of how greatly these rights were valued. A marginal comment in the Pentice Cartulary put it thus: 'See how precious the mayor and sheriffs were of their liberties then to deny the prince's writs, and how loth the prince was to have them infringed.'[9]

The Portmote

From the 1370s the mayor presided over the Portmote, which sat on Mondays every two or three weeks in the common hall on the west side of Bridge Street. Sessions were suspended at Christmas and at Easter, and for several weeks during the midsummer fair. The mayor also presided over the Crownmote, held in the common hall on Mondays every six weeks or so,

6 CALS, ZSB 1, fols 115–118; ZSB 3, fols 22v, 25, 99, 101v.

7 See Jane Laughton, 'The alewives of later medieval Chester', in Rowena E. Archer (ed.), *Crown, Government and People in the Fifteenth Century* (Stroud, 1995), pp. 203–5; and Laughton, *Life in a Late Medieval City*, pp. 40–59.

8 CALS, ZMB 1, fol. 16; ZMB 2, fol. 19v.

9 CALS, ZCHB/2, fols 66v, 68–68v, 79, 82v–83 (case of 1405), 85–86 (petition from mayor, sheriffs and commonalty, and reply of Prince of Wales); British Library (hereafter BL), Harleian MS 2057, fols 156–157v.

occasionally coinciding with the Portmote. The sheriffs acted as executive officers at both courts.[10]

Some fifty Portmote court rolls survive for the period from 1390 to 1503, many of them devoted solely to enrolments of property transactions. Occasionally a will was enrolled, with the date of grant of probate in the archdeacon's court duly added.[11] Pleas of real estate formed the bulk of legal business and were subject to numerous adjournments, usually caused by the absence of one or other of the parties.[12] If the wife owned the property, it was customary for her to accompany her husband to court and for the mayor to question her carefully to ensure that she had not been coerced into the transaction. In the case of a widow, half a dozen or so aldermen and other worthy citizens were also present, their names listed below the mayors and sheriffs. The widow had to swear on the bible that she would answer as on Judgement Day.[13]

If the parties failed to agree, a jury was selected, assessed and sworn. The twelve jurors came to the bar to deliver their verdict, after which the doomsmen (*judicatores*) pronounced judgement. The obligation to provide a doomsman remained attached to certain properties within the city, but many owners routinely appointed an attorney to represent them.[14] In October 1398 three owners appeared before the mayor in 'full' Portmote, and each named the individual chosen to pronounce or correct judgement in his name. The choice regularly fell on an experienced court official, whom plaintiffs and defendants perhaps preferred because of his familiarity with court procedures.[15]

A short and untidily written court roll recording pleas of debt and trespass heard at the Portmotes of May, June, July and October 1427 is the first evidence of such causes. Each was adjourned until the following Portmote by the procedure of 'knowenburgh', perhaps only available to citizens; next came a series of distraints, with fines doubled each time (3d, 6d, 12d, 2s), presumably in an attempt to force the litigants to appear. At Portmotes held in March and May 1449 and in November 1450, the mayor heard forty-five pleas of debt, trespass, detinue and broken agreement. Almost half saw the plea adjourned by 'knowenburgh' until the following Portmote, when most failed to come to judgement; either the plaintiff failed to prosecute, the defendant

10 *VCH Cheshire*, vol. 5, part 1, pp. 39, 43. For Chester's medieval law courts, see *VCH Cheshire*, vol. 5, part 2, pp. 21–4.

11 CALS, ZMR 75, m. 1; 77, m. 1.

12 CALS, ZMR 61, m. 1d; 62, m. 1; 64, mm. 1–1d; 67, mm. 1–1d; 76, mm. 1–1d; 81, mm. 1–1d; 95, m. 1.

13 CALS, ZMR 70, m. 1; 76, m. 1; 83, m. 1; 85, m. 1; 91, m. 1.

14 CALS, ZMR 61, m. 1; ZMB 2, fol. 54v; ZMB 5, fols 1, 39v, 41v; ZMB 7, fols 80, 118.

15 CALS, ZMB 1, fol. 64v; ZMB 2, fol. 84v.

acknowledged the trespass, or agreement was reached out of court.[16] After the mid fifteenth century, business in the Portmote was largely restricted to the issuing of mainprizes, legal instruments which bound individuals or groups of individuals to keep the peace.[17]

On Monday 4 November 1448 the mayor and sheriffs presided over a judicial inquiry in 'full' Portmote (*pleno Portmote*) in the common hall. On Monday 22 September 1449 they presided over a *Magna Inquis* in the same location.[18] These sessions came to be held four times a year, at intervals indicating that they were quarter sessions in all but name; business included infringements of civic ordinances, immoral behaviour, assaults and theft. Jurors selected from each quarter presented offenders whose punishment was almost invariably a monetary fine, recorded by street.[19] Thieves were sent to the gallows located at the boundary of the city liberties in Boughton. No record survives of any use of the pillory in the central marketplace opposite St Peter's church.

The standard fine evidently ranged between one and two shillings, but there are examples of the mayor imposing a higher sum should he deem it warranted. In 1464/5 he demanded forty shillings from an individual who failed to appear; in 1469/70, the same sum was paid by a barber indicted for usury and a cook who broke the assize of fish.[20] Marginal entries noted those who had not yet paid their fine in full and those excused payment because of poverty. Occasionally the mayor dismissed a case because he considered the indictment unfair, as happened in 1494 when he pardoned a felt-capper all payment, because his indictment was based on malicious information from the city's textile workers. In c. 1493 one man was pardoned in honour of St George, patron of a fraternity closely linked with Chester's ruling elite, the guild's chapel being in St Peter's church.[21] Others were not so fortunate: the female servant charged in 1468 with stealing money, bedding and two girdles embellished with silver went to the gallows, as did the local weaver indicted for theft of a metal bowl and twenty shillings in February 1485. In neither case was there mention of doomsmen, just a laconic 'hanged by the neck' (*sus' p' col'*) in the margin.[22]

16 CALS, ZMR 83–83d; ZMR 92.

17 CALS, ZMB 4, fols 18v, 59–61v; ZMB 5, fols 48–54v; ZMB 6, fols 41v–57; ZMB 7, fols 19v–28; Jane Laughton, 'The control of discord in fifteenth-century Chester', in Richard Goddard, John Langdon and Miriam Müller (eds), *Survival and Discord in Medieval Society: Essays in Honour of Christopher Dyer* (Turnhout, 2010), pp. 217–23.

18 CALS, ZMB 4, fols 7v, 34.

19 CALS, ZSB 2, fols 39v, 45v, 59, 87v; ZSB 3, fols 60–60v, 65, 93v; ZSB 4, fols 10, 38.

20 CALS, ZSB 2, fols 41v, 89, 90v.

21 CALS, ZSB 3, fols 24, 91v, 94v, 97; ZSB 4, fols 8, 50v.

22 CALS, ZSB 2, fol. 60v; ZSB 3, fol. 97v.

The Crownmote

For the period from 1316 to 1506, just thirteen Crownmote court rolls survive, four of them relevant for this discussion. The roll of 1393/4 recorded indictments for regrating and forestalling, encroachments on the common soil and, on the barely legible dorse, one or two assaults and infringements of the curfew. The roll of 1406/7 was similar; that of 1435 reported an attack on the mayor, but is so damaged as to be more or less unreadable. The final roll contains details of the Crownmote held in August 1488 which considered one case, the death of a draper from a sword-wound inflicted by a fletcher on Trinity Sunday (1 June) 1488. The mayor and coroners requested the presence of twenty-four honourable and worthy (*probos et legales*) citizens as potential jurors for the session arranged for 12 July 1488, presumably to give the draper's widow and the defendant the opportunity to reject any whose impartiality was questionable. A partly illegible list of names followed, listed by street, seven of them marked by a dot, possibly indicating selection. In April 1489 the defendant was finally brought to the Crownmote by the keeper of the Northgate gaol, and the coroners repeated details of his felony. When asked by the mayor how he wished to plead, he declared his innocence and asked for trial by jury. The jurors, his fellow citizens, found him not guilty and the *judicatores* announced his acquittal.[23]

Fortunately, these meagre records can be supplemented by details of Crownmote sessions entered in the Mayors' Books, demonstrating the links between the city's various jurisdictions, officials and records. Only three records of the Crownmote pre-date the mid fifteenth century: those of January 1405, April 1410 and February 1420. In January 1405, after dealing with routine matters including mainprizes and debt recognizances under the heading in 'full' Crownmote, the court heard the case of the city shipman who had dealt a colleague a mortal blow with a poleaxe twelve months earlier. Although bailed to appear at subsequent sessions, he had failed to do so and at this session he was outlawed. Richard II's grant of the process of outlawry to the city in 1398 was recorded in the Pentice Cartulary, but as it lasted only three years the city authorities took care to forward details of this case to the Crownmote session of the county court in March 1405. In 1420 a few breaches of the peace and violent assaults were reported, and one case of regrating and forestalling. The *judicatores* deemed that the Irish woman found not guilty of theft should be acquitted.[24]

23 CALS, ZQCR 10, 11, 12; ZQSF 1, fols 1–4v; ZMB 7, fols 75v, 79; The National Archives (hereafter TNA), CHES 29/108, m. 15d.

24 CALS, ZMB 2, fols 31–31v, 83v; ZMB 3, fols 78v–79; ZCHB 2, fols 43v–44; TNA, CHES 29/108, m. 15d.

Crownmote records survive for twenty-six other years before the Great Charter of 1506. After 1420 there is a gap until 1452/3, by which time much business had passed to the 'full' Portmote. In 1452/3, six sessions had nothing to report and others only a handful of mainprizes. Nine sessions were held in 1459/60, again with little or no business until the session of September 1460 when two cases of theft were heard. The first involved a stringer from Caernarfon, who had stolen money and a silver ring from a fellow countryman on Easter Day and had been imprisoned in the Northgate gaol ever since. The Northgate Street bailiff brought him to court and, when the mayor asked how he wished to plead, he protested his innocence and requested a jury trial. Twelve jurors from the four quarters of the city were selected, assessed and sworn; they found him guilty. He had no goods, chattels, lands or tenements and was sentenced to be hanged. The bailiff then brought in the labourer Margery Scot, indicted for the theft of six yards of woollen cloth. The procedure was identical, and the same jury delivered the same verdict. She too had no possessions and she too was sent to the gallows. In neither case were the doomsmen mentioned.[25]

References to the Crownmote are occasionally found in Chester's Sheriffs' Books, the first recording the session held on 3 November 1427 when no business was transacted. Offenders were punished by fine, listed under street headings by the sheriffs from 1451 to 1452, with a decided emphasis on *p' mercand' suis* (for permission to sell retail within the liberties).[26] On Monday 18 June 1464, the mayor presided over a full Crownmote; twelve named jurors heard three cases of assault, committed by local townspeople on 12 June. The Crownmote of Monday 15 January 1471 was similar: the twelve jurors determined a dozen or so recent cases of assault committed by locals within the liberties in recent weeks, and some breaches of civic ordinances.

The Pentice Court

From the mid 1390s, sessions of the Pentice court were held on Tuesdays, Thursdays and Fridays, a routine confirmed in the 1506 charter. The sheriffs were assisted by the four bailiffs, one from each city quarter, whose duties included issuing summons, making attachments, assembling jurors and collecting fines. Litigants were given a specific time to appear: at the eighth hour, the ninth hour, the first or second hour after noon. Fortunately, the adjoining St Peter's church tower housed a clock by the 1420s, maintained by a cooper for sixteen shillings a year.[27]

25 CALS, ZMB 5, fols 59v–60.

26 CALS, ZSB 1, fols 81, 158; ZSB 2, fols 21–23v, 27v; ZSB 3, fols 6–8, 99; ZSB 4, fol. 30.

27 CALS, ZMB 3, fol. 81; ZMB 4, fols 12, 57; ZSR 196, m. 1d.

The Pentice dealt with all personal pleas except those concerning real estate: debt, trespass, detinue and broken contract. Pleas of debt were always the most numerous, rarely less than 50 per cent of the total in the 1450s and 1480s, and regularly exceeding 70 per cent. Pleas of trespass came second, ranging between 10 and 30 per cent of the total in the same decades. Trespass covered petty pleas of interpersonal violence: assault, larceny, housebreaking and bloodshed.[28] Suits were begun by plaint, occasionally in writing, and most ended at an early stage, when either the plaintiff failed to prosecute or the defendant acknowledged the debt, or agreement was reached out of court. One suspects that the plaint was often lodged solely to put pressure on the defendant to come to terms.[29] The threat of litigation therefore proved an effective strategy in the resolution of disputes.[30] Research elsewhere has shown that only a small proportion of medieval lawsuits ever came to judgement: possibly 20 per cent of crown pleas in the court of King's Bench in the fifteenth century, and barely 1 per cent of private suits.[31] Chester's experience was, therefore, far from unique.

As the sheriffs determined each case, speedy judgement was assured – but trial by jury was always an option. Jury trials slowed down procedures, as indicated by marginal notes. A case first heard in October 1449 was deferred to Tuesday, then to Thursday after 10 November, to Thursday after 6 December, and finally to Tuesday after 25 March 1450. Litigants were not deterred. Twelve jurors at the bar gave their verdict in a case of armed assault in 1394, and jurors continued to decide individual pleas throughout the fifteenth century. A reference to 'the revenues of the panels in the Pentice' (*exitoribus panellorum in Penticio*) in October 1426 reveals that this was the 'panels' court, an alternative name for the 'passage' court. How the jurors were selected is unknown, possibly on an *ad hoc* basis.[32] Jurors also assessed the damages due from plaintiffs who failed to prosecute, from defendants who acknowledged the offence, or from both parties if settlement was reached out of court.[33]

The necessary paperwork for each plea (lists of stolen items and detained goods, for example) was kept on file in the Pentice. In debt cases it was evidently normal for plaintiffs to bring the obligation with them as proof.[34] Litigants stood at the bar and occasionally swore on the bible to tell the truth. In such cases the verdict went their way, be they plaintiff or defendant.[35]

28 CALS, ZSR 281–313, 331–68.

29 CALS, ZSR 126, m. 2; 132, m. 1d.

30 CALS, ZMR 92.

31 Edward Powell, 'Arbitration and the law of England in the late Middle Ages', *Transactions of the Royal Historical Society*, 33 (1983), pp. 49–67.

32 CALS, ZSR 106, m. 1; 161, m. 1; 280, m. 1d.

33 CALS, ZSR 114, m. 1; 123, m. 3d; 185, m. 1d.

34 CALS, ZSR 157, m. 1; 166, m. 1; 175, m. 1d; 240, m. 1; 388, m. 1.

35 CALS, ZSR 157, m. 1; 158, m. 1d; 166, m. 1; 200, m. 1d; 345, m. 1; 351, m. 2; 422, m. 1.

Sometimes the sheriffs ordered an individual convicted of debt or detinue to be detained in the Northgate gaol to ensure payment, usually when expensive items or large sums of money were involved.[36] However, the standard penalty imposed by the sheriffs was a monetary fine, though this sometimes proved difficult to collect. Many pleas of debt in the Pentice court were initiated by former sheriffs attempting to recover these fines, sometimes several years after their term in office.[37]

Fears about the sheriffs' probity were forcibly expressed in a petition to the mayor in 1456/7. The defendant claimed that he would not receive justice from the sheriffs, who were not only in the plaintiff's affinity but had also been approached by wealthy non-citizens related to the plaintiff by marriage. 'May it please you [the right wise and discrete mayor]', the petitioner entreated, 'in your great wisdom to take and remove the case to the common hall to be determined as law will, where every party may have justice and right witness done.'[38]

Surviving Pentice court rolls record the removal of twenty-six pleas to the Portmote during the 1450s, nine of them in 1452.[39] On three occasions the removal took place after the shrieval verdict, and a superscript noted the annulment of that judgement in the Portmote by the city's *judicatores*. Twelve pleas were removed in 1460/1, but then there was a gap until 1477.[40] It is perhaps not coincidental that records of the sheriffs' 'passage' court first appear in 1463. Jurors were assembled by the bailiffs, assisted by four assessors (*triatores*) drawn from each quarter of the city. Thirteen passage court rolls survive for the years from 1463 to 1505. The cases are recorded on one side of the membrane, with the judgements subsequently added below. On the verso, eligible jurors are listed by street and typically include middle-ranking butchers, bakers, tailors, capmakers, coopers and glovers. The marginal dots beside each name probably indicate the number of times an individual had served; 'sworn' (*jur'*) indicated those selected. Jury service was time-consuming and probably resented by men who needed to earn a living. The heavy fines imposed on jurors who failed to appear were an additional disincentive,[41] perhaps partly relieved by the knowledge that they would be excused service once they reached the age of seventy.[42]

36 CALS, ZSR 191, m. 1; 280, m. 1d; 295, m. 1d.

37 CALS, ZSR 150, m. 1; 163, m. 1d; 189, m. 1; 249, m. 1d; 290, m. 1d; 317, m. 1.

38 CALS, ZMB 2, fol. 5v; BL, Harleian MS 2046, fol. 33.

39 CALS, ZSR 288, 291, 293, 294–99.

40 CALS, ZSR 309, mm. 1, 1d; 312, m. 1; ZSR 329, mm. 316–20, 325–6.

41 CALS, ZSR 1–13; ZMB 5, fol. 103v; ZMB 4, fol. 22v; ZMB 7, fol. 1; ZSB 1, fol. 136; 3s 4d demanded in the mid 1450s from the man who did not appear in panels court.

42 CALS, ZMB 5, fol. 103v; ZCHB 2, fols 71, 80v–81.

Officers and Court Personnel

The plaintiffs and defendants who received urban justice naturally viewed that justice very differently from the judges on the bench. Elite citizens could be reasonably confident that their pleas would be judged favourably by their peers, while wealthy townsfolk (accepting litigation as an inevitable fact of life) routinely appointed general attorneys to represent them in Chester's courts. They did this by appearing in person, either before the common clerk in the Pentice exchequer or in 'full' Portmote before the mayor. Each attorney undertook to represent his client, whether plaintiff or defendant, in the Portmote or Pentice court for the whole civic year.[43] The few women who appointed attorneys were mainly wealthy widows.[44] Henceforth, these individuals no longer needed to waste time following the plea along its often tortuous course through the legal system.[45] Occasionally a litigant appointed a friend or fellow craftsman, but it was more usual for civic officers to be chosen: bailiffs and collectors from the four main streets, the city gaoler, the catchpoll, men surnamed 'le Cryer' who presumably broadcast civic proclamations.[46] They were paid for the service and some acted as attorneys for several years, in effect becoming professional pleaders. Roger Holden was attested from 1451/2 until 1464/5, and was perhaps succeeded by Alexander Holden, named in 1469/70.[47]

All litigants were required to nominate a pledge, although the poor were occasionally accepted on trust (*fides quia pauper*).[48] Townspeople commonly found pledges among their family, friends and neighbours; husbands acted for their wives, parents for their children, masters or mistresses for their servants. Craftsmen regularly served as pledges for their fellows, and men working in linked occupations also helped each other out: a dosser for a waterleader, a hosteller for a carrier, a lorimer for a saddler, a butcher for the cook at the Franciscan friary.[49] Townspeople also acted as pledges for non-residents with whom they did business: butchers for Welsh drovers, fishmongers for Manx traders, smiths for carters, an alderman for the Devonian whom he knew through the wine trade.[50] Women were able to act as personal pledges, unlike

43 CALS, ZMB 1, fols 29v, 49v, 66; ZMB 2, fols 29v–30; MB/B 3, fols 3, 49v, 50, 70, 70v, 87–87v; ZMB 4, fols 22v, 39, 41v.

44 CALS, ZSB 2, fol. 3; ZSB 3, fols 3, 62; ZMB 1, fol. 49v.

45 CALS, ZMB 2, fols 29v, 32, 53v, 83; ZMB 3, fols 12, 69v–70v, 87–87v; ZMB 4, fols 22v, 39–41v, 85.

46 CALS, ZSB 3, fol. 62; ZMB 2, fols 95v, 32; ZMB 3, fols 12, 32v, 70v; ZMB 5, fol. 60v; ZMB 6, fol. 41.

47 CALS, ZSB 2, fols 3, 39; ZSB 2, fol. 84.

48 CALS, ZSR 132, m. 1d; 149, m. 1d.

49 CALS, ZSR 71, m. 1d; 178, m. 1; 239, mm. 1d, 3; 242, m. 1d; 245, m. 1; 337, m. 1; 339, m. 1d; 353, m. 1d; 357, m. 1.

50 CALS, ZSR 152, m. 1; 230, m. 1; 261, m. 3; 277, m. 1d; 282, m. 1; 300, m. 1v; 353, m. 1v; 356, m. 1d; 378, m. 1d.

in manorial courts which only accepted widowed heads of households. In Chester a woman's pledging role was usually restricted to family members, household servants and women who did business on their own account (*femmes soles*); they almost invariably acted for defendants.[51] The city gaoler and officers of the Pentice court offered pledging services for which they were paid, and some townsmen also served as pledges in return for payment. The sum of one shilling a week was recorded in the 1450s. Pledges ran risks. Their goods were distrained if a defendant defaulted and they became liable for the fine imposed by the court. They could end up in the Northgate gaol.[52] If a litigant failed to find a pledge, an item of property was taken in lieu: a chaplain's gown, a minstrel's horse, a smith's anvil, a furbisher's plate, cap and sword. In 1443 the Carmelite prior handed over two books, and in 1460 the prioress relinquished the convent cart.[53] The loss of clothing and books was inconvenient, but the loss of tools or means of transport could prove ruinous.

Chester's mayors presided over the city's Portmote and Crownmote between thirty-five and forty times a year. As they also gave judgement, the question of their competence so to do needs to be addressed. It should be noted that the vast majority already had experience of judicial proceedings, either through service as sheriff or, for some, through tenure of rural manors and knowledge of procedures in manorial courts. Additional support was set in place in the early 1390s, when the body known as the Twenty-Four was formed and the city's Assembly was established. This became an extremely powerful institution, composed almost exclusively of men who had served as mayor or sheriff. The numbers of aldermen fluctuated between twenty-six and more than thirty, in spite of their name; these men were consulted by the current office-holders when new ordinances were proposed, and met with them on a regular basis to determine the common good.[54]

The thirty-five aldermen of 1476/7 may be taken as typical. They were named in chronological order of their tenure of office: seven ex-mayors followed by twenty-seven ex-sheriffs. Only the Cheshire gentleman George Bulkeley had not held high office, but he became sheriff the following year and went on to serve twice as mayor. He and the sheriffs of 1475/6, assuredly not political novices, were the new members of the Assembly. Nine aldermen in contrast had experience of high office stretching back to the 1450s, and

51 Jane Laughton, 'Women in court: some evidence from fifteenth-century Chester', in Nicholas Rogers (ed.), *England in the Fifteenth Century: Proceedings of the 1992 Harlaxton Symposium* (Stamford, 1994), pp. 91, 95.

52 CALS, ZSR 105, m. 1d; 107, m. 1; 165, m. 1; 215, m. 1; 253, m. 1d; 258, m. 1d; 268, m. 1d; 295, m. 1; 387, m. 1; 413, m. 1.

53 CALS, ZSR 164, m. 1d; 178, m. 1; 196, m. 1; 214, m. 1; 227, m. 1d; 242, m. 1; 245, m. 1; 251, m. 1d; 261, m. 3; 263, m. 1d; 321, m. 1.

54 *VCH Cheshire*, vol. 5, part 2, p. 59.

may have been in their late sixties. The old had status in medieval society, seen as repositories of custom and precedent, and were regularly consulted by the mayor. In July 1477, for example, when two prominent citizens were embroiled in a property dispute, the mayor decided the issue 'by the advice of his breder and learned counsel of the said city'.[55]

The 'learned counsel' included the 'common clerk of the city', a civic office newly established in the 1390s. The first one known by name is John Hatton, appointed common clerk with custody of the seal of statute merchant during pleasure by Richard II in March 1394.[56] He was possibly followed by the clerk William Hawarden, who oversaw the enrolment of a debt recognizance in 1405. In 1409/10, with the sheriffs, he supervised the appointment of attorneys in the Pentice exchequer and in 1410/11, again with the sheriffs, he oversaw a debt of statute merchant. In the civic year 1415/16, it was noted that a portion of the fines collected from Eastgate Street was to be used for his salary.[57] William and his brother John, 'man of law', were sons of William Hawarden, Chester's mayor in 1416/17 and justice at the session of the county court disrupted by an outbreak of violence instigated by the two.[58] Office-holding ran in the family, and members of the family had been recorded as custodians of the seal of statute merchant from the 1350s until 1387, when they may have been replaced by John Hope, granted a life annuity by Richard II in 1397 in recognition for his ten years' service as exchequer clerk.[59] In 1436/7 John Hawarden received a fee of ten shillings, plus forty shillings for making an ordinance. By 1458/9 the clerk's fee had risen to forty shillings, and three other men were paid for counsel: one received twenty shillings and the other two 13s 4d each. The John Hawarden who received £3 6s 8d for 'City Councell' in 1480/1 was presumably the recorder, an office first recorded in the 1506 charter. Three entrants to the freedom in the 1480s had their entry fines waived because of good counsel, either 'before the justice in the hall of pleas and elsewhere', or 'in diverse matters beneficial to the commonalty', or 'in matters concerning the city's liberty'.[60]

Chester's mayors could also consult the three serjeants-at-law appointed to serve at Cheshire's palatinate court. The letter sent by the mayor to Sir Hugh Holes in 1405, discussed previously, provides a telling example of recourse to their expert legal advice. Sir Hugh had trained at Gray's Inn and was appointed

55 CALS, ZMB 6, fols 4, 37.

56 *Reports of the Deputy Keeper of the Public Records, Appendix II: Calendar of Recognizance Rolls of the Palatinate of Chester, to the End of the Reign of Henry IV* (London, 1875) (hereafter *DKR*), p. 224.

57 CALS, ZMB 2, fols 33v, 83v, 86v; ZMB 3, fol. 20.

58 TNA, CHES 25/11, m. 9.

59 CALS, ZSR 70, m. 1d; 76, m. 1; 81, m. 1d; 101, m. 1; *DKR*, p. 245.

60 BL, Harleian MS 2158, fols 192, 196, 203, 205, 209, 215, 215v, 221, 224; CALS, ZMB 5, fol. 46v; ZMB 6, fol. 86v; ZMB 7, fol. 7v; ZMB 9, fol. 12.

justice of the King's Bench in 1394. He occupied a handsome mansion close to the county court, located just outside the castle gate. Elite lawyers served the shire court throughout the fifteenth century.

Jurors were carefully selected, with consideration made for their reputation and experience within the judicial system. After a plea of land was heard in the Portmote on 26 July 1395, the bailiff was ordered to assemble twelve upright and honourable men (*probos et legales homines*) and bring them to court on 22 November. Eight ex-sheriffs headed the list of those who were chosen. Two sets of jurors were named for a plea of unjust disseisin heard at the Portmote on 5 December 1412, and the mayor added six men of similar quality (*tales*). After several adjournments, ten new men were elected, assessed and sworn, with the consent of the plaintiff and bailiff.[61] Presenting jurors at 'full' Portmote were chosen to represent the four quarters of the city, and offenders brought to court could therefore be assured that charges were based on local knowledge. Conversely, some charges may have been based on local animosities.

The sheriffs' judicial duties were onerous. Not only did they preside over the Pentice court every Tuesday, Thursday and Friday (with no recess during the midsummer fair), they also assisted the mayor in the Portmote and Crownmote on Mondays at three-weekly intervals. This gave them the opportunity to acquire considerable legal expertise, doubtless augmented by their association with the common clerk in the Pentice exchequer, alongside whom they appointed attorneys and registered debts. They may have dispensed summary justice, but it was not uniform, and a growing lack of satisfaction is recorded. In April 1402, a chaplain stood just outside the Pentice in the city centre and loudly denounced the current sheriffs for subverting the course of justice. From the mid fifteenth century, the number of pleas removed to the Portmote increased, suggesting dissatisfaction with the legal process. This dissatisfaction could sometimes turn to violence. In 1432 one sheriff was confronted in the city exchequer by a man wielding a dagger, and would have been killed had the bystanders not intervened. One evening in November 1454, two brothers violently attacked the sheriffs and their bailiff in the street and succeeded in forcibly removing their prisoner. Sheriffs, bailiffs and constables regularly encountered resistance during the course of their duties: doors were slammed in their faces, seals were broken on tavern doors, stolen goods were not handed over.[62] These protests demonstrate the importance of town courts in everyday urban life, and the city's inhabitants' desire for (hopefully) impartial dispute resolution.

61 CALS, ZMR 62, m. 1d; 72, m. 1.

62 CALS, ZMB 2, fol. 110; ZMB 3, fols 71v, 84, 101v; ZSB 3, fol. 96.

Conflicting and Competing Jurisdictions

Despite Chester's ruling body's determination to ensure that the city's laws and customs were respected, their commitment to the protection of their franchise never achieved complete success. Not only were they thwarted on occasion by the townspeople, but they also had to contend with the jurisdictions in which their writ did not run. There were six manorial jurisdictions within the city that were, in a sense, immune from the urban jurisdictions discussed above. The tenants from these, often very small, urban manors could not be prosecuted or fined in the city courts. The existence of these independent jurisdictions highlights the convoluted nature of urban justice in large urban centres, and illustrates the potential for conflict between the city authorities and these enclaves of discrete jurisdiction within the city.

The County Court

The most important of these independent jurisdictions was the county court. This was the superior court for the whole palatinate, with full jurisdiction over all criminal and civil proceedings. The justice presided over the sessions in the shire hall, located since 1310 just outside the castle gate. This area, like the castle itself, lay outside the city's franchise.[63] As the court exercised some jurisdiction over the city, the mayor and sheriffs were regularly required to forward details of indictments and coroners' inquests; they responded promptly to writs of *corpus cum causa* and in December 1482 readily accepted the halting of a case in the Pentice court when the Prince of Wales (as earl of Chester) reminded them of the law and custom that no-one could be attached at any other court while the county court was in session. Cases could be moved from the Portmote to the county court by writ of error, costing 3s 4d in 1442/3 and 6s 8d by 1460.[64]

Eight sessions of the county court, each lasting two or three days, were normally held each year, the first soon after Epiphany and the last a couple of weeks before Christmas. For each session twelve individuals were summoned to form a grand jury, composed of two or three knights and leading gentlemen from the different hundreds. Sir Thomas Manley headed the list of jurors for the session held on 11 April 1469, having travelled the six miles or so from Manley with his daughter Alice. They possibly arrived in time to celebrate Easter on 2 April and were certainly in Chester by 6 April, when Alice's valuable snow-weasel (*letys*) fur was stolen by a group of townsmen and women. Alice had evidently anticipated mingling with other aristocratic

63 *VCH Cheshire*, vol. 2, pp. 15–18, 21–2; *VCH Cheshire*, vol. 5, part 2, pp. 20, 209.

64 TNA, CHES 25/10, mm. 26d, 33; 25/12, m. 31; 25/14, mm. 7d, 20; CALS, ZMB 2, fol. 89; ZSR 340, m. 2; *VCH Cheshire*, vol. 5, part 2, p. 22.

families and possibly meeting her brother James, delegated with a company of twenty to guard the castle in 1468/9 as the rift between Edward IV and Warwick the Kingmaker worsened.[65] Some jurors found accommodation in their own property in the city. At the time of his death in October 1433, Sir Peter Dutton's property in Chester included a messuage called Bartholomews Inne. The regular influx of aristocratic and gentlemen jurors boosted Chester's trade, particularly for those who dealt in merchandise unavailable on rural manors: mercers and drapers who sold cloth of superior quality, tailors who found willing customers for fashionable garments.[66] The serious outbreaks of violence which inevitably erupted when feuding gentlemen met face to face, and which occasionally spilled over onto the city streets, were perhaps viewed as no more than an occasional nuisance. As armed retinues could number three hundred men or more, opposing parties were sometimes ordered to come to Chester on different days 'in esy wysse', each attended by no more than twelve supporters.[67]

The Court of Dee Mills

Chester's justice or his deputy presided over the court of Dee Mills, probably held at the corn mills at the city end of the weir or causeway close to the Dee Bridge. Surviving records suggest that it was held once a year, in different months and on different days, and occasionally timed to fit in with the county court. City officials played no part in the administration, and the townspeople were only involved as the jurors who presented offences committed against them by the millers.[68] The civic officers were ever vigilant, however, and took care to ensure that the city's rights were respected. In December 1406, the serving mayor and sheriffs queried the ancient custom of an annual gift of scarlet hose to the presiding officers, their clerical staff and the chief clerk of the mills, claiming that the custom had ceased in 1397. A jury composed of men from various Cheshire hundreds decided that the gift had always been voluntary and accordingly acquitted all three.[69]

Outbreaks of violence were common. Court records reveal that Chester's bakers, millers and servants regularly came to blows, drawing blood with knives or sticks. Similar assaults took place in the fulling mills, located in Handbridge at the eastern end of the causeway. Bakers accused the millers of taking more than their fair share of multure, of stealing their flour or allowing

65 TNA, CHES 25/15, m. 15d; SC 6/780/7, m. 1d; A. J. Pollard, *The Wars of the Roses* (Basingstoke, 1988), p. 29. The fur was worth five marks.
66 CALS, ZSR 153, m. 1; ZSR 158, m. 1.
67 TNA, CHES 25/12, mm. 12, 12d, 3.
68 *VCH Cheshire*, vol. 5, part 2, pp. 24–5.
69 TNA, CHES 25/10, mm. 22–22d; CHES 29/110, m. 16d.

it to fall into the Dee. Millers regularly complained that the bakers came to the mills armed in order to avoid payment. In June 1422 the millers reported an audacious incident that had occurred the previous April. During the night six bakers had come to the mills *modo guerrimo*, wearing hauberks and metal caps and carrying weapons; they stole large quantities of the king's multure. The city's bakers naturally attempted to evade the millers' extortions, either by buying flour from strangers or by taking their grain to be milled elsewhere, either at the abbot's mill at Bache or at his windmill, immediately north of the city's liberties, but the mills at Trafford and Eccleston were also used.[70]

The malt mills handled the malt required for the production of ale, a trade exclusively in female hands. The brewsters were represented in court by a handful of high-status wives, who would have supervised the preparation of malt in their households and whose husbands were among the jurors. On 4 October 1400, one of Henry IV's earliest ordinances was that the mill's sack-carriers (dossers) should give priority to those of the brewsters, but at the court held in September 1406 it was claimed that some always refused to comply. At other courts the elite wives routinely complained that the miller would not allow grain to be picked up from the floor and charged 1d from every sack in addition to the sixteenth grain. At the court held on 15 January 1428, the millers were accused of having demanded 8d from each brewster in the run-up to Christmas and of having charged extortionate sums for sacks of holly.[71]

The Dee court also dealt with offences at the fulling mills located in Handbridge, at the eastern end of the causeway, where extortions and assaults were similar. Townsmen involved in the cloth trade attempted to evade the high charges by taking their 'rawe clothe' to the fulling mill at Marford in Flintshire, over six miles away. The fishery at the Dee Bridge known as the King's Pool, together with stretches of the river upstream and downstream, were within the franchise of the Dee Mills. Those who put fishing nets in these stretches of the Dee also appeared in court.[72]

The Manorial Court of St Mary's Priory

The lands in Handbridge granted to the Benedictine nuns of St Mary's in the mid thirteenth century came to be regarded as a manor. The tenants were exempt from local levies and, although they were few in number and mostly poor, the civic authorities nevertheless resented these privileges and chal-

70 TNA, CHES 25/10, mm. 14, 22; 25/11, mm. 5, 8, 19, 22; CHES 12, m. 18d; CHES 25/13, mm. 18, 22.

71 TNA, CHES 25/10, m. 22; CHES 25/12, m. 18d; Laughton, 'Alewives', pp. 196–7.

72 TNA, CHES 25/10, mm. 9d, 33; CHES 25/12, m. 38d; CHES 25/13, m. 1; CHES 25/14, m. 3d.

lenged them on occasion. In 1391/2, the prioress agreed that her tenants would appear in the city courts and pay dues like other citizens, but this arrangement proved short-lived. Thereafter, her jurisdiction was respected by the governing body and the fifteenth-century Pentice court rolls regularly noted cases in which the defendant could not be fined because he was a priory tenant. The sheriffs could not arrest anyone on the nuns' land, and their attempt to do so in October 1493 resulted in their indictment in the county court on a charge of breaking and entering.[73]

The Manorial Court of the Bishops of Coventry and Lichfield

St John's had been the principal church of Lichfield diocese from 1075 until 1102 (or possibly 1087), when the see was moved to Coventry. The bishops nevertheless retained their residence within the precincts, and also their manor of 'Redcliff' with its holdings in St John's Lane and Foregate Street. Their claim to view of frankpledge, and to the fines and amercements of their tenants and of other residents in Foregate Street, was resented by the civic authorities; in 1357 the mayor and commonalty petitioned the Black Prince, asking him to help them maintain the city's franchises. They alleged that neither the present bishop nor his predecessors had enjoyed these privileges since the city was let to farm to the petitioners, and they prayed for assistance from the prince's council and lawyers. The absence of further references suggests that the petition succeeded.[74]

The Archdeacon's Court

The principal archdeaconry of the diocese had its seat at Chester, and from 1315 the archdeacon exercised jurisdiction in the first instance throughout the archdeaconry. In later years the archdeacons acquired all powers of probate and intestate administration and, in the mid fifteenth century, the right to try matrimonial causes.[75] Although the dean of St John's claimed exemption from the archdeacon's jurisdiction for his church in 1318 and again in 1542, it seems that the court was held in St John's from the start, as it was in later years. Locally based officials administered the court because the archdeacons were usually absentees, spending most of their time in Lichfield.[76] Chester's townspeople came to the court to settle testamentary and matrimonial affairs. Some may have been unable to write, and it is perhaps no coincidence that the

73 B. E. Harris (ed.), *VCH Cheshire*, vol. 3 (London, 1980), p. 147; CALS, ZSR 205, m. 1; ZSR 208, m. 1; ZSR 245, m. 1; TNA, CHES 25/16, m. 19d.

74 Michael Charles Burdett Dawes (ed.), *Register of Edward, the Black Prince, Preserved in the Public Record Office: Palatinate of Chester, A.D. 1351–1365* (London, 1932), vol. 3, fol. 141v.

75 *VCH Cheshire*, vol. 3, pp. 8–9; *VCH Cheshire*, vol. 5, part 2, p. 25.

76 *VCH Cheshire*, vol. 3, p. 10.

majority of scriveners recorded in the late medieval city lived in St John's Lane. Recent excavations at the nearby amphitheatre unearthed a medieval pen, a parchment clip and an inscribed seal matrix of Robert the chaplain, '*s. Roberti capll'i*'. Occasionally a court official was brought before the mayor and sheriffs and charged with extortion. In October 1437, for example, a former dean was accused of demanding one shilling from a citizen for his wife's will and three shillings from another for probate.[77]

The Court of the Benedictine Abbot of St Werburgh

The immune jurisdiction which provoked most conflict in late medieval Chester was that held by the Benedictine abbot of St Werburgh. In 1092 the founder had granted the abbot the right to hold a manorial court for his tenants, and to have a three-day fair focusing on the feast of St Werburgh (21 June), with jurisdiction over all pleas arising in fair-time except manslaughter. By the early thirteenth century, the city held a fair on 24 June; conflict inevitably arose when the length of the June fair was extended, by the 1290s lasting a fortnight either side of Midsummer Day.[78] Disturbances in 1379/80 resulted in the mayor and commonalty being bound over in a sum of £3,000 to desist from similar acts in the future. On 22 June 1406, theoretically the final day of the abbot's fair-time jurisdiction, the mayor, sheriffs, prominent citizens and a 'multitude' of townspeople broke into the abbey *modo guerrino* during divine service, assaulting the abbot and monks with such ferocity that they feared for their lives and (allegedly) dared not celebrate mass for three months. The civic authorities then gathered at the abbey gates with bundles of wood, determined to burn all the buildings within the precinct to the ground. The ringleaders were questioned separately at a gaol delivery on 7 December and declared their innocence; they appeared in the county court in April 1407, but the jurors were dismissed as they were believed to be favourable to the accused.[79]

The abbot's manor of St Thomas was the most important manor within the liberties. Some tenants lived in Parson's Lane and Northgate Street, but the majority resided in the suburb beyond the Northgate, the site of St Thomas's chapel where the courts were held.[80] This jurisdiction inevitably created friction between the abbot and the city's governing body, and was increasingly challenged over the course of the fifteenth century. These challenges may have been deliberately designed to provoke conflict in order to define and consolidate the powers of their franchise *vis-à-vis* those of the abbot. In the

77 Laughton, *Life in a Late Medieval City*, p. 54; BL, Harleian MS 2020, fol. 18.

78 *VCH Cheshire*, vol. 3, p. 133; *VCH Cheshire*, vol. 5, part 2, pp. 100–1.

79 TNA, CHES 29/110, mm. 4d, 6, 7d, 13.

80 *VCH Cheshire*, vol. 5, part 2, pp. 25, 322–3.

1420s the sheriffs demanded payments from abbey tenants – small sums, but demanded on several occasions, in an attempt to establish their right to such payments. On 4 July 1477, the Friday before the translation of St Thomas the Martyr, the two sheriffs broke into the home of a resident of Northgate Street and assaulted the bailiff of the abbot's liberties and franchise, arrested him and removed him to their own liberty. The timing suggests that their intention was to disrupt preparations for the manorial court in St Thomas's chapel.[81]

Challenges grew ever bolder. On 24 June 1482, the sheriffs seized metal bowls and other items from five men living in St Thomas's manor. That same year, the abbot accused a former mayor and thirteen other citizens of expelling him forcibly (*manu forte*) from forty acres of his lands at Boughton. On 22 June 1485 the sheriffs arrested two women who had come to blows in Northgate Street, one the wife of an abbey servant, and handed them over to the city gaoler. A marginal note beside the entry in the Mayor's Book encapsulated the city's triumphal reaction to this curtailment of the abbot's fair-time jurisdiction: 'Note Note NB on behalf of our liberty against the abbot at fair time' (*Nota nota nota bene: pro libertate nostra contra abbatem tempore nundinarum*).[82] Complete victory was not yet assured. In answer to a *Quo Warranto* enquiry in 1499, the abbot claimed jurisdiction over all pleas except manslaughter during his fair, and view of frankpledge in his chapel of St Thomas the martyr before his steward every fortnight on Saturdays. A dispute in 1509 resulted in the question of the abbot's jurisdiction being put to arbitration. His right to hold a court during the fair was abolished; his jurisdiction within the precincts and in Northgate Street was limited, and the superior authority of the city's mayor, sheriffs and coroners was established.[83]

Conclusion

Chester's wealth of judicial records has allowed the key issues of the functioning of urban justice in Chester to be explored. These records demonstrate that plaintiffs and defendants evidently considered that urban justice worked in their favour – most of the time – and thus routinely turned to the city's courts to resolve their disputes. Both parties would incur costs for attorneys, pledges, fines and damages, but the high level of engagement with urban justice suggests that these were deemed worthwhile in the pursuit of justice. Urban justice often depended upon who you knew: jurors, for example, may have seized the chance to decide in favour of friends and neighbours, while others found the responsibilities of jury service more onerous. Complaints of

[81] TNA, CHES 25/15, m. 39; *VCH Cheshire*, vol. 3, p. 142.

[82] TNA, CHES 25/12, m. 17d; CHES 29/187, mm. 5, 5d, 6, 8, 8d, 28d.

[83] *VCH Cheshire*, vol. 3, p. 142.

unfair treatment by the courts suggest that partiality could have an impact on the outcome of at least some cases. Court officials, predominantly comprising the civic elite, profited from court service and the powers of patronage, influence and enhanced *dignitas* that this brought. These were beneficial returns for the hours spent presiding over the courts and giving judgement. City officials guarded the privileges granted to the various jurisdictions and contested any perceived challenges, sometimes succeeding in extending their privileges at the cost of other neighbouring and competing jurisdictions. In working their way up the ladder of judicial officialdom, city elites had, however, come into close contact with the urban community, meaning that they did not represent an oligarchic group completely separate from the townspeople over whom they presided. As a result, their justice was generally tempered by an awareness of those likely to make a malicious plea, or those who were too poor to pay the fine. The existence of independent islands of jurisdiction, each with its own court – some manorial, such as those of the local religious lords, and others palatinate, such as the county court – emphasises the interlocking complexities of urban justice within a city like Chester. Both officials and residents were aware of these multiple jurisdictions and the correct forum in which to deal with the numerous disputes and complaints that arose from urban life. The existence of, and challenges to, these multiple jurisdictional boundaries once again demonstrate the importance of a working system of justice, mediated through the courts, to medieval townsfolk. The records created by these courts reveal many details of the lives of the city's inhabitants, both rich and poor, that are only recoverable by studying its surviving court records. The courts' officers came into close contact with much of the urban community, and this is reflected in the records they committed to parchment. Analysing these urban court rolls allows Chester's townsfolk to be set within their urban milieu and thus allows the most rigorous appreciation of medieval city life.

9

TRUST: BUSINESS NETWORKS AND THE BOROUGH COURT

RICHARD GODDARD

The idea that businessmen and women were part of a network of fellow business people who shared information and resources is not a new one. Historians have discussed business relationships as networks of people, but networks might also describe patterns of distribution, credit or information. Networks of business people have the effect of increasing the collective knowledge base, conferring status or respectability and lowering transaction costs. Historians of later periods have demonstrated how merchants came together to share skills and capital, and that networks often included people they had never met but rather knew by their association with the network.[1] Networks, across all historical periods, are considered – theoretically at least – to be beneficial to businesses. Merchants are supposed to feel safer when going into business with someone with whom they have some fraternal connection, or who has been recommended to them by a person whom they trust. Networks are valued because they foster trust and solidarity. Indeed, whilst the word 'network' is a modern creation, the importance of collective endeavour or fraternal association – or indeed just the importance of family and trust, which lie at the heart of network analysis – are ideas that were profoundly medieval. Gervase Rosser has eloquently described how medieval guilds fostered new

1 John Haggerty and Sheryllynne Haggerty, 'Visual analytics of an eighteenth-century business network', *Enterprise and Society*, 11 (2010), pp. 2–3; John Haggerty and Sheryllynne Haggerty, 'The life cycle of a metropolitan business network: Liverpool 1750–1810', *Explorations in Economic History*, 48 (2011), p. 190; Emily Buchnea, 'Networks and clusters in business history', in John F. Wilson, Steven Toms, Abe de Jong, Emily Buchnea (eds), *The Routledge Companion to Business History* (Abingdon, 2016), pp. 259–73; Emily Kadens, 'Pre-modern credit networks and the limits of reputation', *Iowa Law Review*, 100 (2015), pp. 2440–1.

business relationships and allowed horizontal and vertical networks to be created and reinforced.[2] However, commercial networks did not always benefit their members. Many transactions were undertaken by incompetent, quarrelsome and unscrupulous people who broke agreements and failed to repay the money they owed. For medieval historians this is something of a boon, as these people generally ended up being sued in borough courts and elsewhere, with the records of their failed transactions being recorded on the court's rolls.

This chapter examines business networks using debt litigation in later medieval Nottingham. It uses, for the first time in medieval studies, a methodology that is known as 'visual analytics'. Visual analytics represents data graphically in order to reveal hidden properties within that data. The goal of this methodology, which is a complementary tool to traditional statistics, is to discover patterns and isolate idiosyncrasies within the data, and to allow users to interact more intuitively with arid and remote statistical evidence. Visual representations therefore make it easier for users to perceive salient aspects of their data. It is particularly useful when handling large volumes of high-level and complex data, by representing a large amount of it within a small space. The method employed here is known as 'social network analysis'. This characterises networked structures in terms of 'nodes' (individual actors within a network) and the 'edges' (the relationships or interactions) that connect them.[3] Social network analysis is used to identify key actors or important communities within a network, as well as the network's critical properties, such as its structural stability or robustness. It is commonly used to investigate, amongst other things, social media networks, friendship and acquaintance networks and disease transmission, but it has also been successfully utilised in historical research. Studies on the international trade of the Quakers, on risk, credit and kinship in early modern business and on Jewish merchants in nineteenth-century America, to name but a few, have all benefited from network or cluster analysis.[4] This chapter considers whether social network analysis might be a useful tool for medieval historians, and how it might assist the study of borough courts and the individuals who attended them.

This chapter analyses the debt plaints which were enrolled in Nottingham's borough court in the mid 1370s. In doing so, it seeks to identify networks of business people who extended credit to each other during the course of their

2 Gervase Rosser, *The Art of Solidarity in the Middle Ages: Guilds in England, 1250–1550* (Oxford, 2015), p. 159.

3 Charles Wetherell, 'Historical social network analysis', *International Review of Social History*, 43 (1998), pp. 125–44.

4 Jordan Landes (ed.), *London Quakers in the Transatlantic World* (Basingstoke, 2017), pp. 22–36; Peter Mathias, 'Risk, credit and kinship in early modern enterprise', in John J. McCusker and Kenneth Morgan (eds), *The Early Modern Atlantic Economy* (Cambridge, 2001), pp. 15–35; Rowena Olegario, '"That mysterious people": Jewish merchants, transparency and community in mid-nineteenth-century America', *Business History Review*, 73 (1999), pp. 161–89.

trade. Furthermore, it attempts to identify 'central actors' who were facilitators within a network – those with a good reputation and an expert knowledge of local trading conditions.[5] Fundamentally, it asks what role Nottingham's borough court played in facilitating the business relationships found within the network. Furthermore, it seeks to measure that most intangible notion of 'trust' within the network. Trust in their customers and suppliers allows merchants to trade more confidently. Business historians have identified two different types of trust recognised by merchants in the past.[6] The first might be described as 'interpersonal' or 'informal' trust, whereby a merchant expects a customer to act honestly, based upon their reputation for prompt payment, their actions in the past or their business connections. This type of trust is based upon personal relationships and cultural constructions of morality, and it is distinct from a second type of trust afforded by creditable institutions, such as borough or other courts.[7] This second type of trust might be described as 'assurance', which goes beyond personal trust; it provides an institutional level of security that can enforce trading regulations and thereby infuse the system with confidence.[8] This chapter investigates the extent to which this community of business people had faith that interpersonal trust would assist them in achieving their commercial objectives – in this case, either finding creditors or ensuring that their money was paid back promptly – or whether they relied instead on the institutional trust provided by the borough court. The speed with which creditors turned to the borough court to resolve debt disputes might suggest something about the efficacy of the interpersonal network as a cohesive, beneficial association, with the capacity to resolve problems amongst its members without recourse to law. On the other hand, does litigation indicate a lack of trust in the efficacy of interpersonal networks? Conversely, do out-of-court settlements indicate that these informal relationships still had some teeth?

Nottingham was a medium-sized administrative centre, being a county town and the residence of the sheriff of Nottinghamshire and Derbyshire. The office of mayor was instituted in the late thirteenth century.[9] It was ranked as England's twenty-sixth wealthiest town in 1334 and is estimated to have

5 For reputation and creditworthiness, see Craig Muldrew, *The Economy of Obligation: The Culture of Credit and Social Relations in Early Modern England* (Basingstoke, 1998), pp. 147–57, 182, 186–8, 194–5.

6 Sheryllynne Haggerty, *'Merely for Money'? Business Culture in the British Atlantic, 1750–1815* (Liverpool, 2012), pp. 70–2.

7 For choice in litigation venues, see Chris Briggs, 'Seignorial control of villagers' litigation beyond the manor in later medieval England', *Historical Research*, 81 (2008), pp. 399–422.

8 Haggerty, *Merely for Money*, pp. 84–5.

9 Stephen N. Mastoris, 'Regulating the Nottingham markets: new evidence from a mid-thirteenth-century manuscript', *Transactions of the Thoroton Society*, 90 (1986), p. 79.

had a population of between two and three thousand people in the 1370s.[10] This chapter analyses pleas of debt recorded in Nottingham's borough court rolls between 3 October 1375 and 17 September 1376, in order to expose the commercial interactions and networks within the town at that time.[11] Debt pleas were regularly the most numerous suits at borough courts, due to the commercialised environment in which they were held.[12] In Nottingham in the late fourteenth century, debt pleas represented 80 per cent of the court's business. Richard Britnell has shown that, by the end of the 1370s in Colchester, there was at least one plea of debt for every eight adult residents of the borough, clearly demonstrating the ubiquity of credit in urban society at that time.[13] Debt amounts in Nottingham ranged from 4d for a wooden tub bought on credit, to forty shillings for a consignment of nails; the mean sum was 5s 8d but amounts varied widely, with 62 per cent being below five shillings.[14] Towns like Nottingham were not only the sites of markets, fairs and shops, but were also home to large numbers of merchants, traders and craftsmen. Being in debt in the Middle Ages, as both Maryanne Kowaleski and Chris Briggs argue, should not be interpreted as dire financial straits for debtors, but rather is evidence of regular participation in the local economy, even if these pleas represent debtors' waiting until the last possible moment to pay off what they owed.[15]

The pleas of debt analysed here are therefore the records of *failed* transactions pursued in Nottingham's borough court. These were circumstances where goods were bought on credit, often with a small down payment, and a (generally oral) contract was negotiated between the seller and the buyer, whereby the balance of the price for these goods was deferred, to be repaid at a specified future date. On 29 September 1375, for example, the merchant Matthew Skegby sold a large consignment of garlic and onions worth ten shillings to Nottingham garlic-monger John Sutton and his wife Alice, presumably

10 Alan Dyer, 'Ranking of towns by taxpaying population: the 1377 poll tax', and Christopher Dyer and T. R. Slater, 'The Midlands', in D. M. Palliser (ed.), *The Cambridge Urban History of Britain*, vol. 1 (Cambridge, 2000), pp. 627, 758.

11 Nottinghamshire Archives (hereafter NA) CA 1279 fols 1–26. The Nottingham court rolls are calendared here: <https://www.nottingham.ac.uk/ucn/onlinesources/index.aspx>.

12 Maryanne Kowaleski, *Local Markets and Regional Trade in Medieval Exeter* (Cambridge, 1995), pp. 202–5; Richard H. Britnell, *Growth and Decline in Colchester, 1300–1525* (Cambridge, 1986), pp. 98–9, 107–8; E. B. Dewindt (ed.), *The Court Rolls of Ramsey, Hepmangrove and Bury, 1268–1600* (Toronto, 1990), pp. 51–3.

13 Britnell, *Colchester*, p. 106.

14 Richard Goddard, *Credit and Trade in Later Medieval England, 1353–1532* (Basingstoke, 2016), p. 149. However, borough court rolls are notoriously unforthcoming in terms of details like debt amount. In the sample year (1375/6), only 39.2 per cent of the individual cases supply the amount being sued for.

15 Kowaleski, *Exeter*, p. 349; Chris Briggs, *Credit and Village Society in Fourteenth-Century England* (Oxford, 2008), p. 152.

to market within the region. Sutton and his wife failed to pay for this prodigious consignment of garlic and so Skegby sued them for the amount, using a plea of debt, in Nottingham's borough court in the following February.[16] What we have in these records, therefore, are genuine commercial transactions: the buying and selling of goods using deferred payment on credit in Nottingham in the mid 1370s. In the sample year (1375–6), there were 318 individual debt pleas, many of which returned to court several times in order to resolve the dispute. In this analysis, each transaction is counted only once. These 318 transactions need to be considered against Nottingham's relatively small population of around two to three thousand. There were 295 unique individuals suing, or being sued, for debt in the borough court in this sample year. This could therefore represent about 12 per cent of Nottingham's medieval population. Again, these facts tend to reaffirm the notion that, if these data represent only the transactions that failed, then not only was there a considerable traffic in goods and services in the town at that time, involving many individuals, but also that credit was vital to the efficient conduct of Nottingham's medieval commerce.

Nottingham's Commercial Network

One of the advantages of using network analysis to study court rolls is that it makes all of the actors in the network equally visible, as they resolve their various disputes in the full public glare of the court, rather than viewing a network from a particular person's perspective, such as through an individual merchant's account book. What the court rolls can show, therefore, are the principal mercantile actors in this community, by seeing who traded with whom, who extended most credit and who borrowed most in the course of their trading year. By examining this material graphically, network analysis indicates connections, networks and hierarchies within this medieval trading community.

The nodes (black dots) in the diagrams below correspond to every litigant involved in a debt plea in Nottingham in the sample year. The size of the nodes simply represents the number of connections extending to and from that node (known as 'degree'). The bigger the node, the more interactions are recorded in the borough court rolls for this individual. The edges (the thin black lines connecting the nodes) depict the credit agreements undertaken by these individuals. The direction of the transaction (the creditor extending sales credit to a customer, making that customer the borrower or debtor) is also recorded in these data. The relative position of each node on the diagram is calculated using the principles of 'centrality'. This is perhaps best explained

[16] NA CA 1279/12.

using an analogy, rather than maths. Consider the movement of information or gossip around an office. For all businesses, access to information is key. Information about the cost and supply of credit and the creditworthiness or reputation of customers are prime concerns for anyone operating in a market wherein credit is used. When commercial information like this flows easily around a network of business people, it has the effect of reducing uncertainty and risk and thus reduces a business's transaction costs.[17] This information moves like a virus through the population, infecting one person after another. Those close to the centre of the network are those who will hear the news first. Those at the centre of the network are also those with most control over information and the flow of that information. This demonstrates that they are well connected and therefore central to the network, and that they act as bridges as they transfer knowledge between others within the network. Those at the centre of the network are also able to interrupt the flow of information between nodes, should they so desire. As the information travels from person to person throughout the network, more members of the network become informed. Eventually, even those who rarely interact with the network obtain the information in passing. These misanthropic individuals would be placed in a peripheral position at the edge of a network diagram. Nonetheless, centrality also measures the number of connections (edges) to the most distant peripheral node (known as 'eccentricity'). This means that the jump of information from node to node, from those in control of that information out to the furthest reaches of the network, is quantified. Those with the fewest jumps to the outer rim of the network are considered to be the best connected.

The figures displayed below are graphical representations of the credit network of Nottingham in 1375–6. The network is presented in Figure 9.1. The names of all the individuals who were involved in debt pleas in this year are recorded in these data. However, for clarity, in these diagrams only those individuals discussed in the text have their names attached to their nodes.

To take one example from the network diagram, represented by edges and adjoining nodes, Richard Hopwell was sued by the following individuals for debt in the borough court in the sample year (circled in Figure 9.1): Geoffrey Pulter, John Lawson (for a tunic worth 11d which Lawson had contracted Hopwell to sell) and Richard del Wold (for half an ell of cloth), who all lined up to sue Hopwell on 17 October 1375; Robert de Kegworth on 14 November; William Remay on 28 November and Richard Netherd on 2 April 1376.[18] Apart from informing us that Hopwell was a fairly frequent user of sales credit, that he was involved in the making and selling of clothing in

17 Steven G. Marks, *The Information Nexus: Global Capitalism from the Renaissance to the Present* (Cambridge, 2016), pp. 75–7, 82.
18 NA CA 1279, fols 1, 2, 4, 5, 13.

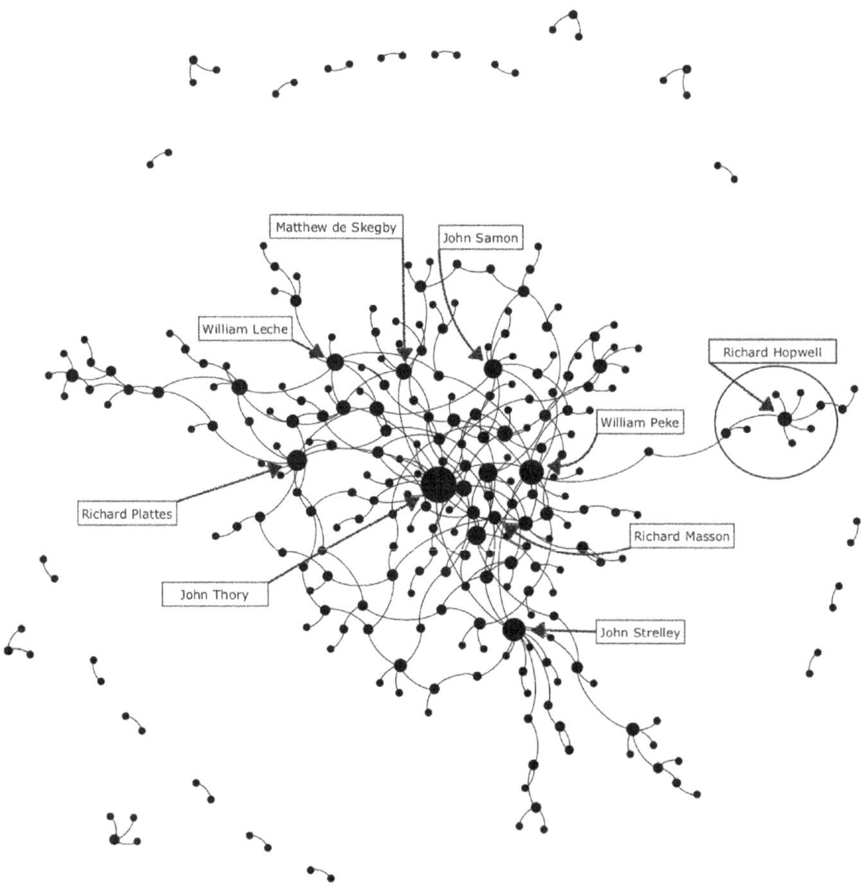

FIGURE 9.1: NOTTINGHAM'S CREDIT NETWORK, 1375–6

Nottingham, and that he was somewhat dilatory in repaying his suppliers, the diagram also demonstrates how this schematic representation should be interpreted. The size of Hopwell's node indicates that he had a number of interactions within the network with all those who were suing him. His node is larger than many of those who had extended him credit and who are thus connected to him by black edges. These individuals (Pulter, Lawson, del Wold, Kegworth, Remay and Netherd) seem to have little contact with anyone else in the network. Of these, Remay and del Wold had slightly wider commercial orbits. William Remay extended credit to Robert Eyton, and Richard del Wold lent to the appropriately-named pouch-maker, Walter Pouch, and another trader called John Roper.[19] As a result of these connections, Hopwell is located

19 NA CA 1279, fols 2, 21.

in the diagram in a peripheral position within the network as a whole. He is not considered to be central to the network, nor a key facilitator within it. He did not transact business as often as other more centrally-placed individuals within the network (those with larger nodes). Furthermore, the people Hopwell dealt with were also marginal or lower-order traders who had very few, if any, business contacts within the network. Those on the peripheral rim of Figure 9.1 are those who are found only once conducting debt pleas in the court rolls; they are therefore almost entirely disconnected to the rest of the network. Contrarily, the grouping of nodes at the very centre of the diagram identifies those individuals at the heart of Nottingham's credit network in the mid 1370s. These are discussed in more detail below. The other salient feature of Figure 9.1 is the size of some of these individuals' (most commonly men's) nodes.[20] Thus those individuals with the largest nodes, such as Richard Plattes and William Peke, lent and borrowed more often than most others in the network.

In 1375–6, one of those in the first division of Nottingham's credit network was John Thory. He both transacted large numbers of credit agreements (which he later pursued through the borough court) and was centrally placed within it (see Figure 9.1). Figure 9.2 shows Thory's immediate business relationships: the individuals to whom he extended sales credit (eight individuals, although he lent to [and sued] one man – William Peke – twice in the sample year) and those from whom he received it (fourteen individuals who sold him goods on credit and later took him to court for failing to pay for these goods at the appointed time). As stated above, these transactions represent only a proportion of his business dealings that required litigation in Nottingham and its region. It is difficult to estimate the ratio of successful credit transactions, repaid in full and on time, to those that defaulted and ended up in the borough court. Pamela Nightingale has suggested that the certificates of defaulted high-value debts using written instruments (thus making them unlike those generally pleaded in borough courts and in royal statute merchant and staple courts) represent about a fifth of all credit in the later fourteenth and early fifteenth century.[21] If this default rate was similar to those lower-value debt pleas found in borough courts, then it suggests that Thory's credit dealings extended much more widely than the borough court evidence indicates.

20 Not all debtors and creditors were men. Agnes Halum, the subject of chapter 4 of this volume, regularly engaged in credit transactions in this period and was an active member of this network (see Figure 9.4).

21 Pamela Nightingale, 'Money and credit in the economy of late medieval England', in D. Wood (ed.), *Medieval Money Matters* (Oxford, 2004), p. 63; Pamela Nightingale, 'Monetary contraction and mercantile credit in later medieval England', *Economic History Review*, 43 (1990), p. 566; Goddard, *Credit and Trade*, pp. 15–16.

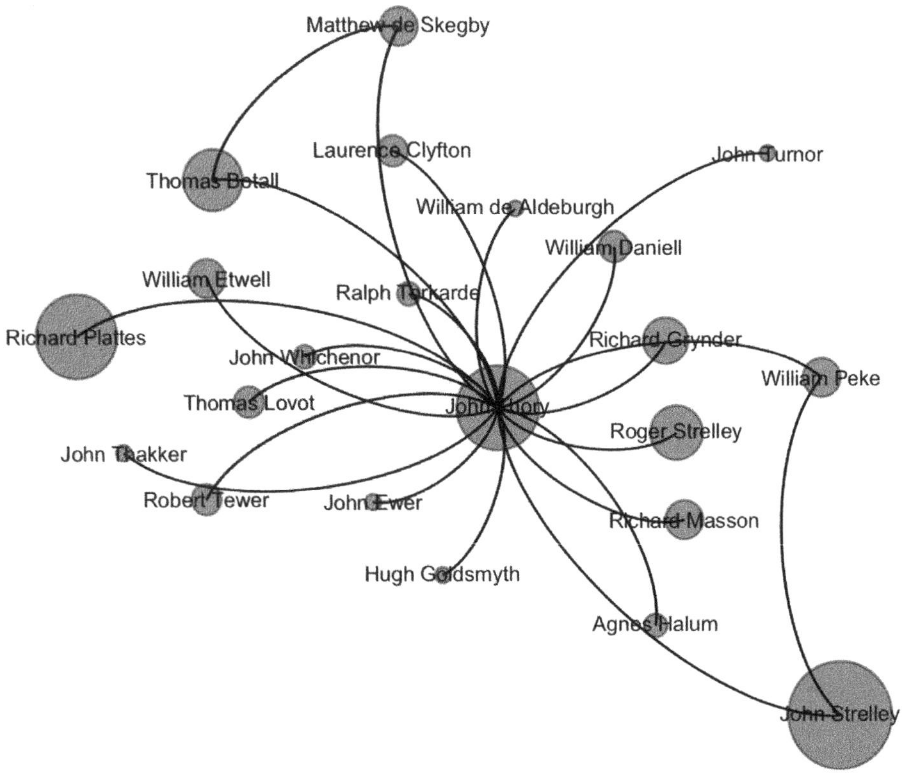

FIGURE 9.2: JOHN THORY'S SUB-NETWORK

The average amounts that John Thory lent were below the 5s 8d late-fourteenth-century mean, at 4s 6d. His principal business involved the buying and selling of horses (no other goods are mentioned) and he worked as a farrier, shoeing and treating horses. His expertise was also used to appraise and value horses on behalf of the borough court.[22] He extended credit to those who bought horses from him, such as Hugh Goldsmyth (for 3s 4d) and William Peke (for 4s 6d) (see Figure 9.2).[23] These amounts must have been the remaining outstanding payments for the horses these men bought (rather than the full price), as a good horse could cost about £1 (or twenty shillings) in the 1370s.[24] John Thory was also regularly granted credit in the course of this horse-trading. For example, he bought a black horse from Richard Plattes

22 NA CA 1279/1; NA CA 1279/3; NA CA 1279/9. For Thory's work as a farrier, see W. H. Stevenson (ed.), *Records of the Borough of Nottingham*, vol. 1 (London, 1882), p. 192.
23 NA CA 1279/6; NA CA 1279/11.
24 David L. Farmer, 'Prices and wages', in Edward Miller (ed.), *The Agrarian History of England and Wales*, vol. 3 (Cambridge, 1991), p. 475.

on 24 January 1376 for twenty-one shillings, which he should have paid off by 2 February (see Figure 9.2).[25] He borrowed more than he lent, with a mean amount borrowed of over fifteen shillings, compared to the mean amount lent of 4s 6d.

John Thory's extended network comprises 158 individuals. This includes his immediate business contacts (as in Figure 9.2), as well as the people that they did business with – and then, finally, his customers' customers' buyers and sellers, three times removed from John Thory's immediate sub-network shown in Figure 9.2. The size of this extended business network – the largest of any Nottingham business person in this year – demonstrates clearly how well connected he was to the whole of Nottingham's business community. One of John Thory's business contacts was Richard Grynder (see Figure 9.2). Grynder was quite well known in Nottingham's court. He spent the 1370s stealing (on one occasion coverlets, linen sheets and other necessaries, worth ten shillings, from Henry de Maisseham's house), getting into fights (one of them with Henry de Maisseham, who was attempting to stop Grynder stealing from him) or withholding cock-fight (*ad pugna gallorum*) winnings from punters. On one occasion, possibly as a result of his quarrelsome brawling, he required the healing services of the leech and widow, Alice Harby, who charged him 32d for her services. Typically, Grynder refused to pay. Alice Harby sued him for the amount.[26] But Grynder was not some low-life criminal. For example, he was often represented in court by his attorney. He was also a businessman. In May 1376, Grynder extended 20d credit to John Thory (Figure 9.2).[27] Grynder had a number of other customers who, like Thory, failed to repay what they owed and were thus sued by him: Robert Blythe, Richard Chilwell and Nicholas Tayt.[28] Grynder's best connected customer was Robert Blythe.[29] One of Blythe's suppliers was Thomas Taverner, a relatively minor player extending credit only to Blythe and two others.[30] This example of an extended network – albeit prodigious – thus demonstrates the potential reach of just one individual (John Thory) from the centre of the network out to its periphery (as seen in Figure 9.1), through the credit transactions undertaken by him and his customers and suppliers.

The discussion above suggests that buyers and sellers were constantly juggling their various obligations and transactions, and managing multiple credit relationships over the year. It would have needed an alert business mind to keep one's eye on all the balls that were in the air at one time. All these

25 NA CA 1279/9.
26 See, for example, NA CA 1277a/23; NA CA 1278/11.
27 NA CA 1279/17.
28 NA CA 1279/1; NA CA 1279/15; NA CA 1279/17.
29 NA CA 1279/12; NA CA 1279/13.
30 NA CA 1279/24.

traders and shopkeepers faced the same exigencies at once: how much was owed and by whom, when was the debt due, what proportion of the goods' price had been deferred, how likely was the debtor to pay up on time, could the agreed repayment terms be extended, and at what point should a creditor go to court to recover the debt? Yet this is what John Thory, and many of the others, seem to have done. Thory had been an active litigant, predominantly in pleas of debt, from 1371; this continued until June 1379, after which he disappears from the record. Furthermore, despite being sued regularly for debt, his credit rating does not seem to have suffered as he continued his trade in horses. A person's reputation was a culturally constructed form of social capital, based upon financial creditability and prompt payment, that gave lenders added confidence that debtors would pay what they owed in the future.[31] At Michaelmas 1378, he borrowed 33s 4d from John Strelley (despite having been sued by Strelley two and a half years earlier), suggesting that Thory's reputation remained secure.[32] This, and Thory's two seemingly unconnected suits against William Peke, indicate that the borough court provided a venue for resolving commercial disputes in an orderly, disciplined way, thus allowing for regular transactions to take place in Nottingham, even if some of the traders had suffered financial setbacks in the past.

The above analysis demonstrates that Thory was centrally placed within the network, and that he was connected (albeit through his customers) to most of the centrally-placed actors in the network. This is confirmed by other measures used in social network analysis. The measurement known as 'betweenness centrality', which measures the level at which any node acts as a bridge connecting other nodes, calculates that Thory, William Peke, Nicholas Gay and Richard Masson were the most connected. The 'betweenness centrality' measurement is displayed in Figure 9.3. Those with the highest level of 'betweenness centrality' are identified by the largest nodes on this diagram. This means that, because these centrally-placed nodes lie between other nodes in the diagram, they have greater ability to control market information (for example, on prices, on customers' creditworthiness or on the cost of credit), because they have the capacity, should they so wish, to obstruct information passing throughout the network. Despite judgements on creditworthiness being made in irregular, informal and often inaccurate ways by these traders, great advantages could theoretically accrue for those who possessed the latest and most accurate information concerning goods, prices and credit.

The second principal actor in Nottingham's business network examined here is John Strelley. Despite the large number of transactions that he pursued

31 Haggerty, *Merely for Money*, pp. 98–101, 120; Muldrew, *Economy of Obligation*, pp. 153–4, 160.

32 NA CA 1279/15.

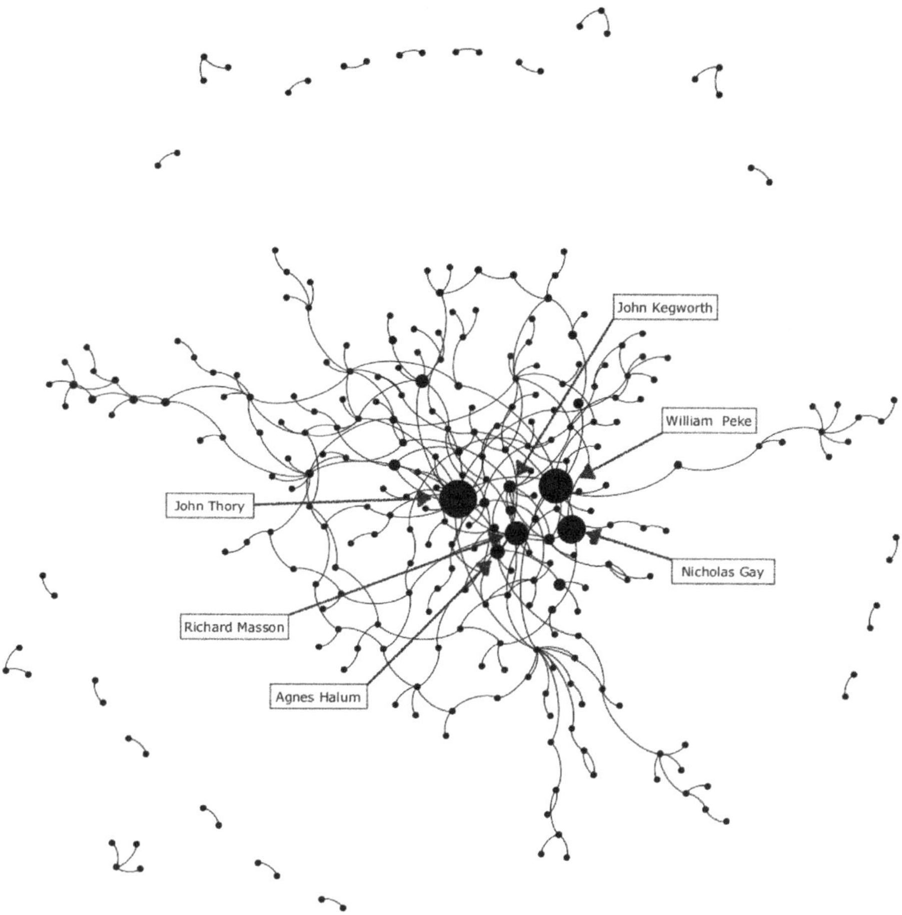

FIGURE 9.3: THE 'BETWEENNESS CENTRALITY' MEASURE OF THE NOTTINGHAM NETWORK

through the borough court, Figure 9.1 places him outside the central core of the network, in an enclave towards the bottom of the diagram, at some distance from the most 'connected' individuals such as John Thory, William Peke and Richard Masson. Figure 9.4 identifies the direct, first-order connections to Strelley – in other words, all of those with whom he personally did business. Strelley lent to people like John Thory, who (as seen above) were central actors within the network. Others to whom Strelley lent, such as Robert Blythe and Joan Lemeryng, also had a few connections (smaller nodes) and so might be considered lower-order participants within this network. Some of the people to whom Strelley lent money or extended credit – such as Geoffrey Lorymer (sometimes known as Ostler), William Suell, John Gateford and William Cole

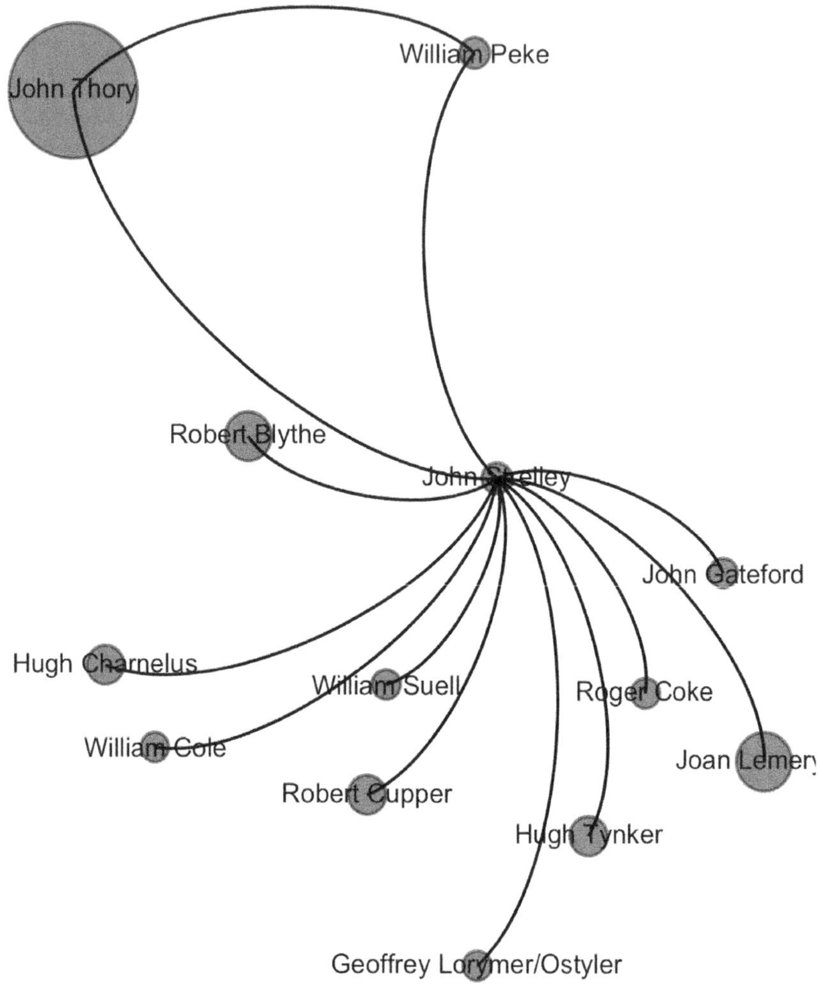

FIGURE 9.4: JOHN STRELLEY'S SUB-NETWORK

– transacted business with nobody other than Strelley in this particular year. This suggests that, whilst he was an important lender, many of those with whom he did business had only a superficial attachment to the network, reducing Strelley's access to, or control over, market information. Despite this, here is seen one of the intrinsic features of a business network like this. John Strelley, like most of the other principal actors in this network, extended credit to a wide variety of customers. The choice of whether or not to extend credit was not made on account of a customer's status or standing as a Nottingham burgess, oligarch or landholder; rather, in this face-to-face business environment, it must have been made simply according to the customer's reputation in the market for creditworthiness.

With twelve individual debt suits to his name, John Strelley was single-handedly responsible for 3.8 per cent of the debt pleas in the sample year, making him the biggest lender. The amounts he extended in credit were slightly above the late-fourteenth-century mean, at 8s 8d.[33] Particularly telling is John Strelley's loan transaction with Geoffrey Lorymer/Ostler. On 28 May 1376, Strelley sued Geoffrey Lorymer for 13s 4d. Lorymer, as his surname suggests, made spurs, bridles, stirrups, keys and locks.[34] In this transaction, Strelley lent money to Lorymer. What seems to have happened in this case was that Lorymer (who came from Lenton, about two kilometres outside Nottingham) had acted as a pledge for a man called John Stanfale, in another court, possibly acting as a surety for a loan.[35] The details of the case are unknown, but Lorymer, as pledge, seems to have been required to pay Stanfale's debt. In order to do so, he borrowed the 13s 4d from John Strelley. What this complicated series of events suggests is that Strelley's reputation for having liquid capital available for lending and being able to extend credit at short notice was widely known, and partly explains his position as Nottingham's pre-eminent lender. No one sued John Strelley in the borough court for debt, so, in terms of both liquidity and reputation, he must also have been in the unusual position of always paying his debts on time. If the loans of the other principal lenders (see Figure 9.1), John Thory, William Leche, Richard Plattes and John Samon – where they extended, rather than received, credit – are added to Strelley's, then these five men were responsible for roughly 14 per cent of the lending in this year.

Network analysis might be able to identify Strelley as a principal lender, but it will never be able to answer questions about his business assets or liquid resources, or the money he was able to lend to people like Geoffrey Lorymer. This requires historical research. There is some evidence that Strelley might have owned a tavern in St Mary's Street in the town. As is well known, these were the sites of much informal marketing in the period.[36] His surname might also suggest that John was related to the minor knightly family of de Strelley, who lived in the moated manor house in Strelley village, situated 6.5km north-west of Nottingham.[37] Evidence of the more senior, knightly branch of the family is seen in Samson de Strelley, who was sheriff of Nottingham in

33 The late-fourteenth-century mean was 5s 8d. However, Strelley's mean loan amount is taken from only two recorded amounts: 4s and 13s 4d.

34 NA CA 1279/18. For Geoffrey Lorymer, see Stevenson, *Nottingham*, vol. 1, p. 251.

35 NA CA 1279/23.

36 For Strelley's fine for breaking the assize of ale, see Stevenson, *Nottingham*, vol. 1, p. 204.

37 For a pedigree of the Strelley family (although excluding John and Roger, another relation in the Nottingham credit network), see Robert Thoroton, 'Strelley', in John Throsby (ed.), *Thoroton's History of Nottinghamshire: Vol. 2, Republished with Large Additions by John Throsby* (Nottingham, 1790), pp. 218–22 <http://www.british-history.ac.uk/thoroton-notts/vol2/pp218–222> [accessed 11 March 2016].

1375.[38] Conjecturally, therefore, John Strelley might have acquired the capital to fund his lending through his gentry family connections. He certainly seems to have been a noted businessman in the community, but certainly not one at the centre of Nottingham's political life. He was one of the town's bailiffs for only one year, in 1366–7, and acted as a witness to the enrolment of a charter in the borough court in September 1376.[39] However, like many of the town's leading businessmen (except John Samon, discussed below), that was the extent of his administrative commitments. Richard Plattes, for example, was, like Strelley, bailiff for only one year (1389–90), and John Thory never held office of any kind in the town. Strelley, and many of those like him, seem to have concentrated instead upon their business or money-lending activities; it is these, rather than a significant administrative role, that placed these men in important positions within Nottingham's credit network.[40]

Unlike these men, John Samon was very active in the town's administration. He was mayor at least seven times and held the office more times than anyone else in Nottingham's medieval history. He was mayor of Nottingham in the sample year of 1375–6. John Samon is the only one of these business people who could be considered to have been involved in what might be described as 'high finance'. Indeed, his business interests were of an entirely different magnitude to most of the other traders using the borough court. He dealt in a range of goods and exported wool to Flanders; he was a wealthy, multi-property holder and he lent large sums using the statute staple court.[41] The statute staple court in Nottingham was part of a royally-sanctioned, kingdom-wide debt registration system, which provided for the efficient recovery of high-value defaulted debts (over forty shillings) using written instruments known as recognizances. These were used predominantly to fund English domestic trade.[42] In these documents, Samon is described as a merchant. Between 1361 and 1378 he extended between £5 and £80 in credit three times to local business people from Nottinghamshire and Derbyshire, using the Nottingham staple court – commonly single-handedly, but on one occasion in partnership with another notable Nottingham citizen called John Ingram (for £20).[43] One of these, for one hundred shillings in 1373, was to Richard Chilwell; two years later, Samon also sued Chilwell for a separate debt of nine shillings in the

38 NA 1279/5/attached piece.

39 Stevenson, *Nottingham*, vol. 1, p. 425; NA CA 1279/26.

40 For the contrasting experience of the oligarchs of Exeter, see Maryanne Kowaleski, 'The commercial dominance of a medieval provincial oligarchy: Exeter in the late fourteenth century', *Mediaeval Studies*, 46 (1984), pp. 355–84.

41 For John Samon, see Richard Goddard, 'Medieval business networks: St Mary's Guild and the borough court in later medieval Nottingham', *Urban History*, 40 (2013), pp. 3–27.

42 Goddard, *Credit and Trade*, pp. 29, 52–3, 63, 84.

43 The National Archives (hereafter TNA), C 241/141/86 (with John Ingram, 1361, £20), C 241/155/4 (1373, one hundred shillings), C 241/165/51 (1378, £80).

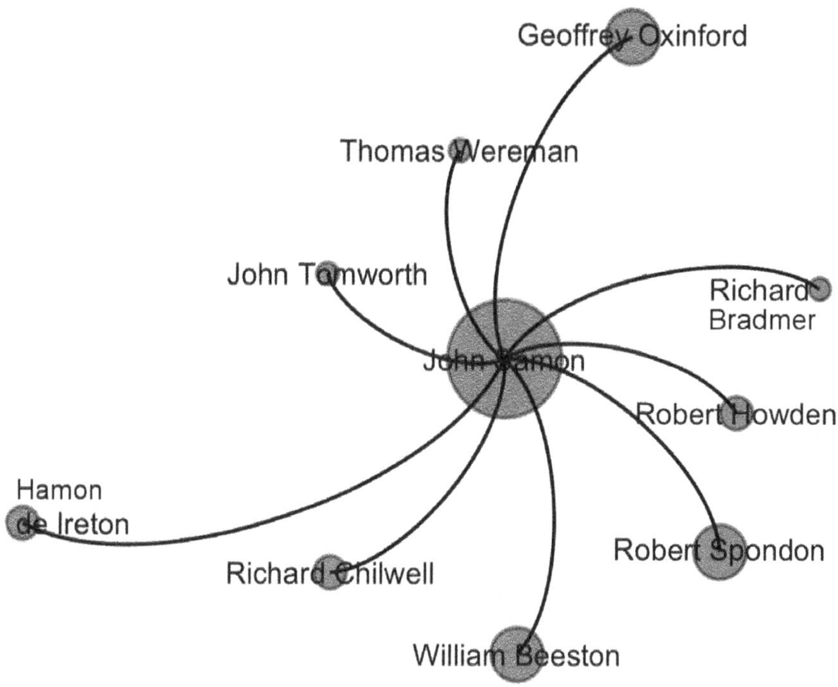

FIGURE 9.5: JOHN SAMON'S SUB-NETWORK

borough court (see Figure 9.5). In the local borough court, Samon similarly sued for amounts that were higher than the late-fourteenth-century average (a mean of 91s 10½d) and, for those over forty shillings, he used recognizances as he had in the more senior staple court to prove the debt in the borough court.[44] For example, in August 1376 he sued two, or possibly three, individuals for ten marks each.[45] These transactions seem to be a continuation of his larger-scale mercantile business, which he pursued in the borough court rather than the staple court, because the borough court was geared to resolving disputes between Nottingham citizens. He may have chosen this court because his pleas might have met with more success in the borough court, in the town where he was, as mayor, a well-known, high-status, 'worthy man'.[46]

Figure 9.5 identifies the nine customers sued for debt by John Samon in this sample year. Few of these people were major lenders or borrowers,

44 The late-fourteenth-century borough court debt value average was 5s 8d. However, Samon's mean debt amount is reconstructed from only three of his nine transactions recorded in the court.

45 NA CA 1279/22.

46 Samon's success in the borough court is discussed in Goddard, 'Medieval business networks', pp. 18–19. For wealth and office-holding conferring reputation, see Muldrew, *Economy of Obligation*, pp. 153–4, 160.

which tends to explain Samon's distance from the network's core in Figure 9.1. Geoffrey Oxinford, for example, extended credit to three other people and borrowed from John Samon. Other customers of Samon, like Thomas Wereman, were very minor players who rarely lent or borrowed (Wereman only borrowed on one other occasion).[47] So these individuals might therefore be considered part of Samon's business sub-network, in that he was in a position to control the amount of credit passing between them; but the fact that many of his customers were disconnected meant that he possessed relatively little integration within the network as a whole, when compared to men like William Peke or John Thory. John Samon was thus in a different league to the horse-traders, artisans and shopkeepers of later medieval Nottingham. It seems likely therefore that Samon's grander business interests required a different level of security than the use of written recognizances and the statute staple court, which were more typical of high-status wholesale merchants engaged in domestic and international trade; the latter were thus engaged in wider, extra-urban business networks that are imperceptible using just the Nottingham court evidence. It was exactly men like this who made up the ranks of the English mayoral elite. Intriguingly, many of Samon's transactions (44 per cent) in the borough court were with other late-fourteenth-century bailiffs: Robert Spondon (bailiff, 1365/6); Richard Bradmer (bailiff, 1374/5); William Beeston (bailiff, 1374/5) and Robert Howden (bailiff, 1380/1) (see Figure 9.6).[48] Thus John Samon's immediate business circle, or sub-network, comprised many of those who, like him, had been involved, or would become involved, in the government of the town.

The network analysis can certainly identify key players within Nottingham's commercial network. It indicates those who controlled the amount of credit flowing through the system. These are useful markers within a large and disparate group of business people. However, using the borough court evidence to more closely examine these individuals' credit transactions demonstrates that business in medieval Nottingham was much more intricate, complicated and impenetrable, and the relationships much more convoluted, than the rather attractive network diagrams produced above suggest.

Trust: How Successful was Nottingham's Commercial Network?

If a business network can be defined as a loose collection of people, buying and selling goods using credit, with a collective knowledge concerning its members' status, respectability or creditworthiness, then Nottingham's commercial

47 NA CA 1279/4; NA CA 1279/21.
48 Stevenson, *Nottingham*, vol. 1, pp. 424–6.

network might well be a business network of sorts.[49] Indeed, as discussed below, to what extent might the borough court have acted as a location where this network met? However, this was not a network in a medieval sense. It was not a voluntary association born out of collective identity or fraternity. These were basically unconnected members of the public, going about their daily business, as all the above examples clearly demonstrate. There is little sense of 'community' here, to which these people voluntarily belonged. They might well have been Nottingham citizens, and thus connected geographically, but they were not linked in any other particular way – for example, by guild membership. To what extent can the modern criteria or designation 'network' be applied to this ill-defined collection of individuals, who used the court to resolve their debt disputes?

Arbitration in out-of-court settlements was a common feature of borough courts. These were known as 'love days' (*amor'*). In 1375/6 in Nottingham, forty-seven cases were granted love days by the court. For example, on 3 October 1375, William Beeston and Simon Roper were granted, 'at the wish of the parties (Beeston and Roper) … a day of concord (for a second time) until the next court', concerning a plea of debt. In February 1376, the court granted Robert Alfreton and John Kegworth a similar period of arbitration.[50] Might this be interpreted as a choice or preference for mediation over litigation? Was arbitration seen as an effective alternative to suing customers through the borough court? This seems unlikely for two reasons. Firstly, arbitration was rarely used for debt pleas, especially those supported by writs or tallies, due to their inherent lack of complexity.[51] In the sample year at Nottingham, only nineteen borough court debt pleas were granted love days. More convoluted pleas of trespass, and particularly pleas of covenant (where agreements had been broken), were more commonly granted love days by the court.[52] Arbitration therefore was used in only 6 per cent of the debt pleas registered in the borough court in the sample year, suggesting that litigation was the first, rather than last, resort for these traders. The source material does not allow access to the informal arbitrations relating to debt that might have taken place between members of the network that were not court-sponsored. Indeed, this may be considered a flaw in the methodology. However, using the available borough court evidence, it is clear that arbitration was a component of borough court procedures, rather than a process separate to it. It is likely (although no evidence exists for Nottingham) that the arbitrators were chosen,

49 Buchnea, 'Networks and clusters', pp. 259–60, 262–3.

50 NA CA 1279/1; NA CA 1279/11.

51 Derek Roebuck, *Mediation and Arbitration in the Middle Ages* (Oxford, 2013), pp. 21–33, 84–6, 385–6; Edward Powell, 'Arbitration and the law in England in the late Middle Ages', *Transactions of the Royal Historical Society*, 33 (1983), pp. 52–3.

52 See, for example, NA CA 1279/2.

not by the parties in dispute, but rather by the court. In the absence of more complete records, the balance of evidence suggests that debt litigation at the borough court which included love days was a central constituent of business life in Nottingham.

The borough court was the principal venue for resolving disputes between the burgesses of Nottingham. Therefore, the sessions of the borough court were regularly attended by Nottingham's traders, as they pursued their cases through that court. Might it be possible, therefore, to see the court as a public area where regular attendees – like Strelley, Thory and Samon, who spent much of their time suing or being sued – obtained and passed on business information, particularly on creditworthiness, and gained new trading contacts? For example, John Strelley attended court, pursuing his debt cases through the system, at least twenty-seven times in this one sample year. In other words, merely being litigious placed these actors at the centre of this commercial network. Should the court itself be considered a proxy networking institution, or a networking hub for the central actors of the network? This was certainly not its function.

This proposition can be tested. William Peke was both a litigious businessman (Figure 9.1) and held a commanding position within the network (Figure 9.3). William Peke's sub-network – those people with whom he personally transacted business – is identified in Figure 9.6. As a result, he is regularly recorded as being in court, pleading his cases or, more commonly, being sued by traders from whom he had bought goods. William Peke dealt in sheep- and calf-skins and sold cloth.[53] Nottingham's borough court was held every two weeks between 3 October 1375 and 3 September 1376, totalling twenty-five court sessions. William Peke is cited in fifteen of these sessions, representing 60 per cent of the total. Thus, beyond Peke's personal, face-to-face contact with his customers and suppliers, his cases were heard at the same time as those of many of the other plaintiffs and defendants involved in debt cases when they attended the guildhall, waiting for their cases to come before the bailiffs. The network, after all, comprises *only* these individuals who used the borough court to recover their debts. Perhaps whilst standing around waiting for their cases to be heard, these traders discussed credit, prices and reputations. If so, it suggests that the most litigious were also, potentially, the best informed – simply because of the inherent attributes of medieval borough court proceedings. Indeed, as Figure 9.3 suggests, Peke's dealings with well-connected people who all frequented the court give him a high 'betweenness centrality' score and place him close to the centre of the network.

However, a note of caution needs to be sounded here. The networking algorithm counts all of the connections recorded in the court rolls. It is not

53 NA CA 1279/1; NA CA 1279/10; NA CA 1279/18.

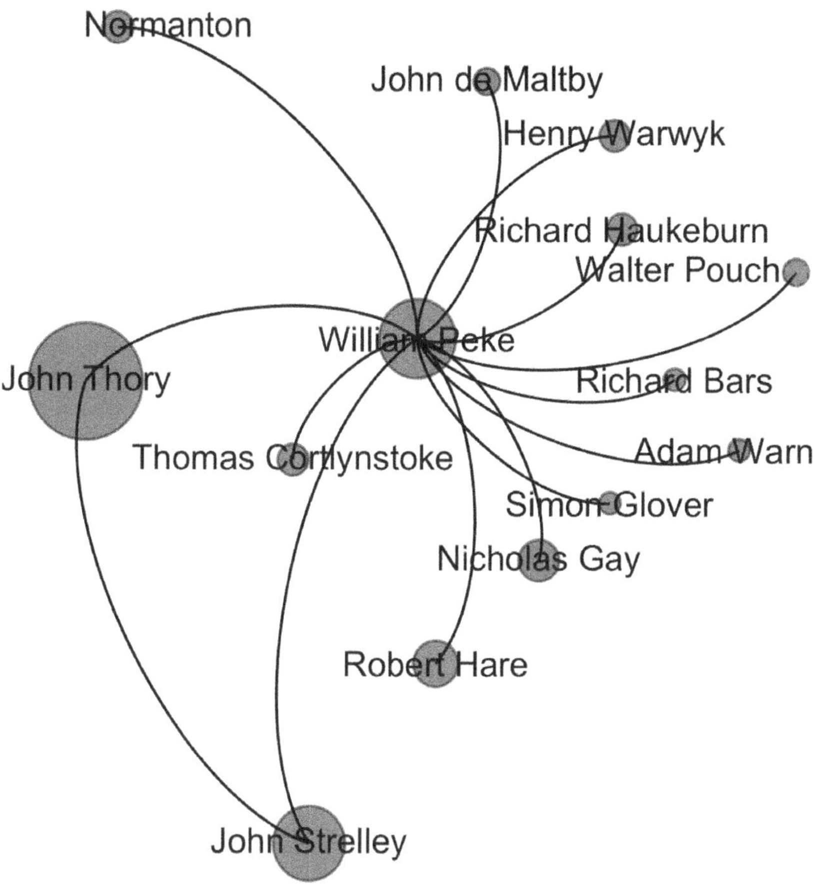

FIGURE 9.6: WILLIAM PEKE'S SUB-NETWORK

sophisticated enough to distinguish between a name recorded in a debt plea and the physical presence of the litigants in the court itself. William Peke did not always turn up at court. He was recorded as being absent when he was the one being sued (and thus fined) seven times – sometimes with, but often without, an essoin. If William Peke's absences and essoins are included in the analysis, then he is recorded as actually being in attendance in the guildhall at only eight (32 per cent) of these sessions. Peke may well have been well informed about the performance of the local market, and the borough court may well have informally functioned as a venue wherein business information could be more easily exchanged, but it is likely that Figure 9.3 overestimates Peke's 'betweenness centrality' rating and therefore places him closer to the core of the network than perhaps he was in reality. The complexities of real-world relationships, especially when viewed nearly 650 years later, are difficult to describe in a graph.

Even if, conjecturally, the court itself acted as a networking venue, to what extent did the members of this network have confidence that the network could aid them in achieving their commercial objectives?[54] This too can be tested, with reference to the speed with which these traders turned to litigation rather than allowing personal or informal networks to resolve their problems. To what extent does litigation indicate a lack of trust in the efficacy of the network? Out of the 318 transactions recorded in the sample year, twenty-four (7.5 per cent) give information concerning the date at which the debt was to be repaid. For example, on 28 May 1376, Alexander Esterlyng sued John Kegworth (possibly related to the Robert de Kegworth cited above) for woad (*wad*) and madder (*mader*) – raw materials used in the cloth-dying process – worth thirty-six shillings, which Kegworth ought to have paid at the previous Easter (13 April 1376).[55] Therefore, Esterlyng brought this plea to court for the first time forty-five days after the debt had fallen due. If the five-year outlier, wherein the same John Kegworth was sued by Robert Hare for failing to dye 7lbs of blanket yarn (*Chalon yern*) is excluded, then the mean period between default and court proceedings was 72.1 days, with the most common period, as with the Esterlyng case, being between forty-three and forty-seven days (in about one third of the cases).[56] Some people – like Richard Plattes when suing John Thory, who hadn't paid for the black horse he had bought – sued very quickly, in just thirteen days.[57] The servant John Smyth sued his employer (and presumably relative) Geoffrey Smyth for 30d wages and a tunic worth 20d, which was also probably part of his remuneration, only eighteen days after this payment was due.[58] The fact that it took an average of between one and a half and two months to recover debts through the court – bearing in mind that the court was only held every two weeks – suggests that these traders turned to the law relatively quickly. Even if they had attempted to recover their money informally before going to court – perhaps using friends, associates and other members of their informal network to help or intercede in the recovery process – they tended not to keep this up for very long. This suggests, of course, that the Nottingham burgesses had relatively little confidence that personal or informal networks could resolve their disputes, and so turned instead to the borough court, which provided an institutional level of security.

54 Kadens, 'Pre-modern credit networks', pp. 2440–3.
55 NA CA 1279/18.
56 NA CA 1279/1.
57 NA CA 1279/9.
58 NA CA 1279/11.

In order for a network to be of real benefit to its members, those individuals need to be well connected and interact regularly. Network analysis of the type employed here has the potential to identify the extent to which the group interacts, and it can therefore suggest how cohesive and successful the network actually was. There are a number of ways of quantifying these factors. 'Modularity' qualifies the number of communities or sub-groups that exist within the data. In the Nottingham debt data, there is less than one. This means not only that no smaller clusters of traders can be identified within the network as a whole, but also that the elements within the network itself are relatively disengaged. This can be further examined using the 'eccentricity' measure, which identifies the outliers in a network. In the Nottingham evidence, the fact that 39.7 per cent of the nodes require no jumps to reach the peripheral rim (because they are already there), and that a further 26.8 per cent require only one short hop to do so, indicates that there is a large number of peripheral members of the network. This means that 66.5 per cent of the members of Nottingham's credit network should be considered marginal or extraneous (see Figure 9.1). In fact, only five people (1.7 per cent) – men like John Thory and William Peke – had eight or more steps to the outer rim, and so would be considered to have a dominant or pivotal role within the network. The data again indicates, therefore, that the majority of the network was disconnected. The measurement of 'graph density' is the final nail in the coffin of Nottingham's credit network. A value of one would indicate that all (or 100 per cent) of the nodes in the diagram are connected. The Nottingham data yields a graph density of 0.008 – meaning that only 0.8 per cent of the nodes are connected, and suggesting an inordinately disconnected and dysfunctional group of people. According to the statistical analysis proffered by the visual analytics methodology, these medieval business people did not trust that the network would work to their advantage. This might help to explain why they turned to litigation in the borough court so quickly.

Conclusion

Using visual analytics and network analysis, it has been possible to identify 'central actors' and facilitators within a credit network, with good reputations and an expert knowledge of local trading conditions in Nottingham in the later fourteenth century. These were people like John Thory and William Peke, who had influence beyond their own sub-networks of direct customers or suppliers, and connections to the wider set of business people in Nottingham. It identifies important lenders like John Strelley and John Samon as the high-level players within the network, although not necessarily centrally placed within it. It is certainly possible that these important actors had greater authority and control over the trade they undertook – perhaps, as network studies suggest, placing them in a position whereby they could dictate the terms of their contracts more easily (although in this case we have no direct evidence of that).

The network analysis methodology has presented the evidence in an intriguing and easily digestible way. It has revealed questions and approaches that might not have been discerned in a traditional analysis of borough court rolls, particularly in terms of perceiving the network as a whole and levels of connectivity within it. It has suggested that Nottingham traders, especially those who attended the court often, did not require personal trust or informal networks because they trusted in the institutional security afforded by the court. Furthermore, the court militated against a collapse in a trader's reputation by effectively enforcing broken agreements. This allowed trade to continue in the town, even if reputations became tarnished. The court might be seen, therefore, as an arbiter of trust or a surrogate for interpersonal trust within the community.[59]

But this study has also revealed the care that needs to be taken when adopting new methodologies. This is demonstrated in William Peke's over-valued 'betweenness centrality', discussed above. Furthermore, the network analysis may be distorted by the cost of litigation, a factor that is not included here.[60] Wealthy, highly-capitalised merchants such as John Samon or John Strelley might have sued more often, rather than using their informal network associations to resolve their debt problems, simply because they could more easily afford litigation than lower-order traders. If cost was a factor in the decision to litigate for some of the members of the network, then this has the effect of bending the true dynamics of the network out of shape. Furthermore, the intricacies and subtleties of medieval commerce in conjunction with the personal relationships and foibles of its merchants remain hidden from us. Individuals' idiosyncrasies are difficult to factor into a network analysis of this kind. Finally, historians need to be wary of applying the attractive concept of a 'network' where none actually existed. However, network analysis has allowed Nottingham's business people to be studied as though they were a network. The analysis itself reveals this to have lacked any real cohesion. These individuals probably never considered themselves to be associated in this way – unlike, for example, the members of a local guild or fraternity. Historians have suggested that networks based upon trading relationships (rather than ethnicity or religion) are, in some ways, more 'modern'.[61] Perhaps, therefore,

59 For the increasing use of informal networks to resolve commercial disputes in the eighteenth century, see Haggerty, *Merely for Money*, p. 146.

60 Tom Olding and Penny Tucker (eds), *The Common and Piepowder Courts of Southampton, 1426–1483*, Southampton Record Series, 45 (2011), part 1, pp. xxx–xxxi.

61 Robin Pearson and David Richardson, 'Business networking in the Industrial Revolution', *Economic History Review*, 54 (2001), pp. 657–79.

seeing these traders in a modern sense – of merchants coming together to share skills and capital, and including people known only by association (rather than personally) – might be slightly misleading in this medieval case.[62] But networks have also been described as patterns of distribution, credit or information. Viewing the participants of this network in that way may be of more value. The network analysis traces these business connections and analyses the strength of these interconnections in a novel and useful way. These relationships and links are viewed through the lens of the town's foremost urban institution: the borough court. This methodology, when used cautiously and in conjunction with a diligent and keen analysis of the rolls themselves, has the potential to reveal much about urban society in the later Middle Ages.

62 Haggerty and Haggerty, 'Visual analytics of an eighteenth-century business network'; Haggerty and Haggerty, 'The life cycle of a metropolitan business network'.

10

SOCIETY, STATUS AND THE LEET COURT IN MARGERY KEMPE'S LYNN

SUSAN MADDOCK

Lynn's borough leet court rolls from 1309 to 1434 comprise the most socially inclusive record to survive from late medieval Lynn.[1] In the late 1370s, for example, they name over a thousand individuals who lived or traded in the town: many more than the sole surviving (but incomplete) poll tax return of 1379, and close to one third of the likely adult population.[2] Described by Henry Harrod, who catalogued the rolls in 1867, as containing 'very few entries of any moment',[3] the leet rolls have never been published, with the exception of a short run of entries from part of a single roll.[4] Nor have they previously been subjected to systematic study, although Stephen Alsford included material from the court rolls in his online history of medieval Lynn,[5] and Kate Parker considered the status of the leet officers as part of a study of the town's government and politics.[6] The purpose of this chapter is to demonstrate how, despite their seemingly mundane contents and chronological gaps, the leet records can enlarge

1 King's Lynn Borough Archives (hereafter KLBA) KL/C 17/1–22 and 41; Norfolk Record Office (hereafter NRO) DCN 44/76/176; the Duke of Norfolk's archives at Arundel Castle (hereafter ACM) MD 1475 and MD 1478. There are complete (or almost complete) leet rolls for twenty-one years and incomplete ones for nine more.

2 Carolyn C. Fenwick, *The Poll Taxes of 1377, 1379 and 1381: Part 2, Lincolnshire-Westmorland* (Oxford, 2001), pp. 180–5.

3 Henry Harrod, *Report on the Deeds and Records of the Borough of King's Lynn* (King's Lynn, 1874), p. 125.

4 A transcript, not wholly accurate, of the first twenty-one of 140 entries for a single constabulary, from an undated roll [1379], in Dorothy M. Owen, *The Making of King's Lynn: A Documentary Survey* (London, 1984), pp. 420–1.

5 Stephen Alsford, *History of Medieval Lynn*, <http://users.trytel.com/~tristan/towns/lynn1.html> [accessed 29 September 2017].

6 Katharine M. Parker, 'Lordship, liberty and the pursuit of politics in Lynn, 1370–1420' (unpublished doctoral thesis, University of East Anglia, 2004).

our understanding of the social make-up of one of England's leading port towns and throw new light on the internal political conflicts which plagued Lynn during the adult lifetime of Margery Kempe. Famous as the author of the earliest autobiographical text in English, Margery Kempe (c. 1373 to c. 1440) was the daughter of one of Lynn's leading townsmen, John de Brunham (or Burnham), wife to another merchant-burgess of Lynn, John Kempe, and the mother of fourteen children. Her book, rediscovered as a single complete manuscript in 1934, centres on her spiritual experiences and aspirations, but also contains vivid glimpses of everyday life in the early fifteenth century.[7]

Lynn Bishop, despite its status as a 'free borough' under royal charters from 1204 onwards, remained a seigneurial borough until 1537, and the near-complete loss of records of episcopal administration in Lynn, including the local courts of pleas,[8] has left a major gap in the archival evidence. Kate Parker expressed regret that 'it has not been possible … to map family and other kinship and friendly relations between the leading personalities in the town for more than a few isolated instances [and] the paucity of local court records has also resulted in evidence for the lower social *strata* being meagre'.[9] The wide social reach of the leet records appeared to offer potential for remedying this gap; perhaps even for 'placing Margery Kempe securely within broad family and social networks',[10] something which has previously proved elusive, provided one, apparently intractable, obstacle could be overcome.

The medieval borough, which was coterminous with the parish of St Margaret, was divided into constabularies for the purposes of neighbourhood policing and taxation. There were ten of these divisions until the late 1340s. By 1350, there were nine; the same number as in the early modern period, but whether their boundaries were the same was unknown, the medieval divisions being identified in the borough records only by the constables' names. Even to match a constabulary in one roll with the same one in the next surviving roll was, in most instances, impossible, depriving the entries of meaningful context. Through transcription and comparative analysis of the entire text of the leet rolls, however, the constabularies have now been identified topographically and do appear to correspond with the modern wards (North End, Kettlewell, Paradise, Jews Lane, New Conduit, Chequer, Trinity Hall, Sedgeford Lane and Stonegate), as shown on the map.[11]

7 Sanford Brown Meech and Hope Emily Allen (eds), *The Book of Margery Kempe*, Early English Text Society, original ser., 212 (London, 1940); the most recent translation is Anthony Bale (ed.), *The Book of Margery Kempe* (Oxford, 2015).

8 A few scattered records survive for the Steward's Hall court and the Husting, or Monday, court: extracts are published in Owen, *King's Lynn*, pp. 409–18.

9 Parker, 'Lordship', p. 12.

10 Anthony Goodman, *Margery Kempe and her World* (Harlow, 2002), p. 4.

11 The methodology used is described in Susan Maddock, 'Neighbours, nuisances and night-walkers in early-fifteenth-century Lynn', *The Annual: The Bulletin of the Norfolk Archaeological and Historical Research Group*, 24 (2015), pp. 44–51.

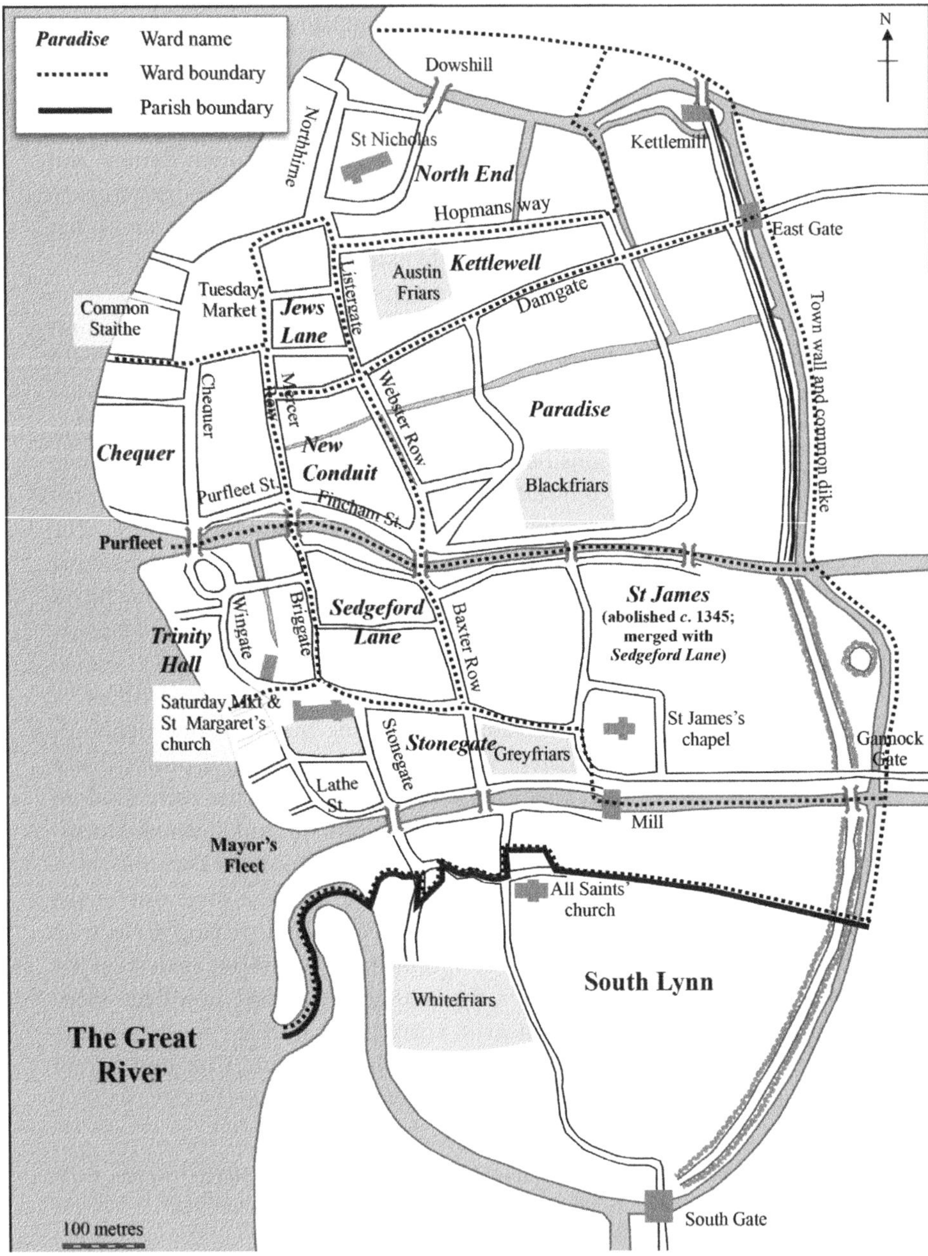

MAP 10.1: MAP OF LYNN IN THE LATE MEDIEVAL PERIOD, SHOWING THE WARD BOUNDARIES

The Leet Court Processes

The leet court, like the other local courts, belonged to the bishop of Norwich, but, by an agreement made in 1309, its administration was split between the bishop and the town.[12] The court was held annually in the Steward's Hall, the bishop's administrative headquarters in Lynn, on the feast of St Simon and St Jude (28 October). The bishop's steward presided, but the mayor and burgesses were required to be present. All resident male householders were also supposed to attend, and those traders using weights and measures were expected to bring them to the court for inspection. By the mid fourteenth century, the leet jury comprised eighteen men: two capital pledges, or headboroughs, from each of the nine constabularies. The constables and headboroughs were chosen by the town's governing body, as were the four affeerers, whose job it was to set the amercements for each infringement. The income from leet amercements was farmed to the mayor and community for an annual payment of £40, but it was the bishop's bailiff who actually collected the money.

In drawing up their bills of presentments, the headboroughs had guidance in the form of a list of 'all manner of articles that belong to the leet'.[13] Some of their enquiries required active scrutiny, and the headboroughs are described in several of the chamberlains' accounts as having been sent around the town to carry out an inspection, a task for which they were fortified by drink to the total value of two shillings.[14] Informants might be amerced for failing to respond, usually at the same level as those who failed to attend the court itself, but sometimes at a much higher sum, especially if they behaved obstructively or offensively, like Godfrey Bolde the tailor, who not only refused to appear before the New Conduit headboroughs in 1400, but couched his refusal in offensive language and additionally refused to give the names of his two servants, who were of an age (twelve years or more) at which they should have entered into a tithing.[15] Nor could headboroughs expect compliance even from their own constable: Robert Burgeys, constable of the ward later known as Paradise, flatly refused for two years running to appear before his headboroughs himself, or to let his servants do so.[16]

Attention was drawn to the leet day by proclamation, made either by the bishop's bailiff or by the town's bellman. The headboroughs' presentments

12 KLBA KL/C 10/5–6 (copies of a composition between John Salmon, bishop of Norwich, and the mayor and burgesses of Lynn, 6 October 1309); abstract in Owen, *King's Lynn*, pp. 379–80.

13 NRO NCR Case 5C/10. Containing forty-five articles, the list is undated but in the hand of Thomas Burbage, town clerk of Lynn, 1457–79.

14 In 1374, for example, the customary payment of two shillings was made to the capital pledges for drink at the time of the visitation of the town to view divers defects (KLBA KL/C 39/34).

15 ACM MD 1478 (leet roll, 1400).

16 Burgeys was amerced two shillings in 1403 and 40d in 1404 (KLBA KL/C 17/14 and 15), compared with the routine 2d or 3d for failure to attend.

were made public and any further additions, such as traders failing to bring their weights and measures for inspection, were either added to the bills of presentments or noted separately. The annotated rolls were then submitted to the affeerers, who were selected a few days after the leet day, perhaps to minimise the risk of bias or embarrassment. More than half the surviving leet records are final copies, written out at the town's expense by one of the bishop's clerks at the Steward's Hall, and identifiable by their relative neatness and the occasional scribal error in copying. In 1404, for example, William Asshebourne, then still in the bishop's service (from 1408 he was the town's common clerk), was paid 6s 8d for the town's copy of the leet record that year, which is recognisably in his hand, as is the previous roll from 1403.[17] Other leet records are the annotated bills which had been exhibited at the court, one for each constabulary, filed together; presumably the borough decided against paying for a fair copy in those years, instead retrieving their own originals for preservation.[18] There is also one instance of what appears to be a first draft of a bill of presentments, without any affeerers' annotations, and one roll of estreats, heavily annotated by the collecting bailiff.[19]

The court processes involved a number of people and incurred substantial costs. In addition to the two shillings which encouraged the headboroughs on their initial survey, they were entertained to the total value of fifteen shillings at the presentation of their verdicts. A higher sum per head, a total of ten shillings, was expended on the affeerers. These were all customary payments, unchanged from year to year. Clerical assistance had to be paid for, too, and any special diligence exercised by the bailiff in collecting the sums amerced might be recognised by a payment of up to twenty shillings, but even in the years when the bailiff had put in extra effort to collect the money due, the expenses should not have amounted to more than £3. In the 1360s and early 1370s, however, as the borough's profits from the leet reached a sum in the region of £30 a year, the amount spent on entertaining at the time of the leet, both in the mayor's house and at the Steward's Hall, crept up, until the total expenses of the leet were recorded in 1374 at more than £6. The town's governing body put a stop to this not long afterwards: an ordinance made in 1378 noted that 'great, various and excessive' expense had been lavished in recent years on food and drink on the day of the leet and afterwards, and made clear that this was to cease. From then on, only the long-established expenses, such as the seventeen shillings for the headboroughs, would be allowable.[20]

17 KLBA KL/C 39/45 (chamberlains' accounts, 1404/5); KL/C 17/14 and 15 (leet rolls, 1403 and 1404).

18 Examples are the rolls for 1391 and 1422 (KLBA KL/C 17/11 and 13).

19 KLBA KL/C 17/7 m. 3 (presentments for Wyth [Kettlewell] constabulary, c. 1361); NRO DCN 44/76/176 (account of revenue from the leet of Lynn Bishop, 1311).

20 KLBA KL/C 39/23–36 (chamberlains' accounts, 1360–77); Holcombe Ingleby (ed.), *The Red*

The Court's Officers

What kind of men were the leet headboroughs and affeerers, and how did they relate to the borough's governing elite? Stephen Alsford, who has carried out the most thorough study to date of office-holding in medieval Lynn, concluded that service as a headborough was neither a qualification nor a prerequisite for higher office, while Kate Parker noted that, unlike the constables, who were men of real power and substance in the borough hierarchy, the headboroughs were lower-ranking burgesses, unlikely ever to be elected as mayor.[21] They were, however, always burgesses, and so drawn from a relatively small group of men.[22]

A snapshot of the comparative wealth of the leet officers can be viewed in the late 1350s, thanks to a tallage assessment from 1357 which enables almost all the constables, headboroughs and affeerers at the 1359 leet to be identified. The constables were all men assessed at between two shillings and eighteen shillings; the affeerers between five shillings and 13s 4d; the headboroughs between one shilling and 6s 8d.[23] The distinction was not one just of wealth, however: the headboroughs were also much more likely to be artificers, or tradesmen. Artificers could purchase their liberty at the same price (forty shillings) as merchants but, unlike their merchant counterparts, artificer-burgesses would rarely be considered for any office above that of headborough. In that role, however, they could participate in local government and judicial administration at a modest level, cooperating with their cohort, receiving guidance from the town clerk[24] or his assistants, and appearing at the court on the leet day with the mayor and the bishop's steward. A sign that the headboroughs could have minds of their own and a sense of solidarity as a group appears in the heading to the leet roll from 1403, which states that the capital pledges had refused to take their oath of office. No reason is given, but tensions were building at this time: relations between the borough and Bishop Henry

---

Register of King's Lynn (King's Lynn, 1919–22), vol. 2, p. 135.

21 Stephen Alsford, 'The men behind the masque: office-holding in East Anglian boroughs, 1272–1460', <http://users.trytel.com/~tristan/towns/mc5_pt1.html> [accessed 29 September 2017]; Parker, 'Lordship', pp. 63–5.

22 As Alsford has pointed out, it is hard to determine the number of burgesses: a list of burgesses alive in 1440 runs to around 250, but this was a generation after a large influx of new entrants; there may have been only half as many in the late fourteenth century. See 'The monopolisation of office', <http://users.trytel.com/~tristan/towns/mc3_pt5.html> [accessed 29 September 2017]; Norfolk and Norwich Archaeological Society, *A Calendar of the Freemen of Lynn, 1292–1836* (Norwich, 1913), pp. 299–303.

23 KLBA KL/C 37/7 (tallage roll, 1357): the assessments range from one shilling (110 names, and much the largest group) to thirty shillings.

24 The rare survival, at Peterborough, of leet presentments in English and judiciously recast in Latin, indicates how great an influence a clerk might exercise: Mary Bateson, 'The English and Latin versions of a Peterborough court leet, 1461', *The English Historical Review*, 19, no. 75 (1904), pp. 526–8.

Despenser were at a very low ebb, while the mayor, Robert Botekesham, was one of five whose expenses claims and high-handedness were to be subjects of scrutiny during the conflicts which erupted in Lynn from 1405 onwards.[25]

If the men who served as headboroughs failed, in the main, to progress to higher office, did they lack higher political ambitions or the financial means to pursue them, or were their aspirations frustrated by the borough's ruling oligarchy? This question is best considered after taking into account the wider social picture which the leet rolls can help to construct.

Patterns of Settlement and Wealth Distribution

The identification of the wards of medieval Lynn impacts most obviously on our understanding of the town's topography. The varied size of the wards (as shown in Map 10.1) reflects the pattern of settlement within the borough boundaries: with the exception of Damgate, the direct route into the town from the East Gate, most of the eastern half of Lynn retained an open, even pastoral, character until the nineteenth century. This explains the much larger territories belonging to the wards which lay on that side of the town. The developed area was, however, expanding westward throughout the medieval period: thanks to a combination of natural silting and the active deposit of sand and other materials, what had been quays belonging to houses along the waterfront streets and marketplaces were transformed between the thirteenth and fifteenth centuries into lines of new houses and warehouses.[26] As a result, the ground occupied by the riverside wards gradually expanded: Chequer and Trinity Hall wards, in particular, would originally have been similar in area to Jews Lane and New Conduit.

In relation to the lost tenth ward, the only location clues in the surviving leet records are two references in 1346 to a bridge opposite the Blackfriars, but personal names from the ward can be linked through property deeds to tenements south of Purfleet, north of the fleet near St James's chapel, and adjoining Baxter Row.[27] This suggests that the ward covered the area east of Sedgeford Lane, into which it merged by 1350. St James's chapel, one of two daughter chapels to the parish church of St Margaret, was founded in the twelfth century, presumably to serve a sizeable population in the area at that time. By the end of the thirteenth century, however, tallage assessments (which are arranged, like the leet rolls, by constabulary, and so can now also be analysed by ward) show that this tenth ward had far fewer taxpayers than

25 KLBA KL/C 17/14 (leet roll, 1403).

26 The topography of medieval Lynn is described in Owen, *King's Lynn*, pp. 13–19, and Vanessa Parker, *The Making of King's Lynn: Secular Buildings from the 11th to the 17th Century* (Chichester, 1971), pp. 19–29.

27 Ingleby, *Red Register*, passim; NRO DCN 44/76/76 and 78, and KLBA KL/C 50/421.

any of the other nine: from a total sum across the borough of £70 18s in 1298, St James's could muster a contribution of only 4s 6d.[28] Evidently, this area was in serious decline a generation before its constabulary was abolished in the late 1340s, almost certainly as a result of a shift to the more desirable land being reclaimed along the waterfront.

The tallage assessment of 1357 (the only surviving near-complete tallage roll after 1306) and those complete, or nearly complete, leet rolls which provide totals of the amercements due from each ward, although created on different principles, show a fairly consistent pattern throughout the fourteenth and early fifteenth centuries. North End ward, which included the largest of the two markets, prime access to the river and the homes of some of the richest merchants, was the wealthiest, closely followed by Chequer.[29] Together, these two contiguous wards offered the greatest opportunities for developing new land along the waterfront, in locations particularly attractive to merchants. The levels of income from Jews Lane, New Conduit, Trinity Hall, Sedgeford Lane and Stonegate were variable, but the two remaining wards, Kettlewell and Paradise, show as consistent a ranking at the bottom of the scale as North End and Chequer at the top. Paradise was the poorest of the nine wards from the mid fourteenth century onwards: in 1357, its taxpayers could muster barely half the contribution made even by Kettlewell, the next lowest. No further amalgamations or changes in ward boundaries were made, however, after the St James's ward was abolished. Presumably the disparities between wards were not considered too great an inconvenience, though the town's governing body appears to have struggled in some years to find a Paradise resident of sufficient status to serve as constable. John Ditton, for example, served as its constable for two years from 1379, despite his being resident in Kettlewell ward, of which he was made constable in 1381; and John Tygo, a Paradise headborough from 1422 to 1425, made the unusual step up to the role of constable in 1426.[30]

Occupational Distribution

The attraction of waterside properties to Lynn's merchants is well known and has already been mentioned. The distribution of artisans and tradesmen across the town has previously proved more difficult to plot,[31] but it is evidenced

28 KLBA KL/C 37/2 (tallage roll, 1297–98).

29 KLBA KL/C 37/7 (tallage roll, 1357). Of the five men with the highest assessments across the borough, four (Thomas Ryghtwys senior, Laurence de Reppes, William de Biteringge and Reginald de Sisterne) were North End residents. Alsford's *History* made use of the tallage rolls, but he was not able to identify the entries by ward.

30 Ingleby, *Red Register*, vol. 2, pp. 140 and 159; KLBA KL/C 17/8, m. 2 (Kettlewell presentments, including John de Ditton); KL/C 17/13 and 18–22 (leet rolls, 1422–34).

31 Parker, *Making of King's Lynn*, pp. 33–8.

to some extent in the leet records. The use of supplementary occupational descriptions in the leet records grew from 1309, when none were cited, to a single-year peak of 170 individuals in 1422, reflecting growing ambiguity as simple descriptions such as Robert Le Tylere (1309) metamorphosed into inherited family names, creating a need by the 1420s to specify (for example) John Barker the baker, and Robert Carpenter the barker.[32] The use of such descriptors remained patchy, but the survival of three consecutive rolls (1425–27) provides the means of identifying the maximum number of individuals and their trades with some confidence.

Of 237 individuals, all men, whose occupations are given in 1425 to 1427, butchers are the largest category, at thirty-one. Ten were based in Jews Lane ward, adjoining the eastern side of the Tuesday Market; another six in the southern half of the borough, close to the earlier, and smaller, Saturday Market. The remaining fifteen were regular visitors from Terrington, five miles west of Lynn: they operated on the northern side of the Tuesday Market, in North End ward. The visibility of butchers in leet records is explained by the public health challenge presented by waste from the slaughter of animals, and butchers in Lynn were typically amerced for leaving their beasts' entrails on a common watergate, or failing to deposit them in a marked location from which they would have been washed away by the tide. Bakers, by contrast, have a relatively low profile, because the assize of bread was dealt with by the bishop's officers throughout the year, and only four bakers (three in Kettlewell and one in New Conduit) are identified in 1425 to 1427.[33]

Kettlewell was the town's main industrial area, at least by the early fifteenth century: fifty-eight craftsmen in that ward are named in leet presentments (1425–27), more than twice the number in any other ward. The majority (thirty-three of the fifty-eight) were engaged in the production of cloth or leather, or of finished clothing or footwear. In general, however, most occupations do not appear to have been grouped together: street names such as Listergate (dyers' street) and Webster (weavers') Row may reflect occupational zones at an earlier period.

Immigrants from the continent were part of the social make-up of Lynn from an early phase of its development, and, from the mid fourteenth century, increasing numbers of foreign craftsmen can be identified in the leet rolls.[34] The clearest picture of the borough's immigrant residents emerges in the fifteenth century, however; partly because their numbers are greater,

32 KLBA KL/C 17/1, 18 and 19 (leet rolls, 1309, 1425 and 1426): Barker and Carpenter were both amerced for refuse left in Kettlewell ward.

33 KLBA KL/C 17/18–20 (leet rolls, 1425–27).

34 In c. 1361, for example, Reynkin of Brabant, webster, drew blood from a fellow weaver named Claus (KLBA KL/C 17/7).

but also because the status of some can be clarified from other sources, both local and national.[35] Between 1400 and 1434, thirty-nine individuals – thirty-four men and five women – can be positively identified in the leet rolls as resident foreigners. Of these, twenty-eight (twenty-four men and four women) were 'Duche', three were Hollanders, two (a tailor and his wife) Zeelanders, and one a Fleming; the nationality of the remaining five is unidentified. Shoemakers and tailors dominate among the twenty men and women for whom a trade is specified, but there were also specialist craftsmen, including an organ-maker and three lantern-makers. The most striking pattern to emerge from the leet entries, however, is the varied density of foreign residents across the town: more than half (twenty-two of the thirty-nine) lived in Chequer ward. New opportunities for renting premises on the east side of the Chequer (now King Street), in particular, may have arisen from moves by their wealthy owners to newly-built houses and warehouses on the west side, adjoining the river. Trinity Hall and New Conduit had the next highest number of foreigners (five each); there were two each in North End, Sedgeford Lane and Stonegate, one in Paradise and none in Kettlewell or Jews Lane.

One occupational designation, that of merchant, was applied in leet entries to only five men in total, despite its centrality to the borough's economy, society and government. This is a revealing omission, as is the fact that the word appears for the first time at so late a date, in leet entries from 1422, 1425 and 1434.[36] Lynn was a town created by merchants;[37] its ruling elite consisted solely of merchants until the second quarter of the fifteenth century; its merchants were firmly pressured to become burgesses, and fined if they traded on their own account before entering the liberty. Artificers could become burgesses by purchase, but they were not equal in status: only a merchant-burgess could be a mayor, or a 'meyrs pere', in Margery Kempe's telling phrase.[38] In Lynn, the word 'burgess', unless qualified, generally meant a burgess who was a merchant, at least until the early fifteenth century. This division between the merchant-burgesses and the artificer-burgesses appears to be deeper and more significant than has previously been recognised, and may be unique to Lynn. The merchant guild of the Holy Trinity was 'as masterful and wealthy as any in England':[39] its vast reserves of wealth enabled

[35] Annual assessments of borough fines on aliens, recorded consistently from 1424 (KLBA KL/C 7/2, p. 54); University of York and The National Archives, *England's Immigrants 1330–1550*, database <https://www.englandsimmigrants.com> [accessed 19 April 2017].

[36] KLBA KL/C 17/13, 18 and 22 (leet rolls, 1422, 1425 and 1434).

[37] An incomplete description of the key role of 'merchant folk' and their 'great Gild' in the development of the town appears in William Asshebourne's book (KLBA KL/C 10/2, fol. 117); the extract published in Owen, *King's Lynn*, pp. 316–17, is unreliable.

[38] Meech and Allen, *The Book of Margery Kempe*, p. 56.

[39] Alice Stopford Green, *Town Life in the Fifteenth Century* (London, 1894), vol. 1, p. 286.

the guild to act as the town's bankers, and it had an extensive portfolio of properties long before the town's governing body acquired estates of its own. The guild also had a firm grip on the borough's political processes (the council of twenty-four jurats were all guild members; the guild's alderman initiated the mayoral election process each year and also acted as the mayor's deputy), while as Lynn's leading religious guild, it employed no fewer than thirteen chaplains.[40] By contrast, craft guilds were non-existent in Lynn: even those guilds which recruited members from a single craft were purely religious and social in character.[41] In contrast to Gervase Rosser's findings in London and some other English towns, Lynn's governing body was actively involved in regulating industrial and trading practices, including the framing of statutes for individual crafts.[42]

The leet court and view of frankpledge sat outside the institutions of borough government run by the burgesses and doubtless pre-dated the earliest borough charter,[43] so it is unsurprising that the word 'burgess' was never used in the leet records: merchant-burgesses are generally identified in the leet rolls by name only. Margery Kempe's father, John de Brunham, for example, was one of the wealthiest Lynn merchants, and at the top of the borough hierarchy for many years (mayor five times between 1370 and 1392, and alderman of the merchant guild of the Holy Trinity for several years from 1393 onwards), but, like any resident, he could be amerced by the leet court for trading offences and public nuisances. He was probably the John de Brunham amerced for regrating bread in New Conduit ward in 1352, and we can be confident that it was he who was amerced for failing to bring his stone and half-stone weights for inspection on a leet day early in the 1360s, because he is listed among weights defaulters in Chequer ward, where he had lived since at least 1357. His tallage assessment that year places him among the three wealthiest men in Chequer, and among the nineteen richest across the borough. Already, John de Brunham had a high profile in Lynn and needed no additional description to identify him, in contrast to another man, identified in the North End in 1359 as 'John de Brunham, servant of John Congham'.[44]

40 Charles Gross, *The Gild Merchant: A Contribution to British Municipal History* (Oxford, 1890), vol. 2, pp. 151–70.

41 For example, the tilers' guild in honour of the Purification (Owen, *King's Lynn*, pp. 319–21).

42 Gervase Rosser, *The Art of Solidarity in the Middle Ages: Guilds in England 1250–1550* (Oxford, 2015), pp. 162–3; KLBA KL/C 7/2–3 (Hall books, 1422–50), passim: some examples are in Owen, *King's Lynn*, pp. 264–8.

43 King John's charter, 1204 (KLBA KL/C 2/1–2), which does not mention the leet or view of frankpledge, but expressly reserved the (undefined) existing liberties of the bishop of Norwich.

44 KLBA KL/C 17/5–7 (leet rolls, 1352, 1359 and c. 1361); KL/C 37/7 (tallage roll, 1357).

The Rise of Artificer-Burgesses and the Role of Leet Headborough

The terms of burgess admission, qualifications to take part in mayoral and other elections, and eligibility for selection as one of the council of twenty-four jurats were issues running through more than a decade of 'discords, strife, controversies, riots, dissensions and quarrels' in the early fifteenth century.[45] Accusations of financial maladministration by mayors who served between 1399 and 1406 rapidly mutated into pressure for constitutional reforms, including wider participation in electoral processes.[46] More than 150 artificers – 112 of them in 1412 alone – were admitted to the liberty between 1412 and 1415, which may well have doubled the total number of burgesses. The new entrants were scornfully described by a leading merchant-burgess, John Wentworth (a former mayor and former constable of North End), as 'cobblers, tailors, etc.; unfit people, twenty of them not worth a penny'.[47]

The reforms were annulled in 1416, but the restored status quo was modified in favour of the artificer-burgesses by two important changes over the next few years. The first was the creation in 1418, confirmed by Bishop John Wakeryng in 1420, of an annually elected common council of twenty-seven men, three from each ward.[48] The second was the introduction of a new form of admission of artificers' apprentices in January 1425, following representations made to the mayor by seventy-three burgess-artificers, thirty-three of whom had been admitted to the liberty between 1412 and 1415. Most of the seventy-three had either taken part in ward elections for the common council or served as one of its number, or both, while thirteen had served at least once as headboroughs, seven of them (a coverlet weaver, chaloner, glover, goldsmith, hosier, shearman and wax-chandler) at the previous leet in October 1424. Nine artificers were chosen to negotiate with the twenty-four jurats and common council of twenty-seven, and they attended the next Hall meeting to put their case. Their spokesman, Robert Brod the glazier, asserted that there was (or should be) 'one liberty in the town, one oath and one fine'. Despite some opposition from the merchants, the proposal was agreed: henceforward, apprentices of artificer-burgesses were entitled to be admitted as burgesses

45 Historical Manuscripts Commission, *Eleventh Report, Appendix 3: Manuscripts of the Corporations of Southampton and King's Lynn* (1887), p. 202.

46 Two recent narratives and assessments of this period of conflict in Lynn are by Goodman (*Margery Kempe*, pp. 35–48), who also notes the involvement of well-to-do artificers in riots and disturbances several years earlier, and Kate Parker, 'A little local difficulty: Lynn and the Lancastrian usurpation', in Christopher Harper-Bill (ed.), *Medieval East Anglia* (Woodbridge, 2005), pp. 115–29.

47 KLBA KL/C 6/3 m. 2 (Hall roll, 1412–13). These words (*Sutores taillours etc. inhabiles, xxti non de valor unius denarii*) were reportedly spoken by Wentworth to the bishop of Norwich.

48 KLBA KL/C 4/11.

on completion of their apprenticeships without paying a fee, thus removing a formal difference between the privileges of artificer-burgesses and their merchant counterparts.[49] This discrimination between the rights of merchants' and artificers' apprentices may have been unique to Lynn, and its implications seem not to have been noticed previously, perhaps because records of burgess entries, like the leet rolls, do not include the word 'merchant' as a descriptor until well into the fifteenth century: until 1419, new burgesses were merchants unless otherwise stated.[50]

The men who benefited from these reforms were the kind who typically served as headboroughs. Over the next decade, as members of the twenty-four died, artificer-burgesses began to work their way into the inner circle of town government. The first to become mayor appears to have been William Palmer, whose name was at the head of the list of seventy-three artificers who came before the mayor in 1425, and who was also the first-named of their nine negotiators.[51] Palmer was admitted as a burgess in 1424, elected to the common council in 1425, chamberlain in 1426, coroner and one of the twenty-four jurats in 1429, and finally mayor in 1436: he died early in 1437, part-way through his year of office. His will shows us his estates in Lynn and Lincolnshire and his family connections, but gives no hint as to the nature of his business: it could easily be the will of a prosperous merchant, were it not that three of his five executors were artificer-burgesses, each of whom had served as headboroughs for their wards. The others were his wife, Emma, and Margery Kempe's highly regarded confessor, Robert Spryngold.[52] Leet records show that William Palmer was engaged in brewing: he first appears in 1422, when he was already much the largest brewer in New Conduit, and thereafter he was consistently the leading brewer in his ward. He was also the biggest in the borough until he was overtaken in 1426 by the brewing partnership of John Ashenden and Edward Mayn. Operating by 1422 in Trinity Hall ward, in 1434 this pair incurred one of the highest amercements recorded in any of the surviving medieval leet rolls.[53] Ashenden and Mayn, brewers, were among the 112 burgesses admitted in 1412; both were among the artificer-burgesses lobbying for equal treatment in 1425 (Mayn as one of the deputation of seven-

49 KLBA KL/C 7/2 (Hall book 1422–29), pp. 29–33. Stephen Alsford's online *History* includes a translation of the new 'Manner of enrolment and admission of apprentices', <http://users.trytel.com/~tristan/towns/ly1425a.html> [accessed 6 October 2017].

50 Norfolk and Norwich Archaeological Society, *Calendar of the Freemen of Lynn*, p. 32.

51 I am indebted to Michael Begley for identifying Palmer as the first non-merchant mayor of Lynn.

52 KLBA KL/C 7/2–3 (Hall books, 1422–50), passim; The National Archives PROB 11/3/371 (will of William Palmere, 1437).

53 KLBA KL/C 17/13 and 18–22 (leet rolls, 1422, 1425–27, 1430 and 1434, when Ashenden and Mayn were amerced at £3 21d in 1434 for brewing sixteen quarters of malt a week, keeping horses, leaving rubbish, and for roping ale).

ty-three; Ashenden as one of the nine negotiators), and they progressed as rapidly through the borough hierarchy as a merchant might have expected to do, Ashenden always in the lead. He served as chamberlain in 1420/1; Mayn in 1424/5; both by-passed the common council to become jurats (Ashenden early in 1435; Mayn eighteen months later), and in 1440 John Ashenden was elected mayor. Within a generation, the artificers had transformed their career prospects within the borough hierarchy.[54]

The Kempe Family Brewery and Residence

One of the first editors of Margery Kempe's *Book*, Sanford Meech, searched those leet records which had then been identified as covering the period of Margery's lifetime, and found the only two references to brewing by John Kempe, Margery's husband, in 1403 and 1404.[55] Meech speculated that these entries relate only nominally to John Kempe and may reflect his wife's activities. He also incorrectly expanded the abbreviated verb *braciavit* (brewed), the usual form throughout the Lynn leet records, as the noun *braceator* (brewer): a distinction which is more significant than it may appear. As we have seen, this was still a period in Lynn at which a 'burgess' was, almost by definition, a merchant-burgess, as opposed to an artificer-burgess like the brewer, William Palmer: John Kempe may not have been an especially successful merchant, but he would never have been defined by contemporaries as 'a brewer'.

A clearer perspective on John Kempe's brewing business can be obtained by looking at all forty-eight leet amercements for brewing in 1403 and 1404. In all, twenty-nine individuals were presented (nine of them named in only one or other of the two years; the remaining twenty in both). Of these twenty-nine, two were women, which suggests that had Margery Kempe's brewery been active in those years, she would have been named. North End ward had the largest number, followed by Stonegate and New Conduit: there were none in Kettlewell or Paradise wards. The amercements ranged from 13d to 46s 8d, the highest sums being due from prominent burgesses who were also wealthy merchants and whose brewing enterprises were profitable sidelines (Richard Denby in Chequer, Robert Salisbury of Stonegate and Thomas Faukes, also in Stonegate); all three were members of the borough's ruling group of twenty-four jurats. John Kempe was one of four men amerced in New Conduit ward for brewing in 1403, and one of five in 1404: at thirteen shillings (1403)

54 KLBA KL/C 7/2–3 (Hall books, 1422–50), passim; Hamon Le Strange, *Norfolk Official Lists* (Norwich, 1890), p. 191.

55 Meech and Allen, *The Book of Margery Kempe*, p. 364. The original entries in KLBA KL/C 17/14 and 15 read as follows: *M' xiij s. Johes Kemp' brac' vj quart' in sept' per am et vend' contra Ass' etc. et t' I equ' et ocup' coem flet' cum fimo etc.* (1403) and *M' v s. Johes Kemp' brac' ij quart' in sept' per am Et tenet equ' Et ocup' coem flet' cum Fim' etc. Et vend' contra Ass'* (1404).

and five shillings (1404), he was paying sums below the average for brewers, both in his ward and across the borough, which suggests that his brewery was a sideline which was ticking over satisfactorily, but no more. He appears to have inherited this New Conduit brewery from his father: a John Kempe was amerced for brewing in the same ward in 1379 at fifty-eight shillings and in 1391 at 6s 6d.[56] The ambitious Margery, impatient at her husband's laid-back approach to business, may have taken over the running of the modest Kempe brewery and scaled it up, in emulation of the most successful merchant-brewers.[57] There is no reason to doubt Margery's statement that she gave up brewing after the business failed: her time as a brewer may have been after 1404, and the next surviving leet records, from 1416 onwards, have no entries relating to a Kempe brewery.

Presentments relating to the brewing and selling of ale and beer are, unsurprisingly, among the most numerous in the leet records, but they are outnumbered by those for domestic and industrial waste deposited in the public streets and fleets. These mundane records usefully connect householders with properties for which they were responsible, and some name the street or other location. Returning to the two entries relating to John Kempe (1403 and 1404), they show that he kept a horse and was responsible for dung or other waste deposited in a common fleet, which could be either Purfleet or the parallel minor fleet which ran through the middle of New Conduit ward. Together (and in combination with the absence of any evidence of Kempe's residence elsewhere in the borough), these strongly suggest that they relate to a house in which he lived, giving greater weight to previous speculation that the tenement on the north side of Burghardeslane, alias Fyncham Street (later New Conduit Street), already known to have been held by a John Kempe from 1391 to at least 1425, was indeed the Kempes' marital home.[58]

A similar approach – matching evidence of property occupation from the leet records with deeds, wills and community rentals – has made it possible to identify with some confidence the house of John de Brunham, Margery Kempe's likely birthplace and her home until she married, around 1393.[59] The Brunhams' was the eighth of thirteen tenements on the west side of Briggate, running north to south from the corner with Wingate (now Baker Lane) towards the north side of St Margaret's church: the site (115–116 High Street) is now part of a modern block of shops and flats.

56 KLBA KL/C 17/8/5; KL/C 17/11, 14 and 15 (leet rolls, 1379, 1391, 1403 and 1404).

57 'Sche wold not … be content wyth the goodys that god had sent hire, as hir husbond was, but euyr desyryd mor & mor': Meech and Allen, *The Book of Margery Kempe*, p. 9.

58 Meech and Allen, *The Book of Margery Kempe*, pp. 366–7.

59 A detailed account of the evidence relating to the Brunhams' and neighbouring tenements in Briggate is in Susan Maddock, 'Mapping Margery Kempe's Lynn', *The Annual: The Bulletin of the Norfolk Archaeological and Historical Research Group*, 26 (2017), pp. 3–14.

The Kempe and Brunham Families

While Margery herself escaped mention in those leet rolls which have survived, there are dozens of entries relating to other Brunhams and Kempes, less than a handful of which have previously been noted.[60] Because the Brunhams came from the Burnhams (a group of seven parishes on the north-west Norfolk coast, also habitually written as 'Brunham' at this period), some of the seventeen men and women called Brunham who appear in the leet records may have no connection with John de Brunham, burgess, mayor and alderman. The links with particular wards and activities evidenced in the leet rolls, however, do enable some tentative connections to be made. During the long lifetime of Margery's father (c. 1330 to 1413), three generations of Brunhams were in Lynn for at least part of their adult lives. Contemporaries of John de Brunham – possibly his cousins – included Robert de Brunham, a skinner who was active in New Conduit between 1349 and 1375 and died by 1405; Edmund de Brunham, admitted burgess as John's apprentice in 1359; and Martin de Brunham, associated mainly with Trinity Hall ward between 1357 and 1366, and a leet headborough there in 1359. A younger man, Lawrence Brunham (a tailor in New Conduit ward between 1375 and 1394 and a Chequer headborough from 1400 to 1403, who was admitted burgess by purchase in 1384), was probably a cousin to Robert de Brunham, John's probable eldest son and Margery Kempe's brother or half-brother.

Two younger Brunhams became burgesses in the exceptional intake of 1412: a hosier named John Brunham, and a burgess and vintner, Thomas de Brunham. The hosier may have had no close relationship with Margery's family, but Thomas did: he was amerced in Chequer ward in 1422 for selling wine in the house of Geoffrey Sutton, the man who married Margery Kempe's mother or step-mother, Isabelle de Brunham, after the death of John de Brunham in 1413.[61]

Those Kempes who appear in the leet records are fewer in number but include a previously unnoticed contemporary of Margery's father-in-law. Geoffrey Kempe was a skinner in North End ward between 1375 and 1379,

60 Charity Scott Stokes, 'Margery Kempe: her life and the early history of her book', *Mystics Quarterly*, 25, nos 1–2 (March/June 1999), p. 59, cites entries relating to Alice Kempe, 1333, and John Brunham ('for obstructing the Tuesday Market with timber'), 1375. I have been unable to identify the 1375 entry in KL/C 17/9, although there is an entry for John Brunham concerning broken paving in Wyngate, and several entries relate to timber left on highways by other men. Goodman refers to leet entries for Edmund Brunham, 1403, and William Brunham, 1404, but these actually relate to men called Runham, not Brunham. See Goodman, *Margery Kempe*, p. 222, n. 138.

61 Maddock, 'Mapping Margery Kempe's Lynn', p. 12, has a chart showing the Brunhams of Lynn. Stokes, in 'Margery Kempe', pp. 19 and 24, speculated that the hosier was John de Brunham's son (and Margery's brother or half-brother), John de Brunham junior, but the latter was admitted burgess by right of birth in 1394, and cannot have been the hosier.

and may have been a brother to John Kempe senior, who was described as a skinner when he was admitted to the freedom in 1351, but was clearly a merchant-burgess.[62] He also served as constable of Sedgeford Lane in the mid 1370s. The words 'skinner' and 'pelter' seem to have been used interchangeably in Lynn, both for merchants like John Kempe senior, who presumably specialised in imported pelts (as the vintners did in wine), and for artificers like the skinner John Crosse of Kettlewell ward (1420–34).[63] Three fourteenth-century Kempe women who are named in leet presentments as forestallers of fish (Katherine, 1311; Alice, 1328–33, and Isabel, 1352) may not have been closely related to Margery's father-in-law, although they are likely to have come from the same extended family, but the Agnes Kempe who was amerced for regrating ale and leaving refuse in 1434 could well have been one of Margery's children or a daughter-in-law.[64]

Margery Kempe's book is notoriously silent on the political and social conflicts of her home town, but, given her pride in her father's status, one might expect her to have shared John Wentworth's contempt for the artificers who were admitted as burgesses during the radical reforms of 1412. However, we know that Robert Spryngold, parish priest of St Margaret, and Margery's 'gostly fadyr', was the man she respected above all others, and Spryngold acted as executor to both Robert de Brunham and William Palmer, the first artificer to become mayor. It was also an artificer-burgess, John Ashenden, whom Margery trusted to hand over the final two instalments of her admission fee of one hundred shillings to the Holy Trinity guild. Perhaps she was friendly with, even related to, John Ashenden's wife, Isabel. Isabel, together with Edward Mayn's wife, Joan, entered the Holy Trinity guild at much the same time as Margery: their names were entered together in the guild accounts for 1437/8, just as their husbands' names were (uniquely) paired in the leet rolls.[65] Despite Margery's privileged background, it appears that she had embraced the new order, in which the merchant-burgesses no longer ruled supreme.

62 KLBA KL/C 17/9 and KL/C 17/10/1 (leet rolls, 1375 and 1379); Ingleby, *Red Register*, vol. 2, p. 171 (John Kempe's entrance by purchase, 29 January 1351). Maddock, 'Mapping Margery Kempe's Lynn', p. 8, has a chart showing the Kempes of Lynn.

63 KLBA KL/C 37/7 (tallage assessment, 1357, in which the terms 'pelter' and 'skinner' are both used, but vary by ward, not by the individuals' status); KLBA KL/C 17/13 and 17–22 (leet rolls, 1420–34) and KL/C 7/2 (Hall book, 1422–29), p. 30. Crosse was one of the seventy-three artificer-burgesses who appeared in the Hall in 1425 to put their case for equality with the merchants.

64 NRO DCN 44/76/176 and KLBA KL/C 17/2–3, 5 and 22 (leet rolls, 1311, 1328, 1333, 1352 and 1434).

65 Meech and Allen, *The Book of Margery Kempe*, pp. 358–9; KLBA KL/C 7/2, p. 90 (reference to Robert de Brunham's executors, 1424), KL/C 38/16–17 (Holy Trinity guild accounts, 1437–39) and KL/C 17/13 and 18–22 (leet rolls, 1422, 1425–27, 1430 and 1434).

Conclusion

The creation of a database of leet court entries, ordered by name and ward location, is now beginning to provide the fuller picture of the social make-up of late medieval Lynn which has previously eluded historians. Paradoxically, perhaps, this new evidence has reinforced just how overwhelming was the dominance of merchant-burgesses in the town's society and governing group. By enlarging on previous analysis of the social standing of those burgesses who served as leet headboroughs, it has also illuminated the political challenge to the merchant elite by better-off artificers who had purchased the burgess-ship, or who were admitted to the liberty following the short-lived constitutional settlement of 1412. Family connections between merchants and artificers, such as those implied by leet entries relating to the Brunhams, together with respect for successful professional brewers like William Palmer and John Ashenden, whose dominance of the trade in early-fifteenth-century Lynn is revealed by records relating to the assize of ale, may also have played a part in overcoming the conservative view that artificers were unfit for higher office, enabling them, by the mid fifteenth century, to participate fully in the governance of the borough.

TABLE 10.1: INCOME BY WARD FROM TALLAGE ASSESSMENTS AND LEET AMERCEMENTS, 1349–1434 (COMPLETE AND NEAR COMPLETE YEARS ONLY)

	North End	Kettlewell	Paradise	Jews Lane	New Conduit	Chequer	Trinity Hall
Leet 1349	£4 7s 5d	£1 12s 0d	£1 7s 3d	£2 13s 0d	£1 12s 9d	£5 6s 11d	£1 12s 0d
Tallage 1357	£14 0s 8d	£4 12s 0d	£2 7s 6d	£5 3s 2d	£4 12s 8d	£10 13s 0d	£5 12s 4d
Leet 1359	£15 6s 1d	£3 13s 6d	£2 8s 11d	£9 10s 1d	£5 10s 1d	£6 12s 5d	£4 9s 7d
Leet 1375	£8 18s 4d	£4 18s 5d	£3 7s 4d	£7 5s 9d	£8 11s 6d	£9 0s 9d	£4 4s 10d
Leet 1391	£5 5s 6d	£4 0s 11d	£1 5s 2d	£5 8s 10d	£6 16s 9d	£8 7s 9d	£4 19s 2d
Leet 1400	£6 10s 3d	£4 8s 8d	£2 5s 5d	£4 19s 11d	£6 12s 4d	£9 14s 10d	£4 1s 0d
Leet 1425	£8 19s 8d	£3 6s 3d	£3 7s 6d	£2 17s 0d	£5 0s 14d	£6 16s 0d	£4 3s 10d
Leet 1426	£8 3s 3d	£3 5s 5d	£2 6s 9d	£3 17s 9d	£5 14s 10d	£6 17s 4d	£4 13s 5d
Leet 1427	£8 13s 3d	£2 5s 8d	£3 2s 3d	£3 19s 0d	£5 5s 5d	£6 17s 10d	£4 15s 8d
Leet 1434	£6 19s 5d	£3 9s 11d	£1 16s 6d	£4 8s 4d	£6 7s 3d	£4 19s 4d	£5 17s 5d

edgeford Lane	Stonegate	10th ward	Total	Document references	Notes
9s 10d	£2 1s 5d	1s 0d	£22 6s 7d	ACM, MD 1475	Ward sums and total calculated from individual amercements
13s 2d	[£6 ap-prox.]	NA	[£57 ap-prox.]	KL/C 37/7	Total estimated, as Stonegate list is incomplete (extant Stonegate entries amount to £3 2s 8d)
17s 8d	£5 13s 4d	NA	£60 11s 2d	KL/C 17/6	Total includes defaulters (£1 10s 6d)
6s 9d	£9 7s 3d	NA	£66 5s 11d	KL/C 17/9	Total includes defaulters (£2 3s 6d)
6s 6d	£7 15s 5d	NA	[£51 8s 0d]	KL/C 17/11	Total calculated from ward sums
19s 10d	£6 21s 0d	NA	£52 4s 0d	ACM, MD 1478	
4s 0d	£5 4s 9d	NA	£44 2s 5d	KL/C 17/18	
7s 5d	£4 13s 1d	NA	£43 19s 8d	KL/C 17/19	
18s 9d	£4 8s 6d	NA	£42 15s 4d	KL/C 17/20	
19s 4d	£4 4s 1d	NA	[£42 1s 9d]	KL/C 17/22	Total calculated from ward sums

Appendix

AN ANNOTATED LIST OF PRINTED OR ONLINE TRANSCRIPTIONS AND TRANSLATIONS OF MEDIEVAL TOWN COURTS IN BRITAIN TO 1500[1]

MARYANNE KOWALESKI

Medieval town or borough court records have rarely been printed *in extenso* because they are so long and contain more names than details of legal matters. As a result, many of the borough courts in print consist of extracts, abstracts or abbreviated summaries. These transcriptions and translations can, however, still offer instructive material, so this appendix provides annotations on town courts in print or available online in order to illustrate their wide variety, provide examples of the types of business they treated, and stimulate more comparative studies. Town courts are defined here as meetings identified as 'courts' by contemporaries, which included 'legal' matters (such as presentments, indictments or pleas) and operated under the authority of town officials – a definition that excludes most guild courts, unless they were meetings of a guild merchant that essentially served as the town's government.[2] The bibliography, which is organised alphabetically by town, encompasses

1 I thank Christopher Dyer for checking this list and making additional suggestions.

2 For this reason, most of the guild courts of Scottish boroughs have been excluded, including Thomas Dickson, 'Proceedings of the gild court of Ayr, from the Ayr manuscript', *Archaeological and Historical Collections Relating to the Counties of Ayr and Wigton*, 1 (1878), pp. 223–30, and *The Gild Court Book of Dunfermline, 1433–1597*, ed. Elizabeth P. D. Torrie, Scottish Record Society, new series, 12 (Edinburgh, 1986).

town courts in England, Scotland and Wales, up to about 1500.[3] The second part of the appendix lists references to extracts of borough courts printed in the appendices of the *Reports of the Royal Commission of Historical Manuscripts*.[4] Those interested in borough courts for which no or few records are extant should also be aware of detailed references to business in these courts collected by scholars of English common law, who have tracked writs of error that required the local court to provide a record of a particular case to the appellate central court.[5]

Annotated List

Aberdeen

Aberdeen Guild Court Records 1437–1468, ed. Elizabeth Gemmill, Scottish History Society, 5th series, 17 (Edinburgh, 2005). Transcription of the proceedings of the court of the guild of the burgh, which handled both guild and burgh business, including admission of new guild members and burgesses, enforcement of guild and burgh trading regulations, leasing of burgh property and presentments of offences (particularly forestalling), but no personal pleas. The alderman and/or dean of the guild presided over the court, which met at least once a week in between meetings of the town council (which was elected by the guild). Entries in Latin and increasingly in Scots.

Early Records of the Burgh of Aberdeen 1317, 1398–1407, ed. William Croft Dickinson, Scottish History Society, 3rd series, 49 (Edinburgh, 1957). Latin transcripts of the burgh courts for 1317 and 1398 to 1400 are complete; later records include only extracts. The burgh court was presided over by the town's four bailies, who were the king's officials. There were three types of burgh court, each entered chronologically on the same court roll: the *curia legalis* met every two weeks on Mondays; three of these were head courts (*curia*

3 The older editions (published before 1923) are usually available online, especially through the Internet Archive, at <https://archive.org/index.php>, which allows downloads in PDF and other formats. Many of the volumes for London courts have been digitised for British History Online: <http://www.british-history.ac.uk/>. Other volumes may be found online via the Hathi Trust or Hein Online (especially those in the Selden Society).

4 Borough records discussed in the earliest reports are listed in Charles Gross, *A Bibliography of British Municipal History* (London, 1897), pp. 10–12, but fewer than half of these publications include actual extracts from the town courts.

5 For example, E. W. W. Veale, 'Introduction', in E. W. W. Veale (ed.), *The Great Red Book of Bristol: Text (Part III)*, Bristol Record Society, 16 (Bristol, 1951), pp. 2–55; S. Jenks, 'Picking up the pieces: cases presented to the London Sheriffs' courts between Michaelmas 1461 and Michaelmas 1462', *Journal of Legal History*, 29 (2008), pp. 99–145; J. H. Baker, *The Oxford History of the Laws of England: 1483–1558*, vol. 6 (Oxford, 2003), pp. 291–319.

capitalis); the most important was the Michaelmas court, at which the alderman and bailies were elected. By 1398, there were also courts held by the bailies to deal with business in between meetings of the *curia legalis*. The court handled personal pleas, actions begun by royal writ, registration of deeds and limited criminal jurisdiction.

Extracts from the Council Registers of the Burgh of Aberdeen, vol. 1, 1398–1570, ed. John Stuart, Spalding Club, 12 (Aberdeen, 1844). Extracts from the first twenty-seven volumes of the council registers, which include civil and criminal court proceedings in the burgh courts and guild court, as well as council discussions of civic policy, regulations, debts, properties and disputes initiated by city officials or individuals, elections, royal letters and taxes, among other matters.

'Law in the Aberdeen council registers, 1398–1511', Research Institute of Irish and Scottish Studies, University of Aberdeen, at <https://aberdeenregisters.org/>. Project funded by the Leverhulme Trust (for 2016–19) to make transcripts of extant Aberdeen council registers available online in TEI (Text Encoding Initiative) format; see entries above for the contents of these registers. There are also digitised copies of these eight volumes (minus vol. 3, which is missing) available online at <https://scotlandsplaces.gov.uk/digital-volumes/burgh-records/aberdeen-burgh-registers>.

Andover

'Andover', in Charles Gross, *The Gild Merchant*, vol. 2 (Oxford, 1890), pp. 3–12, 289–351. Latin transcriptions of the Morghespeche (or *Maneloquium*) of the guild merchant, which dealt mainly with guild business (especially admissions to membership) but which had a wider jurisdiction over other crafts and heard cases of trespass and debt, though it is unclear if the plaintiffs had to be members of the guild to bring suit. An unusual number of women appear in these courts, which date from 1262 to 1348 (along with a few extracts from the fifteenth century). There are also transcripts from a small number of Hundred courts (1304–05) presided over by the bailiffs.

Atherstone

Select Pleas in Manorial and Other Seignorial Courts, ed. F. W. Maitland, Selden Society, 2 (London, 1888), pp. 25–6, 40–1. Latin and facing English translation of pleas in 1285 and 1291, mostly about property, from a small Warwickshire borough of the abbey of Bec.

Barnstaple

Reprint of the Barnstaple Records, ed. J. R. Chanter and Thomas Wainwright, 2 vols (Barnstaple, 1900). Includes English translations of extracts from a variety of mayor's court rolls and books from the early fourteenth into the fifteenth century. An index is available at <https://www.genuki.org.uk/big/eng/DEV/Barnstaple/>.

Basingstoke

A History of the Ancient Town and Manor of Basingstoke in the County of Southampton, ed. F. J. Baigent and E. J. Millerd (London, 1889), pp. 221- 356. Translated extracts of the weekly Hundred court and the leet court with view of frankpledge (held twice a year) from 1386 to 1558, including the town and manor of Basingstoke and some of the other manors in the hundred. The civic authorities farmed the town, manor and hundred from the king, which explains why the bailiffs of the town presided over both courts. A good example of how the business of a small town court was part of a larger rural area.

Bridgwater

Bridgwater Borough Archives, ed. Thomas Bruce Dilks, 5 vols, Somerset Record Society, 48, 53, 58, 60, 70 (Frome and London, 1933–71). The following volumes include court rolls, mainly transcripts from the original Latin, some of them also translated into English, and others only briefly summarised: *1200–1377* (1933): Latin transcript of courts of Bridgwater castle (with the manor of Haygrove), 1371/2. *1377–99* (1938): courts of the castle (with the manor of Haygrove); a Durneday court held in January 1388, when burgage holders who had failed to pay the rents due to the lord and the chaplain of Our Lady's chantry at Michaelmas were amerced 6d; courts of the borough held before the steward of the lord regarding debts, trespass and other pleas, as well as (twice a year) view of frankpledge with a wide variety of presentments typical of leet courts, and profits of the piepowder court. *1400–45* (1945): no courts. *1445–68* (1948): court session of the common steward (1446) and extracts of the same (1453/4), including personal debt pleas. *1468–85*, ed. R. W. Dunning and T. D. Tremlett from transcripts by T. B. Dilks (1971): court of the chantry of Holy Trinity (1473), presided over by the mayor and feoffees of the chapel, dealing with entry fines and presentments and fines for failure to repair tenements and lands of the chapel.

Caernarvon

Caernarvon Court Rolls, 1361–1402, ed. G. P. Jones and Hugh Owen, Caernarvonshire Historical Society Record Series, 1 (Caernarvon, 1951). Includes translations from three courts. The Great Tourn, held twice a year before the town bailiffs with the constable of the castle as chief magistrate, recorded the admission of burgesses and jurors' presentments of minor trespasses and infringements on the town's rights. The town court, which met roughly every three weeks, treated personal pleas, especially debt, and the assize of bread. The fair courts dealt primarily with commercial matters arising during the fairs. The relationship between the piepowder courts and fair courts is unclear; they could have been the same.

Cambridge

Cambridge Borough Documents, ed. W. M. Palmer, vol. 1 (Cambridge, 1931). Latin transcription of the proceedings (mostly personal pleas) of one court in 1294 (pp. 2–6) and selected cases from subsequent courts in 1294/5 (pp. 6–10).

Chester

Calendar of County Court, City Court and Eyre Rolls of Chester, 1259–1297, ed. R. Stewart-Brown, Chetham Society, new series, 84 (Manchester, 1925). English calendar of pleas of the crown for the city for 1288 to 1296, including felonies, trespass, nuisance and some personal pleas of trespass and detention, held before the justiciar of Chester.

Selected Rolls of the Chester City Courts: Late Thirteenth and Early Fourteenth Centuries, ed. A. Hopkins, Chetham Society, 3rd series, 2 (Manchester, 1950). Latin transcripts of proceedings in the Pentice court of 1317/8, which dealt with debts, petty crime and misdemeanours, and was presided over by the sheriff; the Crownmote court for 1316/7, which heard crown pleas before the mayor and bailiffs; and the Portmote for 1295, 1297, 1320/1 and selected cases between 1299 and 1304, over which the mayor presided, which dealt with land disputes as well as trespass, debt and covenant.

Colchester

Court Rolls of the Borough of Colchester, translated and epitomised by Isaac Herbert Jeayes, with introduction and corrigenda by W. Gurney Benham, 4 vols (Colchester, 1921–41): vol. 1 (1310–52); vol. 2 (1353–67); vol. 3 (1372–79); vol. 4 (1379–83). Includes English translations of the Hundred court of Colchester, which met every two weeks and was presided over by the bailiffs to deal with personal pleas (contract, debt, detention of chattels and trespass), actions initiated by writs regarding property disputes, and presentments of minor market infractions, among other business; a thrice-yearly Law Hundred court, which handled typical leet court presentments; and the Court of Pleas (by 1409/10 called the Foreign court), which included speedier procedure for personal pleas.

Coventry

The Coventry Leet Book; or Mayor's Register, Containing the Records of the City Court Leet or View of Frankpledge, A. D. 1420–1555, ed. M. D. Harris, 2 vols in 4 parts, Early English Text Society, nos 134, 135 in vol. 1; nos 138, 146 in vol. 2 (London, 1907–13). By this period, the leet court had lost most of its judicial functions in favour of a greater legislative role in terms of ordinances and mayoral proclamations, many of which stemmed from petitions presented at the leet. Other business includes jurors' presentments, civic elections, decisions about town lands and finances, and reviewing town accounts. In Middle English and some Latin (translated in facing column).

The Statute Merchant Roll of Coventry, 1392–1416, ed. and trans. Alice Beardwood, Dugdale Society, 17 (London, 1939). Contains a record of recognizances of debt according to the Statute of Merchants (although they did not all involve merchants or commercial debts), made before the mayor of Coventry and the clerk of the statute merchant or his deputy. Cases dealing with non-payment mostly appeared in the king's Court of Common Pleas.

Criccieth

'The court rolls of the borough of Criccieth', ed. W. Garmon Jones, *Bulletin of the Board of Celtic Studies*, 2 (1923), pp. 149–60. Latin transcription of seventy courts for five years between 1320 and 1330 for the Small court (*curia parva*), which mostly recorded fines for convictions of trespass and some debts (many courts record no business at all), along with four (very short) fair courts. There was also a 'Great court' whose business was similar to that of the Small court, though it usually named seven jurors.

Dartmouth

Dartmouth. Vol. 1: Pre-Reformation, ed. Hugh R. Watkin, Parochial Histories of Devonshire, 5 (Exeter, 1935). Translated extracts from the town's first volume of the Proceedings of the Mayor's Court, 1484–1511 (pp. 192–255).

Doncaster

A Calendar to the Records of the Borough of Doncaster, 3 vols (Doncaster, 1899–1903). Vol. 2 contains the (manorial) Great court (of the duke of York in 1454–57 and the king in 1495–1503) at which civic officials (including the mayor) were elected and jurors presented infractions of the assize of ale, nuisances and assault. After 1505, when the town became a borough, the business of what was called the Great court with view of frankpledge expanded. It is unclear whether the printed proceedings are extracts or a complete transcription.

Durham

Records of the Borough of Crossgate, Durham 1312–1531, ed. Richard Britnell, Surtees Society, 212 (Woodbridge, 2008). Latin transcriptions of court rolls (including leet courts) from 1312 and 1390 to 1400, and court books covering 1498 to 1531. Crossgate, one of four jurisdictions in the town of Durham, was in the lordship of Durham Priory.

Hedon

The Early History of the Town and Port of Hedon, in the East Riding of the County of York, J. R. Boyle (Hull, 1895). Includes extracts in Latin from the Communitas (the c. 1360 court of the burgesses) in the footnotes, to provide evidence on observations made in the main text. There were other courts, including a Court of Pleas, but Boyle makes far less use of them.

Henley

Henley Borough Records: Assembly Books i–iv, 1395–1543, ed. and trans. P. M. Briers, Oxfordshire Record Society, vol. 41 (Banbury, 1960). Includes admissions of burgesses, election of civic officials, enrolment of property transactions, ordinances on sanitation and trading, and accounts of borough officials. Offenders were brought for punishment to the court of the lord of the manor, which was coterminous with the borough. Latin transcript, with entries increasingly in English from the 1490s onward.

Ipswich

The Ipswich Recognizance Rolls 1294–1327: A Calendar, ed. G. H. Martin, Suffolk Records Society, vol. 16 (Ipswich, 1973). Originally enrolled in the Portmanmote (later called the Great court) and the Court of Petty Pleas, these transfers of title to burgage tenements and proof of testaments were recorded separately by the early fourteenth century in what came to be known as the Petty Court of Recognizances. Particularly interesting are the formal renunciations by wives of title. The conveyances and testaments are translated into English, but the headings of the rolls and marginal notes by the clerks are in the original Latin.

King's Lynn

The Making of King's Lynn: A Documentary Study, ed. Dorothy M. Owen, British Academy Records of Social and Economic History, new series, 9 (London, 1984). Latin transcription of pleas (assault and debt) in the Monday court for the southern half of the town (pp. 409–11); extracts (personal pleas) from a Stewards' Hall court in 1318 for Newland (pp. 411–14); details of litigants and procedure in an account of profits of the Hustings court in 1347, when the courts were in royal hands (pp. 414–18); selected presentments and orders at leet courts (pp. 419–22); coroners' inquests, 1291–1304; and gaol delivery before the justices of the peace, including the mayor (pp. 429–30).

Lanark

Extracts from the Records of the Royal Burgh of Lanark with Charters and Documents Relating to the Burgh: A.D. 1150–1722 (Glasgow, 1893), pp. 1–10. Proceedings of the borough court and Head court of the borough (*curia capitalis burgi*), both held by the bailiffs, in Scots with Latin headings, for 1488, 1490, 1498, and many years in the sixteenth century and beyond. The extracts (it is unclear how much of the original records are printed here) consist mainly of property transfers and disputes, burgess entries and burgh business, including the filing and auditing of accounts, rents on town property, and occasionally presentments for market infractions.

Launceston

The Histories of Launceston and Dunheved in the County of Cornwall, Richard Peter and Otho Bathurst Peter (Plymouth, 1885), pp. 116–23 passim. English translation of extracts from the Mayor's courts of 1413, 1418, 1420, 1430.

Leicester

Records of the Borough of Leicester: Being a Series of Extracts from the Archives of the Corporation of Leicester, ed. Mary Bateson, revised by W. H. Stevenson and J. E. Stocks, vol. 1: *1103–1327*, vol. 2: *1327–1509* (London, 1899–1901). Extensive extracts in Latin with English translations of the Guild Merchant Rolls (the first is for 1196 to 1225), also called Pleas of the Merchant Guild and the Morningspeech, which heard presentments of market offences and pleas of debt and trespass, as well as recording guild admissions, fines and trade ordinances. Vol. 2 also includes proceedings of the burgesses' court of record (for 1378/9 and a fragment from 1269/70), called the Portmanmoot (the first, c. 1260, is in vol. 1), which heard personal and property pleas and met weekly by 1377, when its profits were transferred from the earl of Leicester to the borough, along with a fragment of a frankpledge (1443) and pleas in a fair court (1347, 1446). There are coroners' rolls in vol. 1 (1297–1327) and vol. 2 (1327), noted as pleas of the crown, but the coroners were two burgesses,

London

Calendar of Early Mayor's Court Rolls Preserved among the Archives of the Corporation of the City of London at the Guildhall A.D. 1298–1307, ed. A. H. Thomas (Cambridge, 1924). The only surviving rolls of the Mayor's court, though some later proceedings are recorded in the Letter Books and the Plea and Memoranda Rolls. Originating in the thirteenth century, it became the city's most important court for personal actions, especially debt. It did not deal with cases involving property ownership.

Calendar of Letter-Books of the City of London, A–L, ed. R. R. Sharpe, 11 vols (London, 1899–1912). Among the memoranda and notes recorded by various town clerks in these folio volumes are early records of the Court of Common Council and the Court of Aldermen, as well as numerous debt recognizances, deeds, ordinances and the assize of bread. The eleven medieval volumes (of a total fifty volumes in the series) cover the period from 1275 to 1496.

Calendar of the Plea and Memoranda Rolls of the City of London, 6 vols. Vols 1–4 were edited by A. H. Thomas and published in London: vol. 1, *1323–1364* (1926); vol. 2, *1364–1381* (1929); vol. 3, *1381–1412* (1932); vol. 4, *1413–1437* (1943). Vols 5–6 were edited by Philip E. Jones and published in Cambridge: vol. 5, *1437–1457* (1954); vol. 6, *1458–1482* (1961). Detailed abstracts of actions in the Mayor's court that medieval clerks chose to include as legal precedents or as examples of the city's rights. Latin entries are translated into English, but entries are increasingly in Middle English. Vol. 3 is titled *Calendar of Select Pleas and Memoranda of the City of London* because it excludes smaller debt actions and some formal entries. Vol. 4 contains presentments of the Wardmotes in 1422 and 1423. Valuable introductions on specific issues are included in each volume.

Calendar of the Wills Proved and Enrolled in the Court of Husting, AD 1258–1688, ed. R. R. Sharpe, 2 vols (London, 1889–90). The Court of Husting, the oldest court of record in London, originally handled a wide variety of business, but personal pleas were moved to other courts as the city's population expanded. By the late thirteenth century, the Hustings court was mainly used for wills and conveyances of land. These volumes print English abstracts of the wills, which focus primarily on bequests of rents and tenements, not chattels or personal goods.

London Assize of Nuisance 1301–1431: A Calendar, ed. Helena M. Chew and William Kellaway, London Record Society, vol. 10 (1973). English abstracts of complaints regarding offences against the city's assizes of buildings and nuisance, held before the mayor and twelve aldermen. The complaints usually pitted neighbour against neighbour over encroachments caused by cesspits, gutters and walls; the right to privacy; and danger from fire, among other issues. The procedures to be followed for complaints are also clearly set out.

London Possessory Assizes: A Calendar, ed. Helena M. Chew, London Record Society, vol. 1 (1965). English translations of the assizes of novel disseisin (known in London as assize of fresh force) and a few cases of *mort d'ancestor* held before the sheriffs and coroners, 1340–1451, with individual pleas for 1317, 1380 and 1470 calendared in the appendix. Plaintiffs initiated the complaint (which could involve lands, tenements or rents) at the Monday session of the Hustings Court of Pleas, but it was heard before a jury impaneled by the sheriffs.

'The Portsoken presentments: an analysis of a London ward in the 15th century', Christine Winter, *Transactions of the London and Middlesex Archaeological Society*, 56 (2005), pp. 97–161. English translation of mainly nuisance indictments made by the jurors of a London suburban Wardmote for fourteen years, 1465–83. The jurors' presentments focus in particular on fire hazards and on prostitutes and their maintainers.

Norwich

Leet Jurisdiction in the City of Norwich during the XIIIth and XIVth Centuries, ed. William Hudson, Selden Society, 5 (London, 1892). Facing page Latin and English translation of ten leet courts (1288–1313, 1375, 1391), amercements at a leet in 1364, and a roll of pleas before the bailiffs (1350).

The Records of the City of Norwich, ed. William Hudson and John Cottingham Tingey, vol. 1 (Norwich, 1906). Includes extracts in Latin (with English abstracts) of conveyances enrolled in the City court, 1287–98; English translation of selected civil pleas in the City court, 1329–79 and 1404; selected sessions of the peace and of enquiry, and gaol delivery before various civic officials (1423 to the sixteenth century); examples of litigation in the fifteenth century; and extracts from the leet courts, 1288–1391.

Nottingham

Nottingham Borough Court Rolls, trans. Trevor Foulds and J. B. Hughes, at <https://www.nottingham.ac.uk/ucn/onlinesources/index.aspx>. An impressively full calendar in English of all entries (except for the fourteen annual courts from 1303/4 to 1335/6, which still extract well over ten thousand pleas in this period) for c. eighty-five years from 1303 to 1455. Includes rolls for burgess pleas and foreign pleas (for cases in which one of the litigants was not a city resident). Nottingham has one of the most continuous runs of medieval borough court records, and this project represents by far the most complete transcriptions available of the genre. For more on the courts, see the website users' guide by Richard Goddard.

Records of the Borough of Nottingham, Being a Series of Extracts from the Archives of the Corporation of Nottingham, ed. William Stevenson, 4 vols (London, 1882). Vol. 1 covers 1155–1399; vol. 2, 1399–1485; and vol. 3, 1485–1547. There is a gap in 1457–1481, after which the courts are recorded less carefully in paper books.

Oxford

Munimenta Civitatis Oxonie, ed. H. E. Salter, Oxford Historical Society Publications, 71 (Devizes, 1920). Latin transcripts made by Brian Twyne (d. 1644), with some translations, of a variety of documents, including extracts from Hustings courts, writs, and petitions dealing with business in the civic courts.

Oxford City Documents Financial and Judicial 1268–1665, ed. J. E. Thorold Rogers, Oxford Historical Society, 18 (Oxford, 1891). Includes Latin transcripts of selected coroners' inquests, 1297–1303, 1306–07, 1314, 1319–22, and inquests before the alderman of South ward (1423), and the mayor and bailiffs (1428). Full transcript of the 1285 eyre held in the borough and a 1402 inquest before the mayor on thefts and receivers of stolen goods, among other crimes.

'The view of frankpledge', in H. E. Salter, *Medieval Oxford*, Oxford Historical Society, 100 (Oxford, 1936), pp. 146–53. Latin transcripts made by Brian Twyne (d. 1644) of now lost records; extracts of presentments in eleven courts of frankpledge, 1405–1516.

Peebles

Charters and Documents Relating to the Burgh of Peebles with Extracts from the Records of the Burgh, A.D. 1165–1710, ed. W. Chambers, Scottish Burgh Records Society, 10 (Edinburgh, 1872), pp. 111–99. Extracts in Middle Scots,

1456–98, from the court of the burgh (sometimes called the 'Head court'), held before two bailiffs in the tollbooth. Proceedings mainly include burgess entries and notices of leases and repair of city properties, appointment of town officers and by-laws, especially on commercial matters. Little litigation recorded in these extracts, but there are inquests, most of which concern landed property.

Peterborough

Peterborough Medieval Court Rolls, trans. Margaret Briston, introduction by Nicholas Karn, Northamptonshire Record Society, 48 (2015). English translations of entire courts, including the leet courts (twenty-eight from 1359 to 1538) with presentments of the tithingmen of the town's five wards; the Portmanmoot court (for five years, 1397–1425), which focused heavily on transfers of property; and the Market court (four survive for short periods in 1397–1426), which dealt with personal pleas of all types, but especially debt. Also includes manorial courts of Peterborough estates.

Ramsey

The Court Rolls of Ramsey, Hepmangrove and Bury, 1268–1600, ed. and trans. E. B. DeWindt (Toronto, 1990). Transcripts of views of frankpledge for the small town of Ramsey, including presentments by ale-tasters. Also includes some leet courts and pleas in the courts of the banlieu of the abbot of Ramsey (some with coroners' inquests, pleas of oyer and terminer, assizes and gaol deliveries). The courts often include the nearby villages of Hepmangrove and Bury. Full transcripts are available in microfiche at the back of the book.

Ruthin

The Court Rolls of the Lordship of Ruthin or Dyffryn-Clwydd of the Reign of King Edward the First, ed. R. A. Roberts, Cymmrodorian Record Series, 2 (London, 1893). Includes courts of the borough of Ruthin, presided over by the constable of the castle. Latin (replicating the abbreviations of the original hand) with facing page English translation for 1294/5; the remaining court rolls are simply summarised in English.

The Dyffryn Clwyd Court Roll Database, 1294–1422, ed. R. R. Davies, L. B. Smith, A. D. M. Barrell, O. J. Padel and M. H. Brown [data collection, 1997]. UK Data Service. SN: 3679 <http://doi.org/10.5255/UKDA-SN-3679-1>. A downloadable dataset containing an English language calendar of the Latin court rolls of the lordship of Dyffryn Clwyd, which includes the town of Ruthin.

Southampton

The Common and Piepowder Courts of Southampton, 1426–1483, ed. Tom Olding, 2 vols, The Ames Foundation and Southampton Records Series, 44, 45 (Bristol, 2011). English translations of Latin proceedings in the town court, which by the fifteenth century was divided into three sessions. The Common court met weekly to hear personal pleas and presentments by town officials. The Piepowder court also heard personal pleas, but primarily involving those not resident in Southampton, and administered a swifter justice. Only one record of the court to hear land pleas survives (for the late fourteenth century). Digital images of the original manuscripts of these records are available at <http://amesfoundation.law.harvard.edu/Southampton/>.

Stafford

'Stafford borough court rolls 1396–97', ed. and trans. F. B. Stitt, in *Old Stafford: Essays Presented to J. Sidney Horne, Transactions of the Stafford History and Civic Society* (1974–76), pp. 15–35. English translation of one leet court (called the Great court) with the usual presentments made by a jury of twelve, and fourteen meetings of the 'Small court' or court baron, which heard civil pleas (mostly debt and trespass) and met on Mondays. The editor usefully distinguishes marginal and interlinear material.

Stamford

William Browne's Town: The Stamford Hall Book, Volume 1, 1465–1492, ed. Alan Rogers (Stamford, 2005). The contents include proceedings of the Thursday court of the alderman (the chief official of the borough), which include admissions to the freedom, elections, warrants to keep the peace issued in response to particular suits, personal pleas (mostly debt), some recognizances, and civic ordinances. The court was also called 'sessions of the peace'. English translations of Latin, with some Middle English.

Tamworth

'Court rolls of Tamworth', trans. M. K. Dale, unpublished typescript (Tamworth, 1959). Translated selections from views of frankpledge and the Portmanmoot court, 1289–1320. Available at https://www.keele.ac.uk/library/specarc/collections/tamworthcourtrolls/, along with R. Studd, 'An introduction to the colour microfiche edition published by Ormonde in 1987'; the microfiche edition includes all the court rolls, including some discovered since Dale's calendar.

Totnes

The History of Totnes Priory and Medieval Town, Devonshire, ed. Hugh R. Watkin, 3 vols (Torquay: privately published, 1914–17). English translation of a wide variety of feudal, manorial, borough and ecclesiastical documents. Includes proceedings of the Court of the Community of the Borough (also called the Court of the Community of the Guild Merchant), when it was presided over by the senior steward of the merchant guild. This steward had become the mayor by 1359, after which the court was titled the Law Court of the Mayor. There are proceedings extant from 1313 (with a gap from 1345 to 1404), but they are concerned mainly with guild business, particularly admissions to the guild. The courts extant from 1405 include a wider range of business.

Wallingford

'Extracts from the earliest datable roll of the town assembly (*burgimotus*) of Wallingford', in *Elenchus Fontium Historiae Urbanae*, vol. 2, part 2: *The United Kingdom, Ireland*, ed. Susan Reynolds, Wietse de Boer and Gearóid Mac Niocaill (Leiden, 1988), pp. 121–3. Latin transcript of the earliest datable court, 1231/2, called the Burgimote, held on Thursdays. The seven court sessions include essoins, personal pleas, and prices set for the assize of ale and bread.

Winchester

Town Life in the XIV Century as Seen in the Court Rolls of Winchester City, J. S. Furley (Winchester, 1947), pp. 114–61. Includes extracts in Latin with English translations, organised under headings to illustrate the jurisdictional reach, procedure and different types of personal pleas and presentments made by aldermen and jurors.

York

Sheriffs' Court Books of the City of York for the Fifteenth Century, trans. P. M. Stell (York, 2000). English translation of Sheriffs' courts (1471–79), sessions of the peace (1498–1500), accounts of court expenses, and custumal (c. 1415–33) of the Sheriff's court.

Borough Courts in the Reports of the Royal Commission on Historical Manuscripts

Extracts (often translated into English) from the medieval court rolls of the following towns can be found in the appendices to the reports of the Royal Commission on Historical Manuscripts.[6]

Bridgnorth: H. C. Maxwell Lyte, 'The manuscripts of the corporation of Bridgnorth', *Tenth Report*, Appendix, pp. 424–37

Canterbury: J. Brigstocke Sheppard, 'The records of the city of Canterbury', *Ninth Report*, Appendix, pp. 129–77

Chester: John Cordy Jeaffreson, 'The manuscripts of the corporation of Chester', *Eighth Report*, Appendix, pp. 355–403

Faversham: Henry Thomas Riley, 'The corporation of Faversham', *Sixth Report*, Appendix, pp. 500–11

Gloucester: W. H. Stevenson, 'The records of the corporation of Gloucester', *Twelfth Report*, Appendix, pp. 400–529

Grimsby: Alfred Gibbons, 'The corporation of Great Grimsby', *Fourteenth Report*, Appendix, pp. 237–91

Hereford: William Dunn Macray, 'The manuscripts of the corporation of Hereford', *Thirteenth Report*, Appendix, pp. 292–302-

Hythe: Henry Thomas Riley, 'The manuscripts of the corporation of Hythe, Kent', *Fourth Report*, Appendix, pp. 429–39

Ipswich: John Cordy Jeaffreson, 'The manuscripts of the corporation of Ipswich, co. Suffolk', *Ninth Report*, Appendix, pp. 222–62

Leicester: John Cordy Jeaffreson, 'The manuscripts belonging to the corporation of the borough of Leicester', *Eighth Report*, Appendix, pp. 403–41

New Romney: Henry Thomas Riley, 'The manuscripts of the corporation of New Romney', *Fourth Report*, Appendix, pp. 439–42, and idem, 'Court books of the corporation of New Romney', *Sixth Report*, Appendix, pp. 540–5

6 I checked all reports on the records of boroughs or corporations in England, Scotland and Wales in the Folio Series: the first through ninth reports (1872–84), as well as all volumes published in the Octavo Series (1889–1976). Note that individual reports were often published in multiple volumes and that the transcripts were almost always in the appendices. These reports offer a good guide to extant town records, including court rolls, but are only included here if the report printed actual extracts from the town courts.

Rye: Henry Thomas Riley, 'The manuscripts of the corporation of Rye', *Fifth Report*, Appendix, pp. 488–516

Totnes: Henry Thomas Riley, 'The corporation of Totnes', *Third Report*, Appendix, pp. 341–50

Wallingford: Henry Thomas Riley, 'The corporation of Wallingford', *Sixth Report*, Appendix, pp. 572–95

Weymouth and Melcombe Regis: Henry Thomas Riley, 'The manuscripts of the towns of Weymouth and Melcombe Regis', *Fifth Report*, Appendix, pp. 575–90

Winchester: Henry Thomas Riley, 'The corporation of Winchester', *Sixth Report*, Appendix, pp. 595–605

BIBLIOGRAPHY

Unpublished Primary Sources

Borthwick Institute for Archives, York, CP.F.36, 153

British Library, London, Add MS 46460; Harleian Roll F21, F35; Harleian MSS 2020, 2046, 2057, 2158

Centre for Kentish Studies, Maidstone, Sackville of Knole, U269 M73

Cheshire Archives and Local Studies, Cheshire, MB/B; ZCHB/2; ZMB; ZMR; ZSB; ZSR; ZQCR

Devon Heritage Centre, Exeter City Archives, Mayor's court rolls; Mayor's tourn; CR 227

Dorset Record Office, DC/SYB/B1, B2

The Duke of Norfolk's Archives, Arundel Castle, MD 1475, 1478

Herefordshire Record Office, E12, F5/I/3, 4; E12, F/S/I/4, 5

King's Lynn Borough Archives, King's Lynn, KL/C 2–4, 6–7, 10, 17, 37–39, 50

Lincoln Archive Office, Dij 74/1/8, 18; Dij 74/2/6, 10; Dij 77/1/12, 16, 28–29, 31, 35, 42; FL/TRANSCRIPTS/U/28 (F. W. Brooks, *Calendar of the Rolls of the Lincoln Court of Burghmanmote*)

Lincoln Cathedral Library, Burwarmote Book, MS 169

London Metropolitan Archives, COL/CS/01/010

The National Archives, Kew, C 241/141/86, C 241/155/4, C 241/165/51; CHES 12, CHES 25/10–16, CHES 29/108, CHES 29/110, CHES 29/187; DL30/109/1615; DL 111/1662; E 179/135/12, 16; SC 2/210/71–72; SC 6/780/7; SC 8/57/2819; PROB 11/3/371

Norfolk Record Office, Norwich, DCN 44/76/76, 78, 176; NCR Case 5B/1–11; Case 5C/10; Case 8A; Case 8D/1–7

Nottinghamshire Archives, CA1258a, CA1260, CA1265, CA1273, CA1274, CA1275, CA1277a, CA1278, CA1279, CA1280a, CA1281, CA1282, CA1288,

CA1290, CA1291, CA1292, CA1294, CA1295/I, CA1296, CA1296/II, CA1297, CA3942
Shakespeare Centre Library and Archives, Stratford-upon-Avon, DR 75/4, 7, 8
Staffordshire Record Office, D1333/1; D1333/2; D1337/3; D590/4331, 2, 3; D590/433/6; D590/434; D641/1/4E/2; DC/SYB/B1
Suffolk Record Office, Ipswich, C/4/1/1; HD64/1/2, 28, 29
Warwickshire County Record Office, CR1886/172, 173D
Westminster Abbey Muniments, 21937, 21938, 21939, 21942
Worcester Cathedral Library, C897, E1, E2, E7, E8, E9, E10, E11a, E13, E14, E15, E17, E21, E22, E26, E27, E32, E38, E41, E45, E95, Reg. A IV
Worcestershire Archives, BA 2636 177/92504, 92508

Published Primary Sources

Baber, A. F. C. (ed.), *The Court Rolls of the Manor of Bromsgrove and King's Norton, 1494–1504*, Worcestershire Historical Society, new ser., 2 (1963)
Bailey, Mark (ed.), *The English Manor, c. 1200 – c. 1500* (Manchester, 2002)
Bale, Anthony (ed.), *The Book of Margery Kempe* (Oxford, 2015)
Ballard, Adolphus (ed.), *British Borough Charters, 1042–1216* (Cambridge, 1913)
Ballard, Adolphus, and James Tait (eds), *British Borough Charters, 1216–1307* (Cambridge, 1923)
Bateson, Mary (ed.), *Records of the Borough of Leicester: Being a Series of Extracts from the Archives of the Corporation of Leicester*, revised by W. H. Stevenson and J. E. Stocks, 3 vols (London, 1899–1901)
Bateson, Mary (ed.), *Borough Customs*, 2 vols, Selden Society, 18 and 21 (London, 1904–21)
Bolton, J. L. (ed.), *The Alien Communities of London in the Fifteenth Century: The Subsidy Rolls of 1440 and 1483/4* (Stamford, 1998)
Bracton on the Laws and Customs of England, ed. George E. Woodbine, trans. S. E. Thorne, vol. 2 (Cambridge, MA, 1968)
Britnell, Richard H. (ed.), *Records of the Borough of Crossgate, Durham, 1312–1531*, Surtees Society, 212 (2008)
Calendar of Close Rolls for the Reign of Edward III: 1330–1333, vol. 2 (London, 1898)
Calendar of Patent Rolls for the Reign of Edward I: 1281–1292, vol. 2 (London, 1893)
Calendar of Patent Rolls for the Reign of Edward II: 1317–1321, vol. 3 (London, 1908)
Calendar of Patent Rolls for the Reign of Edward III: 1358–1361, vol. 11 (London, 1911)

Calendar of Patent Rolls for the Reign of Henry IV: 1408–1413, vol. 4 (London, 1909)

Calendar of Patent Rolls for the Reign of Richard II: 1381–1385, vol. 2 (London, 1897)

Chew, Helena, and William Kellaway (eds), *London Assize of Nuisance, 1301–1431: A Calendar* (London, 1973)

Darlington, R. R. (ed.), *The Vita Wulfstani of William of Malmesbury*, Camden Society, 40 (1928)

Darlington, R. R. (ed.), *The Cartulary of Worcester Cathedral Priory*, Pipe Roll Society, new ser., 38 (1968)

Dawes, Michael Charles Burdett (ed.), *Register of Edward, the Black Prince, Preserved in the Public Record Office: Palatinate of Chester, A.D. 1351–1365* (London, 1932)

de Gray Birch, Walter (ed.), *The Historical Charters and Constitutional Documents of the City of London* (London, 1887)

Dewindt, E. B. (ed.), *The Court Rolls of Ramsey, Hepmangrove and Bury, 1268–1600* (Toronto, 1990)

Drinkwater, C. H. (ed. and trans.), 'The merchants' gild of Shrewsbury: the two earliest rolls for 1209–10 and 1219–20', *Transactions of the Shropshire Archaeological and Natural History Society*, 2nd ser., 2 (1890)

Drinkwater, C. H., 'The merchants' gild of Shrewsbury: seven rolls of the thirteenth century', *Transactions of the Shropshire Archaeological and Natural History Society*, 2nd ser., 12 (1900)

Fenwick, Carolyn C., *The Poll Taxes of 1377, 1379 and 1381: Part 2, Lincolnshire-Westmorland* (Oxford, 2001)

Furley, J. S. (ed.), *Ancient Usages of Winchester, from the Anglo-French Version Preserved in Winchester College* (Oxford, 1927)

Furley, J. S. (ed.), *Town Life in the XIV Century as seen in the Court Rolls of Winchester City* (Winchester, 1947)

Goldberg, P. J. P. (ed.), *Women in England, c. 1275–1525: Documentary Sources* (Manchester, 1995)

Gross, Charles (ed.), *Select Cases Concerning the Law Merchant: Vol. 1, A.D. 1270–1638: Local Courts*, Selden Society, 23 (London, 1903)

Hale, W. H. (ed.), *Registrum sive Liber Irrotularius ... Prioratus Beatae Mariae Wigorniensis*, Camden Society, 91 (1865)

Hall, G. D. G (ed.), *The Treatise on the Laws and Customs of the Realm of England Commonly Called Glanvill* (London, 1965)

Hall, Hubert (ed.), *Select Cases Concerning the Law Merchant: Vol. 2, A.D. 1239–1633: Central Courts*, Selden Society, 46 (London, 1930) and *Vol. 3, A.D. 1251–1779: Supplementary Central Courts*, Selden Society, 49 (London, 1932)

Hanawalt, Barbara A. (ed.), *Crime in East Anglia in the Fourteenth Century: Norfolk Gaol Delivery Rolls 1307–1316*, Norfolk Record Society (1976)

Harris, Mary Dormer (ed.), *Coventry Leet Book: Or Mayor's Register, Containing the Records of the City Court Leet or View of Frankpledge, A.D. 1420–1555 with Divers Other Matters*, Early English Text Society, original ser., 134, 135, 138, 146 (London, 1907–13)

Historical Manuscripts Commission, *Eleventh Report, Appendix 3: Manuscripts of the Corporations of Southampton and King's Lynn* (1887)

Hudson, William (ed.), *Leet Jurisdiction in the City of Norwich during the 13th and 14th Centuries, with a Short Notice of its Later History and Decline from the Rolls in the Possession of the Corporation*, Selden Society, 5 (London, 1892)

Hudson, William, and John Cottingham Tingey (eds), *The Records of the City of Norwich*, 2 vols (Norwich, 1906–10)

Ingleby, Holcome (ed.), *The Red Register of King's Lynn*, 2 vols (King's Lynn, 1919–22)

Kowaleski, Maryanne (ed.), *The Havener's Accounts of the Earldom and Duchy of Cornwall, 1287–1356*, Devon and Cornwall Record Society, new ser., 44 (Exeter, 2001)

Leach, Arthur F. (ed.), *Beverley Town Documents*, Selden Society, 14 (London, 1900)

Maidstone, Clement, and Stephen K. Wright (ed. and trans.), *The Martyrdom of Archbishop Richard Scrope* (Washington DC, 1997): <http://english.cua.edu/faculty/wright/maidston.cfm>

Maitland, Frederic William, and William Paley Baildon (eds), *The Court Baron: Being Precedents for Use in Seignorial and Other Local Courts, together with Select Pleas from the Bishop of Ely's Court of Littleport*, Selden Society, 4 (London, 1891)

Markham, Christopher A. (ed.), *The Records of the Borough of Northampton*, vol. 1 (Northampton, 1898)

Marsden, Reginald G. (ed.), *Select Pleas in the Court of Admiralty*, vol. 1, Selden Society, 6 (London, 1894)

Martin, G. H. (ed.), *The Ipswich Recognizance Rolls 1294–1327: A Calendar*, Suffolk Records Society, 16 (Ipswich, 1973)

Meech, Stanford B., and Hope E. Allen (eds), *The Book of Margery Kempe*, Early English Text Society, original ser. 212 (London, 1940)

Nichols, Francis Morgan (ed.), *Britton: The French Text Carefully Revised with an English Translation*, vol. 2 (Oxford, 1865)

Norfolk and Norwich Archaeological Society, *A Calendar of the Freemen of Lynn, 1292–1836* (Norwich, 1913)

Noy, D. (ed.), *Winslow Manor Court Book*, Buckinghamshire Record Society, 35 (2011)

Olding, Tom, and Penny Tucker (eds), *The Common and Piepowder Courts of Southampton, 1426–1483*, Southampton Record Series, 45 (2011)

Owen, Dorothy M., *The Making of King's Lynn: A Documentary Survey* (London, 1984)

Pugh, R. B. (ed.), *Court Rolls of the Wiltshire Manors of Adam de Stratton*, Wiltshire Record Society, 24 (1970), pp. 111–63

Raine, James (ed.), *The Fabric Rolls of York Minster*, Surtees Society, 35 (1859)

Raine, James (ed.), *Testamenta Eboracensia*, vol. 3, Surtees Society, 45 (1865)

Reports of the Deputy Keeper of the Public Records, Appendix II: Calendar of Recognizance Rolls of the Palatinate of Chester, to the End of the Reign of Henry IV (London, 1875)

Richardson, William H. (ed.), *The Annalls of Ipswche: The lawes customes and governmt of the same, collected out of ye records books and writings of that towne by Nathll Bacon serving as recorder and town clark in that towne. Anno Dom. 1654* (Ipswich, 1884)

Riley, Henry Thomas (ed.), *Munimenta Gildhallæ Londoniensis: Liber Albus, Liber Custumarum, et Liber Horn, vol. 1* (London, 1859)

Riley, Henry Thomas (trans.), *Liber Albus: The White Book of the City of London. Comp. A. D. 1419, by John Carpenter, Common Clerk. Richard Whitington, Mayor* (London, 1862)

Riley, H. T. (ed.), *Chronicles of the Mayors and Sheriffs of London* (London, 1863)

Rogers, Alan (ed.), *William Browne's Town: The Stamford Hall Book, 1465–1492*, vol. 1 (Stamford, 2005)

Rowe, Margery, and John Draisey (eds), *The Receivers' Accounts of the City of Exeter, 1304–1353*, Devon and Cornwall Record Society, 32 (1989)

Schopp, Jacob Wilhelm (ed.), *The Anglo-Norman Custumal of Exeter* (Oxford, 1925)

Sellers, Maud (ed.), *York Memorandum Book: Lettered A–Y in the Guildhall Muniment Room*, vol. 1, Surtees Society 120, 125 (1911–12)

Sharpe, Reginald R. (ed.), *Calendar of Wills Proved and Enrolled in the Court of Husting, London, 1258–1688*, 2 vols (London, 1889–90)

Sharpe, Reginald R. (ed.), *Calendar of the Letter-Books*, vols A–K (London, 1899–1912)

Stell, P. M. (trans.), *Sheriffs' Court Books of the City of York for the Fifteenth Century* (York, 2000)

Stevenson, W. H. (ed.), *Records of the Borough of Nottingham*, vol. 1 (London, 1882)

Thomas, A. H. (ed.), *Calendar of Early Mayor's Court Rolls, 1298–1307* (London, 1924)

Thomas, A. H. (ed.), *Calendar of Plea and Memoranda Rolls: A.D. 1413–1437*, vol. 4 (Cambridge, 1943)

Thomson, Reginald M., *Catalogue of the Manuscripts of Lincoln Cathedral Chapter Library* (Cambridge, 1989)

Throsby, John (ed.), *Thoroton's History of Nottinghamshire: Vol. 2: Republished with Large Additions by John Throsby* (Nottingham, 1790)

Torrie, Elizabeth P. D. (ed.), *The Gild Court Book of Dunfermline, 1433–1597*, Scottish Record Society, new ser., 12 (Edinburgh, 1986)

Toulmin Smith, Lucy (ed.), *Leland's Itinerary in England and Wales* (London, 1906)

University of York and The National Archives, *England's Immigrants 1330–1550*, database <https://www.englandsimmigrants.com>

Wadley, T. P. (ed.), *Notes or Abstracts of the Wills Contained in the Volume Entitled the Great Orphan Book and Book of Will: In the Council House at Bristol*, Bristol and Gloucestershire Society, 1 (Bristol, 1886)

Weinbaum, Martin (ed.), *British Borough Charters, 1307–1660* (Cambridge, 1943)

Winter, Christine L. (ed.), '*The Portsoken presentments: an analysis of a London ward in the fifteenth century*', *Transactions of the London and Middlesex Archaeological Society*, 56 (2005), pp. 97–161

Secondary Sources

Allen, David H., *Ipswich Borough Archives: A Catalogue*, Suffolk Records Society, 43 (Woodbridge, 2000)

Alsford, S., *History of Medieval Lynn*, <http://users.trytel.com/~tristan/towns/lynn1.html>

Alsford, Stephen, 'The men behind the masque: office-holding in East Anglian boroughs, 1272–1460', <http://users.trytel.com/~tristan/towns/mc5_pt1.html>

Alsford, Stephen, 'The monopolisation of office', <http://users.trytel.com/~tristan/towns/mc3_pt5.html>

Baker, J. H., *The Oxford History of the Laws of England: 1483–1558*, vol. 6 (Oxford, 2003)

Baker, Nigel, and Richard Holt, *Urban Growth and the Medieval Church: Gloucester and Worcester* (Aldershot, 2004)

Bardsley, Sandy, *Venomous Tongues: Speech and Gender in Late Medieval England* (Philadelphia, 2006)

Barley, M. W., and I. F. Straw, 'Nottingham', in M. D. Lobel (ed.), *Historic Towns: Maps and Plans of Towns and Cities in the British Isles*, vol. 1 (London, 1969)

Barron, Caroline M., 'The "golden age" of women in medieval London', *Reading Medieval Studies*, 15 (1989), pp. 35–58

Barron, Caroline M., 'Lay solidarities: the wards of medieval London', in Pauline Stafford, Janet L. Nelson and Jane Martindale (eds), *Law, Laity and Solidarities: Essays in Honour of Susan Reynolds* (Manchester, 2001)

Barron, Caroline M., *London in the Later Middle Ages: Government and the People, 1200–1500* (Oxford, 2004)

Bateson, Mary, 'The English and Latin versions of a Peterborough court leet, 1461', *The English Historical Review*, 19 (1904), pp. 526–8

Beattie, Cordelia, *Medieval Single Women: The Politics of Social Classification in Late Medieval England* (Oxford, 2007)

Beattie, Cordelia, '"Living as a single person": marital status, performance and the law in late medieval England', *Women's History Review*, 17 (2008), pp. 327–40

Beattie, Cordelia, 'Married women, contracts and coverture in late medieval England', in Cordelia Beattie and Matthew Frank Stevens (eds), *Married Women and the Law in Premodern Northwest Europe* (Woodbridge, 2013), pp. 133–54

Beattie, Cordelia, and Matthew F. Stevens (eds), *Married Women and the Law in Premodern Northwest Europe* (Woodbridge, 2013)

Beckerman, John S., 'The forty-shilling jurisdictional limit in medieval English personal actions', in Dafydd Jenkins (ed.), *Legal History Studies, 1972* (Cardiff, 1975), pp. 110–17

Benedictow, Ole J., *The Black Death, 1346–1353: The Complete History* (Woodbridge, 2008)

Bennett, Judith, *Women in the Medieval English Countryside: Gender and Household in Brigstock Before the Plague* (Oxford, 1987)

Bennett, Judith M., *Ale, Beer, and Brewsters in England: Women's Work in a Changing World, 1300–1600* (Oxford, 1996)

Bennett, Judith M., and Shannon McSheffrey, 'Early, erotic and alien: women dressed as men in late medieval London', *History Workshop Journal*, 77 (2014), pp. 1–25

Beresford, Maurice W., and H. P. R. Finberg, *English Medieval Boroughs: A Handlist* (Newton Abbot, 1973)

Beresford, Maurice W., 'English medieval boroughs: a hand-list: revisions, 1973–1981', *Urban History Yearbook* (1981), pp. 59–65

Beresford, Maurice W., *New Towns of the Middle Ages: Town Plantations in England, Wales and Gascony* (London, 1988)

Bolton, J. L., '"The world upside down": plague as an agent of economic and social change', in M. W. Ormrod and P. G. Lindley (eds), *The Black Death in England* (Stamford, 1996)

Bolton, J. L., 'Was there a crisis of credit in fifteenth century England?', *British Numismatic Journal*, 81 (2011), pp. 144–64

Bolton, J. L., *Money in the Medieval English Economy: 973–1489* (Manchester, 2012)

Braid, Robert, 'Behind the Ordinance of Labourers: economic regulation and market control in London before the Black Death', *Journal of Legal History*, 34 (2013), pp. 3–30

Briggs, Chris, 'Manor court procedures, debt litigation levels, and rural credit provision in England, c. 1290 – c. 1380', *Law and History Review*, 24 (2006), pp. 519–58

Briggs, Chris, *Credit and Village Society in Fourteenth-Century England* (Oxford, 2008)

Briggs, Chris, 'Seignorial control of villagers' litigation beyond the manor in later medieval England', *Historical Research*, 81 (2008), pp. 399–422

Britnell, Richard H., 'Colchester courts and court records, 1310–1525', *Essex Archaeology and History*, 17 (1986), pp. 133–40

Britnell, Richard H., *Growth and Decline in Colchester, 1300–1525* (Cambridge, 1986)

Britnell, Richard H., 'Forstall, forestalling and the statute of forestallers,' *The English Historical Review*, 102 (1987), pp. 89–102

Britnell, Richard H., 'The Black Death in English towns', *Urban History*, 21 (1994), pp. 195–210

Britnell, Richard H., 'Town life', in David M. Palliser (ed.), *The Cambridge Urban History of Britain: 600–1540*, vol. 1 (Cambridge, 2000), pp. 134–79

Britton, Edward, *The Community of the Vill: A Study in the History of the Family and Village Life in Fourteenth-Century England* (Toronto, 1977)

Brooks, A., and Nicholas Pevsner, *The Buildings of England: Worcestershire* (New Haven and London, 2007)

Brown, Andrew (ed.), *The Rows of Chester: The Chester Rows Research Project*, English Heritage Archaeological Report, 16 (1999)

Brown, Sandra, *The Medieval Courts of the York Minster Peculiar*, Borthwick Papers, 66 (1984)

Buchnea, Emily, 'Networks and clusters in business history', in John F. Wilson, Steven Toms, Abe de Jong and Emily Buchnea (eds), *The Routledge Companion to Business History* (Abingdon, 2016), pp. 259–73

Butler, Sara M., '"I will never consent to be wedded with you": coerced marriage in the courts of medieval England', *Canadian Journal of History*, 39 (2004), pp. 247–70

Butler, Sara M., 'Local concerns: suicide and jury behavior in medieval England,' *History Compass*, 4 (2006), pp. 820–35

Cam, Helen, 'Northampton borough', in William Page (ed.), *The Victoria History of the County of Northampton*, vol. 3 (London, 1970)

Campbell, Bruce M. S., 'Hundreds and leets: a survey with suggestions', in C. Harper-Bill (ed.), *Medieval East Anglia* (Woodbridge, 2005), pp. 153–67

Campbell, Bruce M. S., 'Benchmarking medieval economic development: England, Wales, Scotland, and Ireland, c. 1290', *Economic History Review*, 61 (2008), pp. 896–945

Campbell, James, 'Norwich before 1300', in Carole Rawcliffe and Richard Wilson (eds), *Medieval Norwich* (London, 2004), pp. 29–48

Cannon, Debbie, 'London pride: citizenship and the fourteenth-century custumals of the City of London', in Sarah Rees Jones (ed.), *Learning and Literacy in Medieval England and Abroad* (Turnhout, 2003), pp. 179–98

Carlton, Charles, *The Court of Orphans* (Leicester, 1974)

Champion, W. A., 'Shrewsbury, 1340–1540', in W. A. Champion and A. T. Thacker (eds), *The Victoria History of the County of Shropshire*, vol. 6, part 1, Shrewsbury General History and Topography (London, 2014), pp. 89–135

Clanchy, M. T., 'The franchise of return of writs', *Transactions of the Royal Historical Society*, 17 (1967), pp. 59–82

Clark, Elaine, 'City orphans and custody laws in medieval England', *The American Journal of Legal History*, 34 (1990), pp. 168–87

Cohn, Samuel K., *Popular Protest in Late Medieval English Towns* (Cambridge, 2013)

Croft, Justin, 'The custumals of the Cinque Ports, c. 1290 – c. 1500: studies in the cultural production of the urban record' (unpublished doctoral thesis, University of Kent, 1997)

Crowley, D. A., 'The later history of frankpledge,' *Bulletin of the Institute of Historical Research*, 48 (1975), pp. 1–15

Cuenca, Esther Liberman, 'Town clerks and the authorship of custumals in medieval England', *Urban History*, 46 (2018), pp. 180–201

Cullum, P. H., 'Vowesses and female lay piety in the province of York, 1300–1530', *Northern History*, 32 (1996), pp. 21–41

Davis, James, *Medieval Market Morality: Life, Law and Ethics in the English Marketplace, 1200–1500* (Cambridge, 2012)

Davis, James, 'Selling food and drink in the aftermath of the Black Death', in Mark Bailey and Steven H. Rigby (eds), *Town and Countryside in the Age of the Black Death: Essays in Honour of John Hatcher* (Turnhout, 2013), pp. 351–406

Davis, Natalie Zemon, *Fiction in the Archives: Pardon Tales and their Tellers in Sixteenth-Century France* (Stanford, 1987)

DeWindt, Anne Reiber, 'Local government in a small town: a medieval leet jury and its constituents,' *Albion*, 23 (1991), pp. 627–54

Dickson, Thomas, 'Proceedings of the gild court of Ayr, from the Ayr manuscript', *Archaeological and Historical Collections Relating to the Counties of Ayr and Wigton*, 1 (1878), pp. 223–30

Ditchfield, P. H., *The Parish Clerk* (London, 1907)

Dodd, Gwilym, 'The rise of English, the decline of French: supplications to the English crown, c. 1420–50', *Speculum*, 86 (2011), pp. 117–50

Donahue, Charles, Jr., 'Female plaintiffs in marriage cases in the court of York in the later Middle Ages: what can we learn from the numbers?', in Sue Sheridan Walker (ed.), *Wife and Widow in Medieval England* (Ann Arbor, 1993), pp. 183–213

Donahue, Charles, Jr., *Law, Marriage, and Society in the Later Middle Ages: Arguments about Marriage in Five Courts* (Cambridge, 2007)

Duffy, Eamon, *The Voices of Morebath: Reformation and Rebellion in an English Village* (New Haven, 2001)

Dunn, Caroline, *Stolen Women in Medieval England: Rape, Abduction, and Adultery, 1100–1500* (Cambridge, 2013)

Dunn, Penelope, 'Trade', in Carole Rawcliffe and Richard Wilson (eds), *Medieval Norwich* (London, 2004), pp. 213–34

Duxbury, Neil, *The Nature and Authority of Precedent* (Cambridge, 2008)

Dyer, Alan, *Decline and Growth in English Towns 1400–1640* (Cambridge, 1991)

Dyer, Alan, 'Ranking lists of English medieval towns', in D. M. Palliser (ed.), *The Cambridge Urban History of Britain: 600–1540*, vol. 1 (Cambridge, 2000), pp. 747–70

Dyer, Alan, 'Ranking of towns by taxpaying population: the 1377 poll tax', in D. M. Palliser (ed.), *The Cambridge Urban History of Britain: 600–1540*, vol. 1 (Cambridge, 2000)

Dyer, Christopher, 'Small-town conflict in the later Middle Ages: events at Shipston-on-Stour', *Urban History*, 19 (1992), pp. 184–210

Dyer, Christopher, *Standards of Living in the Later Middle Ages: Social Change in England, c. 1200–1520* (Cambridge, 1998)

Dyer, Christopher, *Bromsgrove: A Small Town in Worcestershire in the Middle Ages*, Worcestershire Historical Society Occasional Publication, 9 (2000), pp. 12–27

Dyer, Christopher, 'Small towns, 1270–1540', in D. M. Palliser (ed.), *The Cambridge Urban History of Britain: 600–1540*, vol. 1 (Cambridge, 2000), pp. 505–37

Dyer, Christopher, *Making a Living in the Middle Ages* (London, 2002)

Dyer, Christopher, 'Small places with large consequences: the importance of small towns in England, 1000–1540', *Historical Research*, 75 (2002), pp. 1–24

Dyer, Christopher, and Jane Laughton, 'Small towns in the East and West Midlands in the later Middle Ages: a comparison', *Midland History*, 24 (1999), pp. 24–52

Dyer, Christopher, and Jane Laughton, 'Seasonal patterns of trade in the later Middle Ages: buying and selling at Melton Mowbray, Leicestershire, 1400–1520', *Nottingham Medieval Studies*, 46 (2002), pp. 162–84

Dyer, Christopher, Jane Laughton and Evan Jones, 'The urban hierarchy in the later Middle Ages: a study of the East Midlands', *Urban History*, 28 (2001), pp. 331–57

Dyer, Christopher, and T. R. Slater, 'The Midlands', in D. M. Palliser (ed.), *The Cambridge Urban History of Britain: 600–1540*, vol. 1 (Cambridge, 2000), pp. 609–38

Ewan, Elizabeth, '"For whatever ales ye": women as consumers and producers in late medieval Scottish towns', in Elizabeth Ewan and Maureen Meikle (eds), *Women in Scotland c. 1100 – c. 1750* (East Linton, 1999), pp. 125–35

Farmer, David L., 'Prices and wages', in Edward Miller (ed.), *The Agrarian History of England and Wales*, vol. 3 (Cambridge, 1991), pp. 431–525

Fay, Isla, 'Health and disease in medieval and Tudor Norwich' (unpublished Ph.D. thesis, University of East Anglia, 2008)

Fay, Isla, *Health and the City: Disease, Environment and Government in Norwich 1200–1575* (York, 2015)

Fenster, Thelma, and Daniel Smail, 'Introduction', in Thelma Fenster and Daniel Smail (eds), *Fama: The Politics of Talk and Reputation in Medieval Europe* (Ithaca, NY, 2003), pp. 1–11

Finn, Margot, 'Women, consumption and coverture in England, c. 1760–1860', *The Historical Journal*, 39 (1996), pp. 703–22

Flather, Amanda, *Gender and Space in Early Modern England* (Woodbridge, 2007)

Foulds, Trevor, 'The medieval town', in John Beckett (ed.), *A Centenary History of Nottingham* (Manchester, 1997), pp. 56–71

Fox, Harold S. A., 'Medieval urban development', in R. J. P. Cain and W. L. D. Ravenhill (eds), *An Historical Atlas of South-West England* (Exeter, 1999), pp. 424–31

French, Katherine L., 'Well-behaved women can make history: women's friendships in late medieval Westminster', in Charlotte Newman Goldy and Amy Livingstone (eds), *Writing Medieval Women's Lives* (Basingstoke, 2012), pp. 247–65

Frost, Ruth, 'The urban elite', in Carole Rawcliffe and R. Wilson (eds), *Medieval Norwich* (London, 2004), pp. 235–54

Giggins, Brian L., and Jane Laughton, 'Catesby: an interdisciplinary study' [Part II], *Northamptonshire Past and Present*, 56 (2003), pp. 52–5

Gillett, Edward, and Kenneth A. MacMahon, *A History of Hull*, 2nd edn (Hull, 1989)

Goddard, Richard, 'Church lords and English urban investment in the later Middle Ages', *Past and Present*, Supplement 2 (2007), pp. 148–65

Goddard, Richard, 'Surviving recession: English borough courts and commercial contraction, 1350–1500', in Richard Goddard, John Langdon and Miriam Müller (eds), *Survival and Discord in Medieval Society: Essays in Honour of Christopher Dyer* (Turnhout, 2010), pp. 69–87

Goddard, Richard, 'Small boroughs and the manorial economy: enterprise zones or urban failures?', *Past and Present*, 210 (2011), pp. 3–31

Goddard, Richard, 'Medieval business networks: St Mary's guild and the borough court in later medieval Nottingham', *Urban History*, 40 (2013), pp. 3–27

Goddard, Richard, *Credit and Trade in Later Medieval England, 1353-1532* (London, 2016)

Goldberg, P. J. P., 'Urban identity and the poll taxes of 1377, 1379, and 1381,' *Economic History Review*, 43 (1990), pp. 194–216

Goldberg, P. J. P., *Women, Work and Life Cycle in a Medieval Economy: Women in York and Yorkshire c. 1300–1520* (Oxford, 1992)

Goldberg, P. J. P., 'Fiction in the archives: the York cause papers as a source for later medieval social history', *Continuity and Change*, 12 (1997), pp. 425–45

Goldberg, P. J. P., 'Masters and men in later medieval England', in Dawn Hadley (ed.), *Masculinity in Medieval Europe* (London, 1999), pp. 56–70

Goldberg, P. J. P., *Medieval England: A Social History, 1250–1550* (London, 2004)

Goldberg, P. J. P., *Communal Discord, Child Abduction, and Rape in the Later Middle Ages* (New York, 2008)

Goldberg, P. J. P., 'St Richard Scrope, the devout widow, and the Feast of Corpus Christi: exploring emotions, gender, and governance in early fifteenth-century York', in Susan Broomhall (ed.), *Authority, Gender and Emotions in Late Medieval and Early Modern England* (Basingstoke, 2015), pp. 66–83

Goldberg, P. J. P., 'John Rykener, Richard II, and the governance of London', *Leeds Studies in English*, 45 (2016), pp. 49–70

Goodman, Anthony, *Margery Kempe and her World* (Harlow, 2002)

Greatrex, J., *Biographical Register of the English Cathedral Priories of the Province of Canterbury c. 1066–1540* (Oxford, 1997)

Green, Alice S. *Town Life in the Fifteenth Century*, 2 vols (London, 1894)

Griffiths, David, Robert A. Philpott and Geoff Egan, *Meols: The Archaeology of the North Wirral Coast*, Oxford University School of Archaeology, Monograph 68, Institute of Archaeology (Oxford, 2007)

Gross, Charles, *The Gild Merchant: A Contribution to British Municipal History*, 2 vols (Oxford, 1890)

Gross, Charles, *A Bibliography of British Municipal History* (London, 1897)

Hadwin, John F., 'The medieval lay subsidies and economic history', *Economic History Review*, 36 (1983), pp. 200–17

Haggerty, John, and Sheryllynne Haggerty, 'Visual analytics of an eighteenth-century business network', *Enterprise and Society*, 11 (2010), pp. 1–25

Haggerty, John, and Sheryllynne Haggerty, 'The life cycle of a metropolitan business network: Liverpool 1750–1810', *Explorations in Economic History*, 48 (2011), pp. 189–206

Haggerty, Sheryllynne, *'Merely for Money'? Business Culture in the British Atlantic, 1750–1815* (Liverpool, 2012)

Hanawalt, Barbara A., 'Medieval English women in rural and urban domestic space', *Dumbarton Oaks Papers*, 52 (1998), pp. 19–26

Hanawalt, Barbara A., *The Wealth of Wives: Women, Law, and Economy in Late Medieval London* (Oxford, 2007)

Harding, Alan, *The Law Courts of Medieval England* (New York, 1973)

Hare, J., 'Inns, innkeepers and the society of late medieval England, 1350–1600', *Journal of Medieval History*, 39 (2013), pp. 477–97

Harper-Bill, Christopher, 'The English church and English religion after the Black Death', in W. Mark Ormrod and Phillip Lindley (eds), *The Black Death in England, 1348–1500* (London, 1996), pp. 79–123

Harris, B. E. (ed.), *The Victoria History of the County of Cheshire*, vols 1 and 3 (London, 1980, 1987)

Harrod, Henry, *Report on the Records of the Borough of Colchester* (Colchester, 1865)

Harrod, Henry, *Report on the Deeds and Records of the Borough of King's Lynn* (King's Lynn, 1874)

Hastings, Margaret, *The Court of Common Pleas in Fifteenth-century England: A Study of Legal Administration and Procedure* (Ithaca, NY, 1947)

Hatcher, John, 'England in the aftermath of the Black Death', *Past and Present*, 144 (1994), pp. 3–35

Hearnshaw, F. J. C., *Leet Jurisdiction in England: Especially as Illustrated by the Records of the Court Leet of Southampton* (Southampton, 1908)

Helmholz, R. H., *Marriage Litigation in Medieval England* (Cambridge, 1974)

Hemmeon, Morley de Wolf, *Burgage Tenure in Medieval England* (Cambridge, MA, 1914)

Hill, James W. F., *Medieval Lincoln* (Cambridge, 1948)

Hilton, Rodney, H., *A Medieval Society: The West Midlands at the End of the Thirteenth Century* (London, 1966)

Hilton, Rodney, H., 'Small town society in England before the Black Death', *Past and Present*, 105 (1984), pp. 53–78

Holdsworth, William, *A History of English Law*, 2 vols (London, 1956)

Horrox, R. E., 'Medieval Beverley', in K. J. Allison (ed.), *A History of the County of York East Riding*, vol. 6 (London, 1989)

Hudson, John, *The Oxford History of the Laws of England: 871–1216*, vol. 2 (Oxford, 2012)

Hunnisett, R. F., *The Medieval Coroner* (Cambridge, 1961)

Hyams, Paul, *Rancor and Reconciliation in Medieval England* (Ithaca, NY, 2003)

Ibbetson, David, 'Custom in medieval law', in Amanda Perreau-Saussine and James Bernard Murphy (eds), *The Nature of Customary Law: Legal, Historical and Philosophical Perspectives* (Cambridge, 2007), pp. 151–71

Jenks, Susanne, 'Picking up the pieces: cases presented to the London Sheriffs' Courts between Michaelmas 1461 and Michaelmas 1462', *Journal of Legal History*, 29 (2008), pp. 99–145

Johnson, Tom, 'The preconstruction of witness testimony: law and social discourse in England before the Reformation', *Law and History Review*, 32 (2014), pp. 127–47

Jones, Evan T., Jane Laughton and Peter Clark, *Northampton in the Late Middle Ages: The Archaeology and History of a Midland Town*, Centre for Urban History, University of Leicester, Working Paper No. 10 (2000)

Jones, Karen, *Gender and Petty Crime in Late Medieval England: The Local Courts in Kent, 1460–1560* (Woodbridge, 2006)

Jordan, William Chester, *From England to France: Felony and Exile in the High Middle Ages* (Princeton, 2015)

Jørgensen, Dolly, '"All good rule of the citee" and civic government in England, 1400–1600', *Journal of Urban History*, 36 (2010), pp. 300–15

Kadens, Emily, 'Pre-modern credit networks and the limits of reputation', *Iowa Law Review*, 100 (2015), pp. 2429–55

Karras, Ruth Mazo, *Common Women: Prostitution and Sexuality in Medieval England* (Oxford, 1998)

Keene, Derek, *Survey of Medieval Winchester*, vol. 1 (Oxford, 1985)

Keene, Derek, 'Changes in London's economic hinterland as indicated by debt cases in the Court of Common Pleas', in James A. Galloway (ed.), *Trade, Urban Hinterlands and Market Integration c. 1300–1600*, Centre for Metropolitan History Working Papers, ser. 3 (London, 2000), pp. 59–81

Keene, Derek, 'Issues of water in medieval London to c. 1300', *Urban History*, 28 (2001), pp. 161–79

Kellaway, William, 'John Carpenter's *Liber Albus*', *Guildhall Studies in London History*, 3 (1978), pp. 67–84

Ker, Neil R., 'Liber custumarum, and other manuscripts formerly at the Guildhall', *The Guildhall Miscellany*, 1 (1959), pp. 37–45

Ker, Neil R., *Medieval Manuscripts in British Libraries*, vol. 1 (Oxford, 1969)

Kermode, Jennifer, 'Obvious observations in the formation of oligarchies in late medieval English towns', in John A. F. Thomson (ed.), *Towns and Townspeople in the Fifteenth Century* (Gloucester, 1988), pp. 87–106

Kermode, Jennifer, 'The greater towns, 1300–1540', in David M. Palliser (ed.),

The Cambridge Urban History of Britain: 600–1540, vol. 1 (Cambridge, 2000), pp. 441–66

Kissane, Alan, 'Lay urban identities in late medieval Lincoln, 1290–1400' (unpublished doctoral thesis, University of Nottingham, 2013)

Kissane, Alan, *Civic Community in Late Medieval Lincoln: Urban Society and Economy in the Age of the Black Death, 1289–1409* (Woodbridge, 2017)

Klerman, Daniel M., 'Was the jury ever self-informing?', in M. Mulholland and B. Pulman (eds), *Judicial Tribunals in England and Europe, 1200–1700: The Trial in History*, vol. 1 (Manchester, 2003), pp. 123–50

Kowaleski, Maryanne, 'Social groupings and legal participation in a medieval English town', unpublished paper given at the American Society of Legal History Conference (October, 1984)

Kowaleski, Maryanne, 'The commercial dominance of a medieval provincial oligarchy: Exeter in the late fourteenth century', *Mediaeval Studies*, 46 (1984), pp. 355–84

Kowaleski, Maryanne, 'Women's work in a market town: Exeter in the late fourteenth century', in Barbara A. Hanawalt (ed.), *Women and Work in Preindustrial Europe* (Bloomington, 1986), pp. 145–64

Kowaleski, Maryanne, *Local Markets and Regional Trade in Medieval Exeter* (Cambridge, 1995)

Kowaleski, Maryanne, 'The demography of maritime communities in late medieval England', in Mark Bailey and Stephen Rigby (eds), *Town and Countryside in the Age of the Black Death: Essays in Honour of John Hatcher* (Turnhout, 2012), pp. 87–118

Lacey, Kay E., 'Women and work in fourteenth and fifteenth century London', in Lindsey Charles and Lorna Duffin (eds), *Women and Work in Pre-Industrial England* (London, 1985), pp. 24–82

Lambert, T. B., 'The evolution of sanctuary in medieval England', in Paul Dresch and Hannah Skoda (eds), *Legalism: Anthropology and History* (Oxford, 2012), pp. 115–44

Landes, Jordan (ed.), *London Quakers in the Transatlantic World* (Basingstoke, 2017)

Laughton, Jane, 'Women in court: some evidence from fifteenth-century Chester', in N. Rogers (ed.), *England in the Fifteenth Century: Proceedings of the 1992 Harlaxton Symposium* (Stamford, 1994), pp. 89–99

Laughton, Jane, 'The alewives of later medieval Chester', in R. E. Archer (ed.) *Crown, Government and People in the Fifteenth Century* (Stroud, 1995), pp. 191–208

Laughton, Jane, 'The port of Chester in the later Middle Ages', in Peter Carrington (ed.), *'Where Deva Spreads Her Wizard Stream': Trade and the Port of Chester*, Chester Archaeology, Occasional Paper No. 3 (Chester, 1996), pp. 66–71

Laughton, Jane, 'Catesby in the Middle Ages: an interdisciplinary study' [Part I], *Northamptonshire Past and Present*, 54 (2001), pp. 7–32

Laughton, Jane, 'Economy and society, 1350–1500', in C. P. Lewis and A. T. Thacker (eds), *A Victoria History of the County of Chester*, vol. 5, part 1, *The City of Chester* (London, 2003), pp. 64–78

Laughton, Jane, 'Catesby Priory as consumer in the first half of the fifteenth century', in Sylvia Pinches, Margaret Whalley and David Postles (eds), *The Market Place and the Place of the Market*, Friends of the Centre for English Local History, Friends' Paper No. 9 (Leicester, 2004), pp. 35–43

Laughton, Jane, *Life in a Late Medieval City: Chester 1275–1520* (Oxford, 2008)

Laughton, Jane, 'The control of discord in fifteenth-century Chester', in Richard Goddard, John Langdon and Miriam Müller (eds), *Survival and Discord in Medieval Society: Essays in Honour of Christopher Dyer* (Turnhout, 2010), pp. 213–39

Laughton, Jane, 'Mapping the migrants: Welsh and Manx settlers in fifteenth-century Chester', in Catherine A. M. Clarke (ed.), *Mapping the Medieval City: Space, Place and Identity in Chester c. 1200–1500* (Cardiff, 2011)

Laughton, Jane, 'Successful careerists from south-east Cheshire in the years 1383–1403, *Cheshire History*, 57 (2017–18), pp. 8–29

le Strange, Hamon, *Norfolk Official Lists* (Norwich, 1890)

Lewis, C. P., and A. T. Thacker (eds), *The Victoria History of the County of Cheshire*, vol. 5, parts 1 and 2 (London, 2003, 2005)

Liddy, Christian D., 'William Frost, the city of York and Scrope's rebellion of 1405', in P. J. P. Goldberg (ed.), *Richard Scrope: Archbishop, Rebel, Martyr* (Donington, 2007), pp. 64–85

Lilley, Keith, *City and Cosmos: The Medieval World in Urban Form* (London, 2009)

Lilley, Keith, 'Urban planning after the Black Death: townscape transformation in later medieval England (1350–1530), *Urban History*, 42 (2015), pp. 22–42

Lindley, Philip, 'The Black Death and English art: a debate and some assumptions', in W. Mark Ormrod and Phillip Lindley (eds), *The Black Death in England, 1348–1500* (London, 1996), pp. 125–46

Maddern, Philippa, *Violence and Social Order: East Anglia 1422–1444* (Oxford, 1992)

Maddern, P., 'Order and disorder', in Carole Rawcliffe and Richard Wilson (eds), *Medieval Norwich* (London, 2004)

Maddock, Susan, 'Neighbours, nuisances and night-walkers in early fifteenth-century Lynn', *The Annual: The Bulletin of the Norfolk Archaeological and Historical Research Group*, 24 (2015), pp. 44–51

Maddock, Susan, 'Mapping Margery Kempe's Lynn', *The Annual: The Bulletin of the Norfolk Archaeological and Historical Research Group*, 26 (2017), pp. 3–14

Maitland, F. W., 'Leet and tourn', in Helen Cam (ed.), *Selected Historical Essays of F. W. Maitland* (Cambridge, 1957), pp. 41–51

Maklin, Christopher, 'Stability and change in the composition of a "Plague Mass" in the wake of the Black Death', *Plainsong and Medieval Music*, 25 (2016), pp. 167–89

Marks, Steven G., *The Information Nexus: Global Capitalism from the Renaissance to the Present* (Cambridge, 2016)

Martin, G. H., *The Early Court Rolls of the Borough of Ipswich*, Department of English Local History, Occasional Papers, 5 (Leicester, 1954)

Martin, G. H., 'The English borough in the thirteenth century', *Transactions of the Royal Historical Society, 5th ser.*, 13 (1963), pp. 123–44

Martin, G. H., 'The registration of deeds of title in the medieval borough', in D. A. Bullough and R. L. Storey (eds), *The Study of Medieval Records: Essays in Honour of Kathleen Major* (Oxford, 1971), pp. 151–73

Martin, G. H., *The Hustings Rolls of Deeds and Wills, 1252–1485: Guide to the Microfilm Edition* (Cambridge, 1990)

Martin, G. H., 'English town records, 1250–1350', in Richard Britnell (ed.), *Pragmatic Literacy, East and West: 1200–1330* (Woodbridge, 1997), pp. 119–30

Martin, G. H., 'The diplomatic of English borough custumals', in Walter Prevenier and Thérèse de Hemptinne (eds), *La diplomatique urbaine en Europe au Moyen Age: actes du congrès de la Commission internationale de diplomatique, Gand, 25–29 août 1998* (Leuven, 2000), pp. 307–20

Mastoris, Stephen. N., 'Regulating the Nottingham markets: new evidence from a mid-thirteenth-century manuscript', *Transactions of the Thoroton Society*, 90 (1986), pp. 79–83

Mathias, Peter, 'Risk, credit and kinship in early modern enterprise', in John J. McCusker and Kenneth Morgan (eds), *The Early Modern Atlantic Economy* (Cambridge, 2001), pp. 15–35

McClure, Peter, 'Patterns of migration in the late Middle Ages: the evidence of English place-name surnames', *Economic History Review*, 32 (1979), pp. 167–82

McDonagh, Briony, 'Fragments from a medieval archive: the life and death of Sir Robert Constable', *Journal of Historical Geography*, 42 (2013), pp. 50–61

McIntosh, Marjorie Keniston, 'Local change and community control in England, 1465–1500', *Huntington Library Quarterly*, 49 (1986)

McIntosh, Marjorie Keniston, *Controlling Misbehavior in England, 1370–1600* (Cambridge, 1998)

McIntosh, Marjorie Keniston, 'The benefits and drawbacks of *femme sole* status in England, 1300–1630', *Journal of British Studies*, 44 (2005), pp. 410–38

McLoughlin, Sarah, 'Gender and transgression in the late medieval English household' (unpublished doctoral thesis, University of York, 2011)

McRee, Benjamin, 'Peacemaking and its limits in late medieval Norwich,' *The English Historical Review*, 109 (1994), pp. 831–66

McSheffrey, Shannon, 'Men and masculinity in late medieval London civic culture: governance, patriarchy and reputation', in Jacqueline Murray (ed.), *Conflicted Identities and Multiple Masculinities: Men in the Medieval West* (New York, 1999), pp. 243–78

McSheffrey, Shannon, 'Whoring priests and godly citizens: law, morality, and clerical sexual misconduct in late medieval London', in Norman L. Jones and Daniel Woolf (eds), *Local Identities in Late Medieval and Early Modern England* (Basingstoke, 2007), pp. 50–70

McSheffrey, Shannon, 'Detective fiction in the archives: court records and the uses of law in late medieval England', *History Workshop Journal*, 65 (2008), pp. 65–78

McSheffrey, Shannon, 'A remarrying widow: law and legal records in late medieval London', in Kim Kippen and Lori Woods (eds), *Worth and Repute: Valuing Gender in Late Medieval and Early Modern Europe: Essays in Honour of Barbara Todd* (Toronto, 2011), pp. 231–52

Morris, William Alfred, *The Frankpledge System* (London, 1910)

Muldrew, Craig, 'The culture of reconciliation: community and the settlement of economic disputes in early modern England', *The Historical Journal*, 39 (1996), pp. 915–42

Muldrew, Craig, *The Economy of Obligation: The Culture of Credit and Social Relations in Early Modern England* (Basingstoke, 1998)

Müller, Miriam, 'Social control and the hue and cry in two fourteenth-century villages,' *Journal of Medieval History*, 31 (2005), pp. 29–53

Müller, Miriam, 'Peasant women, agency and status in late thirteenth and early fourteenth century England: some reconsiderations', in Cordelia Beattie and Matthew Frank Stevens (eds), *Married Women and the Law in Premodern Northwest Europe* (Woodbridge, 2013), pp. 91–113

Murray, K. M. E., *The Constitutional History of the Cinque Ports* (Manchester, 1935)

Musson, Anthony, 'New labour laws, new remedies? Legal reaction to the Black Death "crisis"', in N. Saul (ed.), *Fourteenth Century England*, I (Woodbridge, 2000), pp. 73–88

Musson, Anthony, 'Appealing to the past: perceptions of law in late-medieval England', in Anthony Musson (ed.), *Expectations of the Law in the Middle Ages* (Woodbridge, 2001), pp. 165–80

Musson, Anthony, *Medieval Law in Context: The Growth of Legal Consciousness from Magna Carta to the Peasants' Revolt* (Manchester, 2001)

Musson, Anthony, 'Lay participation: the paradox of the jury,' *Comparative Legal History*, 3 (2015), pp. 245–71

Neal, Derek G., *The Masculine Self in Late Medieval England* (Chicago, 2008)

Newton, Kenneth C., and Marjorie K. McIntosh, 'Leet jurisdiction in Essex manor courts during the Elizabethan period', *Essex Archaeology and History: Transactions of the Essex Archaeological Society*, 13 (1981), pp. 3–14

Nightingale, Pamela, 'Monetary contraction and mercantile credit in later medieval England,' *Economic History Review*, 43 (1990), pp. 560–75

Nightingale, Pamela, 'Money and credit in the economy of late medieval England', in Diane Wood (ed.) *Medieval Money Matters* (Oxford, 2004), pp. 51–71

Olegario, Rowena, '"That mysterious people": Jewish merchants, transparency and community in mid-nineteenth-century America', *Business History Review*, 73 (1999), pp. 161–89

Oliver, George, *The History of the City of Exeter* (Exeter, 1861)

Ormrod, Mark W., 'The politics of pestilence', in W. Mark Ormrod and Phillip Lindley (eds), *The Black Death in England, 1348–1500* (London, 1996), pp. 147–81

Palmer, Robert C., *English Law in the Age of the Black Death, 1348–1381* (London, 1993)

Parker, Kate M., 'Lordship, liberty and the pursuit of politics in Lynn, 1370–1420' (unpublished Ph.D. thesis, University of East Anglia, 2004)

Parker, Kate M., 'A little local difficulty: Lynn and the Lancastrian usurpation', in Christopher Harper-Bill (ed.), *Medieval East Anglia* (Woodbridge, 2005), pp. 115–29

Parker, Vanessa, *The Making of King's Lynn: Secular Buildings from the 11th to the 17th Century* (Chichester, 1971)

Pearson, Robin, and David Richardson, 'Business networking in the Industrial Revolution', *Economic History Review*, 54 (2001), pp. 657–79

Pedersen, Frederik, 'Demography in the archives: social and geographical factors in fourteenth-century York cause paper marriage litigation', *Continuity and Change*, 10 (1995), pp. 405–36

Phelps Brown, Henry, and Sheila V. Hopkins, *A Perspective of Wages and Prices* (London, 1981)

Phillips, Kim M., *Medieval Maidens: Young Women and Gender in England, c. 1270 – c. 1540* (Manchester, 2003)

Phipps, Teresa, 'Creditworthy women and town courts in late medieval England', in Elise Dermineur (ed.), *Women and Credit in Preindustrial Europe* (Turnhout, 2018), pp. 73–94

Platt, Colin, *King Death: The Black Death and its Aftermath in Late Medieval England* (London, 1996)

Pollard, A. J., *The Wars of the Roses* (Basingstoke, 1988)

Pollock, Frederick, and Frederic W. Maitland, *The History of English Law before the Time of Edward I*, 2 vols (Cambridge, 1898)

Poos, L. R., *A Rural Society after the Black Death: Essex 1350–1525* (Cambridge, 1991)

Post, John B., 'Jury lists and juries in the late fourteenth century', in J. S. Cockburn and T. A. Green (eds), *Twelve Good Men and True: The Criminal Trial Jury in England, 1200–1800* (Princeton, 1988), pp. 65–77

Postles, David, 'Record-keeping in the medieval borough: proof of wills', *Archives: The Journal of the British Records Association*, 16 (1983), pp. 12–15

Postles, David, 'Personal pledging in manorial courts in the later Middle Ages,' *Bulletin of the John Rylands Library*, 75 (1993), pp. 65–78

Powell, Edward, 'Arbitration and the law in England in the late Middle Ages', *Transactions of the Royal Historical Society*, 33 (1983), pp. 49–67

Rawcliffe, Carole, '"That kindliness should be cherished more, and discord driven out": the settlement of commercial disputes by arbitration in later medieval England', in Jennifer I. Kermode (ed.), *Enterprise and Individuals in Fifteenth-Century England* (Stroud, 1991), pp. 99–117

Rawcliffe, Carole, 'Barton, Henry (*d.* 1435), of London', in J. S. Roskell, L. Clark and C. Rawcliffe (eds), *The History of Parliament: The House of Commons, 1386–1421* (Woodbridge, 1993)

Rawcliffe, Carole, 'Sickness and health', in Carole Rawcliffe and Richard Wilson (eds), *Medieval Norwich* (London, 2004), pp. 301–26

Rawcliffe, Carole, *Urban Bodies: Communal Health in Late Medieval English Towns and Cities* (Woodbridge, 2013)

Rawcliffe, Carole, 'Sources for the study of public health in the medieval city', in Joel Rosenthal (ed.), *Understanding Primary Sources* (London, 2014), pp. 183–4

Razi, Zvi, and Richard M. Smith (eds), *Medieval Society and the Manor Court* (Oxford, 1996)

Rees Jones, Sarah, 'York's civic administration, 1354–1464', in Sarah Rees Jones (ed.), *The Government of Medieval York: Essays in Commemoration of the 1396 Royal Charter* (York, 1997)

Rees Jones, Sarah, 'Household, work and the problem of mobile labour: the regulation of labour in medieval English towns', in James Bothwell, P. J. P. Goldberg and W. Mark Ormrod (eds), *The Problem of Labour in Fourteenth-Century England* (York, 2000), pp. 133–53

Rees Jones, Sarah, 'The regulation of "nuisance": civic government and the built environment in the medieval city', in Maria do Carmo Ribeiro and Arnaldo Sousa Melo (eds), *Evoluçãi da Pausagen Urbana: Sociedade e Economia* (Braga, 2012), pp. 283–94

Rees Jones, Sarah, *York: The Making of a City, 1068–1350* (Oxford, 2013)

Rexroth, Frank, *Deviance and Power in Late Medieval London*, trans. Pamela Selwyn (Cambridge, 2007)

Reynolds, Susan, *An Introduction to the History of English Medieval Towns* (Oxford, 1977)

Rigby, Stephen H., 'Urban "oligarchy" in late medieval England', in John A. F. Thomson (ed.), *Towns and Townspeople in the Fifteenth Century* (Gloucester, 1988), pp. 62–86

Rigby, Stephen H., *Medieval Grimsby: Growth and Decline* (Hull, 1993)

Rigby, Stephen H., and Elizabeth Ewan, 'Government, power and authority 1300–1540', in D. M. Palliser (ed.), *The Cambridge Urban History of Britain: 600–1540*, vol. 1 (Cambridge, 2000), pp. 291–312

Roebuck, Derek, *Mediation and Arbitration in the Middle Ages* (Oxford, 2013)

Röhrkasten, Jens, 'Trends of mortality in late-medieval London (1348–1400)', *Nottingham Medieval Studies*, 45 (2001), pp. 172–209

Rosser, Gervase, *Medieval Westminster, 1200–1540* (Oxford, 1989)

Rosser, Gervase, 'The essence of medieval urban communities: the vill of Westminster, 1200–1540', in Richard Holt and Gervase Rosser (eds), *The Medieval Town in England 1200–1540* (London, 1990), pp. 216–37

Rosser, Gervase, *The Art of Solidarity in the Middle Ages: Guilds in England 1250–1550* (Oxford, 2015)

Rutledge, Elizabeth, 'Immigration and population growth in early fourteenth-century Norwich: evidence from the tithing roll,' *Urban History Yearbook* (1988), pp. 15–30

Sabine, Ernest, 'City cleaning in mediaeval London,' *Speculum*, 12 (1937), pp. 19–43

Sagui, Samantha, 'The hue and cry in medieval English towns', *Historical Research*, 87 (2014), pp. 179–93

Sagui, Samantha, 'A prosopography of the capital pledges of medieval Norwich,' *Medieval Prosopography*, 31 (2016), pp. 97–114

Schmidt, A. V. C., '*Lele Wordes* and *Bele Paroles*: some aspects of Langland's word-play', *Review of English Studies*, 34, no. 134 (1983), pp. 137–50

Schofield, Phillipp R., 'The late medieval view of frankpledge and the tithing system: an Essex case study', in Zvi Razi and Richard M. Smith (eds), *Medieval Society and the Manor Court* (Oxford, 1996), p. 408–49

Scott, Joan W., 'Storytelling', *History and Theory*, 50 (2011), pp. 203–9

Shaw, David Gary, *The Creation of a Community: The City of Wells in the Middle Ages* (Oxford, 1993)

Shaw, David Gary, *Necessary Conjunctions: The Social Self in Medieval England* (Basingstoke, 2005)

Shaw, David Gary, 'Social networks and the foundations of oligarchy in medieval towns', *Urban History*, 32 (2005), pp. 200–22

Shaw, David Gary, 'Social selves in medieval England: the worshipful Ferrour and Kempe', in Nancy Partner (ed.), *Writing Medieval History* (London, 2005), pp. 3–21

Shrewsbury, J. F. D., *A History of Bubonic Plague in the British Isles* (Cambridge, 1970)

Shuger, Debora, *Censorship and Cultural Sensibility: The Regulation of Language in Tudor-Stuart England* (Philadelphia, 2006)

Slater, Terry, 'Understanding the landscape of towns', in D. Hooke (ed.), *Landscape: The Richest Historical Record*, Society for Landscape Studies, supplementary ser., 1 (2000), pp. 97–108

Sloane, Barney, *The Black Death in London* (London, 2011)

Smail, Daniel Lord, *The Consumption of Justice: Emotions, Publicity, and Legal Culture in Marseille, 1264–1423* (Ithaca, NY, 2013)

Smail, Daniel Lord, *Legal Plunder: Households and Debt Collection in Late Medieval Europe* (London, 2016)

Stanley, Amy, 'Maidservants' tales: narrative domestic and global history in Eurasia, 1600–1900', *American Historical Review*, 121 (2016), pp. 438–41

Staples, Kate Kelsey, *Daughters of London: Inheriting Opportunity in the Late Middle Ages* (Leiden, 2011)

Stenton, F. M., 'Norman London: an essay', in William Fitz Stephen, *Norman London* (New York, 1934), pp. 1–45

Stevens, Matthew Frank, 'Failed arbitrations before the Court of Common Pleas: cases relating to London and Londoners, 1400–1468', *Journal of Legal History*, 31 (2010), pp. 21–44

Stevens, Matthew Frank, 'Londoners and the Court of Common Pleas in the fifteenth century', in Matthew Davies and James A. Galloway (eds), *London and Beyond: Essays in Honour of Derek Keene* (London, 2012)

Stevens, Matthew Frank, 'London women, the courts and the "golden age": a quantitative analysis of female litigants in the fourteenth and fifteenth centuries', *The London Journal*, 37 (2012), pp. 67–88

Stevens, Matthew Frank, 'London's married women, debt litigation and coverture in the Court of Common Pleas', in Cordelia Beattie and Matthew Frank Stevens (eds), *Married Women and the Law in Premodern Northwest Europe* (Woodbridge, 2013), pp. 115–32

Stocker, David (ed.), *The City by the Pool: Assessing the Archaeology of the City of Lincoln* (Oxford, 2003)

Stokes, Charity Scott, 'Margery Kempe: her life and the early history of her book', *Mystics Quarterly*, 25, nos. 1–2 (March/June, 1999), pp. 9–68

Stretton, Tim, and Krista J. Kesselring, 'Introduction: coverture and continuity', in Tim Stretton and Krista J. Kesselring (eds), *Married Women and the Law: Coverture in England and the Common Law World* (Montreal, 2013), pp. 2–23

Stretton, Tim, and Kesselring, Krista J., *Married Women and the Law: Coverture in England and the Common Law World* (Montreal, 2013)

Stubbs, William, *The Constitutional History of England in its Origin and Development*, vol. 1 (Oxford, 1891)

Tait, James, *The Medieval English Borough: Studies on its Origins and Constitutional History* (Manchester, 1936)

Thacker, Alan, and Dorothy Cromarty, 'Shrewsbury 1200–1340', in W. A. Champion and A. T. Thacker (eds), *The Victoria History of the County of Shropshire*, vol. 6, part 1, Shrewsbury General History and Topography (London, 2014), pp. 31–88

Thompson, Anthony H., 'The registers of John Gynewell, bishop of Lincoln, for the years 1347–1350', *Archaeological Journal*, 68 (1911), pp. 300–60

Thrupp, Sylvia, *The Merchant Class of Medieval London, 1300–1500* (Ann Arbor, 1948)

Tucker, Penny, 'Relationships between London's courts and the Westminster courts in the reign of Edward IV', in Diana E. S. Dunn (ed.), *Courts, Counties and the Capital in the Later Middle Ages* (New York, 1996), pp. 117–38

Tucker, Penny, 'London courts of law in the fifteenth century: the litigants' perspective', in Christopher Brooks and Michael Lobban (eds), *Communities and Courts in Britain, 1150–1900* (London, 1997), pp. 25–42

Tucker, Penny, 'Dunthorn, William (*d.* 1490)', in *Oxford Dictionary of National Biography* (Oxford, 2004)

Tucker, Penny, *Law Courts and Lawyers in the City of London, 1300–1530* (Cambridge, 2007)

Ulrich, Laurel Thatcher, *A Midwife's Tale* (New York, 1991)

Unger, R. W., *Beer in the Middle Ages and the Renaissance* (Philadelphia, 2011)

Unwin, George, *The Gilds and Companies of London* (London, 1908)

Veale, E. W. W., 'Introduction', in E. W. W. Veale (ed.), *The Great Red Book of Bristol: Text (Part 3)*, Bristol Record Society, 16 (Bristol, 1951), pp. 2–55

Walker, Sue Sheridan, 'The action of waste in the early common law', in J. H. Baker (ed.), *Legal Records and the Historian* (London, 1978), pp. 185–206

Walker, Sue Sheridan, 'Free consent and marriage of feudal wards in medieval England', *Journal of Medieval History*, 8 (1982), pp. 123–34

Wetherell, Charles, 'Historical social network analysis', *International Review of Social History*, 43 (1998), pp. 125–44

Willard, James F., *Parliamentary Taxes on Personal Property, 1290–1334* (Cambridge, MA, 1934)

Winter, Christine, 'The Portsoken presentments: an analysis of a London ward in the fifteenth century,' *Transactions of the London and Middlesex Archaeological Society*, 56 (2005), pp. 97–163

Ziegler, Philip, *The Black Death* (Stroud, 1969)

INDEX

Printed and bound by CPI Group (UK) Ltd, Croydon, CR0 4YY

15/09/2026

14962416-0004